Phonographies

Phonographies

Grooves in Sonic Afro-Modernity

Alexander G. Weheliye

Duke University Press

Durham and London

2005

© 2005 Duke University Press

All rights reserved

Printed in the United States of

America on acid-free paper ∞

Designed by CH Westmoreland

Typeset in Minion with

Helvetica Neue display by Tseng

Information Systems, Inc.

Library of Congress Cataloging-in-

Publication Data appear on the last

printed page of this book.

"[The Negro] is not a visitor in the West, but a citizen there, and American; as American as the Americans who despise him, the Americans who fear him, the Americans who love him—the Americans who became less than themselves, or rose to be greater than themselves by virtue of the fact that the challenge he represented was inescapable. . . . The time has come to realize that the interracial drama acted out on the American continent has not only created a new black man, it has created a new white man too. . . . This world is no longer white, and it will never be white again.—**James Baldwin**

Lifting up from the circles and grooves of a record can change the weather. From freezing to hot to cool.
—**Toni Morrison**

Actively we have woven ourselves with the very warp and woof of this nation.—**W. E. B. Du Bois**

Invisibility, let me explain, gives one a slightly different sense of time, you're never quite on the beat. . . . Instead of the swift and imperceptible flowing of time, you are aware of its nodes, those points where time stands still or from which it leaps ahead. And you slip into the breaks and look around.—**Ralph Ellison**

I wanna wind your little phonograph, just to hear your little motor moan.—**Robert Johnson**

Contents

Acknowledgments

The genre rules that I am subject to here require a listing of debts owed to various persons. However, given the stifling economization of so many aspects of life in late capitalism, I prefer to think of such contributions to life and work as aneconomic gifts. As I discuss in my book, the gift, as theorized by Du Bois and several others, functions as both an offering and a poison, and that is what these people have given me, by offering their thoughts, time, energy, and the like while at the same time "poisoning" my thought. They have become voices, apparitions, images, smells, sounds, and so on in my body and mind, enabling me to think and live above, below, beyond, and beside that possessive pronoun "my," and for that I am forever grateful.

Let me commence by thanking a group of intellectuals whose work has sustained me: Stuart Hall, Hortense Spillers, Gayatri Spivak, and Sylvia Wynter. In the years that I have spent thinking about and writing this book, these thinkers, individually and as a group, offered me a vital model for intellectual inquiry. I have also greatly benefited from various mentors and teachers, particularly Elke Stenzel and Ulla Haselstein, who provided challenges and support in high school and college, and Abena P. A. Busia, Bruce W. Robbins, and Cheryl A. Wall, who, as my graduate mentors offered me a mixture of critical acuity, generosity, understanding, and professional support. I can only hope to live up to the example they have set.

At Rutgers I had the good fortune of knowing and working with a group of dynamic graduate students and faculty members: Carol Allen, Deborah Allen, Anthony Alessandrini, Heather Russell Anderade, Kim Banks, Wesley Brown, Elaine Chang, Cheryl Clarke, Joseph Clarke, Sam Elworthy, Donald Gibson, Rachel Herzing, Briavel Holcomb, Myra Jehlen, Jonathan Kahana, Cora Kaplan and David Glover, John Kasparian, Cindy Katz, Samira Kawash, Thomas Keck, Meredith McGill, Jennifer Milligan, Verner Mitchell, Tricia Rose, Julie Skemp, Neil Smith, Sarah Thompson, Michael Warner, and Maire Veith. I will always be immensely grateful for Craig Gilmore and Ruth Wilson Gilmore's hospitality and intellectual generosity. During 1997–1998 I held a fellowship at the Rutgers Center for the Critical Analysis of Contemporary Culture; there the conversations were invaluable for formulating the beginnings of this project. The staff in the Rutgers English Department, Linda Kazusko, Nancy Miller, and Candace Walcott-Shepherd, offered endless help and a sense of humor. Tanya Agathocleous and Chris O'Brien, Joseph Chaves, Erik Dussere and Stephanie Hartman, Lisa Gitelman, Helen Hurwitz, Lisa Lynch, and Tamar Rothenberg will hopefully continue to honor me with their friendship for years to come.

At the State University of New York, Stony Brook, Helen Cooper, E. Ann Kaplan, and (particularly) Ira Livingston welcomed and supported me in a difficult institutional situation, for which I am thankful. I was also fortunate enough to share conversations with numerous outstanding undergraduates at Rutgers, Stony Brook, and Northwestern; special thanks go to the students in my "Sound/Technology/Culture" classes, and particularly those in the "Sonic Afro-modernity" graduate class at Northwestern, for discussing much of the material in this project. Parts of the book have been published previously in the following venues: a much earlier version of chapter 3 appeared in *American Studies/ Amerikastudien* 45.4 (winter 2000), a shorter incarnation of chapter 2 can be found in the summer 2003 issue of *boundary 2: an international journal of literature and culture*, and a condensed version of chapter 3 appears in *Public Culture* 17.2 (spring 2005).

I am grateful also to many people at Northwestern and in Chicago: Jeffrey Masten, Bonnie Honig, Susannah Gottlieb, John Keene, Tricia Dailey, Carole Boyce Davies, Helmut Müller Sievers, Betsy Erkkila, Lynn

Acknowledgments

Spigel, Reginald Gibbons, Sam Weber, Sandra Richards, Jay Grossman, Eric Sundquist, Elzbieta Foeller-Pituch, Miguel Vatter, Regina Schwartz, Tori Marlan, Mary Finn, Harry Samuels, and the members of the Northwestern Theory Reading Group. Particular thanks to Sharon Holland, Jennifer DeVere Brody, Kevin Bell, Dwight McBride, Dorothy Wang, E. Patrick Johnson, and Michael Hanchard for their collegiality and friendship. The staff in the Northwestern English and African American Studies departments provided smooth operations; many thanks to Kathy Daniels, Natasha Dennison, Marsha Figaro, Stacia Kozlowski, Nathan Mead, and Marilyn Williams. Jules Law and Jennifer Brody deserve special mention for being such exceptional mentors. A great deal of the final work on the manuscript was made possible by a generous fellowship from the Alice Berline Center for the Humanities at Northwestern.

Much gratitude goes to all those who read parts of manuscript and/or discussed its arguments with me at one point or another: Jonathan Arac, Kevin Bell, Lawrence Ytzak Brathwaite, Jennifer DeVere Brody, Joseph Chaves, Erik Dussere, Brian Edwards, Robert Gooding-Williams, Lisa Gitelman, Michael Hanchard, Kodwo Eshun, Ronald Judy, Andrea Kleinhuber, Jules Law, Ira Livingston, Ruth Mayer, Charles Mudede, Alondra Nelson, Ulfried Reichardt, Ryan Snyder, and the readers at Duke University Press and the University of Minnesota Press. I thank Ken Wissoker for believing in this book as it currently stands and the staff of Duke University Press for their patience and expertise. A heap of gratitude goes to Sonia Nelson, who undertook the gargantuan task of proofreading an earlier incarnation of the whole manuscript, and Abigail Derecho, who compiled the index. Many thanks go out to Nadine Robinson for the permission to use her artwork and to Alondra Nelson for suggesting Robinson's work. I cannot do justice to the depths of Fred Moten's engagement with the conceptual architecture of this book.

The folks who are last on my long list deserve so much more than mere thanks, since they have been such a forceful presence in my life and will I hope continue to be so for a variety of futures: Patricia Bembo, Arndt Weisshuhn and Miriam Schmidt, Manfred Bertelmann, Christian Schwabe and Jamilla Al-Habash, Patrick Hosp and Roya Djaberwandi, Aki Hanne and Andrea Wiedermann, Frank Kohlgrüber, Aicha Muthukumupe Katjivena; many thanks also go out to Wendy Gold, Yves Clement, Leonie Baumeister, Sonja Boerdner, and Julia Kühn and Peter Krauskopf.

Acknowledgments

I am enormously appreciative of my family's inspiration and support, especially to my parents, Nuur Ahmed Weheliye and Barbara Christine Weheliye, for being model organic intellectuals, for bestowing upon me the pleasure (and pain) of cultural nomadism, for teaching me how to make hard decisions, and for making of me always a man who questions. My siblings Daud Ahmed, Asli-Juliya Weheliye, and Samatar Weheliye deserve a great deal of gratitude for being co-conspirators and teachers. Thanks also to my uncle Said Ahmed and my sister-in-law Qadiiya Ahmed. I wish my grandmother Margarete Wittkat had been alive to see the publication of this book. My other family also deserves my great appreciation: E. Nancy Markle, George Enteen, Sharon Enteen and Doug Prusso, Alice and Bernie Learman, Henrietta and Morris Mitzner, and George and Sylvia Levy.

This book is dedicated to the two people from whom I have learned the most in my time in this galaxy: my mother, Barbara Weheliye, and Jillana Enteen. My mother has always given me the freedom to explore, a trait at once more generous and rigorous than mere encouragement, because it allowed me to make my own mistakes, and hopefully to get some things right as well. It is far from easy to describe her pervasive influence on my life and work, but I want to single out her fearlessness. Although she herself would never claim that particular quality, her strength, courage, and erudition will never cease to amaze me. This book could not have been written without Jillana Enteen, whose presence sounds from every page of this book; I look forward to many more years of collaborative endeavors in life *and* work.

Intro

It's Beginning to Feel Like . . .

Prolegomena Beginnings and introductions are occasions for sonic events or apparitions — and song intros are no exception: the soft, mid-tempo, yet insistent drum-machine rumblings and water tap sounds of Mtume's "Juicy Fruit" that prolong the wait for the grand entrance of the bass, especially in the extended twelve-inch version; the lengthy cinematic string section of Phantom/Ghost's "Perfect Lovers (Unperfect Love Mix)"; the looped invocations of "love ya babe" in conjunction with the crisp, syncopated snare drums and sampled bird sounds that introduce Aaliyah's "One in a Million." I could continue this list indefinitely, but I trust that you get the picture, or the sound as it were, of the allurements that lurk in the crevices of sonic beginnings, those sonorous marks that launch new worlds, holding out pleasures to come while also tendering futurity as such in their grooves. My all-time favorite in this category is Harold Melvin and the Blue Notes' "Wake Up Everybody," which gently burrows into the tympanum with its harp swooshes, a tambourine, and two different piano motifs, to then guide us into the pièce de resistance: a very subtle bass solo that never reappears in the duration of this 7:33-minute masterpiece. These fifteen seconds invite repetition by virtue of denying the listener recurrence and as a result haunt and shadow the remainder of the track, compelling him/her to return the needle to the first grooves of the record, rewind the tape, or push the back button on the CD/MP3 player. Because these sounds defy reiteration in the musical text, they compel the listener to actively intervene in its structure via the tools of technological re/production, which in turn calls attention to their singularity and the singularity of all sounds. These resonant instigations also amplify the integral enmeshment of sound and technology in the modern era, underscoring some of the ways sound technologies are a vital element of the musical text rather than supplementary to its unfolding.

If the coexistence of the "human" with various "technological" structures and processes presents one of the central challenges of the contemporary world, then Afro-diasporic subjects and cultures surely form a crucial part of this mix. But perhaps we should begin differently, since this statement already assumes too much, or too little, depending on your viewpoint. It presumes that the human and the technological represent separate, if not antagonistic stable entities, which at this point, and perhaps always already, seems untenable, to say the least, given that one is hardly conceivable without the other. Why then does black cultural production still function as a convenient outside to this interface that will not quite listen to the catachrestic nominalism "cyborg"? For all intents and purposes, it seems to be a resolutely stubborn child. Recent debates about the "digital divide," while surely drawing much needed attention to certain politicoeconomic inequities, cannot but reinforce the idea that Afro-diasporic populations are inherently Luddite and therefore situated outside the bounds of Western modernity. Samuel R. Delany, for instance, distinguishes "the white boxes of computer technology" and "the black boxes of modern street technology." The former, particularly in the form of the Internet and World Wide Web, are deemed central to the techno-vanguard of a continually progressing machine, while the latter — sound technologies for instance — are not regarded as technological at all.[1] Too often this bifurcation locates black cultural production beyond the pale of what counts as technological in contemporary critical discourse. Routinely, most academic considerations of technology, especially those found in studies of cyberculture (where the term "digital divide" was coined) remain deaf to the sonic topographies of popular music, which is not surprising, given the general hegemony of vision that permeates Western modernity. Yet popular music offers one of the most fertile grounds for the dissemination and enculturation of digi-

2

tal and analog technologies and has done so at least since the invention of the phonograph at the close of the nineteenth century. Pop music also represents the arena in which black subjects have culturally engaged with these technoinformational flows, so that any consideration of digital space might do well to include the sonic in order to comprehend different modalities of digitalness, but also to not endlessly circulate and therefore solidify the presumed "digital divide" with all its attendant baggage.[2]

Phonographies hopes to circumvent and reroute this path by examining the numerous links and relays between twentieth-century black cultural production and sound technologies such as the phonograph and Walkman. Recognition of these connections will in turn lead us away from the assumption that black cultures are somehow pre- or antitechnological. That is not to suggest, however, that this project reduces black cultural production to an "objective" technological sphere; it is neither a strict history of black people's involvement in the processes of sound recording and reproduction nor a comprehensive survey of representations of sound recording and reproduction in black culture.[3] Rather, I assess specific instances in the technological and social histories of sound recording and reproduction as they cut across twentieth-century black cultural production in order to suggest that the interface of these two discourses provides a singular mode of (black) modernity.[4] *Phonographies* imagines not a strict historicist account of the interface between sound technologies and black culture but instead a conceptual intervention into the fields of African American studies, musical histories of the twentieth century, and cultural studies. Black culture's reciprocal engagement with sound technologies amplifies this formation's indicativeness of and centrality to modernity rather than affirming its status as a minor modernity or countermodernity.[5] That said, this modernity appears not as an overparticularized and identitarian minority configuration as much as modernity per se, which, although marked by certain particularisms (as all cultural formations are), cannot and should not be wholly contained by them. What is generally at stake are the fates of black sounds in the age of mechanical, electrical, and digital reproduction. And, while the appearance of the phonograph suggests the most obvious point of entry into "sonic Afro-modernity," given the clearly technological dimensions of this summit so central to twentieth-century global culture, we will have to cast a wider and differently tuned historical net that considers the vexed place of writing—both in a limited and general sense—and orality vis-à-vis New World slavery, in order to come to grips with the singularity of black sounds as they ricochet between "humans" and modern informational technologies. The phonograph and other sound technologies in its wake offer prime loci from which to consider the ineluctable imbrication of black cultural formations with technology and Western modernity.

Although there exist many theories of modernity, three moments are commonly taken to be the grounds upon which this *longue durée* is erected: first, the beginnings of secularization in the Renaissance; second, the Enlightenment, as well as the rise of capitalism and the Industrial Revolution in the eighteenth century and early nineteenth century; and third, the proliferation of information technologies such as the phonograph, telegraph, telephone, and cinematograph at the end of the nineteenth century. All these prostheses of modern origins emphasize the ascent and proliferation of reason, secularization, progress, humanism, individualism, rationalization, industrialization, and so on.[6] Yet—as writers such as Walter Benjamin, Aimé Césaire, W. E. B. Du Bois, and Sylvia Wynter, to name but a few, have argued—slavery, colonialism, scientific racism, and the Holocaust are not, as has often been assumed, aberrations from the "higher" ideals of the modern but lie at its molten nucleus. In fact, these supposed archaisms provide the props, both conceptually and sociohistorically, upon which the hubristic edifices of unmitigated reason and progress rest, if uneasily so. Modern discourses and institutions have found it necessary to produce and project their own outsides in various guises—the contemporaneousness and codependency of industrialization and anthropology is a prima facie case in point—the primitive or insane serving as some obvious candidates.[7] Afro-diasporic subjects and blackness in general have had to bear the burden of being cast in the role of the other to Western modernity in numerous ways, heightening the bitter irony that marks the fractured dialectic of Enlightenment, since spatial proximity had to be compensated by a temporal displacement that deems blackness beyond the epistemological and ontological reach of the West even while this category is a fabrication of its discourses, practices, and institutions.[8] *Phonographies* surveys some of the mechanics by which (technosonic) blackness came to be fashioned as antithetical to modern structures, asking why it seemed, and in some ways still does seem, imperative to stress ad nauseam these anti- and/or premodern facets of black cultural production if, indeed, these were thought to reside beside reason, progress, and rationality. Phrased differently, how does blackness operate paradoxically as both central to and outside of Western modernity? The node of black cultural practices and sound technologies acts as one of the chief areas for examining this conundrum in the twentieth century.

The sonic remains an important zone from and through which to theorize the fundamentality of Afro-diasporic formations to the currents of Western modernity, since this field remains, to put it bluntly, the principal modality in which Afro-diasporic cultures have been articulated — though clearly it has not been the only one. Consequently, it seems only fitting that I center my analysis on the cultural, political, economic, and epistemological complexities that ensue from the new-fangled technologization of black sounds beginning at the end of the nineteenth century. Even though my argument will most clearly be situated in the last of the three models for the origins of modernity (see the beginning of the preceding paragraph), I do not want to construct a decisive rift, choosing instead to trace the rhizomatic reverberations of sonic Afro-modernity through a variety of historicocultural patterns. For instance, the volatile liaison between racial formation and vision would not appear quite comprehensible without nods to the structuration of the scopic as the disembodied sense of reason par excellence since the Renaissance. Similarly, my discussion of race, writing, and difference draws on debates about the status of black subjects as (non)human in the Enlightenment and after.

At its broadest, *Phonographies* hopes to establish the centrality of both sonic blackness — here characterized as an unwieldy compound comprising all the discourses (black and nonblack) that imagine and circumscribe racial formation within Western modernity — and black culture (the totality of cultural marks produced by those who have been labeled and/or define themselves as black) to Western modernity. The very category "black" is an invention of Western modernity, which does not mean that it can be reduced to a mere colonialist imposition on empirically verifiable black beings that preexist this classification, but that this arrangement defies any sort of quasi comprehensibility, if it does so at all, outside the modern West. In this regard, Ronald Judy, in *(Dis)forming the American Canon*, makes an important intervention in the debates concerning the function of writing in the New World slave narrative.[9] Hitherto, critics have assumed that because of the interfacing and/or equating of writing with reason the slave narrative facilitated black peoples' ingress to the domain of the human, since their ability to master alphabetic script proved their humanity. Judy, however, maintains that "the humanization in writing achieved in the slave narrative required the conversion of the incomprehensible African into the comprehensible Negro" (92). This subtle and supple syncopation of emphasis is vital because it does not suppose *the Negro* and *the African* to be fungible, even if they occupy the same continuum, while also making possible the conjecture that Afro-diasporic cultural formations are not intrinsically beside Western modernity. Instead, the argument magnifies the ways in which blackness becomes (il)legible from within this assemblage; paradoxically, this decipherability rests on the supposed externality of black culture to Western modernity, amplifying the manifold ways in which the inside always already discharges the outside and vice versa. Or, in Ralph Ellison's phrasing, "Black is . . . an' black ain't."[10] And while Judy is chiefly concerned with the figuration of "the Negro as a trope, indeed as a misapplied metaphor" (94) in the realm of the writing, my endeavor lies in scrutinizing the in/audibility of blackness in this field, which designates how blackness is sounded and heard by a whole range of cultural, philosophical, political, social, and economic discourses. What strikes the auditory apparatus via this line of inquiry is not so much a monolith of negritude as a series of compounded materiodiscursive echoes in and around black sounds in the West, what Edouard Glissant would call an opacity. In this way, the dub version or remix of blackness precedes and envelops both temporally and conceptually any putative original over the last hundred years or so; this is what I term "sonic Afro-modernity," no more, no less.

Prior to the twentieth century, orality and music served as the main modes of dissemination for New World black cultural productions. In the twentieth century, we see the indexing of music and orality in the aesthetic productions of major black authors such as W. E. B. Du Bois, Ralph Ellison, James Weldon Johnson, Paule Marshall, and Toni Morrison. In addition, black music from ragtime to hip-hop has enjoyed massive success on a global scale over the last century. The engagements with sound technologies are both an extension of and a divergence from these pre-twentieth-century musical and oral *technes*. While many studies of black culture and literature discuss the two concepts, these works frequently posit music and orality as static constants, mapping one particular form of music, such as the blues, onto all of black culture, or locating a pre-technological orality in black cultural history. As a result, these theories do not fully account for the overdetermined contingency of orality or particular genres of black music, and, most important, they seldom address their technicities. We find these complexities both in the continuities between nineteenth- and twentieth-century formations and in the ruptures created by modern sound technologies. The advent of technological sound recording embodied in the phonograph made it possible to split sounds from the sources that (re)produced them, creating differently pitched technological oralities and musicalities in twentieth-century black culture. In other words, oralities and musicalities were no longer tied to the immediate presence of human subjects, a situation that occasions not so much a complete disappearance of the human as much as a resounding through new styles of technological folding.

On the one hand, this (dis)juncture between sound and source rendered sound more ephemeral, since it failed to provide the listener with a "human" visual point of reference. On the other hand, sound gained its materiality in the technological apparatuses and the practices surrounding these devices and in the process rematerialized the human source. We should understand this disturbance of the alleged unity between sound and source not as an originary rupture but as a radical reformulation of their already vexed codependency, which retroactively calls attention to the ways in which any sound re/production is technological, whether it emanates from the horn of a phonograph, a musical score, or a human body. The singularity of the technological instantiation, however, does not remain the same. This interplay between the ephemerality of music (and/or the apparatus) and the materiality of the audio technologies/practices (and/or music) provides the central, nonsublatable tension at the core of sonic Afro-modernity.[11] The novel cleft between sound and source initiated by the technology of the phonograph in twentieth-century black culture supplies the grooves of sonic Afro-modernity. By drastically re/constructing the flow between sounds and an identifiable human source, the technology of the phonograph worried the complex intersection of orality, music, and writing. This joint proves particularly pertinent to black culture since music and orality carried a different weight in nineteenth-century African American culture. Because alphabetic script did not represent the primary mode of cultural transmission, the phonograph did not cause the same sorts of anxieties about the legibility of music as it did in mainstream American culture. Instead, black cultural producers and consumers productively engaged the split between sound and source in order to create a variety of musics, literary texts, and films. The nexus of black culture and sonic technologies tenders notions of temporality, spatiality, and community unlike those that insist on linearity, progress, and the like, but without renouncing these *tout court*, thus enabling black subjects to structure and sound their positionalities within and against Western modernity. The chapters that follow isolate some major currents within sonic Afro-modernity that boost the ephemoromateriality of sound transmitted through technology and reveal how black cultural producers have created a plethora of practices and objets d'art that (re)mix the divide between the ephemerality and materiality of technologized sound in the twentieth century.

Surveying literary texts, films, and sound media that highlight the recording and reproduction of sonic material provides the occasion to explore the ways in which black culture has utilized and created the technological innovations that now characterize sound technologies' central features. I draw on these cultural representations, because sonic technologies and their attendant listening practices have received scant attention in analyses of black music or, until recently, of music in general. While some studies have begun to address the new technological developments and their cultural ramifications, few works thoroughly probe the explicit connection between black culture and developments in sound recording and reproduction.[12] My method, although situated within (black) cultural studies, is not beholden to one particular school of thought. As an alternative, I establish a dialogue between literary texts and current popular culture to conjecture how sonic technologies and black cultural production have fruitfully contaminated each other, analyzing specific musical practices and their technological (un)folding. *Phonographies* practices what I dub—with all its resonances of echo, delay, and Afro-diasporic studio tricknology—"thinking sound/sound thinking." This approach eschews a strict opposition between popular culture and canonical forms of cultural expression, without erasing their differing institutional articulations; it involves using the insights of each field to critically reconfigure the other. Like the practices of disc jockeys, it juxtaposes historically and formally (supposedly) disparate artifacts and methodological approaches to yield new meanings, intensities, and textures in the field of sonic Afro-modernity. This style of inquiry not only offers different modalities for probing the crosscurrents and discontinuities of twentieth-century black cultures as they intersect with the histories of sound technologies, but also, and perhaps more significantly, transacts different registers for apprehending modern cultural formations in the Western world (readers interested in a more elaborate discussion of these methodological questions might want to jump ahead to the outro).[13] Framed by this intro and the outro, the core of the book takes up specific concerns central to Western modernity (subjectivity, temporality, spatiality, and community) from the conceptual purview of sonic Afro-modernity, adding new interpretive layers to the initial argument instead of "applying" the theoretical insights developed at the onset. In short, this book elaborates both the black cultural specificities and general modern Western provenances of these patterns and asks whether the distinctions between the two are as steadfast as we would like or assume them to be.

Phonographies also contains substantial (re)readings of African American canonical texts by W. E. B. Du Bois and Ralph Ellison from a techno-auditory standpoint. Ellison has emerged as a central figure in the process of writing, since he, more than any other writer, engages the poetics of sonic Afro-modernity by returning time and again to questions of sound, technology, and (black) culture. My engagements with Ellison and Du Bois provide occasions from and through which to think and hear both lyrically and critically the three fields that form this book's core: sound, technology, and black culture. Just as important are the popular works of art and practices, which, on their own and in their interfacing with Ellison's and Du Bois's texts, form the other archive of this book. And while I am aware of the differential positions occupied by the bibliotheques and discotheques "out there," in here they meld into a splintered totality that cannot be encapsulated by either field separately. What is more, my analysis takes the purportedly ephemeral cases as seriously as those already enshrined in consecrated timelessness, insisting, as I mentioned above, on their singularity. Discussing popular culture only qua popular culture commonly leaves unsullied the orders of discourse that relegate noncanonical formations to the dustbin of "history" until they are excavated as important texts in the future at the same time as neglecting pop culture's constitutive conceptualness. In other words, *Phonographies* does not celebrate popular cultural resistance; nor does it scrutinize its ideological containment or hegemonic rearticulation. More exactly, I ask what new modes of thinking, being, listening, and becoming, what Amiri Baraka terms "the flow of *is*," are set in motion by all the cultural idioms included here.[14] The answer: sonic Afro-modernity.

Since the Enlightenment, the sonic, especially in the form of music, has led a strange existence in the annals of Western thought, functioning concurrently as the most abjected and most exalted of the arts. Beginning with Plato, music was thought to have no significance without the accompaniment of words. Since sound by itself could only generate affect and not linguistic meaning, Plato and many after him feared the abandon and sensory pleasure derived from pure sonorousness.[15] During the "Ensoniment," however, music came to be heard as the most rarefied of the arts, but only insofar as it interfaced with the mathematicism of certain types of classical music that eschewed sensory pleasure and the body in favor of the "higher" regions of the mind; thus the idea of "absolute music" was born.[16] Yet, as many recent writers have pointed out, "absolute music" remains an impossibility due to the necessary material manifestation of any sound whether in human bodies, written scores, on phonograph records, compact discs, or MP3 files. But the phantoms of these post-Enlightenment discourses concerning music's asocial purity still indefatigably haunt both popular media and academic arguments.[17] What remains to be interrogated is the embodiment of sonic matter in a variety of forms without resorting to any a priori suppositions of the figuration these materialities will assume, if they do so at all. Jacques Attali's *Noise: The Political Economy of Music* remains an important text about the place of the sonic in Western culture(s) since the Middle Ages, even while it succumbs at points to an unnecessary economic functionalism. The gauntlet Attali has thrown before traditional musicology has found its most attentive listeners among academic and journalistic popular music critics, who have taken seriously the sociality of the auditory. For Attali, *pace* conventional musicology, the main factor in establishing an ontological rift between noise and music is culture, or rather the totality of a given sociohistorical formation. According to his argument, "we must learn to judge a society by its sounds, by its art, and by its festivals, [rather] than by its statistics," that is, by instigating a style of cultural analysis that carefully and boisterously lends its ear to the sounds produced within a sociohistorical context as well as their mutual enmeshment.[18] Attali tends to emphasize the primacy of the political and economic, especially in its determination of the aural; a shortcoming, to be sure, but not so grave as to render his arguments useless. This obsession with the socioeconomic is most clearly articulated in the principal narrative of *Noise*, which begins with the sonic at the center of social life in the Middle Ages (here music serves as ritual sacrifice), moving to its abstraction from the quotidian and reification in scores and concert halls (Attali terms this the epoch of representation), followed by music's utter and devastating commodification at the hands of the recording industry (the age of repetition), culminating, finally, in an era of composition made possible by new sound technologies.

To any reader of Marxist theory this story of an Edenic and precapitalist world where the people fall from grace as they are colonized by capital and then only after a while reclaim their place in an utopian future hardly contains any surprises; we might even say that it is as comforting as a fairy tale. In each of these stages recounted by Attali—in a rather circular and perhaps even tautological fashion—the sonic simply mirrors/redacts the social contexts from which it initially welled up. To Attali's credit, he actually takes a slightly different stance, rendering music as prophetic of social formations rather than representing them a posteriori. This is a welcome change, even if it just reverses the order of things by positing the aural to herald future social and political constellations: "Music is prophecy. . . . [I]t makes audible the new world that will gradually become visible" (11).[19] At the very least, this puts a heavy burden on music while also making it a cog in a quasirepresentational apparatus. Perhaps we should tune Attali's interpretive framework to another pitch or dub his steady Marxist beat a bit by not reading the prophetic vicissitudes too literally, but keeping in play the imbrication of the social and the sonorous—what distinguishes noise from music in the first place. Put differently, maybe the sonic does not harbor so much a sheer image—its figuration as sound qua sound would in many ways preempt this pictorializing gesture—of what is to come as much as it renders futurity audible in its circumvention of strictly mimetic technes. In sonic Afromodernity, sound, for a variety of social, ontological, historical, and aesthetic reasons (as a general rule, the *why* is never quite as important as the *how* here), holds out more flexible and future-directed provenances of black subjects' relation to and participation in the creation of Western modernity. I am by no means, at least not by any necessary ones, propagating a sonic idealism or hierarchy of the senses with their attendant structuration in the West since the Enlightenment, but instead welcome

Attali's challenge, albeit without resorting to the functionalism that intermittently mars *Noise*. What I take from Attali are the jerky perimeters of the noise/music bifurcation within modernity and black cultures' fundamental part in its fluctuation; as Attali himself observes, the global dominance of the recording industry was made possible by "the colonization of black music by the American industrial apparatus" (103). My argument versions Attali's work by hearing the flux of the world in the traffic between music and a variety of social formations, minus any representational or idealist guarantees, choosing instead to dwell on the singularity framed by their close encounters (of the third kind).

Chapter 1 of this book, "Hearing Sonic Afro-Modernity," commences with a discussion of recent theories of "minor" modernities as they interface with sonic technologies and follows with a short history of the phonograph. Then the argument turns to the thorny intersection of speech and writing—as framed by debates in African American literary studies and poststructuralist theory—to analyze how this bifurcation is both compounded and reframed by the technology of the phonograph. Relating these debates to a number of contemporary writings on race, modernity, and sound situates my concept of "sonic Afro-modernity" within a broad theoretical field. These thoughts are followed by a discussion of W. E. B. Du Bois's concept of double consciousness as put forth in *The Souls of Black Folk* (1903). I scrutinize the role of vision and sound in the construction of modern black subjectivity, amplifying both the materiality of the visual by way of racial formation and suggesting different ways of combining the phono and the optic. Overall, I take the phonographic technologization of black music and speech not as an instance of "inauthenticity" but as a condition of (im)possibility for modern (black) cultural production.

"I Am I Be" (chapter 2) draws on the prologue of Ralph Ellison's *Invisible Man* (1952) to query the vexed intersections of sound, technology, and black subjectivity in the twentieth century. I investigate how Ellison's nameless protagonist's subjectivity is framed by his engagement with Louis Armstrong's recording of "(What Did I Do to Be So) Black and Blue." Ellison's insistence on sound and technology as forceful modalities in the construction of black selfhood suggests a path that circumvents, or at least refigures, the identity/subjectivity split by refusing to pit one against the other. Armstrong's voice on a phonograph provides an acoustic mirror for the protagonist's social invisibility and serves as the structuring metaphor for the protagonist's subjectivity. The resulting increased technological audibility provides the necessary backdrop for the social invisibility of black subjects. The chapter then considers more generally how *identity*, as a particular, local, and minoritized category, is often construed against the *subject*, as its universal and disembodied other within academic discourse. Thus, the "sounds of blackness" articulated through constantly shifting sonic technologies represent a crucial signifying locus for the formation of (black) subjectivities throughout the twentieth century and help recalibrate the identity-subject gulf by calling attention to their mutual interreliance.

"In the Mix" (chapter 3) links the formal structure of W. E. B. Du Bois's *The Souls of Black Folk* to the contemporary mixing practices of DJs. First, the argument returns to Ellison's *Invisible Man*, where he imagines history in the form of a groove inscribed on the surface of a phonograph record, offering a model of temporal change that "spins around" a linear and progressive version of history. Ellison's description of the "groove of history," I argue, locates black culture in the technologized sounds of the phonograph. Du Bois's text suggests a continuous mix of different genres and media (sociology, history, narrative fiction, poetry, and music). Moreover, the musical bars at the beginning of each chapter of *Souls*, quotations from the vast archive of spirituals, appear in the text not as accurate mimetic representations but as distorted, layered, lingering traces that disrupt the flow of words. "In the Mix" then surveys the history and mechanics of disc jockeying as an art form in contemporary (black) musical culture in order to conjecture how this practice is echoed in Du Bois's textual strategies and vice versa. My analysis shows that one of the major currents of sonic Afro-modernity is "the mix" as it appears in *Souls* and DJing, for it offers an aesthetic that realigns the temporalities (grooves) of Western modernity in its insistence on rupture and repetition. If, in Ellison, history appears in the form of a groove, then the mixing tactics of Du Bois and DJs provide ways to noisily bring together competing and complementary beats without sublating their tensions.

While the first three chapters dwell in the dominion of the primarily conceptual (and in some ways literary), the final two chapters draw on a more clearly discernable cultural studies approach, in part because the works discussed therein are not as well known as those central to the earlier arguments, so contextualization seems more paramount here. Nevertheless, I want to caution against the easy opposition of the "theoretical" and "cultural" that so often occurs in contemporary debates; rather, my approach queries the foundations upon which these distinctions are routinely administered. In other words, in the recent history of the Anglo-American humanities, "theory" and "cultural studies" designate not only two supposedly dissimilar ways of analyzing cultural objects and subjects but also two points in a fairly traditional narrative of supersession, where the more "empirical," "historical," "ethnographic," and so on discourse pays for the "sins" of its "abstract," "lofty," and "elitist" father (maternity—and this will come as no great surprise—remains absent in this context: papa's baby, mama's maybe). Now—according to this account—we are dealing with real people instead of intangible subjects, with politics and history (always functioning as the ultimate guarantors for the real) and not textuality or philosophy, or so we tell ourselves time and again. This story, taken at face value, frequently serves as a safeguard against various criticisms from outside the academy in the wake of the theoretical turn and the culture wars. It also makes "us" feel important, since we are now actually helping "the people" and not just onanistically relishing abstract otherworldly thought. But I have little tolerance for this line of thinking, given that it preempts inventive and idiosyncratic ideas and smuggles in an unarticulated positivism that calcifies how things are instead of imagining how they could be. Conversely, my patience is equally lacking (maybe my problem is that I just don't have enough patience) for the calls for a return to the heady days of "pure theory." *Phonographies* is very much a product of and in dialogue with both of these forces, and, while the chapter structure of this book might indicate a schizophrenic dualism, all the arguments reflect an engagement with a theoretically inflected (black) cultural studies, just differently so. In the end, I hope that readers will discern the cultural dimensions of the first three units and the theoretical spirits of the final chapters, as well as their complementary intersections.[20]

Chapter 4, "Consuming Sonic Technologies," considers Ralph Ellison's essay "Living with Music" (1955) and Darnell Martin's film *I Like It Like That* (1994). These texts exemplify how recorded music and its technological embodiment construct public and private spaces. Ellison's essay meticulously describes his living quarters in terms of the music that emanates from the apartments around him and the manner in which he uses recorded music (phonograph records on his sound system) to distinguish his space from that of his neighbors. Similarly, Lisette, the protagonist of

Martin's film, uses sonic technologies (boom box, radio, and Walkman) to create a space that simultaneously differentiates her from and links her to her family and neighbors. As these texts progress, both characters redefine themselves vis-à-vis their spatial and social surroundings through sound technologies. Where Ellison fetishizes the stereo equipment itself, Lisette deploys audio technologies to access sound and establish a zone of privacy. Still, both instances underscore the integrality of sound technologies in making and recasting modern urban geographies, while also highlighting how these spatialities are inflected by the history of technologies and gendered access to these apparatuses.

The final chapter represents an aberration of an aberration; fittingly it is also the longest of the five. Not only does "Sounding Diasporic Citizenship" focus narrowly on contemporary popular music in a cultural studies fashion; it also includes little deliberation on sonic technologies per se. What this chapter does in fact is zero in on the culturo-political practices initiated by sonic technologies. So, while its analysis of three contemporary Afro-diasporic musical acts—the Haitian and African American rap group the Fugees, the Afro- and Italian-German rap collective Advanced Chemistry, and the black British artist Tricky and his partner, Martina—does not concern itself with the specific machinations of recording and reproducing sonorous material, the very existence of these artists would not have been possible without the technological shifts discussed in the preceding chapters. I begin with a deliberation of current discussions of diaspora and citizenship, coming to the conclusion that both figurations are too narrow to contain the complexities of Afro-diasporic subjectivities. These forms of belonging also belie any easy invocations of hybridity as a cultural and political free-for-all, given that they direct attention to the difficult political, cultural, and affective labor involved in maintaining multifarious forms of association. Music as it is transmitted through different sound technologies provides alternative spaces for the articulation of "diasporic citizenship" and offers avenues for present-day black musical artists to envision and sound their multiple sites of political and cultural membership. The diasporic citizenships of these musical acts imagine black political and cultural subjectivities that encompass local/global and national/transnational affiliations through sonic technologies.

As a whole, my project examines particular instances in black culture that would have not been possible without sound recording and reproduction and their entanglement with the world at large. Yet, rather than merely seeing them as instances of commodification, I have chosen to focus on the conditions of im/possibility these technologies represent for twentieth-century black culture. The bulk of *Phonographies* builds its argumentative intensity by way of examples rather than by attempting any sort of comprehensive overview that assumes to uncritically represent the encased totality of a field already preestablished in "the real world." I cling to the importance of the example, since, as Giorgio Agamben explains, it enhances the singularity of the cases in question: "Neither particular nor universal, the example is a singular object that presents itself as such, that shows its singularity."[21] Insisting on singularity, and not, say, particularity and/or universality with reference to black cultural architectonics offers different styles for thinking this field, modes of inquiry that do not cast black culture as belated or dislocated from some general sphere of Western modernity. In general, my "method" is best described by what Gilles Deleuze and Felix Guattari term *ritournelle*, a rhythmic pattern in a field of chaos, or rather the autopoetic vacillation of the universe. Translated as "the refrain," the ritournelle is for Deleuze and Guattari a "prism, a crystal of space-time. It acts upon that which surrounds it, sound or light, extracting from it various vibrations, or decompositions, projections, or transformations. The refrain also has a catalytic function."[22] The refrain is decisive for the phono-graphic unfolding and folding of this book, because it allows for theorizations from and with the sonic, while also underscoring the singularity of the subjects and objects under scrutiny.

Focusing on the conditions of im/possibility that these technologies engender for twentieth-century black culture and how black cultural sensibilities have shaped the history of sonic technologies accents the complicated rapport among sound, writing, orality, and technology in the twentieth century. Instead of emphasizing either the technological or the cultural, the grooves of sonic Afro-modernity integrate both. *Phonographies* acknowledges the technological mediation of black popular music in the twentieth century but does not relegate these practices to the apparatus itself, at least not any notion thereof in which technology's materiality remains anterior to or outside of the machinations of (black) culture. The grooves of sonic Afro-modernity can be found in the spaces and times between technological change and a variety of cultural practices, and the interplay between the hard- and software poignantly encodes the competing notions of subjectivity, temporality, spatiality, and community without dissolving them.

Post Script   Let us return for a moment to the planet of popular music, if you will permit me to indulge in a further instance of "high-fidelity-ism" before we begin "properly."[23] One of my favorite songs over the last year has been a recording by British R&B girl-group Mis-Teeq. The refrain of this song repeats the phrase "It's beginning to feel like."[24] Of course, what it is beginning to feel like is *love*, the central topos of R&B and perhaps all popular music. Yet, when the lead singer utters the L-word the background harmonies contrapuntally interrupt and/or augment the central voice with the following lines: "Like the sun on my skin on a hot summer's day / Like a song in my head that won't go away / Like a smile on my face coz you make me happy / Ohhh." Here, *love* is indefinitely postponed both sonically and linguistically, lingering in the quagmire of simile and creating aural ellipses by making language stutter (as Nathaniel Mackey and Gilles Deleuze remind us).[25] This musical example, along with the ones invoked earlier, provide fragile complexities from which academic discourses can learn a thing or three, even though there does not seem to be a need to treat academic language and pop culture all that differently. While I surely cannot claim creating something as majestic as Kenny Gamble and Leon Huff's work with Harold Melvin and the Blue Notes on "Wake Up Everybody," or Mis-Teeq's rigorous vocal acrobatics, I take these sonoric flickers as inspirations, since they make perceptible singulars that only signify in their "poetics of relation" to other sounds and matters.[26] A literary approximation of these instances appears in Ralph Ellison's *Invisible Man*: "Instead of the swift and imperceptible flowing of time, you are aware of its nodes, those points where time stands still or from which it leaps ahead. And you slip into the breaks and look around" (9). These lines from Ellison appear, disappear, and rematerialize throughout *Phonographies* as epigraphs, mantras, choruses, or refrains, to heighten the texturality and intensity of my contentions (and to remind myself of the pleasures, responsibilities, and dangers attached to this gliding), honing in on singular temporospatial nodes found in the tumultuous relationship between black cultural production and sound technologies in the streams of the twentieth century, an intimate affair, to be sure, one marked by both soft screams and loud whispers.

1

Hearing Sonic Afro-Modernity

The invention of the phonograph at the end of the nineteenth century offered a different way to split sounds from the sources that (re)produced them, thus generating a new technological orality and musicality in twentieth-century black culture (even though orality is always already techne-logical). Now that the space and time of audition were separated from the contexts of reception, both orality and musicality relied differently on the immediate presence of human subjects. One result of this development is that the technological recording and mass distribution of music are often construed as lacking the authenticity and immediacy of live performances and/or as the wholesale appropriation of musical cultures by various capitalist formations in current critical discourses. Although these interpretations surely possess some value, they tend to neglect the possibilities occasioned by this audiovisual disjuncture for black cultural production, or any form of cultural production for that matter. The complex interfacing of modern black culture and sound technologies in fact provides the venue for imagining and producing a variety of cultural practices, constituting in their open totality sonic Afro-modernity. Nevertheless, while the literature on black musics comprises an expansive and ever expanding archive, encompassing numerous disciplinary approaches and spanning various historical periods, work that considers the technological instantiation of these sounds occurs less frequently. However, if we are to analyze a sounding black modernity, we should strive to understand how technologies have affected the production, consumption, and dissemination of black popular music and vice versa; an endeavor that is even more pertinent today with the increasing globality of black musical practices. In other words, we need to probe the conditions for the im/possibility of modern black sounds: black sounds are made perceptible in the modern era by sonic technologies, and these technologies have been shaped significantly by black music.

Although the phonograph rendered sound more ephemeral — it seemingly removed the performer from view — its materiality was displaced onto the recording apparatus itself and the practices surrounding it and, as a result, rematerialized the sonic source. As we shall see, the putative split between sound and source created anxieties about the writing of sound and the visual dimensions of music, but it also opened new ways to engage these spheres. Sound recording and reproduction technologies have afforded black cultural producers and consumers different means of staging time, space, and community in relation to their shifting subjectivity in the modern world. In fact, sound recordings of African American–derived music have dominated the American and now global record industry. It is my contention that the radical reconstruction of the previous relation between sound and source created fresh cultural spheres that would not have been possible without recording and reproduction technologies, just as these technologies are unthinkable without black music.

Paul Gilroy and Houston Baker attempt to account for the crucial place of sound within modern black culture; yet they gloss over the technelogical aspects (which are never simply reducible to technology) of black popular music.[1] While carefully assessing the effects of the recording, reproduction, and international distribution of black popular music, they stop short of reflecting on the ramifications of these factors themselves. In *The Black Atlantic*, for instance, Gilroy stipulates an integral connection between music and modern black cultural production, granting the sonic a privileged place within Afro-diasporic formations because of its ability to convey the horrors of slavery via its primarily nonrepresentational attributes.[2] Because of these nonrepresentational dimensions, says Gilroy, "engaging with black popular music demands an embarrassing confrontation with substantive intraracial differences that make the easy essentialism from which most critical judgments are constructed simply untenable" (36). Although at pains to stress the musical properties that exceed the strictly textual and literary, Gilroy primarily focuses on the lyrics of black popular music and the interaction of performers with audiences. Sound recording and reproduction are mentioned briefly and do not occupy center stage, an omission that reduces the force of his argument regarding black popular music's intimate relationship to modernity. At the close of his examination, Gilroy asks how contemporary global flows will change the interactive patterns between black audiences and performers, stating that "calls and responses no longer converge in the tidy patterns of secret, ethnically encoded dialogue" (110). However, while current forms of globalization might be reconfiguring certain kinds of "tidy" ethnically marked conversations around black popular music, it is anything but a recent phenomenon. As Gilroy himself shows in a different part of his book, the history of black popular music, from nineteenth-century spirituals to contemporary hip-hop, makes any easy (or even difficult) essentialisms impossible. We can hear the developments Gilroy attributes to the current moment as far back as the 1920s, when African American popular music was first recorded and disseminated on a large scale, or even earlier, with the Fisk Jubilee Singers' global travels, so eloquently elucidated by Gilroy.[3] By enabling disparate audiences in a variety of locations to consume black music, sound technologies assured that local calls and responses would differ according to spatio-temporal coordinates, facilitating the emergence and reconfiguration of numerous cultural practices. The phonograph's recalibration of locality effected changes in its relation to other vicinities rather than erasing the local altogether. Thus black popular music transmitted through sonic technologies failed to generate the same meanings and textures — neither worse nor better, simply different — as those sounds produced and consumed exclusively in geographically circumscribed locales. Nevertheless, we should note that geographic proximity does not guarantee that all present will derive the exact same meaning from the event. When these questions about the recording and distribution of black popular music are relegated to the present and future, previous forms of black popular music remain auratically suspended in an authentic pretechnological bubble. And this bubble appears only as such in contradistinction to the technological — much in the same way as the source of phonographic framing.

Houston Baker describes a "modern Afro-American sound" found in African American literature from Charles Chesnutt, W. E. B. Du Bois, and Booker T. Washington at the end of the nineteenth century, for instance, to Richard Wright's work in the 1940s.[4] Sound functions as a metaphor for Baker, while it does not for Gilroy. Not so much interested in the particular properties of black music itself, Baker contemplates how music and certain black vernacular oral expressions are inscribed in African American literary works. Key to Baker's analysis is how particular sounds are (re)sounded in literary artifacts and the ways in which this resounding bespeaks a specific black American literary modernism. His points, however, remain largely abstract, not probing the changes the incorporated sounds themselves undergo in the process of de/relocalization: what happens if these formerly orally and locally transmitted "modern Afro-American sounds" become nationally consumable as parts of literary texts and recorded on phonograph discs? Such questions are crucial because, instead of leaving the sounds intact, they ask how sonic marks are transformed by entering into the age of mechanical reproduction, either in literary texts or on records. Moreover, by either not thinking the effects of these transformations at all or by pitting them against a prelapsarian instance of spatiotemporal unity, these considerations disregard the constitutive technicity of black music in the modern era. Gilroy and Baker are right to think together black popular music and modernity, since Afro-diasporic musical practices are routinely described as pristine and untouched forms of "vernacular" expression even though they are such crucial parts of modern formations. Still, any consideration of black music might do well to ponder the ramifications of this particular culturoinformational imbrication without succumbing to the pitfalls of technological determinism or celebrating the vernacular authenticity of black popular music; addressing that imbrication would not only broaden the scope of Gilroy's and Baker's arguments but also emphasize the centrality of black musical cultures to modern sonic technologies.

Building on Baker's and Gilroy's concerns about black music's rapport with modernity and the spatiotemporal aperture engendered and amplified by the phonograph, we can come to an understanding of the multifarious ways in which these currents have impacted black music in the twentieth century and vice versa, albeit not in a functionalist manner that emphasizes either technology or culture at the cost of the other. For black music is not merely a byproduct of an already existing modernity, ancillary to and/or belated in its workings, but a chain of singular formations integrally linked to this sphere, particularly as it collides with information technologies. Homi Bhabha offers a conception of such a modernity that differs radically from the hegemonic Western model, imagining the fluid structural position of marginalized subjects vis-à-vis Western modernity as follows: "Modernity . . . privileges those who 'bear witness,' those who are 'subjected,' or . . . historically displaced. It gives them a representative position through spatial distance, or the *time-lag* between the Great Event and its circulation as a historical sign of the 'people' or an 'epoch.' . . . The discursive address of modernity— its structure of authority—decentres the Great Event, and speaks from the moment of 'imperceptibility,' the supplementary space 'outside' or uncannily besides."[5] This "modernity otherwise" disrupts and displaces the grand narratives of reason and technological progress by incorporating those who fall outside of these categories into the mix, which disruption, in turn, revamps the meanings of modernity as it resists separating these two spheres (modernity and minority cultures) into neatly distinct categories, asking us to rethink the very source of this putatively universal and homogenous sphere.[6] Modernity, according to Bhabha, is transformed into a series of competing and, at times, conflicting singular spatiotemporal terrains marked by constitutive lag: "It is the function of the *lag* to slow down the linear progressive time of modernity to reveal its 'gesture,' its *tempi*, 'the pauses and stresses of the whole performance' " (253). This lag, imagined by Bhabha as primarily temporal, suffuses the (anti)ontology of the modern and finds its uncanny home in the poetics of relation that mark the node where the *phono* joins the *graph* and/or *optic*. We will now make a pilgrimage to this spot in order to come to a fuller understanding of sonic Afro-modernity.

For the Record: Phono-Graph The *Random House College Dictionary* gives no fewer than eighteen definitions of "record." The first and most general signification reads as follows: "To set down in writing or the like, as for the purpose of preserving evidence," a definition that stresses writing, but does not exclude other modalities. Written records conserve already existent materials; the act of writing transforms the content of recording into evidence. According to this characterization, writing can stockpile data without the baggage of the reproductive because it seemingly wields an ontological presence beyond its ontic replication: it can exist as such. In the context of this definition, only the act of producing script (or any other form of writing) matters, everything else is simply window dressing; neither the writer nor the reader seem to have any consequence in this assemblage. Definition number 10, the second pertinent one for my purposes, reads: "a disc or other object on which sounds are recorded for later reproduction." Since sound is located in the sphere of the oral and phonic, sound recordings appear to subsist principally for duplication, falling short of standing on their own as records, especially since they constantly have to corroborate their authority via replication; in fact, their *Dasein* seems to emanate from repetition and (re)iteration.

Keeping within the taxonomy of the characterization cited above, sound recordings do not secure evidence of preexisting information but "merely" disseminate recorded sounds: they are forever suspended in a circulatory tide. Hence, writing attains record status in the act of production, whereas sound recordings cannot achieve evidentiariness through production alone: they are permanently lacking, always secondary. Or, put in a slightly different way, in these discourses alphabetic script is construed as a natural extension of the human body, as if there were anything natural about the human or its varying prostheses, where sonic inscription interjects spacing and absence into this flow. These divergent dictionary significations of written and phonic records stem, at least to some extent, from the different sociotemporal contexts in which both emerged: script appeared well before the advent of mechanical reproduction, and sound recording is a product of the late nineteenth century, a period when informational technologies such as the telephone, telegraph, and photography proliferated. Still, the definitions of written and phonograph records summoned earlier were devised at a time when both writing and sound were readily recordable and reproducible via mechanical means; they appear even more startling if we take into account that writing has been in the age of mechanical reproduction at least since the fifteenth century when Gutenberg invented the printing press.[7] Why, then, do written documents conjure the finality of script when sound necessitates reproduction in order to escape the throwness of finitude? It seems that in order for writing not to come into view as a technology, and therefore not a biological extension of homo sapiens, the process of its motorized mediation had to be rendered imperceptible; making it seem as if script exists outside the vicissitudes of history and ideology.[8] As will become apparent, this naturalization had particularly volatile consequences for Afro-diasporic cultural constellations.

An inquiry into the etymology of "phonograph" and the history of the phonograph record can shed some sound on the observation that "writing [apparently] merely stores the fact of its authorization," while sound must be constantly reproduced in order for it to gain the same authority as writing, if at all.[9] *Phonê* in Greek denotes sound and voice; *graph*, on the other hand, signifies writing. Thus, the oral and phonetic are written down (*recorded*) by the phonograph (*sound writer*), imploding the originary aperture between writing and sound by calling attention to the improbability of writing sound in any commonsensical manner. The etymology of "phonograph" and the words used to designate many other nineteenth-century technologies — "photography" (picture writing) and "cinematography" (film writing) — suggest that inscription seems to be at the root of any kind of recording: more than recording itself, it seems that sound necessitates transposition into writing to even register as technology. The place of script as a preferred, if not dominant, cultural technology in the West makes for the authority that it relays in relation to speech and sound, which, in contrast to writing, have to be reiterated and imagined as writing in order to operate as recordings; sonic recordings are the means rather than the end to a status as record. Of the hegemony of writing in Western modernity, Friedrich Kittler writes:

> What will soon end in the monopoly of bits and fiber optics began with the monopoly of writing. History was the homogenous field that, as an academic subject, only took account of literate cultures. Mouths and graphisms were relegated to prehistory. . . . Otherwise events and their stories could not have been linked. This is why anything that ever happened ended up in libraries. . . . [W]riting functioned as a universal medium — in times where there was no concept of medium. (4–6)

In this scheme, something is heaved into the sphere of script and therefore recorded, ensuring its presence beyond the scene of production. Sound and voice, on the other hand, require an audience to guarantee, legally, epistemologically, and ontologically, their continuing being. Hence the written record seems autonomous of any reception and reproduction processes, whereas sound and voice become documents, when and if they do so at all, *only* in the murky domains of reproduction and reception.

If the etymology of "phonograph" implies that sound and voice are not capable of recording independently of writing, since they fall short of record status per se, the early history of the technology of the phono-graph reproduces, as it were, this dilemma, since the machine was judged incapable of securing evidence, although expressly invented with the aim of preserving oral communication, public opinion, and legal discourse. When the phonograph first appeared in the late 1870s it was not intended as a device to record music or as a source of home entertainment; its main function was to record human voices.[10] The phonograph was marketed as an office instrument to record and preserve court proceedings and busi-ness letters.[11] It was not until the turn of the century that the phonograph became a player in the home entertainment market, serving to reproduce music and human voices in domestic settings. Set in 1877, there is some dispute concerning who authored the creation of the phonograph; while Thomas Alva Edison is commonly credited with its invention, a French scientist, Charles Cros, was working on a strikingly similar machine at the same time. Yet Edison was the first to "go on record" with this inven-tion—here the ontological authority of writing meets its doppelgänger in the annals of patent law. In fact, the phonograph was a byproduct of research on the telephone and telegraph and formed a part of the com-plex web of other proliferating informational technologies in the latter half of the nineteenth century. Alexander Graham Bell, Elisha Watson, and Edison were all working on perfecting the telephone, which had been patented by Bell in 1876; however, it was Edison who, in the process of recording telephone messages, "invented" the phonograph. Andre Mil-lard describes Edison's discovery as follows:

> One night in July 1877, his staff rigged up an indenting stylus connected to a diaphragm, which in turn was attached to a telephone speaker. As Edison shouted into the speaker, a strip of paraffin-coated paper was run underneath the stylus. An examination of the strip showed the irregular marks made by the sound waves. When the strip was pulled back under the stylus, the group of men crowded around the laboratory table heard, with disbelief, the faint sound of Edison's shouts from a few minutes earlier.[12]

Yet it took some time to come up with a functional machine that both recorded and reproduced sound, and even more time for one that would allow for large-scale industrial manufacture, which was needed for this appliance to penetrate and appeal to the national populace.

The phonograph led a tenuous existence as an office dictation device for a time before it hit upon its unforeseen entelechy: although it was able to record and reproduce sound, the machinery was too unreliable and expensive for mass production and consumption. The tin foil on which sonic information was by then being imprinted could only sound out what it had recorded twice or thrice at maximum, and the hand crank to power the phonograph was so delicate that slight shifts in speed altered and/or distorted the content completely.[13] Failing as an administrative appliance, the phonograph's purpose changed from recording and reproducing sound in business and court environs to serving as a machine for the mass consumption of entertainment in the domestic sphere. First, however, the phonograph (by now much more robust) accidentally held a role as a successful vehicle for public entertainment in the form of automated slot machines.[14] What began with demonstrations in Edison's laboratories soon spread to traveling phonograph exhibitions, arcades, and train stations during the late 1880s, thus unexpectedly shifting the machine's main utility from recording to reproducing sound. People were not so much interested in hearing their own recorded voices as those of singers and comedians, perhaps because the voice, even more so than writing, represents pure interiority and the proper domain of the sovereign human subject. In addition, the invention of the phonograph coincided with the rise of the entertainment industry in the United States and was taken up by this branch of capital and made into a desirable commodity. By the early 1890s the phonograph primarily brought musical (vocal and nonvocal), spoken word, and comedic entertainment into the homes of middle-class Americans. In 1894 Columbia Records produced the first inexpensive phonograph; prices now ranged from twenty to fifty dollars, compared to two hundred dollars, which was the sum hitherto charged by Edison's National Phonograph Company. Suddenly, the phonograph became a mass-produced and mass-distributed household item, despite the fact that the unreliability and high cost of this young technology complicated its development.

Several critics writing about the wider social and epistemological implications of the technology of the phonograph stress the way in which the machine refigured the connection between sound and writing. For instance, in a discussion about the musical Copyright Act of 1909 (the first such act to include recorded music), Lisa Gitelman shows that the central debate concerned the split between sound and vision, especially writing, in the phonograph.[15] Since musical copyright law was heretofore based on sheet music, in order for recorded music to function as intellectual property, composers—performers did not even merit a footnote—had to prove that the phonograph read their music in the same or a similar way as did consumers who played the music from printed scores. In these debates the sounds contained on phonograph records were only fixable as objects under the purview of copyright law if they were proven to be the mechanical equivalent of written notation and/or script. Record companies, in particular, in order to claim all the profits from record sales, argued that phonograph records did not represent written embodiments of the composer's score since they were not legible by humans. Conversely, composers and publishers, defending their own economic interests, attempted to establish that the phonograph could, indeed, read recordings. This new technology also magnified the embodiment of music per se, because it queried the naturalization of musical notation as the most faithful record of sonic information. The dispute over the Copyright Act revolved around whether recordings based on copyrighted sheet music merely represented the use of the score or a particular performance of a composition as opposed to an altogether different material manifestation of music. Since the phonograph possessed the ability to make sounds audible, even though these noises could hardly be heard as mimetic due to technological limitations in this particular situation, marks on a page now seemed glaringly mute in comparison.

Not surprisingly, unmediated mimetic listening was most habitually ascribed to "others," such as native subjects, women, and black people. The mimetic dimensions of recorded sound were also highlighted in scenes depicting the ascription by "primitives" of paranormal powers to this machinery, which they most often encountered as an instrument of Western ethnography. Michael Taussig writes of these scenarios: "Here every effort is made to represent mimeticizing technology as magical, and the question must be repeated—because phonographic mis-en-scene [sic] is surprisingly common in twentieth-century descriptions of 'primitive' peoples—as to why Westerners are so fascinated by Others' fascination with this apparatus."[16] Gitelman analyzes a 1905 story from the *Edison Phonograph Monthly* in which the listener reacts to a recording of a flogging scene in *Uncle Tom's Cabin* as emotionally as if it were "real" (119–121). As was and perhaps still is often the case—witness current discussions of the digital divide—angst about embryonic technologies is projected onto those subjects already marginal, highlighting not so much the roles of technologies in minority cultures, or the manner in which these are construed as always after the temporospatiality of modernity, as it proves symptomatic of the mainstream anxieties about emergent technologies and minority subjects.

When phonographs began to augment and replace live performances and/or musical scores at the end of the nineteenth century, they created a glaring rupture between sound and vision.[17] Both performer and score clearly provided some discernible human origin for sounds — even though we should not assume this to represent any form of prelapsarian unity and/or simple presence — where the phonograph only gave the listener "a voice without a face," to use David Laing's phrase.[18] Now this newly invented technological apparatus stood as the main visual counterpoint to the sounds emanating from its horn, ostensibly reproducing sonic data without the cumbersome intervention of human subjects. Even the telephone, although similarly disrupting the spatial configuration of linguistic communication, offered a clearly palpable live human source for its sounds at the other end of the line. As a direct reaction to this gash between sound and human visual source, a profusion of cultural maneuvers have sought to yoke the two back together; the iconography of record covers and music videos are some obvious examples. Before these developments, however, records were produced without much graphic and/or visual accompaniment. In this particular historical context written notation suggested the most natural material grounding of music's ephemerality. Because the technology of the phonograph seemingly heightened the nonrepresentational, disembodied, transient qualities of music, almost from its very inception various discourses, more specifically those revolving around questions of copyright, attempted to capture fleeting sounds in writing, extending the linkage between writing and sound already embedded in the designation "phonograph." The phonograph suggested a machinic materiality, one that acutely destabilized any notion of an "absolute music" and called attention to other forms of aural embodiment, whether a concert stage, a musical score, or a human body. It is precisely this conflict between the phonograph's material and ephemeral dimensions, as well as the machine's worrying of the immediate connection between sound and writing, that makes it such a crucial site for the articulation of black cultural practices in the twentieth century.[19] For, in many ways, the phonograph refracts technosonically the shape-shifting textures of blackness in Western modernity as hyper(dis)embodied and (in)human.

Source Material The act of writing signals truth-value and indestructibility, while sound and voice are rendered effervescent. In other words, writing "must be repeatable—iterable—in the absolute absence of the addressee or of the empirically determinable set of addressees."[20] This remains one of the most crucial insights of Jacques Derrida's early work, which insists on the endemic absence that authorizes writing qua writing; *that is*, writing needs to be discernible beyond the immediate context of its re/production. Yet we should not understand writing to only be synonymous with alphabetic script: "This iterability . . . structures the mark of writing itself, and does so moreover for no matter what type of writing (pictographic, hieroglyphic, ideographic, phonetic, alphabetic, to use old categories). A writing that was not structurally legible—iterable—beyond the death of the addressee would not be writing" (315).[21] If writing always already carries a trace of an absence that constitutes its graphematicity, then speech, at least in Derrida's conception of certain Western philosophical traditions, signifies unmediated presence, acting as a humble servant of interiority and meaning.[22] Whereas writing relies on externality and the materiality of the signifier, speech is configured as nonrepresentational, ideal, *that is*, an unmitigated reflection of pure thought. Derrida extends his reformulation of the speech/writing problematic thus: "This structural possibility of being severed from its referent or signified (and therefore from communication and its context) seems to make of every mark, even if oral, a grapheme in general, *that is*, as we have seen, the nonpresent *remaining* of a differential mark cut off from its alleged 'production' or origin" (318). Clearly, Derrida is not after any simple privileging of the written over the oral, rather this argument exhumes the writingness of all linguistic and cultural characters, their difference and deferral, as it were. Following Derrida's formulation of writing in the general sense, the phonograph appears to unearth the iterability of speech by abstracting oral communication (or human sounds in general) from its scene of (re)creation beyond the death of the addressee. This abstraction is magnified by the intrusion of the phonographic machine, both in the limited and general sense, into the flow of oral marks and the human body. As a consequence, the machine and the various abstract machines that frame and produce it not only make sounds mechanically repeatable but also highlight the fundamental iterability of human speech. The phonograph suggests a "space-time distanciation" in which cultural productions are "distanced from this context, both spatially and temporally, and re-embedded in new contexts which may be located at different times and places," introducing a spatio-temporal rift between the moment of production and reception that allows for different conceptions of the cultural object: the absence that enables sound's iterability.[23] Accordingly, the phonograph reconstructs the speech/writing antinomy by disseminating speech in the general sphere of semiosis, although not in the same way as those forms of script listed by Derrida, since the machine actually sounds, which clearly does not imply any form of wholesome mimesis, human speech, albeit under the conditions of iterability and seriality.[24] Thus we can understand the rupture brought about by the phonograph as an anxiety about speech as absence; hence the link between the apparatus and haunting often cited in its early stages.[25] In order for human vocalization to continue in its role as unmediated presence, the sounds of the phonograph had to necessarily be yoked to writing, otherwise the materiality and iterability of the voice would become all too audible.

In *Sound Technology and the American Cinema*, James Lastra provides a much-needed corrective to previous treatments of film sound, not only to earlier film theorists, who heard no difference at all between a sound and its technological (re)production, but also to more recent writers who subscribe to the "nonidentity" conception of film sound.[26] These critics, Rick Altman and Tom Levin among others, postulate no strict correlation between the original sound and its reproduction within the cinematic apparatus, yet, says Lastra, "they too, nevertheless assume a standard, and essentially *prior* sound, which is transformed or violated by recording" (127). Instead of supposing that there exists a crudely mimetic relationship between source and reproduction, "nonidentity" theorists concede the partial and representational dimensions of sound recording and reproduction; still, they leave the original intact qua original. That is, they grant this occurrence an ontological reality above and beyond the intrusive forces of representation and do not conjecture how the original itself only functions as such in relation to its later reproduction.[27] Even so, "original" performances or sound events are often created purely for the purposes of recording and later reproduction (musicians go in the studio

to make a record and perform their music *for* the technological apparatus), and are not always already "out there" configurations waiting to be
represented, even if only partially.[28] Drawing on Derrida's conceptions
of writing and iteration, Lastra comes to the conclusion that it might be
more useful to think of the "original" as an effect of reproduction and
representation rather than its prerequisite (151–153). As a result, we can
begin to perceive the "absence by which we classify representations *as*
representations, recordings *as* recordings [as] a positive condition of possibility rather than a fault" (152). When this absence—which, as we have
seen, not only makes writing possible to operate as writing but also provides the precondition for recording and reproducing sound—is taken
into account, the emphasis shifts from the ways in which the original is
tainted by the technological process to the ways the apparatus and the
cultural practices (re)shape and (re)frame the musical object.

Despite Lastra's divergence from the nonidentity theorists, he insists
on a "theory of representation" that leaves the general economy of "copy"
versus "original" intact (153). Any theory of representation, as unmimetic
as that theory may be, fails to abolish the secondariness of the copy, since
what is repeated remains yoked to a principle of sameness rather than
difference, uncannily mirroring the manifold methods through which
black culture is construed as simply "repeating" hegemonic discourses.
But what if we push the very concept-metaphors of "original" and "copy"
to the side for the time being and think of repetition not as rearticulat-
ing the same but as activating difference? As useful as Lastra's Derridean
model and notions of repetition with a difference are, they mitigate the
intensity and force of difference by virtue of measuring it against a putative origin from which the copy diverges. In contrast, what I am suggesting here is not repetition with a difference so much as the repetition *of*
difference, wherein the original/copy distinction vanishes and only the
singular and sui generis becomings of the source remain in the clearing.[29] This repetition of difference does not ask how "the copy" departs
from "the source" but assumes that difference will, indeed, be different
in each of its incarnations. Here, the phonograph emerges as a machinic
ensemble (to cross-fade Fred Moten's and Deleuze and Guattari's idioms)
that accents the eventness of the (re)production of the source; the source
is always (re)produced as an (anti)origin while also appearing as a differently produced occasion in each of its singular figurations.[30] As a consequence, records, CDs, cassette tapes, or MP3 files should not be thought

as attempting to replicate a lost immaculate source/original but as events in their own right. These questions are not merely abstract and conceptual, since this modality of repetition also significantly recasts how we engage with recorded music in a more quotidian fashion. Most readers will recall moments in which the repeated listening to a musical object (and the same can be said of any engagement with a cultural object, reading a novel, watching a film, etc.) exposed new sounds that they had not heard in previous encounters. These instances of divergence, however, have no home in the representational brand of recurrence, because it only accents what supposedly stays the same; in this differently sounded repetition, however, what remains similar is precisely difference. In addition, as James Snead has shown, this notion of repetition and difference represents one of the hallmarks of modern black cultural production, due to its insistence on nonrepresentational and nonprogressive versions of the said categories.[31] But this model also bears out modes of thought that enable fresh ways to conceptualize the fundamental role of black culture in Western modernity, for often black culture is cast in the role of simply repeating majoritarian formations — I will have more to say about this in my discussion of Du Bois in chapter 3 — rather than as singular figurations of difference. Still, we need to return to the source of phonography, since we've only considered one aspect (iterability) of this abstract machine.

It seems that Derrida can only conceive of the voice as speech and reformulate its function as writing. Or phrased in a different key, this conception of the speech/writing bifurcation that suffuses much of Western thought in some sense domesticates and humanizes the voice by rendering it almost synonymous with linguistic marks, which functioned as the universal data storage and transmission medium up till the end of the nineteenth century. This bifurcation leads Friedrich Kittler, in *Gramophone, Film, Typewriter*, to contend that "writing [can only] store writing — no more no less," thus highlighting that in the Derridean scheme the dimensions of the voice that elude writing cannot but be kept silent (7).[32] Additionally, Kittler observes, "the phonograph does not hear as do ears that have been trained to immediately filter voices, words, and sounds out of noise; it registers acoustic events as such" (23). A striking assertion, no doubt, one that simultaneously gets to the heart of the matter and completely misses the point, as anyone who has heard early sound recordings (think about the lack of lower frequencies on many old recordings, especially those of the acoustic era) or some current MP3s will realize. While it is true that the phonograph's sound perception differs manifestly from human ears, its transmitting of sonic marks per se appears illusory, given the stark limitations in sound "fidelity" throughout the history of sound recording. Instead of dispensing with the original/copy distinction, Kittler desires something like the transcendental omniscience of the phonograph. The insistence on the (in)humanity of the phonograph remains key, for it assists in conjecturing the sonorous dimensions teleported by the phonograph that are elided in script and thus shushed in Derrida's understanding of the voice as speech writing. In this way, Derrida veers perilously close to another strand in Western philosophy, ranging from Plato, to Kant and Rousseau, and more recently to Emmanuel Levinas, who provides the following pithy aphorism: "The sounds and noises of nature are failed words. To really hear sound, we need to hear a word. Pure sound is the word."[33] These thinkers take in music and the voice only insofar as they aspire to and/or attain linguistic signification or mathematical abstraction with the express aim of stifling and silencing embodiment, sensuality, and most important, the sonorous materiality of the aural.[34] Thus, Derrida's influential argument begins to reformulate the status of the voice by underscoring how speech functions as writing in the general sense, something Afro-diasporic cultures have known and enacted for at least three hundred years, yet falls short of facilitating any discussion of the sonorous qualities transmitted by human vocal cords, especially singing, which surely sounds differently in connection with black cultural production.

Put bluntly, Derrida's argument, while attuned to the constitutive writingness of all linguistic signs, redacts these as *only* linguistic marks, all the while placing a significant barrier between signifier and signified. The primacy of this post-Saussurean model, which to this day remains one of the axiomatic cornerstones of literary and cultural studies, still maintains the linguistic as the prima facie spot from which to think and imagine all vocal utterances, or "[the] occlusion that occurs sometimes in the name of a deconstruction of phonocentrism and always within the tradition of logocentrism, which has at its heart a paradoxically phonocentric deafness" (*In the Break*, 185). Moten's perspicacious point directs us to the oft unacknowledged muteness to the lower frequencies (I'm using this phrase in the full Ellisonian sense) that covertly underlie many poststructuralist-inspired academic debates, where language is always already "pure form" (190), in Moten's phraseology, and therefore the sonic is downgraded to its same old place: outside, below, and beyond the strictures of discourse. Although it remains crucial to think the graphicity of all cultural utterances, Derrida's model does not quite allow us to conjecture the very "real" (re)formulation of the sound/source relationship occasioned by the phonograph, since, in Jacques's part of the universe any vocalization always already appears as phonography (as I'm writing this, it strikes me that the problem might be the "always already"). In other words, this mode of thinking disables, or at least is not very interested in making, distinctions between "human" vocalization, written scores, and phonograph records, echoing, albeit sotto voce, the equation of language with "pure form." Although all these factors surely constitute a part of writing in the general sense, they do not do so in the same way. Thus, might it not be possible to insist on the writingness of all vocal acts and their differently calibrated sonic iterability through the technology of the phonograph?

What would a nonlinguistic archetype and/or a theory of (a)signification that considered both these domains sound like? While there are no comfortable answers, here as elsewhere the writings of Deleuze and Guattari and some of their followers suggest a distinct style of thinking about this tricky terrain in which nonlinguistic signs are accorded at least as much, if not more, of a vital force as language as "pure form."[35] These crucial additions to the archive of contemporary critical idioms often appear in the theorization of sensation, expression, affect, and perception. Brian Massumi tenders the following formulation of both the difference between and the codependency of perception and sensation: " 'Perception' [refers] to object-oriented experience, and 'sensation' [to] 'the perception of perception,' or self-referential experience. Sensation pertains to the stoppage- and stasis-tending dimension of reality. . . . Sensation pertains to the dimension of passage, or the continuity of immediate experience. . . . Perception is segmenting and capable of precision; sensation is unfolding and constitutively vague."[36] Sensation thus partakes in the realm of the prelinguistic, alinguistic, and a conceptual, while perception systematizes sensations into recognizable forms.[37] For our purposes, the phonograph sounds both sensation, in the guise of the sonic (phono), and perception, here the sphere of inscription (graph), even though these two energies are not opposed and, in the realm of speech, hardly dissociable to/from each other. Yet graphematicity continues to be seen and read as the sine qua non of human signification, which neglects to take in the phonograph's most radical gesture: its sonic materiality. In other words, writing does not lack sensation ontologically but its reduction to linguistic structures, even if these can never achieve transparency, in the aftermath of structuralism preempts any discussion of the many nonlinguistic ways in which it achieves its effects. So Derrida's notion of graphematicity remains crucial for any consideration of the phonographic-machinic ensemble, since, although it allows us to think the iterability of the graph as part of the equation, it does not offer much in the way of theorizing the endemic difference between reading the score or listening to a recording of a Prince song such as "The Ballad of Dorothy Parker." In order to come to grips with both sameness and difference in these iterations we need a theory of phonography—and of aesthetics in general—that blends sensation and perception and listens to the variety and intensity of their intermingling. The invention of the phonograph and the different status of the speech/writing compound vis-à-vis New World blackness provide the occasion to think and hear these matters in slightly different versions that do not lose sound or sight of the surplus gift inherent to Afro-diasporic double consciousness. One of the prime modes of this excess comes in the form of a phonography that rebuffs any separation of the two forces in this compound, whether it rolls up in the sphere of literature or music.

The Sounds of Blackness Surely, the conjoining of writing and sound has particular ramifications for black cultural production, given the importance of orality as the major mode of cultural transmission in this temporal setting. Because alphabetic writing was such an embattled terrain for black subjects in nineteenth-century America, the phonograph did not cause the same anxieties in black cultural discourses, and musical notation and writing were not necessarily understood as the most natural way of recording music. Much has been written about the fraught status of writing in Afro-diasporic configurations, particularly in regard to nineteenth-century African American literary history, but rather than redacting these arguments here, I will just say that black subjects did not have the same access to alphabetic writing as white subjects and therefore were also barred, both discursively and materially, from writing's attendant qualities of reason, disembodiment, and full humanity by a variety of repressive and at times violent mechanisms. Because graphic mastery functioned as a sign for civilization and humanity, black subjects were placed outside these domains. Some critics, nevertheless, consider the act of writing, chiefly in the slave narrative genre, to be revolutionary, since it not only highlighted black people's "humanity" but also worried the very messy bond between writing and reason; more recently this tenet has come under scrutiny and has been revised significantly.

Lindon Barrett, for instance, maintains that the black voice functions as a figure of value within African American culture, particularly as it is contrasted with the lack of worth ascribed to blackness in American mainstream culture.[38] He distinguishes *the singing voice* from the *signing voice* of Euro-American alphabetical literacy, writing that the singing voice "provides a primary means by which African Americans may exchange an expended, valueless self in the New World for a productive, recognized self" (57). The *signing voice*, on the other hand, represents the literacy of the white Enlightenment subject. The *signing voice* signals full humanity, whiteness, and disembodiment, where the *singing voice* metonymically enacts blackness, embodiment, and subhumanity. For Barrett, corporeality, or "sly alterity" as he terms it, furnishes the black singing voice's most destabilizing feature (58):

> The African American singing voice emphasizes—rather than merely glances at—the spatial, material, dative, or enunciative action of voice. Singing voices undo voice as speech per se. By highlighting the enunciative or vocative aspect and moment of voice, singing voices mark the absence that allows iteration and repetition. They imprint above all the pure sonorous audibility of voice, and not a seeming absolute proximity to fixed meaning and identity. (84)

Thus, the black *singing voice* suggests a rather different access to the Enlightenment category of humanity from the *signing voice*, and in the process undermines the validity of the liberal subject as the quintessence of the human, instead providing a fully embodied version thereof. Black subjectivity appears as the antithesis to the Enlightenment subject by virtue of not only having a body but by being a body. But what happens once the black voice becomes disembodied, severed from its source, (re)contextualized, and (re)embodied and appropriated, or even before this point? All these things occurred when the first collections of transcribed spirituals became readily available for public consumption during the Civil War and continued with the recording and reproduction through various media of the black voice in the twentieth century. Although I endorse Barrett's useful differentiation between the *signing voice* and the *singing voice*, at times it runs the risk of configuring the black singing voice as always already embodied, rather than as a series of strategies and/or techniques of corporeality.[39] Far from being transmitted "in [a] startlingly authentic form," as Barrett will have it (86), the black singing voice, decoupled from its human source — which nonetheless remains a prominent spectral residue — and placed in the context of spiritual collections and, subsequently, phonograph records, insinuates a much more overdetermined and unwieldy constellation within both black and mainstream American cultural discourses. This account also mutes the many ways the singing voice has provided a prime channel for making New World blackness audible from within Western discourses, much in the same way that slave narratives, in Ronald Judy's argument, rendered the African (il)legible as Negro. In the end, despite his nuanced argument, Barrett also thwarts any recourse to writing in his treatment of the si(g)n(g)ing voice — where Derrida can only read the voice as linguistic a/signification, Barrett hears the black voice as pure ludic sonorousness — or rather the coupling of the graphematic *and* the phonic, which represents the prime achievement of black cultural production in the New World. As we shall see in the discussions of Du Bois and Ellison, neither abandons the *graph* for the *phono* or vice versa; this is what we call phonographies.

Surely, this is not to argue that orality and music were the only channels for black culture in this period, but rather that the relationship between sound and writing imploded by the discourses around the phonograph in mainstream American culture carries different cadences in relation to black culture. Consequently, we need to account for how orality and music, the two main cultural techniques in African America, were transformed by the technology of the phonograph.[40] In what sense does the de/re/coupling of sound and source shift the central place of orality and music in the production, transmission, and reception of black culture? According to Edouard Glissant, "it is nothing new to declare that for [black subjects] music, gesture, dance are forms of communication, just as important as the gift of speech. This is how we first managed to escape the plantation: aesthetic form in our cultures must be shaped from these oral structures."[41] How did these modes of cultural transfer, which are always constitutive of the contents they transmit, change at the end of the nineteenth century through the incorporation of orality and music into written texts and the technological recording of sound and speech? In the literary domain, writers such as Pauline Hopkins, W. E. B. Du Bois, Zora Neale Hurston, Ralph Ellison, James Baldwin, Nathaniel Mackey, and Toni Morrison, to name only a few, have "sounded" modern African American culture, utilizing aspects of the varied histories of black music in their writings. In addition, black literature has also produced a multitude of "speakerly texts" by stressing the oral performative dimensions of written language.[42] Understood as sound recordings, then, these writings suggest a different way of merging the *phonê* and *graph* than the technology of the phonograph, underscoring how sound and writing meet and inform each other in the annals of twentieth-century African American literature. These practices serve as ripostes to Derrida and Barrett, who insist on abandoning either the *phonê* or the *graph* in *phonograph*: Derrida by construing the voice as linguistic structure and Barrett by not taking into account how sound suffuses New World black writing.

If African American literature bridges the divide between the sonic and graphic in the realm of textuality, then the invention of the phonograph suggests different ways in which race, writing, and sound interact in late nineteenth-century America. While black performers were a part of the phonograph and recording industry from the beginning of its mass entertainment function, it was not until the 1920s and the coming of the jazz age that they became a substantial part of recording industry.[43] The end of the nineteenth century is marked, not so much by the proliferation of black performers, as in later historical assemblages, but in the way that the newly invented technology of mechanically storing and reproducing sound perturbed prevalent perceptions of race and instantiated a new form of sonic blackness. The immense popularity of a genre, adapted from the minstrel stage and known as "coon songs," ensured that race and the phonograph were thoroughly enmeshed; indeed, according to Andre Millard, "coon songs" made up the bulk of "humorous" recordings at the turn of the century.[44] Lisa Gitelman writes, "The most acute destabilization [between sound and vision], I would argue, . . . took place around the recorded coon song, since the coon song was a complex, late-nineteenth-century survival of an already intricate and naggingly visual experience, the mid-century minstrel show" (276). The "coon song," like the minstrel show, relied on the stability and verifiableness of the performers' racial identity. In other words, the performers needed to stage a particular version of blackness while guaranteeing that their whiteness was still discernible qua essence. The phonograph disturbed this traffic between the sonic and visual by denying the audience, at least initially, any easy way to determine the performer's racial identity. At stake was clearly discerning a white projection of blackness from a black image of blackness.[45] Here, we cannot only surmise that the phonograph's audio-visual rift had particular consequences for both black performers and the phonic performance of blackness, but that, in the U.S. context, race figures prominently in the primal historical scene of this then nascent informational technology — a tendency also manifest in the anxieties about racial and gender passing in the early days of the Internet. It further suggests that blackness necessitated redefinition in relation to this new technology, as it could now be imagined phonographically, and had to therefore be recast in order to fit into the already existing templates for racial formation. In order to better ascertain the parameters of the new audio-visual rift generated by the phonograph, it is crucial to hook up a different loudspeaker, one that takes into account the fraught relation of race and visuality in Western modernity.

Phono-Optics The hegemony of vision in Western modernity, its ocularcentric discourse, has been subjected to much scrutiny, and Afro-diasporic thinkers, in particular, have stressed the centrality of the scopic in constructions of race and racism.[46] In *The Souls of Black Folk*, Du Bois begins his comments on the mechanisms of double consciousness as it pertains to black subjects in the United States with the following announcement: "The Negro is sort of a seventh son, born with a veil, and *gifted* with *a second sight* in this American world."[47] Du Bois posits that black subjects are gifted, not cursed, with a second sight, yet he fails to disclose the precise nature of this second sight and why it is a consecration instead of a burden. Du Bois goes on to describe "a world which yields [the Negro] no true self-consciousness, but only lets him *see* himself through the revelation of the other world" (5, emphasis mine).[48] When Du Bois initially invokes the term "double-consciousness," he implicates sight: "It is a peculiar sensation, this double consciousness, this sense of always *looking* at one's self through the *eyes* of others, of measuring one's *soul* by the tape of the world that *looks on* in amused contempt and pity" (5, emphases mine). Again Du Bois only discusses how vision is at the root of "double consciousness": the black subject observes her/himself as split and doubled because of the look of the white subject. In this way, Du Bois anticipates Sartre's look and Lacan's notion of the gaze, since the eyes evoked here index not so much epiphenomenal eyeballs, at least not primarily, as the structuration of the visual apropos racial subjectivity. The stare that haunts Du Bois is empirical, phenomenal, and (anti)ontological, representing a constitutive feature of black subjectivity that does not stipulate the actual presence of white people, but is nevertheless enacted by and through them repeatedly and thus becomes an integral component of the racial formation feedback loop; in the words of Frantz Fanon, "Not only must the black man be black; he must be black in relation to the white man."[49] Hearing and sound, references to which serve as recto and verso of Du Bois's *Souls of Black Folk*, however, contribute differently to the fractured subjectivity of double consciousness, prompting us to ask about the status of black subjectivity as it passes through the aural, albeit without austerely counterposing these force fields, since, as Du Bois and Fanon among many others bear out, the *phono* and the *optic* cannot materialize without each other.[50]

Robyn Wiegman suggests the following about the slippage between vision and knowledge as it applies to race in what she terms "visual modernity": "The move from the visible epidermal terrain to the articulation of the interior structure of human bodies thus extrapolated in both broader and more distinct terms the parameters of white supremacy."[51] The look of white subjects deduces supposed racial characteristics from the surface of black subjects' skin, which in turn affirms the subjects' whiteness and dominance. In a similar vein to Du Bois, Frantz Fanon shows how vision—the first and only sight of whiteness as it calcifies in relation to blackness—represents an integral part of the racist machine at the heart of the modern West (also known as the jungle), beginning his now famous description of "the fact of blackness," the primal scene of racial subject formation, with the following exclamations by a white person: " 'Dirty nigger!' Or simply, 'Look, a Negro!' " (*Black Skin*, 113). His account demonstrates the leakage from racial identity to assumed inadequacy to be synonymous in the racist imagination. Further in the text, Fanon accentuates the effects of, as well as the reactions to, this look on the part of a black subject: "My body was given back to me sprawled out, distorted, recolored, clad in mourning on that white winter day. The Negro is an animal, the Negro is bad, the Negro is mean, the Negro is ugly" (113). This is the moment of double consciousness in which the white gaze is introjected and becomes a cornerstone for the construction of black subjectivity. Du Bois confirms Fanon's invocation of the distortion against a lily-white canvas both in terms of process (something being taken away and returned in a different form) and visual light/dark imagery (dimness takes over a formerly clear space). When describing his own racial primal scene, Du Bois writes: "I remember well when the shadow swept across me. . . . Then it dawned upon me with a certain suddenness that I was different from the others" (*Souls*, 4, see also 7).[52] Coming to this conclusion because he is denied access to cross-racial (proto)heterosexuality (if you recall, he is refused by a presumably, although not explicitly described as such, white girl), Du Bois marks the rupture of this event as resolutely ocular.[53] Du Bois and Fanon are literally recolored by the shadow only to internalize it in their newly fashioned sense of (non)being; hence the look of the white subject interpellates the black subject as inferior, which, in turn, bars the black subject from seeing him/herself without the internalization of the white gaze. Plus, if, as Judith Butler remarks, the Althusserian moment of interpellation—the decisive reformulation of the primal scene/mirror stage as enmeshed in and constituted by totality of the sociopolitical assemblage (remember "Hey, you"—no, not the Rock Steady Crew), which in Althusser bears the name ideology—provides "a visual rendering of an acoustic scene,"[54] then Fanon's theory might be said to acoustically depict a visual scene. Where Fanon's white voice projects racial identity, it casts a shadow on the black subject in Du Bois's framework. As opposed to standing on its own, it auratizes and therefore amplifies the visual components of racism. In other words, the white subject's vocal apparatus merely serves to repeat and solidify racial difference as it is inscribed in the field of vision; yet in doing so, it lays bare the structural methodology of race in Western modernity by piercingly calling attention to how whiteness is just as dependent on blackness in order to appear and function as whiteness, much in the same way "the original" is framed in the phonographic primal scene.

The look of white folks implies power over black subjects that cannot return the look. Du Bois writes this against the backdrop of numerous lynchings. One of the main "reasons" given for these lynchings was the look of black subjects (most often male) vis-à-vis white subjects (mainly women); Robyn Wiegman describes these lynchings and their relation to the ocular thus: "We encounter the landscape overseen by the

Ku Klux Klan: lynched, castrated, raped, and charred bodies ceremoniously strung up for public view — images that would increasingly circulate as detailed descriptions of torture found their way into local newspapers and as photographs of the event were mass produced for commercial entertainment value" (*American Anatomies*, 39). These lynchings, then, formed a crucial part of the black subject's ecology both as physical threats and media representations, making them *subject* to the look of white folks, yet unable to return the look. Indeed, "looking" as the act of looking at another subject and "looking" as the wielding of power over subjects through the extrapolation of "inferior" characteristics coexist in Du Bois's definition of double consciousness, not randomly, but because historically these apparatuses of power have played a major role in constructing race discursively and materially in the Western world, especially in the United States. Ultimately, vision, in Du Bois's scheme, can only provide space where black people are *subject to* racial interpellation, and not *subjects of* this process, which nevertheless does not preempt the making usable of the sonic.

Instead of thinking his recently darkened self as pure lack, or rather, letting his being be overshadowed by deficiency, Du Bois overdubs double consciousness with a different riddim: "I had thereafter no desire to tear down that veil; I held all beyond it in common contempt, and lived above it in a region of blue sky and great wandering shadows" (4). Even though this passage attempts to negate the world external to the veil, Du Bois's dwelling habitus betrays a duality in its evocation of "blue skies" and "wandering shadows," which though surely not tantamount to black and white, nonetheless harks back to the color scheme set out earlier in the text. How to make the originary negativity of double consciousness usable without abolishing its ontico-ontological scorn, that's the question. On the one hand, Du Bois's contempt becomes an engine that fuels his ambition — notice how an increase in coloration serves as an index of his frame of mind — a somewhat different spin on the coupling of *dark* and *blue* than Armstrong, Ellison, and after them Curtis Mayfield: "The sky was bluest when I could beat mates at examination-time, or beat them in a foot-race, or even beat their stringy heads" (*Souls*, 4). Here, the supposedly benign cruelty of competition forms a cluster with physical aggression in correspondence with the strictures of racial formation, transforming ressentiment into a desiring machine of negativity that creates and produces at factory speed. On the other hand, Du Bois's derision is

augmented by, but not reducible to, "the gift of story and song" (214).[55]
This endowment undergirds much of Du Bois's text, as can be gleaned in
the musical epigraphs and the centrality accorded to the aural in the fore-
and afterthought of *Souls*: contrasted with the discussion of the visual
qua racism, sound and hearing emerge as differently pitched modalities
in the domain of a black subject.

Donald Gibson explains that "the 'veil' is not indicative of prescience,
but of blinding," though, this should not exclude the "second sight" from
laboring as a sound system, for, crudely put, blindness does not necessarily connote deafness and/or dumbness; in fact, the sensibilities allotted
to vision are often displaced onto the other senses, particularly hearing.[56]
Also, the blind have often been associated with a different sort of seeing, prophetic vision or second sight, which finds its double in Du Bois's
secular messianism.[57] Reading and listening to the otherworldly sight as
gift, especially considering the various uses of music in the text, lets us
understand second sight not only as ancillary to a handicap but also as Du
Bois's attempt to make black history, culture, and subjectivity audible in
the text. What remains unanswered though, is who or what bestows the
gift on the black subject: is it a divine source, a sociological condition, an
aesthetic stance, or a combination of all these factors? The origins of this
blessing, however, seem to interest Du Bois far less than its articulation as
an offering — and a much exploited one at that — to U.S. and world culture
and politics. Nevertheless, we should pause here to include the German
cognate of the English-language term gift, *das Gift*, that is, "poison." The
poisoned blessing or blessed poisoning manifests as both a hindrance to
full subjecthood and suffrage and a surplus/excess that structures Western modernity, for it is "in 'blood-poisoning' that human promise is to be
found."[58] As a result, these sanguine harmonies and melodies "poison"
the body politic of U.S. national culture by suffusing it with other ways of
becoming human, which is to say that black subjectivity not only functions as a constitutive trace or outside of whiteness, reason, citizenship,
full humanity, and so on, but as an event horizon for "human promise."[59]
Possibly, this is what Du Bois has in mind when writing "Negro blood
has a message for the world" (5). Here, poisoning and offering concoct an
alchemic brew of blackness — a *pharmakon*, as Plato and Derrida would
call it — that recolors, via the sonic (the gift of song), the very grounds of
Western modernity.[60] In the end, double consciousness does not so much
critique as *gift* (poison and bless) the disembodiment of vision and by

extension the human in modernity in its excavation and amplification of aural materiality, the "tremulous treble and darkening bass" (*Souls*, 215) veiled by scopic racial formation, as it throws phono-optics into the mix of the phonographic grooves of sonic Afro-modernity.

Ultimately, it is not sound as an idealized, authentically vernacular, or discrete sphere that distinguishes Afro-diasporic cultural production in/as Western modernity but the use of the sonic to both create and re-calibrate some of its central topoi, such as the equation of script with reason and humanity, narratives of unmitigated progress, and the con-figuration of vision as incorporeal and therefore the apex of scientific rationality. Black cultural production casts a sonic shadow on Western modernity only to return it recolored to its (im)proper place within said galaxy. Put differently, these discourses are neither erased nor suspended; rather, they are significantly (re)created in their encounter with auditory blackness, which also undergoes substantial shifts in this assemblage. In this way, neither of these energies can materialize without its spectral doppelgänger: no Western modernity without (sonic) blackness and no blackness in the absence of modernity. The phonograph — both as an ob-ject and a machinic ensemble — and many of the culturotechnological formations after it — intimate a prima facie crossroads from and through which to theorize the intricate codependency of blackness and the mod-ern, since this apparatus, in its catachrestic naming, technological capa-bilities, and cultural discourses, directs our ears and eyes to the grounds of blackness' materialization and figuration in the West. Phonography, as a sounding Barakian movement of *is*, circles around the doubleness (the primary and secondary riddim of modern blackness), the vacillation between *phono* and *graph*, human and inhuman, sound and vision — that has been muted in and estranged from many modern discourses for far too long.

2

"I Am I Be"

A Subject of Sonic Afro-Modernity

Surely, "the subject" represents one of the more embattled concepts in the recent history of the Anglo-American humanities; structuralist and poststructuralist discourses were almost singularly concerned with dissolving and/or resituating the self-same subject (in some cases putting it under erasure) as it appeared in Western thinking, idealist philosophy in particular.[1] The main thrust of these debates troubled the coherence and unmediated presence of the subject, seeking to displace this category as the uncontested center in a variety of thought systems, with different structures (linguistic, anthropological, political, psychic, economic, etc.), or, in the poststructuralist case, rendering palpable the fissures, traces, and ruptures contained within and undermining these very structures that enabled the subject's putative intelligibility and therefore, constrained its ability to appear as the center from which all movements flow.[2] If the advent of structuralism and its subsequent postformations provides one of the crucial re/formulations of the humanities project since the 1960s, then the coming to the fore of minority discourses stands as the other major shift in this context.[3] Although some scholars have thought these two developments together fruitfully—Hortense J. Spillers and Sylvia Wynter immediately come to mind—usually they are perceived as mutually exclusive, at least contra-

dictory. In most instances, however, and this bears stressing, the two processes are not thought related at all.[4]

One version of this argument discerns the irony in the dissolution, and
perhaps even abandonment, of the subject as a category of critical thinking just as minorities are being recognized as subjects within academic
discourse. In fact, uttering "minority" and "subject" in the same breath
seems counterintuitive, if not paradoxical.[5] While I do not seek to address that critique here, or, for that matter, reinstate an earlier and more
innocent version of the subject, I would like to take the occasion to think
about the subject from the perspective of the minoritarian by investigat-
ing why the minoritarian is automatically linked to the category of identity rather than the subject. These reflections will be preceded by an analysis of the prologue of Ralph Ellison's 1952 novel, *Invisible Man*, and will
conjecture the way Ellison imagines a subject of sonic Afro-modernity.
Ellison constructs a model of subjectivity that augments, but does not
displace, the Du Boisian subject of double consciousness outlined in the
previous chapter, bearing witness to specificities of black life while ges-
turing toward a more general condition of Western modernity.

Ralph Ellison's poetics, situated at the interstices of music and technology, bridge the assumed divide between black cultural production
and modern informational technologies, probing their textural and overdetermined interdependencies rather than their contrasting natures. In
Invisible Man, his essays, and numerous interviews, Ellison consistently
turns to questions of sound recording and reproduction. In this way, Ellison not only insists on the sociality of sonic technologies but also bears
witness to the numerous ways in which they structure modern (black) life
worlds, conceptually heaving black life out of a mythic, Luddite, unusable
past and into the center of Western modernity. Sadly, critics have paid
scant attention to Ellison's engagement with sonic technologies, zeroing
in only on his thoughts about jazz and the blues, rather than the interplay
of content *and* transmission so crucial to the Ellison oeuvre. We might
even say, *pace* Walter Benjamin, that Ellison locates the aura not in the
original musical utterance but in the mode of mechanical reproduction
itself, making him one of the foremost intellectual architects of sonic
Afro-modernity.[6]

Moreover, *Invisible Man* lends itself to the theorization of subjectivity
because the nameless protagonist functions as a shifting structural loca-

tion, an empty signifier, if you will, that resists the strictures of any standard notion of character. The protagonist, by virtue of not possessing a predetermined identity, is thrown into numerous situations that momentarily define him as subject within these contingent configurations. This, on the one hand, assures that the protagonist's subjectivity cannot be disentangled from its singular material and discursive instantiations and, on the other, points to some general laws of subject(ivat)ion. As a whole, the novel transacts the problem of the subject as a process and in doing so allows us to surmise how a subject comes to be rather than how it is. While the protagonist's much commented-on interpellative encounters with Mr. Norton and the Brotherhood, for instance, remain germane in the context of the protagonist as subject, for my purposes, his engagement with Louis Armstrong's phonographic voice represents a crucial moment in probing the critical importance of the subject for the field of black studies and conjecturing the centrality of sound technologies in twentieth-century black culture.[7]

Throughout his work, Ellison listens carefully not only to the complexities and subtleties of black musical expression but also—and this distinguishes him from other writers—the intricate manner in which these sounds are intertwined with informational technologies in the modern era. This sensibility enables Ellison to suggest a grammar for thinking, if not hearing, a subject of sonic Afro-modernity located in that explosive audiovisual disjuncture engendered by the phonograph. In the force field of sonic Afro-modernity, sound technologies, as opposed to being exclusively determined or determining, form a relay point in the orbit between the apparatus and a plethora of cultural, economic, and political discourses. And insisting on the central place of technology in this formation goes a long way toward ascertaining how musical production and structures of listening have shifted over the course of the last century. At the very least, this might move us away from the zero-sum game of authenticity versus commodification, which will surely entail letting some of the old "bad air" out without losing its entire funk.

Listening around Corners *Invisible Man* is framed by the protagonist's consumption of and engagement with Louis Armstrong's recording of the Andy Razaf and Fats Waller song "(What Did I Do to Be so) Black and Blue."[8] Armstrong recorded several versions of this piece after he encountered it as part of the stage musical *Hot Chocolates* in 1929; legend has it that the song was composed because the financier of the show, the mafioso Dutch Schulz, demanded a humorous musical rendering of the black experience.[9] While Ellison's protagonist draws on "Black and Blue" as "one of the first instances of racial protest in American popular music," he emphasizes the quality of Armstrong's voice embodied in the particular performance rendered on record and not primarily the signification of the song's lyrics (115). The prologue establishes the protagonist's social invisibility, the major theme of the novel, by depicting his hibernation in a hole, the basement of a "whites only" building, describing his condition in the following fashion: "I am a man of substance, of flesh and bone, fiber and liquids—and I might even be said to possess a mind. I am invisible, understand, simply because people refuse to see me" (3).[10] By way of explicating how he is refused representation in the field of vision, the protagonist also insists on the intersubjective workings of his invisibility, rather than construing it as an ontological absolute. This is imperative since, according to Sylvia Wynter, the prologue as a whole performs "the possibility of their/our recognition of this imposed 'invisibility,' which leads to a new demand for another concept of freedom, another possibility of a livable being that culminates in [the protagonist's] recognition of his alterity."[11] Wynter's invocation of the protagonist's "alterity" appears at the interstice of self and other, which is to say that the protagonist remains foreign to himself as much as he does to others, although evidently not in the same way. This alienness is also patent in the hall of mirrors that reflect and shape the protagonist's visual imperceptibility: "It is as though I have been surrounded by mirrors of hard, distorting glass. When they approach me they see only my surroundings, themselves, or figments of their imagination—indeed, everything and anything except me" (3).[12] Here, the nucleutic structuration remains undetectable, a *lumen* of blackness, a veritable black hole around which meaning spirals in the cross-reflections of the surrounding mirrors, but which cannot be accessed itself. While the racial metaphorics of this predicament—white subjects' inability and/or outright refusal to recognize black people's subjectivity—appear abundantly clear, the question of visuality merits more than a brief glance here, since Ellison explicitly situates the protagonist's nonsubjectivity in the ocular domain. Surely, Ellison's utilization of invisibility takes into account the vexed vicissitudes of race and visuality in Western modernity, while also insisting on a sonic-cum-technological formulation of a black subject.

While the sonic may indeed provide a more receptive metaphor for the subject, it does so only in relation to the visual. That is to say, rather than repeating the fallacy of current critical idioms that locate the subject *only* in the fields of language and/or the visual, focusing on sound not only opens our ears to the opacities of the sonic but also, and no less germane, necessitates a reconfiguration of the visual and the linguistic, in that they fail to function as the sole determinants of subjectivity. Once the sonic is introduced into this mix, the category of the subject transmutes into a multifarious constellation that does not rest on mutual exclusives but instead enables particles to bounce off one another and bring to the fore their vortexes. Stuart Hall gives the following description of black cultural strategies that have arisen in the wake of the racializing mechanisms of visual modernity: "to subvert the structures of 'othering' in language and representation, image, sound, and discourse, and thus to turn the mechanisms of fixed racial signification against themselves, in order to begin to constitute new subjectivities, new positions of enunciation and identification."[13] In the history of twentieth-century black cultural production, the "new positions of enunciation and identification" identified by Hall have been most forcefully articulated in and through sound. Sound occupies a privileged place precisely because it manages to augment an inferior black subjectivity — a subjectivity created by racist ideologies and practices in the field of vision — establishing venues for the constitution of new modes of existence called for by Hall. Thus a (black) subject inhabits the spatiotemporal terrain between sonic modernity and visual modernity: the crossroads of subjection and subjectivation.

Sonic modernity and visual modernity do not stand as diametrical opposites, but they articulate different modes of becoming-in-the-world for modern black subjects in the West, which, although not entirely the same, cannot quite be disentangled from one another. Steven Connor persuasively argues that due to the proliferation of auditory technologies such as the telephone and phonograph at the turn of the century, modern subjectivity might be best thought of as a "modern auditory I."[14] This "auditory I," in Connor's view, offers a different notion of subjectivity than visually and linguistically based ones: "Where auditory experience is dominant, we may say, singular perspectival gives way to plural, permeated space. The self defined in terms of hearing rather than sight is a self imagined not as a point, but as a membrane; not as a picture, but as channel through which voices, noises and musics travel" (207). Following Connor, then, we might designate a subject of sonic Afro-modernity as a channel through which voices, noises, and music pass. However, this subjectivity does not displace a black subject in visual modernity as much as it highlights the particular mechanisms of the visual as it cuts across the mechanics of racialization. Ellison masterfully stages the interdependency of the sonic and the visual by charging both sound and vision with the electrical currents of modern technologies, namely the phonograph and the lightbulb. The problematic of visuality is picked up again a little later in the prologue when the protagonist reflects upon his desire for brightness: "My hole is warm and full of light. Yes, *full* of light. I doubt if there is a brighter spot in all New York than this hole of mine. . . . Perhaps you'll think it strange that an invisible man should need light, desire light, love light" (6). Yet, the desire for light only seems noteworthy in a world where social visibility is a given. As an a priori, social discernibility already functions as light by legislating the boundary between the visible and invisible, therefore it does not oblige further illumination. Here, *lux* (the physical experience of light) and *lumen* (the disembodied ideal of light) are both severed from and returned to each other in order to shine a spotlight on the luminosity of white supremacy or, in the more genteel Derridean formulation, white mythology.[15] For, as the protagonist points out, and as we have seen in Du Bois and Fanon, it is not sight as such that is at stake in this surge of in/visibility, but rather the intangible version thereof that banishes the black subject from the sphere of *lumen*, which in turn leaks into the province of *lux*. The text proceeds: "But maybe it is exactly because I am invisible. Light confirms my reality, gives birth to my form. . . . Without light I am not only invisible, but formless as well; and to be unaware of one's form is to live a death. I myself, after existing some twenty years, did not become alive until I discovered my invisibility" (6–7). This contradictory insight underscores the protagonist's urgency to comprehend his invisibility while simultaneously reformulating that predicament by consuming light, since he needs to look at himself through the eyes of others in order to not disappear from his own line of sight. Illuminated by the 1,369 lightbulbs covering the ceiling of his hibernation hole, the protagonist pilfers the electricity that powers them from "Monopolated Light & Power," which ensures, both literally and metaphorically, that his illumination cannot be disentangled from his invisibility.

In this scene, Monopolated Light & Power, as the modernized and electrified capitalist reformulation of Western-style heliocentrism, caustically encodes the structures at the root of the protagonist's invisibility. The electricity rechanneled from the company is turned against itself, because instead of presenting his visual nonpresence as an ontological and political fait accompli, it allows him to illuminate, and thus verify, the very fact of his invisibility, which disenchants the truth-value of light. In other words, if the protagonist's invisibility can be set alight, then maybe seeing the light does not always already imply luminosity as self-evidence, or, in Ellison's formulation, "Truth is the light and light is the truth" (7). Similarly, in terms of a philosophical optics, Jacques Derrida differentiates between the "sun," as the center of Western metaphysical meaning-making, and a "star" that wades, as it were, in the muddy waters of catachresis: "As soon as one admits that all terms in an analogical relation already are caught up, one by one, in a metaphorical relation, everything begins to function no longer as a sun, but as a star, the punctual source of truth or properness remaining invisible or nocturnal."[16] Thus, Monopolated Light & Power, which remains invisible but nonetheless central, ceases to operate as the "sun" of invisibility, since the 1,369 "stars" displace the "truth" of the protagonist's invisibility in order to shed a different light on his be(com)ing. In effect, the lightbulbs disperse the supposed central facticity of the protagonist's invisibility across 1,369 different punctures, enabling a new understanding of the singularity of his predicament, which moves back and forth between the sun and stars, vision and sound, invisibility and visibility. Moreover, we should not overlook the texturality of light in this context, since "light is not a transparent medium linking sight and visibility. . . . In its texture, light is a fabrication, a surface of a depth that also spills over and passes through the interstices of the fabric."[17] Hence the ideological and material currents of subordination electrically and texturally cross the protagonist's inscription as lack in the field of vision, in the meantime giving birth to his sonic interpellation, a movement further evident in his identification with Thomas Edison, the "father" of both the lightbulb and the phonograph (7).

The electricity the protagonist reroutes from the large company also powers his radio-phonograph, assuring that the aural component of the protagonist's subjectivity and his scopic invisibility are fully interfaced. A single radio-phonograph, however, does not do the job; the protagonist yearns for five machines: "I'd like to hear five recordings of Louis Armstrong playing and singing '(What Did I Do to Be So) Black and Blue'—all that at the same time" (8). The reason, he claims, stems from the sonic characteristics of the basement: "There is a certain acoustical deadness in my hole, and when I have music I want to feel its vibration with my whole body" (8). If the multiplicity of lights reflects the protagonist's craving to understand his social invisibility, then the corporeal viscerality of the protagonist's ideal listening scenario manifests an intense longing to experience his body *in* sound in ways that he cannot do visually. Wanting to embody and be embodied by sound (sensation), the protagonist imagines his flesh as an eardrum—he's literally all ears— transforming his corporeal schema into a channel for his sonic subjectivity, which, in turn, only emerges in relation to his scopic interpellation (perception). Here, we see and hear the continuum of sensation and perception. Thus the sonic and the scopic, far from being diametrically opposed, provide occasion for each other: visual subjection begets sonic subjectivation. In this way, formlessness elides the protagonist only insofar as the music re/sounds his invisibility, particularly Louis Armstrong's voice: "Perhaps I like Louis Armstrong because he's made poetry out of being invisible. I think it must be because he's unaware that he *is* invisible. And my own grasp of invisibility aids me to understand his music" (8). On the surface, the protagonist detects similar qualities of invisibility in Armstrong's recorded voice, so that it presumably serves as an aural mirror of his own predicament. Yet, despite this strong identification, there exists a crucial difference between them: Armstrong has no conception of his invisibility, at least according to the protagonist, which powers the poetic motor of his music. In the earlier, visually mediated passages, the protagonist's condition was predicated upon others' negation of his optic presence; in this case, however, his invisibility is instantiated via the sounds of another invisible subject. As a result, sound, particularly recorded and mechanically reproduced sound, grants the protagonist access to his invisibility in a different fashion than the not-so-soft glow afforded by the 1,369 lightbulbs. Even though this aspect of the protagonist's becoming is staged intersubjectively—his invisibility is amplified by the effect of Armstrong's voice on the phonograph—it differs quite significantly from the visual one because it relies not on negation and abjection but recognition, or rather the protagonist's recognition of Armstrong's supposed misrecognition. More than simply identifying with the singer, the protagonist recasts Armstrong in the role of his former self, the self not able to ascertain its own invisibility.

Apart from filling the dead air in the basement with music, the phonograph stages Armstrong's (non)presence just as much as it allows the protagonist to reside within the contours of his invisibility. Armstrong's invisibility manifests itself in several ways: the manner in which his racial identity figures in the musical text, both in terms of lyrical content and vocal delivery, in addition to Armstrong's visual absence, since he cannot see Armstrong but only hears how the phonograph re/presents his voice. The protagonist's emphasis shifts from the visual to the aural because being unable to visually face Armstrong makes him more susceptible to the quality of invisibility transported by Armstrong's voice. This characteristic becomes even more indicative of the social imperceptibility faced by black subjects due to its phonographic transmission. Since there are no optic cues, only Armstrong's phantomic voice accompanied by instrumentation on the recording, the protagonist projects his own invisibility onto Armstrong's vocal apparatus. We should return to Barrett's argument in *Blackness and Value* concerning the ways in which the voice functions as a figure of value within African American culture, particularly as it is contrasted with the lack of value ascribed to blackness in American mainstream culture. The characteristics Barrett ascribes to the black voice are magnified in the phonographic listening scenario when the singer's embodiment rests chiefly in his/her voice. When the visual props disappear, the ghostlike ruminations of the voice stand as the last and only vestiges of the corporeal, sonically folding the body into the voice and vice versa. In the process of this folding, the ear is directed toward the sound process itself, that is, the ways in which a black voice performs and constructs its corporeality.

The phonograph's ability to disconnect the singing voice from its face, or rather to replace it with a technological visage, further heightens its materiality, which impels the protagonist to imbue Armstrong's voice with a surplus of signification. In order to achieve this feat, however, light cannot function as the sole source of illumination: "It was a strangely satisfying experience for an invisible man to hear the silence of sound. . . . I've illuminated the blackness of my invisibility—and vice versa. And so I play the invisible music of my isolation. The last statement doesn't seem just right, does it?" (13). Taken literally the statement does seem just right though, for the phonograph provides, if anything, invisible music, since it denies the listener a visual representation of the performer. What initially seems oxymoronic actually provides the most succinct description of the protagonist's invisibility in relation to Louis Armstrong's voice flowing from the phonograph's speaker. The protagonist and Armstrong are joined not only by their social concealment as black subjects but also in their reliance on sound to enact this condition — Armstrong by vocally projecting his invisibility and the protagonist by listening to Armstrong. In this way, Barrett's scheme calls for an ear that recognizes the value of the African American singing voice, and the protagonist has just that ear, or in the extreme, is that ear, one that aurally "illuminates the blackness of [his] invisibility." As a consequence, the value of Armstrong's voice lies in his skill at sonically channeling his invisibility. Nevertheless, in a moment of disavowal, the protagonist casts Armstrong in the role of the naïf, rather than skilled performer, in order to better understand the parameters of his own imperceptibility in the field of vision. For the protagonist hears not an eternal spring of blackness welling from Armstrong's throat but the deftness and grace with which Armstrong manipulates his voice in relation to the sonic apparatus.

Still, Armstrong's voice should not be understood as the only form of embodiment in this scene. At the most basic level, the sonic apparatus itself provides a material grounding for the ephemeral "voice without a face" inasmuch as it replaces Armstrong's appearance as the visual counterpoint to his voice, substituting a machinic for a human presence and inducing the protagonist's urge to hear and feel Armstrong's voice more ardently in an effort to counterbalance the paucity of visual stimuli. Because Armstrong remains visually absent, he imagines being both assailed and enveloped by the sound of Armstrong's voice from five directions. The protagonist realizes that there is no chance for visual accompaniment to the sonic in his situation; therefore his desire migrates to the apparatus itself. Yet the machine, even if multiplied by five, supplies principally aural information, which explains why his fantasy involves his hearing Armstrong further amplified, not his looking at five phonographs. Hearing Armstrong intone from so many different machines at once, even if only in the realm of the phantasmatic, produces an aural materiality. As opposed to grounding sound in writing, the protagonist acutely positions the palpable dimensions of sound within the phonographic voice: the realm of sensation. Accordingly, he does not suggest hearing five different singers or even five different Armstrong recordings, but the same five Armstrong recordings simultaneously. Possibly, more than Armstrong's voice itself, it is the "voice without a face" — the voice of the phonograph — that grounds and transacts both Armstrong's and the protagonist's invisibility. Rather than dissipating into thin air, as early cultural and legal discourse on the phonograph suggested, the dis/re/embodied voice is precisely what frames the social in/visibility of a black subject in this scene. As a consequence, the phonograph does not so much occasion a faceless voice as it transforms the voice into a face. In this particular instance, the phonograph reconfigures the protagonist's invisibility via sonic (de)facilization; denied representation in the field of vision, Armstrong's phonographic voice facilitates the protagonist in recognizing the mechanics of his invisibility, his aural face, as it were. Here, the radio-phonograph serves as a Deleuzo-Guattarian "abstract machine of facialization," since it amplifies both the manner in which the protagonist's face deviates from "the White-Man face" — or "Jesus Christ Superstar" as they also designate this façade — in the racial epidermal schema and how it figures differently in the jurisdiction of the sonic.[18] This alternative visage, however, should not be construed as replacing the non-materialization of the black face in the field vision, its hypervisibility and invisibility, as much as its intensive sonic companion and similar to the way deterritorialization and reterritorialization go hand in hand in Deleuze and Guattari's discography. Overall, light projects the silhouette of his invisibility, where Armstrong's voice fills the visual contours with sound, or to put it crudely, where light confirms invisibility as fact, the phonographic voice sonically reticulates imperceptibility as process, enabling a two-way sonic flow between the two elements of *I am I be* — taken together they provide the textural contingency for a subject of sonic Afro-modernity.[19]

Oceanic Moments The scenario Ellison envisions almost screams for a psychoanalytic treatment, given the womblike basement, the retreat from the social, the phantasmatic ruminations of the protagonist, and the seemingly disembodied voice of Armstrong on the phonograph, which, following Hortense Spillers's suggestive remarks, enacts not so much the traditional law of the father as "a cultural situation that is father-lacking."[20] Indeed, the novel in toto stages a series of the protagonist's failed father figure cathexes, none of which amount to anything but disappointment, except for Armstrong's phonographic absent presence. These factors could easily be subsumed under the rubric of an "oceanic fantasy" in which the boundaries of the protagonist's subjectivity blur in relation to his musical consumption. While most psychoanalytic cultural criticism does not listen to the sonic, except for human speech as it interfaces with language and (the failure) of meaning making, especially in the clinical scenario, there have been some considerations of the interconnection between sound, hearing, and the psychic machine. David Schwarz, for example, argues that "the all-around pleasure of listening to music is one of many 'oceanic' fantasies. . . . Although these fantasies are quite different from one another, they share one common feature: the boundary separating the body from the external world seems dissolved or crossed in some way."[21] While this part of the equation appears somewhat self-evident (although it does beg the polemical question, What social situation does not dissolve the threshold between self and external world?), what distinguishes these moments as "oceanic" requires a bit more scrutiny here.

Following developments in French film theory and psychoanalytic criticism, both Schwarz and Kaja Silverman theorize an "acoustic mirror stage" that temporally precedes the visual mirror stage in the Lacanian theory of the subject.[22] In this phase, the child hears him/herself reflected in the voice of its mother, but the acoustic mirror stage does not denote the same sort of rupture in the subject as the visual one; instead, it represents a period before the splitting of the subject, an instant in which the precincts between the subject and its surroundings remain plastically malleable. All this changes when the child enters the visual mirror stage, occurring between the ages of six and eighteen months, which marks the point in which the child simultaneously recognizes and is severed from its imaginary image. Now the child sees itself for the first time as fractured, because the mirror image does not correspond to his/her imagined image. In the Lacanian scenario, the mirror stage signals the move, if not progression, of the child from the imaginary realm into the symbolic order — "the register of language, social exchange, and radical intersubjectivity" — which splits the subject once and for all, while contemporaneously constituting the child as subject.[23] Typically, the mother's voice defines the earlier imaginary stage, and as a result, these theories of the acoustic mirror stage taxonomically link the mother rather than the father to this "bath of sound," wherein the mother denotes freedom and bliss, while the father signifies language, law, and restriction.

Far more critical than Schwarz, especially in terms of the gendered hierarchy transported by the antinomy mother/voice/pure sonorousness and father/vision/meaning, Silverman distinguishes between two schools of analysis regarding the female voice within psychoanalysis and cinema studies. The first, associated with Michel Chion, partners the mother's voice with the entrapment and darkness of the womb; in Silverman's words, "The conceptualization of the maternal voice as 'uterine night' of non-meaning effects a similar displacement; once again the infant's perceptual and semiotic underdevelopment are transferred onto the mother" (75). Here, the mother's "babble" traps the child in a menacing web of sound, whereas in Guy Rosalato's and Didier Anzieu's mise-en-scène, the maternal voice supplies a "sonorous envelope" that engulfs the child in presymbolic bliss. Even though these versions of the maternal voice differ in their effects on the child, they posit the mother's voice as always already anterior to the symbolic order and meaning, or something the child leaves behind once constituted as subject through the machinations of the visual mirror stage and only retroactively accessible via the listening experience. Silverman is right to chide both of these "fantasies of the maternal voice" for not taking into account that the mother also teaches the child language and aids in interpreting the child's visual mirror stage, and is thus not only a sign for plenitude and bliss but also tied to the symbolic order, which Silverman sees "as part of a larger cultural disavowal of the mother's role both as an agent of discourse and as a model for linguistic identification" (100). However, Silverman can articulate her, granted very useful, critique only from within the psychoanalytic narrative apparatus. Consequently, she leaves intact the bonding of the listening experience to a regression of the subject into its psychic history: nowhere does Silverman conjecture what might happen if the listening experience were wrested from the throes of the restrictive structures of Oedipalization. All roads still lead to the child's mirror stage and subject formation within the confines of the nuclear family; it is just that for Silverman, the female voice plays a more robust role in the family drama, rather than serving as a mere antithetical babbling foil to the father's position within the symbolic sphere.

Although, as we have seen, Silverman complicates this trajectory in certain ways, both Silverman and Schwarz stress the fluidity of the acoustic mirror stage in contrast to the visual mirror stage because of the child's inability to distinguish between itself and its environment. But how does this inflect the experience of listening once the subject has entered into the symbolic order via the visual mirror stage and sees itself as severed from its own mirror image? These psychoanalytic theorizations of sound and subjectivity suggest that all listening experiences hark back to this instant in which the child cannot distinguish between itself and its mother's voice. Listening thus always recovers, even if only phantasmatically, a lost moment for the subject that can be retroactively represented by the experience of listening itself, but cannot return as such.[24] Put differently, listening to music transports the subject's unconscious to a time when s/he was united with her/his mother in a state of bliss or terror. This is where these analyses lose their force, since they routinely reduce listening to a particular lost configuration securely contained in the traditional mapping of subjectivity within psychoanalytic discourse. Why should such a wide range of events be explained by one particular formation in the psychic history of the subject?

Let us turn to a scene in the prologue of *Invisible Man*, which might be said to imagine an "oceanic moment" within the overall oceanic constellation of the protagonist's brightly illuminated basement/womb, and sardonically inverts the previously discussed "uterine night" scene in its substitution of darkness with the electrified "violence of light."[25] Of course, what will amount to the protagonist's descent into a Dantean imaginary purgatory, comes to be by way of his interaction with Louis Armstrong, now intensified after his intake of a potent psychoactive substance: "Under the spell of the reefer I discovered a new analytical way of listening to music" (8). As another cultural technology of dislocation and intensification, marijuana grants the protagonist a different way of apprehending his surround-sound bath, which feeds into the oceanic dimensions of this scene, as psychoactive drugs generally do.[26] Like the music, the reefer induces an extreme moment of desubjectification by realigning the subject's perception and sensation of both the external and internal world. However, that is only if the subject is construed as a self-contained monad and not as always already being enmeshed in the tentacles of some form of sociality. For if the subject ceases to appear as an island, then the reefer and music just unearth and magnify its capacity for deterritorialization, in Deleuze and Guattari's sense, representing, especially in their potent combination, an extreme version of the texturality of subjectivity.

As it turns out, this new analytical approach to the sonic moves from temporal to spatial reconfiguration, as the protagonist encounters three different levels of sound, sending him back not so much to his own onto-genesis, but enabling his understanding, or at least encounter with an altogether different spatiotemporal realm, in which the fast tempo of the music gives way to several competing yet complementary tempi repre-sented as different planes beneath the primary sonic figuration. On one level the protagonist hears "an old woman singing a spiritual full of Welt-schmerz," on another, a young slave woman on the auction block; finally, below all this commotion, lurks a sermon about the "Blackness of Black-ness" (9). This cacophony of voices that occupies different spaces and times within the music transacts a different way of becoming and, thus, understanding of his invisibility for the protagonist, since he can now ap-prehend these forces (almost) simultaneously without having to separate them. The sermon the protagonist hears further emphasizes the para-dox of his invisibility, since blackness, or rather the blackness of black-ness, appears as a series of syncopated contradictions: "It is and it ain't, it will get you and not get you, it will make you and unmake you" (9–10). These paradoxes discharge the nonsensical texture of blackness, in the process also revealing its meaning, which, as it were, has no "real" meaning. As with the hall of mirrors mentioned earlier, here, blackness ceases to radiate any fixed and predetermined signification. It is brought into a representational crisis by virtue of holding all these contradictions together; that is to say, blackness materializes only in its singular articula-tions: blackness de/re/territorialized. But of course things are even more unwieldy and complicated, so let us descend back into the depths.

After the sermon, the protagonist ascends to the level of the female spiritual singer to find out that she is bemoaning the death of her master just as her sons are celebrating his demise in a different realm. Much to the protagonist's surprise and chagrin, the old woman confesses her, grant-edly ambivalent, love for her master, who before his death promised to set her family free but never actually did. The contrast between the woman's lament and the son's jubilation unnerves the protagonist so much that he prompts the woman to describe more succinctly the liberty she so craves, yet the slave woman can offer only an ambiguous answer: "I done forgot, son. It's all mixed up. First I think it's one thing, then I think it's another. It gets my head spinning" (11). Feeling discombobulated, the protagonist is then berated by one of the woman's sons for asking his mother too many

questions, causing in her the same feelings of confusion, and for expect-
ing her to supply answers to queries that remain unanswerable, at least in
the manner the protagonist desires. Since the woman can only delineate
the nature of freedom as elusive, and the preacher cannot offer a fixed
definition of blackness, the protagonist is led to probe this problematic in
a different way, one that demands not only "becom[ing] acquainted with
ambivalence" but dwelling in the very realm of ambivalence, complexity,
and contradiction (10). Were we to place this haze of multiple times and
spaces into the psychoanalytic paradigm, this scene would provide an
"oceanic fantasy" par excellence wherein the protagonist's coherent self
gives way to an anterior subjectivity in which the borders between self
and other blur. This distortion would then lead back to the retroactively
imagined acoustic mirror stage that hallucinates the voice of the protagonist's mother. Clearly, there are numerous details in this scene that would
resolutely contradict this reading, Armstrong's masculine phonographic
voice being the most obvious departure from the maternal. Still, there
remains a nagging methodological point concerning the protagonist's
fantasy space.

Put succinctly, the psychoanalytic framework limits these oceanic fantasies to one particular story within the privatized history of the subject;
it does not furnish the tools for ascertaining how these oceanic moments
might not be about phantasmatic regression at all, or at least not exclusively, but instead a step in the direction of creating hitherto nonexisting
forms of subjectivity. In this way, the protagonist's fantasy encounter with
the preacher, the slave woman, and her sons would enable a different recognition of his becoming rather than merely recovering a lost childhood
moment. Because these theories insist on mapping a stage of the Oedipal
drama onto numerous different experiences, or explaining them through
this stage, they seldom facilitate the emergence of novel configurations
and their being apprehended as such. A more accurate theory of listening might consider the dissolution of subjective boundaries, yet not limit
itself to one "oceanic" pre-Oedipal moment. Simon Frith provides a nuanced description of listening than the psychoanalytic models because he
does not reduce the listening experience to a specific moment within the
history of the subject. He argues: "Music is not, by its nature, rational or
analytic; it offers us not argument but experience, and for a moment — for
moments — that experience involves *ideal time*."[27] Frith's hypothesis, although retaining a level of generality that makes it applicable in multiple

contexts, does not rely on assumptions about the biological or psychic reasons to explain the experience of music. In other words, it highlights *how* we listen instead of tendering a reductive account of *why* we listen to music; however, it does not proffer the tools for considering what conditions of im/possibility this "ideal time" engenders and what role the technological apparatus plays vis-à-vis Frith's suggestive notion of sonic temporality.

While Silverman concerns herself much more with the traditional domain of psychoanalytic cultural theory, the nuclear family, Schwarz actually writes about recorded music (the Beatles, Diamanda Galás, and Peter Gabriel, for example) and its effects on listeners, but he speaks only to the Lacanian concepts of the imaginary, the real, the symbolic, and the gaze in these musical texts without considering how different recording and reproduction technologies frame the listening experience. But surely modern sonic technologies transact, frame, produce, and reflect musical consumption in singular ways that cannot be subsumed by the drama of the acoustic mirror. As we have seen, Ellison's protagonist falls into "ideal time" mainly by way of encountering (with a little help from some marijuana) Louis Armstrong's voice on the phonograph situated in the brightly lit basement; both factors combined clearly represent a recoil from the social in the way suggested by the psychoanalytic oceanic fantasy. The phonograph lends itself well to eschewing the social by allowing the listener to consume music in private, without the presence of a human source responsible for (re)producing these sounds. Historically the phonograph was the first technology to authorize this form of listening (one of the more extreme versions of the privateness of sonic technologies, the Walkman, which enables individual consumption in public, will be discussed at length in chapter 4). So, in short, without the phonograph, there would be no "ideal time" for the protagonist, since (and this is a fairly obvious point) the presence of a human sound source would undoubtedly have altered this listening event.

Yet the phonographic listening modality also bears the traces of sociality, which paradoxically constitutes this scene as private, since the listening subject is drawn out of him/herself by encountering the technologically mediated sounds of other subjects — we might even go so far as to suggest that the phonograph itself functions as a subject, especially in its interfacings with various humans. When the protagonist emerges from his Dantean whirlpool, the first thing he hears is Armstrong: "Somehow

I came out of it, ascending hastily from the underworld of sound to hear Louis Armstrong" (12). Here, the twinning of Armstrong and the general qualities of the sonic machinery provide the condition of im/possibility for the protagonist's "ideal time." Therefore, any conceptualization of listening should ponder both the technological materialization of musical consumption and the particular musics being transmitted by the apparatus, as this will more effectively ascertain the singularity of the experience in question. This singularity gets submerged when all listening is imprisoned within the mute walls of the very particular psychoanalytic conception of sonic subjectivity that remains local but clothes itself in the language of universality by being used to explain and interpret such a wide variety of configurations. Even though these psychoanalytic cultural theories purport to scrutinize instances of boundary crossing in the form of oceanic moments, ironically, they ultimately foreclose rupture, because Oedipus awaits his entry in one form or another. There are no escape routes, only the inevitable return to and of the same old self. In essence, the psychoanalytic theories in question construe all listening textures as Oedipal nature, thus submerging their singularities in the process of reading them solely as a series of enactments of a universalized particularity.[28]

In addition, these conditions, far from teleporting the protagonist to a previous temporal and developmental stage in his ontogenesis, open his eyes and ears to an altogether different space-time continuum, one in which, according to Ellison, "instead of the swift and imperceptible flowing of time, you are aware of its nodes, those points where time stands still or from which it leaps ahead. And you slip into the breaks and look around" (8). These nodes stage time as time; they generally remain absent from linear and chronological perception so as to enable its ostensibly seamless functioning. Black cultural discourses, those of the musical variety in particular, have repeatedly slipped into these nodes that spatialize time as beginning points for new cultural modalities; we will return to these in the next chapter. Witness, for instance, James Snead's argument about the role of "the cut" in relation to repetition: "In jazz improvisation the 'cut' is the unexpectedness with which the soloist will depart from the 'head' or theme and from its normal harmonic sequence or the drummer from the tune's accepted and familiar primary beat."[29] While the cut or break deviates from the main theme or primary beat, it does so only in dialogue with these forces, serving as the difference that enables repetition, which is itself, according to Deleuze, but another name for "difference without a concept."[30] These breaks, rhythmic ones in particular, act as the building blocks for the whole genre of hip-hop, in which DJs or producers isolate these moments to mechanically repeat (loop) them as the basis for wholly new tracks. In general, hip-hop practitioners focus on those instances on old soul and funk records — James Brown's and George Clinton's oeuvres being the most plundered or revered, depending on where you stand — in which the rhythm section "breaks away" from the rest of the instrumentation to explore different sonic configurations. It also bears stressing that hip-hop DJs and producers utilize old recordings rather than replaying these breaks on "traditional" instruments; they use record players and samplers as their weapons of choice. By doing this they amplify the singularity of the recorded performance instead of insisting on the integrity of composition (in Glissant's terminology, they weave together the textures of old recordings). As a result, the technological reiteration of the "originary" break becomes the basis for the main theme in the new sonic constellation, moving from margin to center. This represents the analogical context in which the protagonist's encounter should be read as the sui generis creation of a new sense of becoming. The phonograph, the reefer, the brightly lit basement, and Armstrong's recording provide the conditions of im/possibility for the protagonist's "slip into the breaks." And this slide facilitates a new grasp of his invisibility as becoming, since "sickness is not unto death, neither is invisibility" (14). Clearly, I want to insist on the phonograph's integrality to this process, especially because the visual present absence of the performer creates such a glaring gash within the audiovisual economies of Western modernity, but without necessarily reducing this constellation to a mere effect of the apparatus. Before concluding this chapter, I would like to take a brief detour through current conceptions of the subject as a category in critical idioms, especially as it interfaces with minority discourses, to suggest that *Invisible Man* might offer a different path to thinking the two together.

Good to Think With   There appears to be an odd lacuna, a curious epistemological and categorical aporia, in Stuart Hall's introduction to the volume *Questions of Cultural Identity*; even the introduction's title "Introduction: Who Needs 'Identity'?" stages this disjuncture defensively, perhaps even ironically.[31] The title concomitantly signifies the importance and obsolescence of identity as a conceptual formulation, a bifurcation also evident in the slippage between notions of identity and the subject in the movement of Hall's discussion. Hall's consideration commences with the place of identity in current debates and then progresses to introduce related terms such as "identification," "the self," and "the subject"; yet identity evaporates at a certain point of Hall's argument, begging the question, Why insist on this term in the first place? The fracture between these concept-metaphors—which occupy the same discursive universe but do not travel the same space ways—far from suggesting a lack of analytical rigor, prompts a productive dislocation that defamiliarizes both categories but does not resolve the friction between them, as in the following moment: "I use 'identity' to refer to the meeting point, the point of *suture*, between on the one hand the discourses and practices which attempt to 'interpellate,' speak to us or hail us into place as the social subjects of particular discourses, and on the other hand, the processes which produce subjectivities, which construct us as subjects which can be spoken" (5–6). If identity serves as the point around which these interpellations and subjectivities congeal, what distinguishes this term/concept from the subject? Not much, according to Hall's scenario, which, in turn, draws attention to the ways in which these concepts often operate as mutual exclusives within academic discourses. In general, identity (I be) refers to empirical social beings and is often thought in relation to some form of identitarian realpolitik, whereas as the subject (I am) remains in the unsullied domain of lofty abstraction. By yoking identity to the subject, as opposed to having one dialectically supersede the other, Hall asks his readers to contemplate how these seemingly contradictory and contentious terms depend upon one another, and therefore bring each other into being. Accordingly, Hall gives us not the last word on either identity or the subject, but a fraught coarticulation of these notions "good to think with" (1).[32]

But let's rewind and come again. In a recent essay concerned with, among other factors, the Du Boisian formulation of "double consciousness," Nahum Dimitri Chandler commences with a startling conceptual and methodological statement about the generalizability of this concept: "We should generalize and therefore radicalize W. E. B. Du Bois's formulation of the African American sense of identity as 'a kind of double consciousness,' experienced under the palpable force of the practice of racial distinction, to American identities as such and modern subjectivi-

ties in general."[33] The causal link between generalization and radicaliza-
tion seems to belie a variety of recent critical pieties that privilege the
local, particular, fragmented, hybrid, and specific as opposed to the universal and general, especially in the cosmos of minority discourse. As a
customary rule in Western modernity, racialized identity does not reside
in the realm of the general or the universal (the subject); in fact, historically it has served as the absolute obverse of these forces, as Sylvia Wynter
observes: "The black population groups of the New World [acted] as the
embodied bearers of Ontological lack to the secular model of being, Man,
as the conceptual Other."[34] So what do we "gain" — or, conversely, lose —
by generalizing and thus radicalizing Du Bois's conception of double consciousness, the disputatious twinning of Americanness and Africanness,
regularly thought to signify the radical particularity, yet often amounting
to nothing more or less than an idealization of the modern *and* Western black subject?[35] In other words, why generalize and radicalize this
concept at the risk of losing precisely that thrust which bears witness to
tricky particularities of modern Afro-diasporic subjectivity?

Chandler invites us to consider that "all critical reflections must pro-
ceed by way of example" and are thus dependent on the very specificity of the example to achieve any level of generality ("Originary Displacement," 250). Thus Foucault's notion of "the disciplinary society"
relies on historical materials from late-eighteenth-century France, just
as Sigmund Freud's theory of the unconscious is articulated in relation
to case studies emanating from Vienna at the turn of the twentieth century, but these theories have been employed widely to describe, some
might even say prescribe, a variety of spatial, temporal, cultural, and
political constellations. Why, then, should the Du Boisian proposition
of double consciousness not enjoy the same generalizability as the Fou-
cauldian and Freudian concepts? Chandler offers this answer: "It is time
that we systematically expose the pervasive operative presumption that
general theory or conceptual reflection is formulated elsewhere than in
African Diasporic (American) Studies, and that it is only applied here"
(250). Although we should locate Chandler's "here" not only in African
American studies, but in the academic disciplines associated with racialized minorities in general, this caveat does not undermine the crucial
point herein, which is the assignation of these intellectual projects to the
prison house of conceptual particularity,[36] in which black life functions
as an example within a conceptual framework only insofar as it pertains

to black life, while theoretical utterances that do not primarily pertain to black culture can be "applied" to it with some minor modifications. Insisting on the subject from the vantage point of black studies transacts at least a repositioning of this unfortunate trajectory. Moreover, because it is uttered from the perspective of the minoritarian, it throws this classification, so very central to Western modernity (at least from Descartes onward), into the maelstrom of catachresis.[37] That is to say, once a subject is articulated in relation to Afro-diasporic life, not only does it remove black life from the shackles of base empiricism, it also calls into question the identity/subject discrepancy as such, as well as the politics of theory in the U.S. academy. In this case, following Hortense Spillers's injunction for "the black creative intellectual to get busy where he/she is" induces claiming the subject, at least throwing it into the critical mix akin to a DJ, without inexorably renouncing the specificities of black life.[38] As a result, the subject proves useful, for both theoretical and practical purposes, in the field of black studies for the very reasons Paul Smith dismisses this category, by stating that "current conceptions of the 'subject' have tended to produce a purely *theoretical* 'subject,' removed almost entirely from the political and ethical realities in which human agents actually live."[39] Even though Smith does not use the term "identity," his contention conjures the binary logic, discussed above, of identity versus the subject, only here "the [real] human agents" are proffered as the favored category, which effects little more than reversing the very reasoning it seeks to disarm. Fabricating "a purely theoretical subject" at least recognizes its productive and generative provenances instead of claiming to represent "real human agents," which veers perilously close to a regression to the pastoral time before the advent of "theory."[40] Instead, we should tread the path (as we should with many of the roads paved by Gayatri Spivak's trailblazing oeuvre) that is very much in line with Hall and Chandler, one that Spivak has recently laid out: "Why have I written largely of women to launch the question of the recognition of ceaselessly shifting collectivities in our disciplinary practice? Because women are not a special case, but can represent the human, with asymmetries attendant upon any such representation. As simple as that."[41] Analogously, wielding the category of the subject from the position of black studies—both as simple and as complicated as that—calls this whole dichotomous enterprise into question (I am not naive enough to think that it could do much more than change things at the level of academic discourse, if that), fusing *I am* and

I be in ways that do not inflict violence upon their fragile, yet potent singularities as modes of becoming-in-the-world.

Recent (post)structuralist inflected theorizations of the subject have almost exclusively zeroed in on the lingual provenances of this formation; Judith Butler, for instance, offers one of the more succinct recitals of this trend: "The subject is the linguistic occasion for the individual to achieve and reproduce intelligibility."[42] Even in its brevity this is a striking statement, especially the invocation of intelligibility, which seems to resolutely contradict the insights of Butler's poststructuralist background. If the various thought systems grouped under the rubric of poststructuralism have taught us anything, it is that clarity, linguistic transparency in particular, cannot but remain, at the most, slippery. But perhaps we need to summon a different witness to make our case: Edouard Glissant, who suggests that transparency has long functioned as the central topos in Western thinking. In its stead, Glissant testifies to "opacity" as that "which is not obscure, though it is possible to be so and accepted as such. It is that which cannot be reduced, which is the perennial guarantee of participation and confluence."[43] Rather than apprehending "opacity" in terms of deficiency or lack, Glissant accentuates how "opacity . . . is not enclosure within an impenetrable autarchy but subsistence within an irreducible singularity" (190). Therefore, a subject can be thought as a singular becoming-opacity, a crystallization that amalgamates in a particular spatiotemporal juncture, an agent (human or otherwise) with some form of noncalcified structure, in which neither structure nor agent dominate but might be said to create a temporary and contingent arrangement that does not wield the hubris of intelligibility.[44]

While contemporary critical vernaculars often take the linguistic sphere as their axiomatic horizon (Butler's statement quoted above stands in for a variety of other thinkers), for my purposes, the sonic, markedly in its nonlinguistic musical forms, provides one of the best tracks to opacity, because it fails to cast either intelligibility or transparency in the role of its logos. By focusing on the sonic I do not want to privilege one mode of discursivity as the preferred figure for the articulation of subjectivity, such as the linguistic; rather, I hope to open up possibilities for thinking, hearing, seeing, apprehending the subject in a number of different arenas that do not insist on monocausality. Along these lines, Deleuze and Guattari link the sonic to conjuring, if not transacting, movements of deterritorialization: "Sound owes this power not to

signifying or 'communicational' values, . . . not to physical properties, . . .
but to a machinic phylum that operates in sound and makes it the cutting edge of deterritorialization."[45] While sound may not signify in the
same manner as language, it does harbor opacities that are not communicational per se but nonetheless transmit intensities, which belong to
the realm of expression rather than content, or, as per Deleuze and Guattari, "the unformed material of expression."[46] This, however, should not
imply that content as such is not a pertinent factor here, but that it ceases
to occupy the principal role in this milieu.[47] Since music does not rely on
meaning making in the same way as language—put simply, humans do
not use music as their main mode of communication—it calls attention
to its texture and confluence rather than striving for intelligibility, networking it squarely within the charged currents of opacity.[48] Locating a
subject in the sonic grants a quite different notion of this concept (which
does not mean that the subject as a linguistic category is rendered null
and void; it just relocates to a new analytic neighborhood without losing
its ties to old friends), one that does not posit meaning and/or intelligibility as its teleological end point, but that enables "opacities [to] coexist
and converge, weaving fabrics. To understand these truly, one must focus
on the texture of the weave and not on the nature of its components."[49]
Perhaps, we can distinguish between *the* subject as a determinate linguistic category and *a* subject as an indeterminate sonic opacity, as long as
we remember that the two are contiguous: "The indefinite as such is not
a mark of an empirical indetermination but of a determination by immanence. . . . The indefinite article is the indetermination of the person
only because it is determination of the singular."[50] Thus, the indefinite
article traces texture and not meaning, as effervescent as it may be, sonically adducing a mode of divining the world that sounds its multitude
of opacities without drowning their singularities in the white noise of
determinate transparency.[51]

Yet I also want to steer clear of construing the sonic as a preconscious,
receptive, fragmented, yet fluid sphere that sounds in strict opposition to
the visual and/or language, as Emmanuel Levinas does to some extent, all
the while offering some cogent observations on the general provenances
of this stratum:

> In sound, and in the consciousness termed hearing, there is in fact a break
> with the self-complete world of vision. . . . In its entirety, sound is a ringing,

clanging scandal. Whereas, in vision, form is wedded to content in such a way as to appease it, in sound the perceptible quality overflows so that form can no longer contain its content. A real rent is produced, through which the world that is *here* prolongs a dimension that cannot be converted into vision.[52]

Levinas underscores one of the reasons sound retains such a crucial place within black cultural formations: openness, particularly when contrasted to the way vision has been codified in Western modernity. Over the course of the twentieth century this openness has been boosted by sound technologies such as the phonograph, which, by disturbing any seemingly predetermined symbiosis between the aural and the visual, have allowed for a multiplication of practices and contexts for both the production and reception of black musical cultures. But it should be noted that my argument endorses neither Levinas's idealization of sound nor the tacit insistence on the present tense, particularly as "presentism" often serves as one of the cornerstones for the "social-scientification" of black life by denying black culture any form of historical genesis.[53] In other words, black cultural production is often construed as something found and immediate (i.e., folksy) instead of having a certain past in which forms have been worked upon and over.[54] In addition, rather than suggest that this dimension (subjectivity) can be converted into or represented in sound, I would like to retain its "scandalous" qualities, since the sonic realm grants aural "opacities" qua subjectivity: pathways to moments of subjectivity set off against subjectivity (*a* subject rather than *the* subject); a sonic subjectivity that does not lose sight of the black subject's visual interpellation but noisily "rings" and "clangs" beyond, above, below, and beside the optic nonetheless. As my reading of Ellison has shown, a subject of sonic Afro-modernity, while breaking with purely visual and linguistic paradigms of subjectivity, comes into being in the crevice made by the audiovisual disjunction engendered by the phonograph (cf. chapter 1).

Where the Du Boisian notion of a second sight — as the gift of a black subject's double consciousness — already put forward a sonic style of apprehending the world, Ellison's phonographic scene directs our ears to the technological embodiment of modern musical production and consumption; in other words, the phonograph makes the audiovisual dislocation usable for black cultural production. Armstrong's mechanosonic absent presence stages his blackness as a contingent process that in turn allows the protagonist to apprehend his subjecthood in a similar manner. Yet, as previously stated, this can only occur against the backdrop of his visual appearance as lack. Had the protagonist encountered Armstrong only visually, he would have only seen proof of his invisibility; the phonographic voice, however, enables the protagonist to hear how Armstrong maneuvers, both literally and metaphorically, his invisibility. Here, scopic indiscernibility ceases to materialize as monolithic nature, appearing instead as a series of textured singularities. This is a subject of sonic Afro-modernity, which emerges at the spatiotemporal crossroads where the performer's ghostly sounds merge with the ear of the listener, on those lower frequencies, which resituate, reframe, and resound a black subject's visual invisibility, producing a flash point of subjectivity gleaned in and through sound.

This modality of subjectivity might help explain the immense global popularity — without inescapably succumbing to the tenacious lure of the empirical — of black popular music over the course of the last century. In other words, rather than exclusively presenting a racially particular identity, black music, in the form of the varying techne-logical structures of sonic Afro-modernity, advances and constructs a singular subject, at once more and less than its attendant minor identity without which it cannot be thought or perceived. Just as this subject occupies the regions between the sonic and the scopic, it correspondingly dislodges the subject/identity bifurcation in current debates within the Anglo-American humanities by refusing to separate *I am I be*. The interface of black music and sound technologies yields a rich, varied, and complex field, which amplifies the opacities included therein, since, in the words of Levinas, "form can no longer contain its content." Even if this constellation could just as easily walk the corners of the earth in the cloak of identity, there is a climacteric theoretical point to be made about wielding the category of the subject from the standpoint of black studies in order to dispel the misconception that "general theory is only applied here," resounding Chandler's earlier point, since this frees black life from the conceptual chains of radical particularity and embarks on a global journey to ascertain how black cultural practices do not merely mimic or recast those of Western modernity but are constitutive of this domain proper.[55] This will not entail abandoning the particularities of black life in favor of a colorblind, "can't-we-all-just-get-along" critical theory and practice as much as it will mean reconstructing black life and Western modernity in their mobile relationality, so as not to construe them as mutually exclusive, or even all that different. More succinctly: *I be* (sojourning—both leisurely and contentiously—in the spaces and times between) *I am.*

3

In the Mix

⊚ This chapter hears W. E. B. Du Bois's *The Souls of Black Folk* (1903) and the contemporary practices of disc jockeying as two central art forms in sonic Afro-modernity, presenting Du Bois's text and disc jockeys' sounds as different manifestations of "the mix." The "mix," as it appears in black cultural production throughout the twentieth century, highlights the amalgamation of its components, or rather the process of this (re)combination, as much as it accentuates the individual parts from which it springs. As a result this "mix" provides us with a model of modern black temporality and cultural practice rooted in and routed through the sonic, although, as we have already seen, the scopic realm is not completely absent from this mise-en-scène. In order to contextualize my argument about the temporalities of sonic Afro-modernity, I return to Ellison's *Invisible Man*, where history appears as a groove that indexes both the indentations found on the surface of phonograph records and those somewhat more elusive grooves in the vernacular sense. In addition, Walter Benjamin's "On the Concept of History" will serve as a sounding board for the consideration of the variable temporalities in the "tradition of the oppressed."[1] Finally, this chapter puts into practice what I call "thinking sound" by interfacing historically seemingly disparate texts in order to excavate their intensities (which only emerge in the process of juxtaposition and recontextualization), much as DJs treat records in their mixes. Overall, this strategy quite intentionally goes against the grain of the current historicist discourses in the U.S. academic humanities and social sciences, where "history" appears as not necessarily progressive in a teleological sense but nonetheless commonsensical and determining in the last and any other instance. This often unarticulated and undertheorized version of historical time leaves intact a fairly staid configuration of temporal movement (if it includes motion at all), one that cannot account for the discontinuities of the temporal. To put it bluntly, Fredric Jameson's injunction to "always historicize" should prompt not the Pavlovian responses it has largely garnered thus far, but rather, the question, Historicize how?[2] When we progress from this question, which neither presumes to know history in an a priori sense nor takes the methods of historicization for granted, history ceases to operate as an axiomatic category brimming with found objects in the inevitable flow of time; instead it functions as a series of vexed knots that require the active intervention of the critic or DJ.

The Grooves of History   Chapter 20 of Ellison's *Invisible Man* suggests a notion of temporality steeped in sound technology that thankfully steers clear of the linear models that stalk current academic discourse. This chapter, generally overflowing with references to records and grooves, opens with the protagonist's search for the missing Tod Clifton; both men belong to the political organization the Brotherhood.[3] In his quest for Clifton, the protagonist is led to Harlem, where "the uptown rhythms were slower and yet somehow faster" than the ones downtown, already indicating a shift in time that will acquire more force as the protagonist's quest continues (423). Once in Harlem, the protagonist visits the Jolly Dollar, a neighborhood bar. Musing on the corporeal features of the bar's owner, Barrelhouse, the protagonist observes, "He looked like that kind of metal beer barrel which has a groove in its middle" (424). Barrelhouse asks the protagonist if he likes "groovy music on the jukebox" (425). After exiting the bar, he returns to his old Harlem office to wait for Brother Tarp, who might reveal some information concerning Clifton's whereabouts. When Tarp fails to surface by 3 A.M., the protagonist consults, unsuccessfully, the district's written records, looking for clues about Clifton. Disillusioned, he "pushe[s] the records aside; for they told [him] nothing of why things were as they were" (428). The protagonist finally locates Clifton selling "Sambo dolls" on 43rd Street.[4] Clifton and his partner accompany their sales pitch with a song about the features of this doll. Comparing Clifton's activities in the Brotherhood with his new role as a Sambo doll salesman, the protagonist ponders Clifton's fate: "It was as though he had chosen . . . to fall outside of *history*," an assertion that queries a common-sense approach to history: how, if history is defined as an autonomous motor which keeps the world running, can Clifton fall out of it? (434). Why and what history does Clifton fall out of when selling Sambo dolls, as opposed to being a member of the Brotherhood? Here the protagonist seems to embody the historicist impulse by virtue of not questioning the version of history fed to him by the Brotherhood, or accepting that there can only be one totalizing historical apparatus that controls the past, present, and future. The operative question is, Are you in or are you out?

Undoubtedly, this query acquires different shades of signification for "the tradition of the oppressed." Two incidents in particular shape the protagonist's movement from—in Walter Benjamin's terminology (about which we will have more to say later)—historicist to historical materialist: his witnessing of Clifton's death and his encounter with three young black men in zoot suits.[5] While selling the dolls, Clifton is threatened by and attacks a white policeman, a confrontation that culminates in Clifton's fatal shooting, which the protagonist unwillingly observes. Forced to bear witness to his friend's violent erasure from history, any history, the protagonist is thrown into a whirlpool of doubt, which sparks a different historical motor: "Why should a man deliberately plunge outside history and peddle in obscenity? Why did he choose to plunge . . . into the void of faceless faces, of soundless voices, lying outside of history?" (439). Still in line with the Brotherhood's teleological conceptualization of history, this rumination on Clifton's motives transmutes into a metadiscussion of history's recording gear: "History records the patterns of men's lives they say. All things, it is said, are duly recorded—all things of importance that is. But not quite, for it is actually the known, the seen, the heard, and only those events the recorder regards as important that are put down, those lies his keepers keep their power by" (439). Clifton's death forces the protagonist to acknowledge that Clifton had no choice in "falling out of history" since there exists no place in the Brotherhood's version of history for black subjects. In this sense they are already belated, "men out of time," in Ellison's words. Here, the teleological model of history ruptures: in its place a more nuanced theory of temporality materializes that takes notice of the complex relations of domination and subordination linked to the inscription of history as it pertains to black people in the United States and the oppressed, in general. For Clifton, a black man in the United States, is already (but not always) beyond and beside the written annals of hegemonic history: the only people present to record his death are the protagonist and the policeman. Since history remains the vestige of those in power, the policeman, as a white man and representative of the repressive state apparatus, is the only person authorized to record Clifton's killing. Accordingly, it is he who expunges Clifton from the history he never had access to. But the policeman functions not only as Clifton's historian but also, as the protagonist notes, his judge, witness, and executioner; thus Clifton suffers a double death sentence: he is murdered and barred from official records. Clifton's discursive demise and physical obliteration represent a significant turning point in the protagonist's weltanschauung. In this configuration, written records, historical narratives in particular, are wrested from the sphere of totality and self-evident truth as they fail and/or violently resist to record histories of marginalized subjects such as Clifton.

After leaving the scene of Clifton's death, the protagonist descends into the nearest subway station, where he stumbles upon the three young black men in zoot suits. He describes them, briefly reasserting his totalizing conceptualization of history in the aftermath of Clifton's murder, as "men out of time—unless they found the Brotherhood. Men out of time, who would soon be gone and forgotten" (441). Here, the zoot suiters are beyond the measure of temporality due to their distance from the Brotherhood. The protagonist, nevertheless, envisions this particular redaction of history as History, eliding the differences between the particular and the universal. Like the advent of Clifton's death, this encounter punctures the seamless weave of history and History:

> What if history was a gambler, instead of a force in a laboratory experiment, and his boys the ace in the hole? What if history was not a reasonable citizen, but a madman full of paranoid guile and these boys his agents, his big surprise! His own revenge? For they were outside, in the dark with Sambo, the dancing paper doll; taking it on the lambo with my fallen brother, Tod Clifton (Tod, Tod) running and dodging the forces of history instead of making a dominating stand. (441)[6]

This set of questions and the final assertion serve to further elucidate the dislocation, if not negation, of the protagonist's model of history by questioning the role of history vis-à-vis the vicissitudes of American culture in general and black subjects in particular: if history were a madman and not a scientific motor, would Clifton still be alive? Once history ceases to bear the semblance of a "reasonable citizen," it unmistakably splinters and falls short of functioning as the single placeholder and point of origin of temporal convergence, which, in turn, pilots the protagonist to a different plane in the realization of his own alienation from this machine. In other words, while the totalizing idea of the historical does not quite vanish from the horizon, it does begin to fade slightly, making room for alternative versions thereof that allocate a place ("his agents") for the zoot suiters in a way that the former cannot. Even though Clifton and the zoot suiters are already "recorded out" of governing historiography, according to the protagonist they may be partially responsible for this positioning, for they do not attempt to alter its course. This recourse to agency underscores the protagonist's continuing belief in the Brotherhood's unilateral notion of history, like a transcendental locomotive that Clifton and the young men can either board or let pass by. To completely, or at least principally, abandon this train of thought regarding temporality and black subjects' status in it, the protagonist will have to tune his ears to the refrain of phonograph records for a dissimilar transaction of this vexed conundrum.

Walking the streets of Harlem, the protagonist asserts: "They were *outside the groove of history*, and it was my job to get them in, all of them. Forgotten names sang through my head like forgotten scenes in dreams" (443; emphasis mine). Unable to relinquish the dominant model of history propagated by the Brotherhood, which can only conceive of these men as embodying CPT ("colored people's time"), the protagonist imagines history as a single groove from which the zoot suiters are barred even while they opt for remaining beyond its borders, thus suggesting a syncopated equilibrium between determining structure and human agency.[7] As he continues his not-so-leisurely stroll, however, the sonic ecology intrudes even more forcefully into the protagonist's historical shield (perhaps it's a certain kind of deafness to the lower frequencies that he'll come to embrace?): "I moved with the crowd, the sweat pouring off me, listening to the grinding roar of traffic, the growing sound of a record shop loudspeaker blaring a languid blues. I stopped. *Was this all that would be recorded? Was this the only true history of the time*s, a mood blared by trumpets, trombones, saxophones and drums, a song with turgid, inadequate words?" (443; emphasis mine).[8] What distinguishes this insound from the totality of epochness promulgated by the Brotherhood is not only its imagining of an alternative historical sphere but also, and more important, the appearance of a sonic aperture that shifts the terms of the game altogether.

In what amounts to no less than an instance of a linguistic-cum-historical sublime, the clarity of traditional historiography is momentarily displaced by the "blaring of a loudspeaker" transmitting a variety of instruments and "turgid, inadequate words." The loudspeaker shocks the protagonist to a realm beyond (or possibly adjacent to?) the reach of linguistic signification (inadequate and turgid), wherein aggregations of letters from the alphabet cease to function as the sole determinants in the gamble of time, since they fall short of discharging the interlocking and clashing folds of temporal confluence. Put simply, the brand of history the protagonist has been hitherto accustomed to in his association with the Brotherhood cannot but redact only one modus of historical change, leaving by the wayside those aspects too promiscuous to fit its single purpose teleological sequence of events, which has particular ramifications for those subjects who have access to neither historiographical nor scriptural technes (that is, most markedly, black people in the United States). Nonetheless, the written annals of history are not simply exchanged for a more authentic Afro-diasporic oral theory of history; rather, Ellison insists on the iterability of sound recording and reproduction and thus refuses to extort the *phono* from the *graph* and vice versa, amounting to an additive code as opposed to an either-or proposition. But before we get ahead of ourselves, we should lend an ear to another sage voice sounding from a different virtual loudspeaker.

The protagonist's reconceptualization of the temporal suggests an instance of peril (Clifton's violent demise) in which the past monadically flares up, as in Walter Benjamin's understanding of history, which opens a different series of doorways to the crinkle of the past while suggesting a nondogmatic and elastic arrangement of temporal confluence rather than "the swift and imperceptible flowing of time" (*Invisible Man*, 8). In his oft-cited essay "On the Concept of History," Benjamin distinguishes between "historicism," which slavishly attempts to recreate the "true past" and a "historical materialism" that "brush[es] history against the grain."[9] Even though the invocation of materialism, especially coupled with the adjective "historical," brings to mind certain dogmatic configurations of

In the Mix

Marxian theorems, Benjamin, while surely drawing on those tenets, is in pursuit of an altogether different historical imaginary. This imaginary, rather than seeking to construe the past "the way it really was," aspires to "seize hold of a memory as it flashes up at a moment of danger" (255). Much commentary about this passage has focused on the conjuring of peril in relation to the Third Reich, reducing the insights to the very historicism Benjamin's labors crave to dislodge, or, as Benjamin argues at a different point, "The tradition of the oppressed teaches us that 'the state of exception' in which we live is the rule" (257).[10] In this way, the historical materialist is always confronted by danger, which is precisely what puts into motion the necessity of "brushing history against the grain." But what does this "brushing against" yield that a "brushing with" does not or cannot?

Where the historicist accumulates facts in order to fill "homogeneous and empty time" that "culminates in universal history," the historical materialist works under the auspices of a "constructive principle" that incorporates its own theoretical production — it reflects its own process of assembling history as opposed to simply retelling the past — and "only approaches a historical entity where it confronts him in the form of a monad" (262–263). This monad appears as a breach (a wounding, as Hortense Spillers might say) in the ostensibly inevitable progressive workings of historical time and gives way to a model of "messianic time" that eschews a linear current in favor of a "cessation of happening" (263).[11] Even though this "messianic time" has religious undertones and certainly reflects Judaic theoretical traditions, it should not be the only context for an exegesis of this segment. The historical materialist faces and therefore inevitably constructs history as a secularized version of messianic temporality in which events do not form a chain like "the beads of rosary"; on the contrary, the past is released from its mimeticist straightjacket and reinvented as "a configuration of the present (*Jetztzeit*) which is shot through with shrapnels of the messianic" (263). The shards of messianism enable a revision not only of the historical but of temporality as such, forming hiccups in the machine of "universal history," hiccups that do not suspend or dispense with this chrono/logical mode as much as they provide pathways to the clefts and folds within its very configurations.[12] In Glissant's terminology: the (weak) messianic imagines temporality as series of opacities, where historicism only apprehends the past, present, and future silenced by the screech of clarity. Nodes, monads, opacities, and folds all offer hypotheses of time not encased by the constraints of linearity and unimpeded progress in their incorporation of the active production of temporality. They conjure a different form of temporal materiality, in which the material is interrupted and in constant flux rather than held in the abyss of universal time. We might even say: matter (time) is released from a particular form (historicism) that cloaks itself in truth and universality in order to appear as series of singularities. In an attempt to perforate "the swift and imperceptible flowing of time," Ellison, much like Benjamin, tenders an arrangement of temporal change that bypasses quasipositivist ideas concerning history, especially with regard to "the tradition of the oppressed."

Ellison's insistence on the sonic's traversing the phonograph, proves decisive, as it recalibrates not only temporality as such but also the function of *graph* in historiography rather than claiming an authentic orality uncontaminated by the modern technological viruses for black cultural purposes. Hence, Ellison's "hero" comes upon Benjamin's flash in a moment of danger—Clifton's death—via the electric amplification of a phonograph record and not, to put it briefly, a "real" live singer and/or musician. The retention of the letters *g* and *r* in the shift from "historiography" to "groove" serves as a road sign for the graphematicity of the phonograph, while the addition of "oove" might be said to conjure the sonic as well as other similarly elusive facets of temporality relegated to the borders of hegemonic notions of history *and* time. Clearly, blackness and alterity in general are inscribed in and sound from the sonorous fissure of the "grooves of history." These grooves, in turn serve a double purpose: they displace—once again it is necessary to insist that they do not replace—a historicist model of time, but they also sharply suggest how in the processes of sound recording and reproduction, the production of black history transmogrifies from absolute erasure in writing to sounding from loudspeakers on any given urban corner. And these amplifiers echo not only "turgid and inadequate words" but also predominantly nonlinguistic sonic marks. In this way, black subjects are not intrinsically outside of history, as Hegel would have it a century before Ellison, but are actively and oftentimes ferociously "recorded out" of it, which, in turn has lead to forging other means to record black history.[13] In the Ellisonian cosmos, these instruments appear in, through, and with the phonographic sounds because of, and not despite, the iterability the machine introduces into the realm of black aurality. As we shall see, Du Bois claims the Western musical notation of spirituals in a similar fashion. In other words, the repetition thrown into the whirlpool of transversal movement by this particular technicity of black music in the age of mechanical reproduction — that, here, should not be equated with technicity per se as with a new form of technological folding — enables a fresh recording and sounding of black history. Neither an authentic black orality nor a thoroughly commodified and inauthentic version thereof suffices to stage black history qua history or the temporal; instead, we are confronted with a sounding black history that hinges on mechanical and electric iterability, suggesting a different form of writing than the fraught domain of alphabetic script, one that makes black sounds mechanically repeatable. Consequently, these sounds act as history, without abolishing their sonic dimensions.

If we consult two of the most prominent definitions of "groove," we can better surmise how history might operate as groove. First, the word refers to the channels on the surface of phonograph records, or any long, narrow depression, and second, to the more colloquial "groove" of a particular piece of music or "getting into the groove" of someone or something. These definitions of "groove," if not directly related to the sonic, are at least derived from musical expressions.[14] While the grooves on records present a seemingly straightforward traffic between word and object, the other signification of "groove" proves slightly more intangible (a more Du Boisian and Derridean signifier/signified relationship than a Saussurean one, to be sure), if not elusive; for instance, there are no "objective" ways to describe or pin down the groove of a James Brown track. This, however, does not imply complete incoherency; rather, it highlights the difficulty in transfiguring the exact characteristics of "the groove" into the realm of linguistic meaning making: the groove contains a significant measure of opacity because it registers in the domain of affect and sensation rather than (linguistic) signification. For Steven Feld and Charles Keil this can be attributed to the "collaborative expectancies in time" that lead to an agreement between musicians and their audiences on the affective groove that unites them in an open-ended and unevenly striated rapport, thus amplifying the "ephemeral," nonrepresentational aspects of sound.[15] These "expectancies in time" are also mediated if not constituted by the grooves of phonograph records; they provide the material groundings for the intersubjective grooves while the bass-boom overflows and reconfigures their presumed fixed substance.

The "groove of history" allows for both the materiality and intersubjectivity of history, and if black history is, indeed, contained on, or at least summoned by phonograph records, it is only because the discs and their attendant discourses and practices harbor all these vital forces. Ellison's protagonist comes upon this recognition in an instance of peril, which promotes his recognition of temporality as series of monadic cross-currents and discontinuities, as opposed to a single and totalizing genus of history. These grooves of relation, however, cannot be consigned to the realm of the purely subjective, since they direct our awareness to those dimensions of temporality that are not signified by the strictures of written history or the indentations on phonograph records alone. Therefore, both forms of grooves, at least in the universe of recorded music, are not only constitutive of each other, but bring each other into productive crisis; here the sensational and ephemeral is the material and vice versa, which, to borrow another crucial concept from Glissant, moves us from a description of "Being" to a "poetics of relation."[16] The groove of history works well in this regard because it fails to neglect one aspect in favor of the other; instead it preserves, or possibly invents, the eventness of temporality as sonically singular. Still, should we not ask what transpires when different grooves of history interface and/or collide? W. E. B. Du Bois's *The Souls of Black Folk* and the rigorous dexterity of DJing in a variety of contemporary musical formations will serve as our phonic guides on this journey back and forth through the assorted time(s) of sonic Afro-modernity.

"There's Not a Problem That I Can't Fix, I Can Do It in the Mix" *The Souls of Black Folk*, "the text that would have been" according to Robert Stepto, inaugurates the mix in sonic Afro-modernity. Just as DJs mix parts of different records, Du Bois's text blends together history, eulogy, sociology, personal anecdote, economics, lyricism, ethnography, fiction, and cultural criticism of black music.[17] Furthermore, Du Bois's textual practice highlights the fissures in the mix in the same manner that hip-hop DJs call attention to their mixes through the rhythmical scratching of records, a result of being played with and against the groove. Du Bois's "scratching," one of the central aesthetic achievements of this epochal text, appears in bars of music placed before each chapter.[18] Both Du Bois and DJs combine different elements—in Du Bois's case genres and different forms of recording, and records with regard to DJs—so as to articulate what exceeds the scopic as it has been formed in Western modernity. Du Bois re-defines the spirituals he employs, making them applicable to the situation of black subjects at the turn of the century, and fusing them with Western canonical literature, rendering these songs usable and audible African American future-pasts that bridge the gap between the nineteenth cen-tury—slavery and white transcribers—and the twentieth century—the color line. Yet, Du Bois's mix is not complete: it is marked by a "failure" to represent sound in writing, which, in turn highlights the audiovisual rift set in motion by the technology of the phonograph.[19] This "failure," or scratching, wherein noise intrudes into the temporal architecture of the linguistic text, allows *Souls* to be audible and legible as the first literary sound recording (phono-graph) of sonic Afro-modernity.

The mix can be found in a number of different spaces and times within the discursive and material arenas of sonic Afro-modernity. It exists in the appropriation of the piano, the main instrument of Western clas-sical music, by ragtime musicians; in the samples of Steely Dan, David Bowie, and Foreigner appearing on rap records; and in the mixing of DJs that work in a variety of contemporary (black) popular music genres. In their art, Jean Michel Basquiat and Renee Green use music to des-sediment calcifications in the visual domain. Music also plays a key role in the literary aesthetics of the mix as it appears in the current work of Toni Morrison, Nalo Hopkinson, Paul Beatty, and Ishmael Reed. The per-sistent presence of the mix in these disparate works illustrates its cru-cial place in the construction of twentieth-century black culture. As a mode of cultural criticism and practice, the mix brings together dispa-rate elements, but not in the manner suggested by the notions of "pas-tiche" and "bricolage" as they appear in postmodern literary theory; the mix offers a strategy for the construction of modern temporality that re-sults not from the randomness or irony evoked by these terms. Instead it creates a transversal, nonempirical space that coexists with its other components. Kodwo Eshun marks the main distinctions between "the mix," or what he refers to as "remixology," and more postmodernist-oriented variants of these forms as follows: "The idea of quotation and citation, the idea of ironic distance, that doesn't work, that's far too lit-erary. That assumes a distance, which by definition volume overcomes. There is no distance with volume, you're swallowed up by sound. . . . It's impossible to stay ironic, so all the implications of postmodernism go out the window."[20] Thus, because it was first articulated in musical practices, the term "the mix," itself, locates temporality and black cultural production primarily at the node of the sonic and modern technologies of sensation/inscription.

Surely, this is not an attempt to erase the long history of African-diasporic writing about music preceding Du Bois; in fact, the whole notion of the "Sorrow Songs," which Du Bois uses so extensively in *Souls*, comes, at least in part, from Frederick Douglass's 1845 *Narrative*. Instead I wish to accent the importance of sonic signs to the structural figuration of Du Bois's work. The role that Du Bois ascribes to music, as it relates to U.S. culture, represents a significant departure, while simultaneously drawing on antecedents from nineteenth-century strategies in African American literature, abolitionist rhetoric, and the incipient social scientific discourses — we might add here that Du Bois was one of the founders and most astute critics of the U.S. social scientific discourse. Where black writers in the nineteenth century drew on Christianity to claim moral supremacy over white subjects, Du Bois puts a different spin on these debates in his deployment of the "Sorrow Songs"; his use of those tropes draws on cultural and political tenets, rather than strictly devout ones as in the earlier cases.[21] *The Souls of Black Folk*, situated at the cusp of the twentieth century, was the first African American text to incorporate music into its structure in such a prominent manner, a sonico-textual strategy that ushered in the modernism of the Harlem Renaissance in the 1920s.[22] Following Du Bois, many of the formal expansions in the literature of this period relied upon the compositional utilization of music and sound in the confines of written texts; Langston Hughes, Georgia Douglas Johnson, and Gwendolyn Bennett, among others, used music in their works to create a black modernist formalism. To boot, Du Bois's theory of racial double consciousness, discussed in chapter 1, has served as one of the most significant conceptualizations of (racial) subjectivity in the twentieth century. The concept has been "remixed" numerous times in black literary production and political theorizing.[23] In this way, *Souls* acts as one of the "originary" grooves for both modern Afro-diasporic thought and sonic Afro-modernity in its theorization of double consciousness apropos black subjectivity and its use of musical bars to fortify and insert sonic pauses into the textual machine. If Ellison theorizes the "groove(s) of history" chiefly via the plot of *Invisible Man* and the protagonist's philosophical musings, then Du Bois, his extensive and moving discussion of the sorrow songs in the final chapter notwithstanding, transacts the grooves of temporality through the palimpsestic musical epigraphs and their rapport with both their poetic counterparts and the essays that comprise the bulk of this magnum opus.

Du Bois first mentions the sorrow songs in what he calls the "Fore-thought" to *Souls*, where he explains his rationale for placing bars of music before the chapters: "Before each chapter, as now printed, stands a bar of the 'Sorrow Songs,'—some echo of haunting melody from the only American music, which welled up from black souls in the dark past" (2). Here, Du Bois asserts that the sorrow songs are the only true form of American, not African American, music. Just as in Du Bois's own text, the spirituals are not only relevant to black culture, but to American culture at large; the fact that they are the only true music produced in the history of the United States makes them an achievement his readers must acknowledge. Instead of beginning his discussion of black subjects' role in the United States with physical slave labor, which would seem to provide their most obvious contribution, Du Bois establishes music as the first and foremost accomplishment. In the last chapter, Du Bois lists slave labor, spirituality, and musical production as the main donations of black subjects to U.S. culture and history, but still insists first and foremost on the sonic: "a gift of story and song—soft, stirring melody in an ill-harmonized and unmelodious land; the gift of sweat and brawn to beat back the wilderness, conquer soil, and lay the foundations of this vast economic empire two hundred years earlier than your weak hands could have done it; and third the gift of the Spirit" (214). Not only does Du Bois project black music as the chief cultural nadir of the American nation, he also constructs—through and around the spirituals—an extended metaphor for black subjects' role in American culture at large.

The U.S. is an "ill-harmonized" and "unmelodious" "wilderness" in which black music singularly conjures melody and harmony. Implicated in the scopic regime of racism (through agency and/or structure), white subjects do not have the same access to the gift of song as black subjects. In fact, the adjectives "unmelodious" and "ill-harmonized" aptly describe the physical and discursive violence inflicted upon black people in the history of the United States. In a fairly obvious, but nonetheless crafty, reversal, Du Bois indexes "harmony" and "melody," the most important attributes habitually assigned to Western music, as opposed to rhythm, which is supposedly the defining feature of most African-derived musical practices; because of their "musicality," black subjects embody

the "harmonious" and "melodic" archetype of U.S. democracy. Hazel
Carby notes the following about Du Bois's strategy concerning the fusion
of black and U.S. national culture: "It is black bodies which offer the
only vision of spiritual sustenance in a desert of rampant materialism,
and it is the conditions of *their* social, political, and economic existence,
Du Bois asserts, which are the only reliable measure of the health of the
national body. In the body of America dwells a black soul" (30). Black
bodies, besides offering "a vision of spiritual sustenance," provide a voice,
or a mélange of voices, which sound the ideals of American democracy,
and as Du Bois, as well as many other black writers before and after him
have pointed out, this catachrestic nominalism remains only idyllic, since
these principles cannot be put into practice through a political system
that endorses Jim Crow and lynching. Black music and spirituality serve
as constant reminders of equality and freedom. Music, then, as it appears in relation to spirituality, becomes Du Bois's metaphor, through
which he not only lays claim to the ethical advantage of black subjects
but also points to the wide gap between the abstract ideals of U.S. democracy (equality and freedom) and U.S. political practice (Jim Crow and
lynching).

In addition to utilizing music to metaphorize the vicissitudes of blackness in the United States, Du Bois implies that black people have shaped
the U.S. economic empire not only through their slave labor, but also,
and more significantly, by means of their songs and spirituality. Hence
cultural labor is placed above economic labor.[24] The prominent position
Du Bois allots to sound inaugurates the use of music as a channel through
which to articulate black subjectivity, temporality, spatiality, and culture
in the twentieth century. Since Du Bois wrote these lines, black American
music has represented one of the key achievements of U.S. culture and
one of its main exports to the world, which is, at least in part, due to the
proliferation of sonic recording and reproduction technologies (phonograph records, tapes, CDs, MP3 files) and their increasingly global distribution; the fact that Du Bois anticipated this trajectory in his argument
concerning spirituals makes *Souls* one of the "originating" moments in
sonic Afro-modernity. Additionally, Du Bois not only recognizes the integrality of black music to American culture, he also recodes the meanings of the spirituals through the manner in which he amalgamates them
in his text. This absorption comprises a mix and a theory of temporal
mixology — "time crystals," in Deleuze's dialect — much in the same way

as the contemporary ritual of DJing; we will take a brief detour through the mechanics of this practice in order to pick the Du Boisian beat back up further along in the mix.[25]

Hey Mr. DJ In general, the historical lineage of DJing as an art form begins with black radio personalities of the 1940s and 1950s and extends into the technical innovations of Jamaican sound system culture, as well as to the amalgamation practices first used in New York black and Latino urban gay clubs in the 1970s. Jamaican sound systems, consisting of traveling discos with self-made and/or altered speakers, usually played records imported from the United States and originated in the 1950s as a result of a confluence of economic and cultural forces. In their history of DJing, Bill Brewster and Frank Broughton show that in Jamaica, mobile sound systems were an alternative for those who could not afford to buy expensive U.S. import records for private consumption.[26] As a result, newly urbanized Jamaicans could publicly partake in the reproduction of recorded music accompanied by the vocalizations of an MC, not unlike the way in which, decades later, early hip-hop operated in U.S. urban centers, particularly New York City.[27] The disco boom of the mid- and late seventies produced club DJing as it has come to be defined — the manipulation and merger of different records, rather than merely playing one record after the other. Describing one of the first New York gay dance clubs, Salvation, in his book *Altered State*, Matthew Collin sees the role of the resident DJ as follows: "The DJ, Francis Grasso, would preach from an altar above the dancefloor. . . . He would layer the orgasmic moans from Led Zeppelin's *Whole Lotta Love* over a heavy percussion break, cutting the bass and treble frequencies in and out to heighten the energy level, segueing from soul to rock then on into hypnotic African drums and chants" (11). Other DJs, such as Walter Gibbons, Tom Moulton, Larry Levan, and Nicky Siano, experimented with similar techniques in the 1970s, each seeking to create a new musical text with their selection and interweaving of previously recorded materials.[28] Hip-hop DJs, providing new musical avenues for producing sound, then took up mixing, although their mixing departed from the smooth flow of the disco DJs, stressing instead the rhythmic components of older records (the break-beat) and the technique of scratching. The breakbeat is usually the moment of old funk and R&B recordings where the melody disappears and is replaced by a rhythmic solo — a technique that was glossed in the previous chapter. DJs isolated and extended these moments to form the basis of new tracks. "Scratching" is the action of moving vinyl records back and forth on one of the two turntables that comprise the basic DJing setup to create a scratching sound that corresponds to the rhythm of the record sounding on the other record player. As a result of this technique, phonographs were no longer only playback devices but had attained instrument status. Although DJing remains a crucial part of hip-hop culture, especially in the turntablism subgenre, in recent years this practice has been most prominent in and through various genres of electronic dance music. Clubs in Britain, continental Europe, Latin America, Asia, Africa, and the United States play a number, if not all of these genres, presented by various DJs. While the overarching category of dance music comprises a multiracial global movement, it is of note that most of these genres and the practices of DJing related to them originated in and still have strong ties with black cultural practices.

Raymond Roker perceives his role as a DJ not only as a dance-floor animator, but also as a sonic educator: "As a DJ, especially, I feel that with each rotation of the decks, I am presenting a musical lesson of sorts. The lessons are by no means always consistent or clear, but still there is an underlying purpose to every record that leaves my box. I want the music—just as it has profoundly affected me over the years—to stimulate others."[29] Here, Roker brings to the fore the two main features of DJing, the archival and the sonic, which continue and reformulate what we have been referring to as the material and ephemeral or graphematic and affective.[30] Corresponding with Du Bois, Roker thinks of mixing as a project with the goal of education and clarification; he chooses records according to his principles and shares his pleasure in and intellectual engagement with music. Du Bois's venture in *Souls* consists of educating his readers about life "behind the veil" using sonic materials (sorrow songs) with different forms of written notation (musical notes and words) as the mixer through which he routes his own voice, that of his grandmother, his dead son, Alexander Crummell, unnamed slaves singing spirituals, Booker T. Washington, and many others: "The direct incorporation of previously existing sound source material into an aural text . . . obeys a logic of bricolage that contains objects at different cultural velocities, and creates a multivalent temporal structure that is presented simultaneously. This is what we call the mix."[31] This mixing becomes significant vis-à-vis *Souls* if we consider that most of the pieces therein were previously published and recombined and augmented for their appearance in *Souls*. Du Bois remixes his own words, or rather, as we shall see, engineers a "dub version" of his own texts and the sorrow songs.[32] Du Bois manages to let all the different aspects of his mix coexist within the confines of the text, incorporating various cultural, historical, and political "velocities." Through his mix, Du Bois shows that different velocities are needed in order to depict the souls of black folk, for they cannot be rendered or contained by the narrow confines of one particular genre or single mode of being in the world. His text is a highly personal and public artifact, just like the mix of a DJ, reconstructing his own information — experiences, family history, already published essays — and that of others — his family, Richard Wagner, Washington, Crummell, nineteenth-century British poets, and so on. Du Bois does this much as a DJ does before an audience, trying to let his fusion interact with their needs and anticipations, while not losing sight or sound of his own mission. As a result, Du Bois takes what is around him and puts it through a textual mix, thereby creating a new chronospatial sphere within black cultural production. Overall, the sonicotextual components in *Souls*, both separately and in their assorted interfacings, function as a mixological groove totality. In order to explore this axiom further, let's head back to the DJ booth and hear the tracks about to be unloosed.

DJing provides two modes of sonic double consciousness: on the one hand, the DJ matches up two different forms of sonic consciousness in his/her mix, and on the other hand, the audience and the DJ have to negotiate their expectations and rituals in the sonic space of a club. These two modes of double consciousness add up to a larger mix that combines DJs, audiences, musics, technologies, and public spaces. Moreover, we should also note the sonic projection of temporality in this scenario, both literally and more abstractly, since one of the paramount objectives of mixing is to synchronize the different beats per minute (BPM) of each track and the grooves of the vinyl, harking back to an Ellisonian modus of time. The setup most DJs use consists of a mixer and two turntables (the decks). The turntables are usually equipped with a pitch control device that lets the DJ adjust the rotation speed of the record in order to match the beats of the two records to be mixed.[33] This enables DJs to conceive of records as raw sonic matter (even if this matter is anything but inert or unformed); records thus achieve their momentary meaning not as individual entities but rather as different parts that constitute the mix.[34] In addition, today, many tracks already feature a multitude of samples from earlier recordings in their structure, contributing to the palimpsestic layers of the mix, which leads Charles Mudede to suggest that "a turntable is forced to . . . make meta-music (music about music) instead of [only] playing previously recorded music."[35] This layered assemblage of sonic information throws us into a heightened Ellisonion-Deleuzian vortex of transversal breaks.

Each turntable is connected to a channel on the mixer, which is where all the sonic information passes through and gets redistributed in the mix. This mix then goes through the amplifier, which connects to the speakers that allow the sound to transmit into the space of the audience. Every channel on the mixer has its own volume adjustment, so that the DJ can decide in what relation s/he wants the two records to be heard. In addition there is a master volume control that determines the volume of the overall sound. The final integral component of the mixer is the crossfader, which enables the DJ to arrange how much sonic space the sound emanating from each channel can occupy in the overall temporality of the mix. In other words, one of the records can take up only 20 percent of the mix in order to amplify the other record. Additional features increasingly supplement this scenario: most mixers now have equalizers on each channel that allow for the adjustment of the bass and treble of the records being played. All these technologies and the various practices connected to them are designed to move DJing beyond simply putting a needle on records and toward manipulating the sonic sources and transforming them into something else within the mix.[36]

The DJ constantly monitors the two channels on the mixer: both the audience and the DJ can hear the first conduit over the sound system, amplified by the speakers. Then the DJ puts on another record for the second channel and listens to it on his/her headphones. At this point, the audience is not privy to the second aural channel and can only hear the first one. The DJ hears both records concurrently, one on the speakers and the other through the headphones, suggesting a literalization of F. Murray Schafer's "schizophonia" or a sonorous double consciousness wherein his/her hearing capacities are utterly reconfigured.[37] In this individual sonic space, the DJ matches up what s/he hears on her/his headphones with the sounds emanating from the speakers. The two tracks do not occupy the same aural area or time for the audience; they exist only in the DJ's reconfigured tympanic machine. The DJ's task is to find the precise instance in the grooves that lends itself to mixing and then to make sure that when the two channels congregate they gel with each other musically. When this point is reached, the DJ releases both channels to the audience through the speakers, and the personal sonic temporality transmutes into a social one—which is not to say that it is not social to begin with, since the whole enterprise of DJing takes place in (for the) public. Although one or both of the DJ's ears are privy to the second track that s/he is about to throw into the mix (s/he can either listen to the submerged track through one side of the headphones or completely immerse him/herself in the second sonic temporality), the moment of the mix itself is shared with the audience; everybody can now hear the two records playing on the different channels at the same time. At some point, the DJ withdraws one of the channels from the mix and the audience only hears the other channel, s/he then chooses another record for the next mix, and the whole process starts over. The audience generally trusts the DJ's selections and his/her mixing skills, and the DJ, at least, in part, anticipates what the audience wants to hear. However, this does not mean that the audience cannot disagree with the DJ and chastise her/him for the selections or leave the dance floor, nor that DJs cannot test their audiences by playing "difficult" selections; in an ideal club, all of these factors are in play. The practice of DJing, then, consists chiefly of two forms of mixing: the mixing of records or sonic information, and the merger of the DJ's and the audience's expectations and practices.[38] In essence, DJing performs clashing, yet complementary, temporalities via its interfacing of different grooves, which constructively combine into a newly minted singular totality.

While there are stark differences in the problem of racial identity as depicted by Du Bois and in the mixing of DJs, both manifest a duality that is to be recalibrated in one way or another. The DJ suspends the problem of duality for a moment, the moment of "the mix." In this mix s/he manages to combine two musical modes of information. S/he matches tracks according to their beat, pitch, timbre, melody, genre, and so on.[39] But this only accounts for one of the mixes in a DJ set that consists of many different mixes that add up to a greater part (although this whole is never absolute or unfractured), the DJ's repeating of the mix. The reconciliation between the two channels is only momentary, so the DJ has to reconcile his/her two warring musical "souls" time after time, anticipating the minute of the mix (as s/he listens on the headphones) in order to discern the semiprecise instance to introduce the personal "sonic consciousness" into the social mix. S/he can weave the personal track (or second musical consciousness/temporality) into the mix in a variety of styles: smoothly blending one track into another so that it becomes hard to hear where one track ends and another begins; scratching one record in time with the rhythm of the other, thus amplifying the mixity by using the turntable as a percussive instrument as well as rhythmically matching the two records; or swiftly switching over from one channel to the other. The DJ, by repeatedly weaving together differing sonic material, manages to create a new musical temporality. This new sonic sphere is then shared with an audience, creating yet another dimension in which the audience and DJ coexist as temperosonic architects. In essence, the DJ, with the help of and in dialogue with the dancers, weaves together the textures of temporal grooves or monads in and through sound. These textures transact a theory of temporal confluence that sounds on the lower frequencies of the historicist and/or chronological time, and in this sounding the thunk of the bass makes time palpable as sensation, which is to say that the complementary yet conflicting times in the mix are heard through the body, much in the same way that Ellison's protagonist is literally shocked out of the Brotherhood's chronology when he hears the blaring loudspeaker.[40] Now that we have ascertained some parameters a propos the creative labor of DJs, we can move to scrutinize Du Bois's beatmatching dexterity.

Phono-Epi-Graphs Clearly, the sorrow songs and the way in which Du Bois threads them through the text are the key to *Souls*'s sonorous ignition. Besides the musical epigraphs, references to hearing and the sorrow songs close both his introductory "Forethought" and the "Afterthought," underpinning the manuscript both graphematically—with musical notes—and, in its content, Du Bois's theorization of black music's place in U.S. culture. When Du Bois first introduces the sorrow songs in the "Forethought," he links them directly to the souls of black folk: "Before each chapter, as now printed, stands a bar of the Sorrow Songs— some echo of haunting melody from the only American music which welled up from *black souls* in the dark past" (2, emphasis mine).[41] Moreover, in the "Afterthought," Du Bois asks his readers to "Hear [his] cry" (217) and the best way to *hear* the souls of black folk, as Du Bois remarks at the end of Chapter 1 ("Of Our Spiritual Strivings") is to listen to the sorrow songs: they provide an approximation of the souls of black folk. Du Bois does not ask his readers to view or see the souls of black folk, but instead to listen: he writes "that men may listen to the souls of black folk" (12). Much in the same way as Du Bois appeals to the ear in his theory of double consciousness and the surplus rather than lack or belatedness it produces in the black subject (as discussed in chapter 1), this injunction to imagine blackness sonically provides a phono-graphic guidepost for reading and hearing *Souls*.

Contemporary critics agree that the sonic signs taken from the Western tradition of musical notation cannot form a mimetic merger with spirituals. Eric Sundquist, for instance, states that "the musical epigraphs are therefore . . . an example of a cultural 'language' that cannot be properly interpreted, or even 'heard' at all, since it fails to correspond to the customary mapping of sounds and signs that make up the languages of the dominant (in this case white) culture" (470). Of course, these notes were/are also not able to reproduce the Western classical music for which they were originally designed; for example, these signs cannot capture the full range of a performance of a Bach fugue, since the piece will be interpreted and performed differently depending on who is playing and when and where it is staged. Alan Durant submits the following about musical notation within the history of Western classical music: "Notation marks an ordering of bodily movements of musical performance in addition to immediate verbal directives, and provided historically the possibility for pieces of music of a specialized, if restricted, kind of permanence. In this sense, notation was one necessary condition to take on, as composition, a temporal and aesthetic independence from particular versions and collaborations of its realization."[42] Here, the putative origin (notation and Western classical music) appears as a dub version or remix, introducing an originary lag, *différance*, if you will, into its mix. By incorporating musical notes into his text as doubles for spirituals, Du Bois makes the musical works that comprise this body independent of their performances and location in history while also ensconcing them in new forms of contextual dependency. Instead of being placed within a particular historical framework, the spirituals now signify and stand in for a general black American future-past. Thus, Du Bois's text takes on phonographic dimensions not only in its compositional absorption of sonic signs, but in its addition of elements of other sound technologies to this recording and de(re)contextualizing: *Souls* severs the sorrow songs from their "prostheses of origin" by transmogrifying them into grooves for its own dub mix.

In his analysis of the different functions of spirituals in nineteenth-century and early-twentieth-century American culture, Ronald Radano begins by charting the white fascination with spirituals after they had been transcribed during the Civil War, arguing that spirituals represented "the outer limits of the Western imagination."[43] This was intimately tied to the conundrum of transcription, as most whites "writing down" the spirituals noted the problems of "capturing" these on paper.[44] In the minds of northern white abolitionists, spirituals became a part of a larger romantic ideology that believed that music was an anticivilization pro-phylactic, countering Western reason, especially since certain strands of romanticism in general were obsessed with replacing reason—the central trope/concept of the Enlightenment—with "untainted" and "natural" cultural productions that led "man" back to "his" original state.[45] Romanticist thinkers, in part because of increased interest in folk culture, argued that these "natural" and "authentic" cultural forms possessed qualities lacking in "spoiled" high-cultural production. As musical ruminations of folk culture, spirituals were doubly coded as "authentic" artifacts that provided a "true" representation of black "humanity." As Radano maintains, "Black spirituals were not simply trivial expressions of 'primitive purity.' In fact they were vital to the Anglo-Saxon psyche precisely because they constituted the alter ego of the white self, representing the supplement or missing link of American national identity" (522). Jon Cruz extends Radano's important argument by showing how spirituals formed a fundamental component not only in romanticist qua abolitionist conversations but also in the burgeoning social scientific discourses (ethnomusicology and anthropology, to be precise), or, in his formulation, in "how romantic antimodernism and rational social science converge and intersect in the discovery of the Negro spiritual."[46] The combined force of these two divergent figurations of discourse, and therefore blackness, projected the spirituals as the "preferred black culture" for both white and black pundits from the mid-nineteenth century onward (7).[47] In this context, musical notation served to amplify both the primitive unrepresentability and the rationalization of spirituals, which is rendered even more overdetermined if we take into account, as Radano does, that in the process of transcription, the spirituals forced some scribes to recast the Western system of musical notation *tout court*. As a consequence, the notations that appear in Du Bois's text are already notations in difference, differential notes, originary (re)mixes, or, as Fred Moten has argued in a different context, "an ongoing event of antiorigin and an antiorigin, replay and reverb of an impossible natal occasion, the performance of a birth and rebirth of a new science, a phylogenetic fantasy that (dis)establishes genesis, the reproduction of blackness as (the) reproduction of black performance(s)" (14). Not only does the presence of fragments of musical bars alter the text of *Souls*, but the notations themselves have transformed into another "writing-down system" by virtue of encoding spirituals and not Western classical music, thus transacting on a different scale the manner in which black culture's entry into and constitutive part of Western modernity shifts its grounding terms.[48]

Du Bois's use of spirituals calls into question their representability in the Western system of musical notation while pointing to the limits of the method itself; as a result, they mirror Du Bois's own double textual strategy, which mixes "major" and "minor" cultural archives as opposed to merely using one to mimic the other. The musical notes, like the entire text, form a mix that transforms two distinct parts — Western musical notation and spirituals — into a temporary fusion that highlights its own impurity.[49] Du Bois heightens the fragmentation of the spirituals by inserting musical bars, and only the beginning of each song, at that, into the text, diminishing the chances of readers' actually recognizing the songs. In fact, the only readers who would have deciphered the sonic signs at the time of the text's publication would have been those who both knew the songs *and* could crack this sonic code, giving rise to a certain disjuncture between *Souls* and its audiences, one that transforms the bars of the spirituals before each chapter into "mute ciphers" that call attention to their own "failure" at representing sound.[50] Furthermore, the role assigned to spirituals in particular, and black music in general, derives from a historically specific process informed by black and white American discourses. Once again, we turn to Radano: "If the image of an immaterial black music was variously constructed according to the particulars of time and place, so it was united by the racialist designation 'black' that ascribed to African American musical creativity unique qualities of performance. . . . [I]t is through this idea of [racial] difference that black America would finally hear its cultural past, discerning the echoes of an ancestral world saturated with textually invented 'Negro sound' " (544).

Du Bois's rendering of spirituals must be read in this context, since he draws on the variety of significations that the spirituals had accrued by 1903. As we have established, the sorrow songs cannot sonically represent a "true" and "authentic" African American past, for the media (written collections) through which they were transmitted had transformed them into something altogether different prior to their Du Boisian figuration; this alteration shapes them into future-oriented artifacts that sound an opaque and fragmented African American past. Consequently, the temporality suggested by Du Bois's textual strategies resemble Ellison's "grooves" and Benjamin's "monadic shrapnel" much more than any protectionist or historicist model, since they render the spirituals as grooves in his own mix. Surely, the sedimented meanings ascribed to and inscribed in these marks well up in the Du Boisian text, though they are significantly resounded by Du Bois's working of the textual decks.

The musical bars function in similar fashion to the scratching of DJs as Du Bois highlights the fissures in his mix by not disclosing the name or the lyrics of the spiritual he is citing. Overall, what is at stake in Du Bois's transcription is not whether these spirituals can find an adequate written home that represents them faithfully, but what their fragmentary status does to the text of *Souls*. The sorrow songs have a Freudian *unheimlich* (uncanny) quality—as opposed to homeliness in any traditional sense— as they intimate quasi-indecipherable musical signs that disrupt the flow of words and add to the texturality of the mix. Situated at the intersection of text (lyrical epigraphs) and words (chapters), these sonorous residues noisily implode the linguistic utterances that frame them and thus launch the structural moment of the mix. Analogously, Dick Hebdige illustrates the contours of mixological time in his explanation of one of the all-time classic mixes in hip-hop, *Adventures of Grandmaster Flash on the Wheels of Steel*. Hebdige describes this mix as consisting of several components: "The record is a startling mix of different sounds: the bass line from the rock group Queen's 1980 hit *Another One Bites the Dust* is mixed with a riff from *Good Times*, Chic's disco hit from 1979. These are mixed with snatches from four or five other rap records. Finally, towards the end of the record, a man and a young child read out extracts from an incomprehensible fairy story."[51] These disparate ingredients are (dis)united in an open totality that constitutes its mixness by virtue of rhythm, "All this is jumbled up and scratched together. The record is full of breaks and silences. But it is held together by a stuttering rhythm."[52] These "jumbled up and scratched together . . . breaks and silences" and their rhythmological coherence coincide with Du Bois's strategy for the spirituals. Just as with the musical epigraphs in Du Bois's text, the scratching noises are at their most extreme when the songs clash, and the noise calls attention to itself by interrupting the flow of music. Likewise, Grandmaster Flash takes existing records and plays them against the rotation of the phonograph, fusing the scratching with the sounds of the record on the second phonograph, which then recasts the musical text of that record. These scratching noises can either become a part of the sonic weave for the listener, only adding to the aural density of the mix, or it can threaten the "pure" listening pleasure if perceived as noise. While the musical epigraphs haunt the whole of *Souls*, by way of suggestion, they stand on their own as booming, yet mute, phono-epi-graphs at the intersection of the poems and the body of the text: rather than serving as mere afterthoughts, the scratches in this textual mix radically alter the significations of the text(s) via their constitutive supplementarity.

Du Bois continues the transformation of spirituals initiated by their improvisatory beginnings and subsequent transcription by fusing them with poems from the nineteenth-century European canon, and as a result, he not only appropriates the meanings attributed to spirituals by transcribers and critics of folk culture, but also throws another dimension into the already existing mix. The flow between the musical bars of the spirituals and the poems from the Western canon (mostly nineteenth-century British poetry) in *Souls* presents the most apparent example of the enactment of the mix, even if the core of the spirituals is already a (re)mix. Here, I am not so much concerned with how the musical epigraphs interact with Du Bois's writing as I am with the sonic signifiers' refiguration of the poems that they trail. Far too often, critics have assumed a certain stability of the poems' significations; nonetheless, just as being placed in a literary context alters the spirituals, it also fundamentally transforms these verses, dislodging them from their enshrined canonicity. Ergo Arthur Symons's poem (which opens the first chapter, "Of Our Spiritual Strivings") becomes legible as a lament against chattel slavery and a testimony to the "Spiritual Strivings" of black subjects. The second stanza reads:

Unresting water, there shall never be rest
till the last moon droop and the last tide fail,
And *the fire of the end begin to burn in the west*;

And the heart shall be weary and wonder and cry like the sea,

All life long crying without avail,

As the water all night long is crying to me. (3, emphasis mine)

Once attuned to Du Bois's mixing maneuvers, these lines do not signify anything before or after *Souls*; indeed, they are another manifestation of the spirituals — Du Bois's incorporation releases the poems' Afroentelechy. Initially, what is most striking is the existential despair of these words that eerily echo many sorrow songs' lyrics, particularly "Nobody Knows the Trouble I Have Seen," with which Symons's rhymes are coupled. The chorus of this spiritual reads as follows:

Oh, nobody knows the trouble I've seen,

Nobody knows but Jesus,

Nobody knows the trouble I've seen,

Glory Hallelujah.[53]

Symons's poem and the lyrics of the spiritual suggest troubles and troubled souls, yet in both instances the reasons for these woes are not disclosed. Clearly, Du Bois takes advantage of this poetic haziness so as to make the words applicable to the souls of black folk, and in this way, the "weariness" and "crying" exhibited by the speaker become testimonies of and to *Souls'* collective black voice. In addition, the line "And the fire of the end begin to burn in the west" from Symons's poem, read in the mixological milieu of *Souls*, offers a pertinent observation concerning the role of race in Western modernity, so central to Du Bois's argument. According to this eschatology, the apocalypse will not be precipitated by biblical sins, at least not in any strict sense, but rather by the secular crimes of the West (the specters of slavery, racism, imperialism, etc.). Where earlier African American discourses (in spirituals, poetry, slave narratives, spiritual narratives, etc.) coded secular problematics in religious language, Du Bois deploys the spirituals in their interfacing with the poems to launch a decidedly nonotherworldly critique of Western modernity, "the problem of the twentieth century is the problem of the color-line, — the relation of the darker to the lighter races of the men in Asia and Africa, in America and the islands of the sea" (13). Du Bois introduces a new temporality into the mix of black culture, a time residually tinged with Christianity, but also decisively profane, which represents nothing so much as a seismic shift in the very foundations of postbellum African American aesthetic and political discourse. The concept of *soul*, so vocal to this text, enters the secular domain, albeit without renouncing — to summon Walter Benjamin — its "weak messianic power." Du Bois, moreover, does not merely quote, at least not in any simple fashion, this poem: by meshing its beat with the syncopated stylings of "Nobody Knows" and his own words in "Of Our Spiritual Strivings," he gives it a new signification leg/audible exclusively in his mix. This splintered synthesis of Western canonical literature and black vernacular musical expression inaugurates all of *Souls'* chapters, save the last, which combines the music from one spiritual with the lyrics of another.

Whereas Du Bois transposes spirituals into the realm of "legitimate" written culture, he "vernacularizes" the European writings. A similar strategy will be later used by many black musicians, most famously John Coltrane in his rendition of "My Favorite Things," or DJs' reformulations of previously recorded grooves in their mixes. Schiller's, Byron's, Lowell's, and Whittier's poems (among others) thus form a symbiosis with the spirituals; Du Bois slyly forces these Western texts to testify to slavery and the absent presence of black subjects, both as empirical entities and as apparitions, as integral *to* and unequivocally *of* Western modernity.[54] Read or listened to in tandem with the musical bars, then, the poems *are* the lyrics to the sorrow songs, creating a new form of spiritual in their admixture.[55] The mix in these phono-epi-graphs consists of a number of different layers. The spirituals change their format because they are recorded via musical notation and mediated by black and white discourses on the role of folk culture in Western modernity. Furthermore, these transcriptions modified this system of notation itself, and finally, the musical bars alter the meanings of the poems from the nineteenth-century British canon and vice versa. All of these layers in Du Bois's textual mix exemplify the aesthetic complexity and cultural flexibility of a sonic (black) temporality. And this sonic-textual temporality does not simply reverse the order of things; it generates a genuinely "new" modality, a different groove, inimitable in its insistence on and performance of the coevalness of the sorrow songs with the annals of literary canonicity. Johannes Fabian has shown that the central discourse of anthropology resolutely denies the West's other (generally the primitive or some reformulation thereof) temporal coevalness, choosing instead to "establish itself as an allochronic discourse; it is the science of other men in another Time."[56] Du Bois's style of coevalness exhumes the internal crises in the still warm corpses of reason and progress even while it constructs a different time in which reason and terror, progress and regress coexist in a momentary détente. Nowhere is this more apparent than in the phono-epi-graphic mix placed before the final chapter of *Souls*, "The Sorrow Songs."

In the last chapter of *Souls*, Du Bois presents a theory of the sorrow songs, discussing their aesthetic, cultural, and political dimensions in addition to providing an autohistorical account of how African songs, in the aftermath of the Middle Passage, eventually transmuted into spirituals. The two epigraphs preceding this chapter fail to comply with the scheme Du Bois has thus far established: both the lyrical and musical headings are drawn from the reservoir of the sorrow songs, unlike the previous chapters, which are introduced by one musical epigraph and one poetic one. At first glance, this might imply that the chapter establishes some sort of unity, in terms of both structure and content, in ways that the other chapters do not, which, in turn, harks back to mechanisms of double consciousness: black sonic marks (the words to a spiritual) erase and replace white words (the epigraphic poems), giving the structural feature of a page back its originary stature as black and white recede to their preordained places in the universe.[57] Still, Du Bois does not tender a conclusion in the likeness of a deus ex machina or a Hegelian *Aufhebung*; for all intents and purposes, there is no end of history in *Souls*—maybe an eternal return, but no closure in sight or sound.

The two epigraphs at the start of the chapter "The Sorrow Songs" implement rupture within this field of presumed unity, given that they do not stem from the same spiritual: the lyrics are from "Lay This Body Down," while the musical notes correspond with "Wrestling Jacob." By juxtaposing two spirituals, Du Bois defies any easy or hard dichotomizing of black and white or major and minor; in the process he affixes yet another stratum to the mix in its staging of an interaction between two spirituals, in the same manner as the spirituals and poems in the earlier parts of the text; Edouard Glissant would call this the creation of an open totality. On the one hand, this feat can be interpreted as Du Bois's deliberate move to substitute Western canonical poems with the words from a spiritual, thereby claiming the spirituals to be as much a part of "high" culture as Lowell's or Byron's poems. Conversely, Du Bois circumvents the closure problematic by not offering a tranquil correlation between musical and textual signifiers but instead by constructing a new system of deferred finality in his (re)mixing of "Lay This Body Down" and "Wrestling Jacob," by treating them as the raw materials of his mega mix.[58] While the mixing might be more obvious in the case of the poems meeting the spirituals, its complexity increases in these final epigraphs, and perhaps this concluding fusion represents the epitome of Du Bois's mastery at the textual turntables. In the end, merging the music of one spiritual with the lyrics of another projects a new spiritual, which encodes the multitude of significations the sorrow songs had acquired at this point, but also, and perhaps more significantly, makes them usable for the future.[59] In this final mix, the past, present, and future coexist to generate the temporal grooves of sonic Afro-modernity.

Overall, Du Bois suffuses *Souls* with the "nonwordness" of sounds — the aspects of sound that cannot be reproduced on the written page, what we have referred to as affect and/or sensation: in Du Bois's formulation, "knowing as little as our fathers what its words may mean, but knowing well the meaning of its music" (207), echoing Ellison's "turgid and inadequate words." Du Bois's attempt to provide written words with a sonorous surplus structures *Souls* as a phono-graph, one that attempts to make the souls of black folk *sound* and be *heard*, which is not so much a strict opposition between notated sounds and written words as an augmentation of words with sounds, of adding back into the mix what gets left out in the equation of language and speech with linguistic structures. Du Bois indexes the sorrow songs he intends to use as epigraphs by stating that "some echo of haunting melody" will appear in his text, implying that melodies, which are not the most important aspect of spirituals anyway, can only be recorded by Du Bois and deciphered by the readers as figural excess. The readers become privy to the titles of the spirituals used as epigraphs in the last chapter, yet even there Du Bois does not disclose all of the spirituals contained in the spectral assemblage of *Souls*, nor does he clarify where individual songs are placed in the text. This reticence, and the confusion it causes, exemplifies the distorted reverberations of black sounds since the spirituals that Du Bois quotes appear in the text not as accurate representations, but as distorted, layered, and lingering traces. Through these melodic fragments, the voices of the slaves that "composed," sang, and improvised upon these songs uncannily haunt the textual house of *Souls*. Du Bois seems fairly certain that no one-to-one likeness of these songs will accomplish his goal, hence the invocation of echo rather than more mimetic techniques.

Using Du Bois's terminology, we can imagine *Souls* as an extended echo chamber in which traces of the spirituals reverberate with and against each other, forming a different textuosonic machine than the compilations of spirituals hitherto available, and paving the way for future African American literary aesthetics, chiefly the Harlem Renaissance. In addition, *Souls* reverberates dialogically with one of the most significant Afro-diasporic aesthetic achievements of the past fifty years: dub reggae, without which most contemporary popular music would simply not exist. In the late sixties, Jamaican producers started messing with the musical text via technological means—loosening its confines, turning up the bass and drum in the mix, distorting and displacing the centrality of the voice, opening it up to the cosmos. These aesthetic formations have cast a midday shadow—much in the same way as Du Bois has in the annals of African American literary and political discourses—over much of popular music history since then, including disco, hip-hop, and contemporary electronic dance music; dub reggae is the mother of all remixes. As Brewster and Broughton explain, "A dub mix is essentially the bare bones of a track with bass turned up. Dub separates a song into its stark component parts, and adds and subtracts each strand until a new composition is made. By adding space to the track, what is left has far more room to breathe."[60] As I've stated, dub mixes were also expressly created for sound system use, so that their primary function was to be part of a mix rather than standing on their own. A couple of points remain salient in the resonance between *Souls* and the Afro-tricknology of dub: the style with which Du Bois recasts the spirituals via the technology of musical notation, and his invocation of echo and haunting in the text. Echo, along with reverb, and delay, to this day, remains one of dub's core features, inserting spatiality into the musical track, while also messing with its temporal dimensions; in fact, the spatial effect of echo is achieved via the stuttering and dispersion of the music's time.[61] Also, the term "dub" itself not only indicates a doubling or copying but carries homonymic overtones of *duppy* (the Jamaican word for spirit and/or ghost) so that the dub version of a song provides not only its shadow but also its spectral other that initially appeared on the flipside of a record, but eventually became much more popular than its "original" source. In this echo box, Freud's theory of the uncanny, especially as it passes through the double (doppelgänger), coexists with Du Bois's notion of doubling and spectrality and returns to us from the margins of the contemporary African diaspora in an altered sonic form: dub, duppy, double consciousness, the uncanny, all unveil the haunting at the center of the "real," which, according to Avery Gordon, "is a very particular way of knowing what has happened or is happening . . . as transformative recognition."[62] This "particular way of knowing" that moves with spirits as constitutive of the totality of social life worlds finds its textuosonic correlative in *Souls*'s figuration of the sorrow songs, since, rather than being auxiliary, their spectral absent presence enables the signification of the Du Boisian text, both in terms of thematics and structure. Thus, the *Geist*—what Du Bois terms "the gift of Spirit"—of dub/duppy allows us to think haunting as echo and vice versa, excavating the sonorous facets of this spectral ontology at the limit of empirical knowledge and livability. Hearing voices will never quite be the same again, for what comprises an echo, always a multiplicity of one (the one?), if not the clashing reverberations of a dead sound that lives in its after-effects and therefore resists finitude, even as mortality forms the core of its spirit.

Walter Benjamin, like Scientist, Ellison, Lee Scratch Perry, Du Bois, and King Tubby, was attuned to the lower sonic-cum-spectral frequencies of the past, writing in "On the Concept of History": "Streift uns nicht selber ein Hauch der Luft, die um die Früheren gewesen ist? Ist nicht in Stimmen, denen wir unser Ohr schenken ein Echo von nun verstummten?" (Doesn't a breath of air around our predecessors graze us? Is not in the voices we lend our ears to, an echo of the now muted?)[63] I reproduce the German here because these two sentences have been omitted from the only English translation available until recently, *Illuminations*, the compilation that precipitated Benjamin's popularization in the Anglo-American academy and beyond. Moreover, these lines' omission from that translation and their concern with sound amplify both the volume of this echo and the spectrality of temporality; they exist only in the dub version, the ghostly shadow of Benjamin's text. Benjamin himself anticipated the spectral resonances of this translation in his essay "The Task of the Translator," where he conjures the "eternal afterlife" (*das ewige Fortleben*) of the art work.[64] Benjamin conceives of translation as echoing the original, thus intensifying the aural components of this hauntology: "The task of the translator consists in finding the particular intention in the

target language through which an echo of the original is activated. . . .
[T]he echo is able to give, in its own language, the reverberation of the
work in the foreign language."[65] Du Bois's use of the spirituals and poetry,
rather than providing a simple act of repetition, appears as a form of
Benjaminian translation in which these artifacts resound and disperse
the originals, all the while (re)producing their sonic after/life. The voices
of the dead phantomically infuse Benjamin's discourse, adding a sonic
dimension to his monadic conception of the historical; in a number of
ways they also remember, repeat, and work through Du Bois's plea for
his readers to hear the souls of black folk and his insistence that only "an
echo of haunting melody" can materialize in the text. Thus *The Souls of
Black Folk* transacts the confluence of differing and differential grooves
that add up to a dub mix, a sonic hauntology of the temporal in which
both the past and the future echo in/the present, only to transform its
status as presence.[66]

If Ellison and Benjamin detonate grooves and monadic shrapnel within
the province of the historicist past, Du Bois performs this temporal explosion, where different flows, velocities, and grooves collide, through the
structural mixology of *Souls*'s epigraphs, particularly the final ones. In
other words, Ellison and Benjamin offer the tools for conjecturing non-
historicist compilations of the temporal, especially apropos the tradition
of the oppressed and the sonic; *The Souls of Black Folk* and DJing enact
these principles in their respective media, which ought not involve any
sort of deep rift between the theoretical and the performative, as opposed
to sundry manifestations of analogous principles vis-à-vis temporality in
different modes of discursive materiality. And while these imaginings of
time are drawn from those oppressed subjects behind the veil and outside
the groove of history, we should not be so quick to relegate these imperative contributions to twentieth-century intellectual and cultural history
to their already established minoritarian status. Instead, we might do well
to think, as Homi Bhabha does in his reconceptualization of Western
modernity, how these formations re/mix the temporality of modernity
per se. DJs, Du Bois, Ellison, and Benjamin ratify Bhabha's "time lag" of
Western modernity by reimagining and morselizing the supposed linearity of hegemonic time from the (aural) vantage point of the oppressed.

Overall, it is sound, especially in its ties to modern technologies, that
allows these diverse laborers in the kingdom of culture to "mess" with
the strict cadence of Western modernity in order to present us with a dis-

jointed, singular, and "mixed-up" modernity: "sonic Afro-modernity," giving credence to Deleuze and Guattari's observation that "meter is dogmatic, but rhythm critical" (*A Thousand Plateaus*, 313).[67] These writings/practices rhythmify temporality via syncopation, taking on variously the form of grooves, monadic shrapnel, and haunting echoes, of the past, present, and future. Time ceases to behave solely as meter only when these three forces coexist, even if unequally and in a fragmented manner, and their contemporaneousness is aided by, even though it cannot be determined by, their proximity to the margins of Western modernity. In a recently unearthed essay about the vicissitudes of positivism in U.S. social scientific discourse at the turn of the last century, Du Bois uses rhythm as a figure to delineate the grounds of empirical knowability: "a primary rhythm depending . . . on physical forces and physical law; but within it appears again and again a secondary rhythm, which while presenting nearly the same uniformity as the first, differs from it in its more or less sudden rise at a given tune."[68] Concluding, we can say that Ellison, Du Bois, DJs, and Benjamin insert this secondary rhythm, or *riddim*, to summon an Afro-diasporic rendition of this term, into Western modernity. Generally, this *riddim* is rendered inaudible—even as it transacts the echoing strain and complementarity between these rhythms. Yet, as all of these figures show, once the latter beat, much like a phantom, is introduced to the mix, it no longer remains secondary or belated; rather, it unbolts altogether new and different versions of time, ones synonymous with the rhythms found in and sounding from the grooves of sonic Afro-modernity.

4

Consuming Sonic Technologies

Modernity, particularly in the form of urbanization, radically altered the perception and construction of space, given the large-scale increase in population density in metropolitan areas. The intensification of noises generated by the burgeoning masses was one immediate effect of this development, which, coupled with industrialization and mechanization, greatly multiplied the sources for noise production. In addition, we should consider the effects generated by the invention and distribution of technologies enabling the recording and reproduction of various human and nonhuman sounds.[1] While these two developments (the higher concentration of humans in urban areas and the intensification and escalation of auditory technologies) can be taken to belong to one main current within modernity—the greater sonic intensity of urban space—I would like to suggest a more dialectical approach, albeit one that never quite reaches sublation: an approach that distinguishes between the sound/noise levels that individual subjects encounter through their environments, particularly in the urban terrain, and the sounding technologies these subjects use to distinguish their own space from that of others. While these noises or musics might be qualitatively the same, they are often not perceived as such by the listeners in question.

This chapter sets out some of the ways in which sound constructs modern spatialities by way of Ralph Ellison's essay "Living with Music" (1955) and Darnell Martin's film *I Like It Like That* (1994), since they illustrate how recorded music and its differing modes of transmission — record player, Walkman, stereo system, and boom box — mediate public and private spaces in modernity. Both Ellison's essay and Martin's film provide detailed depictions of the various ways in which subjects use sonic recording and reproduction technologies in their everyday lives. This chapter, then, echoes both the manner in which sonic technologies are consumed and the ways in which subjects are consumed by these apparatuses. I contend that the spatialities resulting from the juxtaposition of *consuming* sonic technologies and *being consumed* by them suggest specifically modern ways of be(com)ing in the world. These modes of subjectivity differ from the ones outlined in the preceding chapter as they arise from modern spatialities constituted through and magnified by sonic technologies, rather than temporality; which is to say that while these subjectivities take place in time, the sounding spatialities of sonic Afromodernity are what this chapter highlights more forcefully. Focusing on how electronically mediated music plays an integral part in constituting private and public spaces, I analyze the consumption of recorded music and its role in protecting listeners from urban noise, which is not deemed a part of the private space of the subjects in the two texts. "Noise," as opposed to "music," disrupts the privacy of musical consumption; however, these categories are not as stable as they initially seem, since they are both heavily reliant on the perspective of the sonic consumer vis-à-vis the borders between "music" and "noise." Ellison and the main character of *I Like It Like That*, Lisette, use recorded "music" (sounds of their own choosing) to shield themselves from the threat of "noise" (sounds imposed upon them by others), staging the scene of consumption as a reaction to their sonic social surroundings. Thus, the subjects' wish to escape their social sonic space leads them right back to it. In other words, while the deployment of sonic technologies is imagined as an individuating gesture, an aggressive retreat from the communal, it only appears as such in relation to some form of sociality.

After identifying a theoretical gap situated at the interstices of sound and geography, my argument then moves on to discuss Ellison's meticulous descriptions of his living quarters in terms of the music that emanates from the apartments around him. Ellison uses recorded music (phonograph records on his sound system) to demarcate his private space from that of his neighbors. Initially attempting to shield himself from the very loud, and — according to Ellison — not very good, singing of one of his neighbors, Ellison eventually enters into a sonic dialogue, playing "superior" versions of the songs she sings at high volumes on his state-of-the-art sound system. Ellison comes to realize that this friendly "sonic warfare" in fact enhances his milieu, since the music deployed in battle becomes a defining feature associated with his living space. Likewise, Lisette, the protagonist of Martin's film, uses recorded music (boom box, radio, and Walkman) to create a space that simultaneously distances her from and links her to her family and neighbors. Lisette inhabits a very small apartment with her husband and her three children, and the only private space she has is her bathroom, where she isolates herself in order to listen to music. The music transforms the bathroom, allowing Lisette to experience her self in a different manner than when in the midst of her family in the rest of the apartment. As the narrative proceeds, Lisette's intimate knowledge of Afro-Latin music aids her pursuit of a career in the music industry, permitting her to construct, for the first time, an identity beyond the confines of her family. Not only does the film show how music enables her to change her position vis-à-vis her family and the workplace, but it also employs music to illustrate Lisette's shifting identity. I come to the conclusion that the music and the technologies the music is transmitted through provide the means for both Ellison and Martin's protagonist to create and recreate space through sound as it is articulated at the interstices of the private and the social. Just as with my previous ruminations on the temporality of "sonic Afro-modernity," here space appears as a series of competing and sometimes conflicting spheres that cohere at certain junctures only to fall apart or, at other points, vehemently oppose one another.

Sounding Space/Spacing Sound Although there have been numerous critical considerations of space in recent cultural criticism—in fact, the emphasis on geography rather than temporality is often construed as indicative of the "postmodern turn"—there exist few studies that analyze how sound articulates space.[2] Susan Smith, for instance, points out the lacunae concerning the incorporation of sound into primarily geographical studies of current social formations, calling for "the more explicit incorporation of sound generally and of music in particular into research in human geography, and especially into those aspects of the subject concerned with cultural politics. Modern musicology is pre-occupied with the importance of seeing as a supplement to hearing, and we, I feel, might seek the converse."[3] While Smith forcefully brings to the fore the absence of the sonic from the discipline of geography, the editors of a recent collection devoted to interrogating the relationship of sound and space suggest a more nuanced circumscription of this problem:

> *The Place of Music* presents space and place not simply as sites where or about which music happens to be made, or over which music has diffused; rather, different spatialities are suggested here as being formative of the sounding and resounding of music. Such a richer sense of geography highlights the spatiality of music, and the mutually generative relations of music and place. Space produces as space is produced.[4]

This assertion maps/sounds a field of inquiry at the intersection of geography and contemporary music criticism that is yet to come, due to neglect on both sides of this disciplinary divide. In order for critical notions of space and sound to amplify one another, geographers need to consider the ways in which sound produces space and music critics how sound is fashioned by space and vice versa.

Following the lead of Henri Lefebvre, Edward Soja contends that we should conceptualize space not as a static and a priori entity, but rather as a field that is constantly re/produced within the realm of the social. He states: "Spatiality, as a socially produced space, must . . . be distinguished from the physical space of material nature and mental space of cognition and representation, each of which is used and incorporated into the social construction of spatiality but cannot be conceptualized as its equivalent."[5] While the three categories of space are separate and, according to Soja's model, should be treated as such analytically, they may not be as easy to distinguish in theory or praxis. How, for example, can we weed out material nature from its mental or medial representations? Although I would not quite claim that material space only exists in representation, these registers are not easily discernible as individual categories; rather, they present themselves as a cluster through which social space emerges as a conflicted terrain, dynamically marking the inseparability of physical, mental, and social space. Soja does concede that all three forms of space are interdependent: "The social production of spatiality cannot be completely separated from physical and cognitive space," he says, yet he insists on a notion of semidistinct spheres of space, which overlap at certain points but are fundamentally different (93). Instead of seeing social, material, and cognitive space in this manner, I would venture that this trinity contributes to a larger totality of space that represents a dialogue between these forces, inasmuch as all of these factors are relational.[6] Consequently, social space can only be produced through physical and cognitive space, and cognitive space is imagined through physical and social space. Sound fits into these three factors as the mediating conduit because it interfaces physical, social, and cognitive space in relation to the subject. On the one hand, certain physical features can be attributed to sound within the scope of an "acoustic space," which denotes the physical space that the sounds of an object — a radio for example, or a person — occupy.[7] Conversely, the "acoustic space" that the subject or object takes up relates to cognitive space in that it influences how subjects imagine their surroundings. Finally, an "acoustic space" can only be discerned in the context of other ones around it: in this sense, it is quite social. The pertinent question here concerns how sound shapes social space and how the acoustic space of one subject is in dialogue with others. But why give sound a particular relation to the sociality of space? What are the particular properties of the sonic in relation to social space?

In her concern about the neglect of spatiality in writings about music and sound, Jody Berland begins to ascertain the specific role that music plays in constructing private and shared spaces: "We surround the visual object, facing towards it as something other than ourselves; to look at something, even one's own image, is to constitute it as something separate. To listen to something is to forego that separation. Sound comes at us from behind or the back, from any direction, and surrounds us; we are constituted as listeners within its space."[8] Here, Berland establishes that viewers observe visual objects, where listeners are immersed in sound, suggesting a totality in the listening experience, as an effect of the spatial dislocation created by the sonic, that is not congruent to viewing. Sound achieves this feat because its source is not unidirectional, coming instead at the listener from different directions, a form of space that eludes visual objects; sound establishes multiple overlapping spatialities. Nonetheless, Berland does not account for how listeners constitute themselves vis-à-vis sound in addition to being interpellated by sound, given that listeners can choose where and when to immerse themselves in sound, especially with the proliferation of mobile auditory technologies. As my readings show, selecting what music to play, when, where, and at what volume, constitutes not only an integral part of each subject's listening experience, but provides the backbeat of sonic geographies.

Conversely, subjects do not always possess agency in determining what sounds surround them, which results in crises when listeners feel overwhelmed by their sonorous surroundings; Berland further delineates the subject located in sound:

> The listener is immersed in sound; the sound, entering the body, located both internally and externally, is immersed in the listener. It is as hard to describe the immersion as it is to say what music is. But in being so immersed, body and brain are brought to something or someone beyond the self, and the sound in turn is drawn into the body and the mind, who cannot turn or close her eyes to it making music the most intimate yet commandingly social of the arts. (34)

This tense articulation of both the intimacy and the sociality in sound is key, for it highlights the particular manner in which subjects relate to sound in space. Whereas subjects can choose not to look at a certain visual object, it is much more difficult to escape the rattle and hum in the space that they inhabit, particularly if it possesses a certain volume: sound cannot be ignored or screened out as can visual objects; instead, it forces subjects to bear witness to its occurrence and duration. This quality makes the sonic at once more communal — because it draws the subject to something or someone outside her/himself — and more personal, as it manages to engulf the subject in a way that visual items do not. In addition, the inability of the listening subject to disregard sound contributes to the impasse in some forms of listening, for the listener is forced to hear the sounds of others, which in turn dissolves physical and mental boundaries; as Connor remarks, "The vulnerability to the alterity of sound — or to sound as the sign of alterity — is a vulnerability to the doubled self of the man-made; man-made sound emanates from 'us,' but assails and pervades us from an enigmatically indefinite 'out there.' "[9] As we shall see in the discussion that follows, the "out there" is not always enigmatic and irks most often when it is clearly locatable.

Both Ellison and Lisette seek to control and manage the contingencies of sonic otherness by locating it in the sounds of specific subjects, their neighbors or family, for instance; this way, the enigma is transformed into a particular source that can be counteracted, as opposed to an unwieldy mass of noise that renders the listener helpless in the face of its radical alterity. This insight allows us to analyze the double impact of sonic technologies, since subjects use them to create individualized space but do so most often in relation to other people's use of these same technologies. Music, and sound in general, roots subjects in their environment by making that environment audible, while the immersion that comes with the listening experience is always tied to a space from whence it originates, thereby spatially marking the sound. In other words, the listening event varies depending on the venue, so that the subject engages with music differently when at home, in a restaurant, or at a dance club. However, music also influences the spaces we dwell in; thus we can turn our home into a club if we play music at decibels high enough to inspire us to dance. Berland notes that music "distinguishes her [the listener] from still others, including perhaps those who are physically present but aurally eliminated, so to speak, with headphones for instance, or with speakers punctuating an inaudible space between them over the decibels in a larger space" (34). Berland's point highlights how subjects employ music to demarcate boundaries by shutting out other subjects through the volume of the music they play, be it over a speaker system or via headphones. In this way, the popularity of auditory technologies might be taken, at least in part, as a way to soothe the dislocation engendered by the raptness of sonic receptivity vis-à-vis the multiplicity of modern sounds. In this noisy constellation, sonic technologies operate both as sources for the aural onslaught of the modern (noise) and as shields (music) from this very racket.

"A War of Decibels" "Living with Music" is the first in a series of essays on music (entitled "Sound and the Mainstream") in Ralph Ellison's *Shadow and Act*, one of the most influential volumes of nonfiction prose in twentieth-century American letters. In contrast to Ellison's other essays on music, this essay has received scant critical attention.[10] This might seem surprising, but not if we consult the actual content of the piece. Unlike all the other essays in the series, "Living with Music" (first published in *High Fidelity* magazine in 1955 and written during Ellison's tenure at the American Academy in Rome), does not concern itself with specific genres or figures—Mahalia Jackson, Jimmy Rushing, or Charlie Parker, for example—from the reservoir of African American music, as many of the other writings in this series do.[11] Rather, it engages with repercussions of the reproduction of recorded sound as such. Although Ellison alludes to a number of performers (Ma Rainey, Lotte Lehman, Bessie Smith, Louis Armstrong, Kirsten Flagstad, etc.) and composers (Händel, Beethoven, Wagner, etc.) from both the African American and the Western classical canons, the piece itself does not concern these figures. This essay shifts emphasis from the *content* of sonic transmission to the *mode* of sonic transmission, bearing witness to the critical importance of sonic technologies in the mediation and construction of music and modern urban spatiality.

In fact, Ellison is one of the major African American writers to acknowledge not only the value of black music but also the import of sound recording and reproduction on music in the twentieth century. As I noted earlier, in *Invisible Man* he uses the grooves of records as a way to imagine the recording and transmission of black cultural history and offers a model of subjectivity routed through an encounter with the phonographic voice of Louis Armstrong. While Ellison is surely not alone in recognizing the place of sonic technologies in twentieth-century black culture, he has provided some of the most sound forays into the grooves of sonic Afro-modernity. In the fictional realm, Toni Morrison, August Wilson, and Paule Marshall have made sound recordings a major aspect of their works, while writers such as Claude McKay and James Baldwin, for instance, have mentioned the phonograph and phonograph records, though only in passing.[12] To my knowledge only Langston Hughes makes use of autobiographical writing to convey the intimacy of sound and technology in the twentieth century in a way that is comparable to Ellison's; Hughes, however, focuses on the social aspects of consuming recorded music rather than the technological dimensions per se.

Published a year after "Living with Music," Hughes's second autobiography, *I Wonder as I Wander*, chronicles his global travels in the 1930s, a large chunk of the text being devoted to Hughes's sojourn in Russia. Hughes lists what he packed for this long trip when he first leaves the United States: "Driving as fast as I could from coast to coast, I got to New York just in time to pick up my ticket, say good-bye to Harlem, and head for the North German Lloyd, loaded down with bags, baggage, books, a typewriter, a Victrola, and a big box of Louis Armstrong, Bessie Smith, Duke Ellington and Ethel Waters records."[13] Hughes's portable record player and records prove to be particularly convenient when he journeys to the Soviet Central-Asian republics, entertaining Russian folk singers on a train trip (103–104). After leaving Moscow, a bustling metropolis, Hughes's records also keep him company while he is writing in the secluded Ashkhabad (110–113). However, it is not until Hughes, with the help of his portable music, makes the acquaintance of Jewish Hungarian intellectual Arthur Koestler that he realizes the social potential of recorded music (113). Koestler introduces himself to Hughes because he hears the traveler listening to a jazz record in an adjacent room, and as a consequence, Hughes's record player and records become the social center of the hotel: "Perhaps it was because of music that my room became a social center. Everywhere, around the world folks are attracted to American jazz. A good old Dixieland stomp can break down almost any language barriers, and there is something about Louis Armstrong's horn that creates spontaneous friendships" (114). This scene, apart from providing a synecdochic rendering of the global popularity of African American music in the twentieth century, conveys the importance of sonic technologies in enabling its very popularity and global dissemination. Nevertheless, Hughes does not dwell on the technological aspects of this scene; instead, he chooses to emphasize the sociality of the music itself thereby rendering the recording and reproduction apparatuses invisible, or rather inaudible. Conversely, in "Living with Music," Ellison's project consists of making the sonic apparatus discernible not only in order to show that technology enables the consumption of music in various locations and at any time, but also to elucidate how it alters the way music is experienced in the twentieth century.

"Living with Music" constructs a geography by depicting the sonic environment of Ellison's small New York apartment in the early 1950s. The text explores the wavering line between noise and music, in addition to providing a poetic description of living with electronically mediated music. It commences with a retrospective assertion: "In those days it was either live music or die with noise, and we chose rather desperately to live" (187). Ellison, *pace* Attali, does not view silence as death; rather, he sees noise as the negation of life. However, what distinguishes music from noise remains unspoken in this statement: Ellison assumes that the reader will intuitively differentiate between the two. He then shows why and how he chose to live with music rather than surrendering to noise, providing only a minimal portrait of his former apartment in physical terms by telegraphically stating that it was "a tiny ground-floor-rear apartment" (187). Further accounts of Ellison's living circumstances center on the sonic aspects of his surroundings, drawing an aural map for the reader: the juke-box in the neighboring restaurant, the "swing enthusiast to [his] left" and the various singing and preaching drunks leaving the bar at the corner. These details give the reader insight, or more accurately, "inhearing," into the acoustic geography of Ellison's apartment. Highlighting the different sources of sound conveys not only the visual characteristics of the apartment — which he hardly addresses at all — but more important, what this apartment sounds like, which shifts the emphasis from the visual to the aural and reveals that the sonic, be it music or other everyday noises, proves as crucial in structuring space as visual phenomena: colors, walls, and furniture, for instance. The totality of the listening experience explains why Ellison, in "Living with Music," takes issue not so much with the surrounding objects to be taken in by the eye but with the sounds coming from his neighbors' apartments; that is, he simply disregards the visual objects that offend him, but he cannot ignore the sounds he perceives as "noise."[14] All of these elements show the porous boundaries of the music/noise dichotomy as it is constantly renegotiated and displaced, particularly in an urban context where a multitude of noises compete on a daily basis.

This "chaos of sound" hinders Ellison's writing process, but he can accept and/or eliminate most of these factors to a certain extent; only the singer situated in the apartment directly above him remains a major obstacle: "No, these more involved feelings were aroused by a more intimate source of noise, one that got under the skin and worked into the very structure of one's consciousness — like the 'fate' motif in Beethoven's Fifth or the knocking-at-the-gates scene in Macbeth" (189). Even while Ellison associates the singer's effect with the manner in which Beethoven and Shakespeare touch him, her noise perturbs him much more forcefully than any other sounds in the vicinity. Yet, because he himself was once an aspiring musician, and therefore, dependent on the leniency of his neighbors to let him play the trumpet at any time and as loudly as he desired, Ellison proves unable to stop the singer's rehearsals: "After a year of non-co-operation from the neighbor on my left I became desperate enough to cool down the hot blast of his phonograph by calling the cops, but the singer presented a serious ethical problem: Could I, an aspiring artist, complain against the hard work and devotion of another aspiring artist?" (190). In this initial confrontation, Ellison uses sonic means to differentiate strictly between cultural production and consumption: while he has no qualms about reporting to the police neighbors who simply listen to music that is too loud, the singer escapes the repressive state apparatus by virtue of being an artist "at work" rather than a mere consumer. Though Ellison understands that practice is indispensable for the singer, he does not consider listening to phonograph records a necessity, at least for the time being, especially at the volume favored by the fellow city dweller. For Ellison, consumption, at this point in the essay, remains something private, whereas production has communal import, and even though Ellison may not discern the specific social value generated by the singer's rehearsals, or at least the ways in which they affect his own life world, he does appreciate her artistic aspirations. Ironically, as the essay progresses, Ellison realizes that the only way he can sonically compete with the singer is by consuming music himself.

In order to remain productive as an artist Ellison decides that he needs to drown the noise originating outside his apartment with noise from within his apartment, thereby achieving a sonic equilibrium of sorts. The distinction here is he has some choice in the noise emanating from within the confines of his four walls: "Since I seemed doomed to live within shrieking chaos I might as well contribute my share; perhaps if I fought noise with noise I'd attain some small peace" (193). At this point, Ellison's account assumes no "objective" difference between noise and music; instead, it appears as a semiarbitrary divide constructed by culture, history, and personal preference. The major distinguishing feature between noise (the singer above) and music (what Ellison consumes in his home) is Ellison's ability to control the sounds in his living space. But after listening to a recital by Kathleen Ferrier, Ellison, once again, erects a solid divider between noise and music. In his early confrontation with the irksome chanteuse, Ellison's main objective had been to drown out his neighbor's singing with random high decibels; however, after hearing the Ferrier recording on the radio he begins to invest in his sonic shield and find pleasure in it. This shift underscores the arbitrariness of the noise/music divide, because the *noise* Ellison deploys to silence the singer's *noise* has now entered the Helicon of music, radically altering its function for Ellison and his measure of dwelling: "I realized that with such music in my own apartment, the chaotic sounds from without and above had sunk, if not into silence, then well below the level where they mattered. Here was a way out. If I was to live and write in that apartment, it was only through the grace of music" (194). At this juncture, external notes appear as "chaotic sounds," while his apartment is graced by "music"; as a result, listening to music constructs a sonic wall around his personal space, a fifth wall, as it were: Ellison chooses musical sounds to dominate his space and consequently bars other sounds from penetrating his apartment.

Having opened his ears to the gratification of music in his home, Ellison decides to purchase an elaborate and expensive stereo system in order to administer his sonic environment. Once he acquires the system, it takes on a life of its own. First, he becomes devoted to the nuts and bolts of his home "sound system." In trying to manage his sonic ecology, he goes to great lengths in choosing the right aural formations for his apartment, thus systematizing the sounds that surround him, while also assembling his state-of-the-art hi-fi equipment. Thus Ellison dives into the world of the technological sound system in order to create a sonic sound system that aids him to take in his own music and not others' noise. Once Ellison starts to enter into the world of sound systems he realizes that "between the hi-fi record and the ear . . . there [is] a new electronic world" (194). This statement is striking, for it emphasizes the technological mediation at the heart of any consumption of recorded sound, since sound has to be reproduced technologically (either acoustically or through electronics, as in Ellison's case) in order to be heard by the listener. Yet often this intrusion is rendered nonexistent, particularly now, when the technological reproduction of sound has become ever present, relegating these technologies to minor parts of our technoinformational media environs. John Corbett argues that the technology of the compact disc reflects this naturalization most clearly (and we can extend this to the digital distribution of music via the Internet, which seemingly dispenses with material instantiation altogether):

> Turntables generally leave the record in plain view, while the disc machine consumes the CD, removing it visually and further concealing the playback process. . . . It is, however, not only the disc that is taken by the machine; the entire visual structure is supplanted by a prosthetic eye (the laser). No more analogy of material contact (tape/head; needle/groove), but a luminous reading—a seeing—internalized by the technology itself.[15]

Even though Ellison does not write about compact discs, he does participate in the dream of rendering the sonic apparatus invisible; paradoxically, this imperceptibility depends on the fetishization of the sonic reproduction technologies. In the recording process musicians' sounds are recorded in a studio on a master tape that is then used to press these sounds onto records. Afterward, the records are packaged, sold, and shipped to record stores (in some cases wholesalers intervene), which is where the end consumer purchases them. Consequently, Ellison's ability to hold a record in his hands relies on a series of technologies, as well as a confluence of industrial and commercial capitalism. The point to be made here concerns not only the "electronic world" between the record and the ear, but another "electronic world" between the producers and listeners of recorded music, namely that of the phonograph record. Ellison offers meticulous details about the acquisition of the individual components of his hi-fi system: tuner, speaker system, record player, cartridge, tone arm, amplifiers and preamplifiers, record compensators, and a tape recorder. After building the perfect sound system, Ellison, having altogether forgotten about his singing neighbor ("the reason" for all his technological wizardry), comes to realize why he has gone through all this trouble, not to mention the financial burden, of assembling this elaborate machinery: "All this plunge into electronics, mind you, had as its simple end the enjoyment of recorded music as it was intended to be heard. I was obsessed with the idea of reproducing sound with such fidelity that even when using music as a defense behind which I could write, it would reach the unconscious levels of the mind with the least distortion" (195). Earlier in the essay Ellison points toward the double technological mediation involved in the consumption of recorded sounds; now he narrativizes his quest for a sound system in terms of disavowing the materiality of recorded sound in his desire for absolute fidelity, which is clearly tied to his endeavor to drown out the noises invading his apartment; the inside and outside form a feedback loop of noise reduction, a Dolby system *avant la lettre*, as it were.

Keir Keightley suggests that the phenomenon of high fidelity as it appeared in the late 1940s "was meant to refer to the degree of truth-to-reality produced by the system. . . . In other words, hi-fi conceived the faithful reproduction of aural phenomena to be the primary purpose of home audio."[16] The notion of high fidelity rests on the following paradox: the pursuit of a pure, unmediated, and originary sonic source involves a sophisticated technological apparatus and substantial monetary investment. Unlike the neophyte, who contentedly listens to a cheap radio, the audiophile devotes vast amounts of time and capital to the very process of sonic purification. The desire for untainted sound fidelity represents not so much a mere reconstruction of an originary source, but an originary fabrication of the source itself—you may recall my discussion of the source in chapter 1. Consequently, the source, or original performance, is created and constructed in the process of technological mediation, both in terms of production and consumption, and has no ontological status anterior to or beyond this mediation. This process draws attention to the means by which the musical object loses its noisy contaminants and becomes a beacon of putative purity.

Once Ellison descends into the murky depths of fetishizing "pure" sounds, he realizes that his original intent—blasting away the singer—no longer forms a crucial element in his habitus of musical consumption: "I'm ashamed to admit, however, that I did not always restrict [the sound system] to the demands of pleasure or defense" (195). His mastery of the apparatus transforms him, pushing aside any earlier ethical inhibitions:

> With such marvels of science at my control I lost my humility. . . . For instead of soothing, music seemed to release the beast in me. Now when jarred from my writer's reveries by some enthusiastic flourish of the singer, I'd rush to my music system with blood in my eyes and burst a few decibels in her direction. If she defied me with a few more pounds of pressure against her diaphragm, then a war of decibels was declared. (195)

The "sound system," initially erected as Ellison's defensive screen from unwanted noise emanating from outside, now serves the principal purpose of sonic offense. After wielding the sound system for personal pleasure, Ellison decides to share his hi-fi with the neighbors, particularly the singer. Because Ellison is so invested in the sounds from his stereo, he expands the sonic boundaries of his private territory, taking up the position formerly occupied by his neighbors; as a result, Ellison becomes the sonic aggressor as he unleashes his sounds on the environment. Instead of silencing the "noise" from outside through the domestic "music," at this point Ellison's sound system produces "noise" for his neighbors. Although what Ellison sonically consumes in his own home is "music" to him, because he is able to choose the music and the technology of transmission, it is a sonic intrusion, that is, noise, to his neighbors, for they are now subjected to Ellison's system of sound and not their own.

Thus far the tense dynamic between Ellison and his singing neighbor shifted from her attack (practicing her singing at decibel levels Ellison found intrusive) to Ellison's sonic retaliation (his playing records/the radio in order to silence the singer, at least within his home) to a new Ellisonian offensive (playing his music very loudly for the purposes of his own enjoyment); and what can all this lead to but a full fledged sonic warfare? Finally, Ellison begins matching his musical selections with the singer's repertoire: if she sings the blues, he plays Bessie Smith; if she sings classical songs, he retorts with Marian Anderson and Lotte Lehman, all intent on demonstrating the neighbor's lack of talent when sonically confronted with the superiority of these vocalists. Now quite beyond the point of restraint, he takes things one step further and attacks the singer with "I'll Be Glad When You Are Dead" by Louis Armstrong, leaving little to the imagination. As Ellison, himself, states: "Oh, I was living with music with a sweet vengeance" (196). Strangely, Ellison's sweet vengeance does not have the intended effect on the singer: "She astonished me by complementing our music system. She even questioned me concerning the artists I had used against her. After that . . . she'd stop singing until the piece was finished and then applaud—not always, I guessed, without a justifiable touch of sarcasm. . . . [S]he was neither intimidated into silence nor goaded into undisciplined screaming; she persevered, she marked the phrasing of the great singers I sent her way, she improved her style" (196).

Instead of sonically vanquishing the singer, Ellison's music actually improves her craft. While Ellison found her singing to be noisily besetting his sonic environment, the singer not only perceives the noise broadcasting from Ellison's sound system as music, but uses it to improve her own vocalization, and, as a result, Ellison's noise helps her produce better music. Accordingly, their sonic warfare shape-shifts into a conversation, which breaks down the barriers between Ellison and his neighbor and dismantles the general music/noise partition. Because the singer learns from Ellison's "noise" she is able to produce better music, and Ellison, in turn, can conceive of her singing as music rather than the earlier noise. Ellison can now hear his neighbor's singing as music and does not feel compelled to produce noise in order to silence her noise (singing); they can both enjoy their respective sonic productions—Ellison's recorded music and the singer's singing—in addition to each other's music. Therefore the music/noise continuum becomes a collective space to be shared, as opposed to simply designating the firm parameters of individual spaces.

As soon as the singer and Ellison start sharing a sonic space instead of fighting each other by means of sound, Ellison no longer discharges his music with the same fervor and both parties move on to a "live-and-let-live" or "listen-and-let-listen" arrangement. Looking back on this episode, Ellison summarizes what he gained from this experience: "Still we are indebted to the singer and the old environment for forcing us to discover one of the most deeply satisfying aspects [listening to music] of our living" (197). Due to his particular living situation Ellison grasps that sounds play a pivotal role in the way we relate to our environs in the modern era, particularly to our homes. These sonic marks, music and otherwise, help construct space by revealing information and grounding us within various localities, delineating boundaries by distinguishing what sounds are contained within our own space and which ones come from outside. Sonic technologies provide the conditions of im/possibility for this transformation, for instance; Ellison uses the absence of an originary source, due to the peculiar nature of the recording and reproduction process, to mark out private and social space. It is the technological iterability of sound that facilitates these cultural practices.

At first glance, Ellison's use of sonic technologies might fit neatly into the gendered and classed practices of mid-fifties audiophiles described by Keir Keightley, who surveyed several major hi-fi magazines between 1948 and 1959 and concluded that the "conception of home audio as a masculine technology that permits a virtual escape from the domestic space is a significant development in the history of sound recording" (150). Keightley examines the use of high-fidelity equipment by white middle-class men to keep at bay the increasing "feminization" of domestic space in the 1950s (153–155). The "active" engagement with hi-fi equipment offered a masculine sphere of individuality, while the newly available technology of television was coded as "passively feminine" (156–157). These instruments of male individuation, although newly popularized by the availability of hi-fi technology as well as the proliferation of hi-fi ideology, have their roots in the history of early radio hobbyists. These traditionally male tinkerers built their own radios instead of relying on ready-made ones. In "That Same Pain, That Same Pleasure: An Interview," Ellison mentions his early enthusiasm for building radios at several key points in the conversation.[17] When asked by his interviewer, Richard J. Stern, about his encounter with the world beyond his immediate community, Ellison responds: "Ironically, I would have to start with some of the features of American life which it has become quite fashionable to criticize in a most unthinking way—the mass media. Like so many kids of the twenties, I played around with radio—building crystal sets and circuits consisting of a few tubes, which I found published in radio magazines" (4).[18] As opposed to proving that "within the safety of one's own home, and out of public view, one's masculinity could be tested and reaffirmed" (Keightley), Ellison describes the sociality that building radios granted him; he describes having used his hobby not to cut himself off from the world around him but to connect to communities and discourses beyond physical reach (150).

As we have seen in the discussion of his love for the stereo system and the "pure" sounds he wants it to re/produce, Ellison clearly participates in the masculinist hi-fi ethos. This involvement, however, differs from the currents outlined by Keightley in several significant, yet intertwined ways: in Ellison's case, domesticity and individuality—according to Keightley, two of the main players in 1950s hi-fi culture—are given a rather different spin. Keightley argues that hi-fi consumption facilitated "the battle of the sexes" within the domestic sphere, citing fantasy scenarios offered in hi-fi magazines in which husbands either shut out their wives sonically or blasted them away altogether with the might of their stereo speakers. This sonic clash is not directed outside the home but instead seeks to create a male sphere within the home itself. While Ellison fashions his domestic space through sonic technologies, he does not do so against his wife; in fact, Ellison mentions his wife only in passing, stating that she shared his passion for music and helped him to procure his precious stereo system ("Living with Music," 194). As discussed above, Ellison's aggression is squarely aimed at the singer located beyond the confines of his home, and while this could very easily be construed as a battle of the sexes—clearly, Ellison is male and the singer female—it is not an altercation between spouses, even if Ellison, not his wife, operates the stereo system. Unlike the suburban instances cited by Keightley, in Ellison's case mastery is not forcefully aimed at his wife. Rather, Ellison provides an account of the "sonic battle of the sexes" that is more clearly determined by geography than by 1950s domestic gender roles, at least exclusively.

For Ellison's situation decisively diverges from Keightley's scenario in terms of location: while Keightley focuses on suburban domestic space, Ellison writes about a small New York apartment. Ellison simply has less domestic space than the suburbanites in Keightley's argument, and the urban locale also signals the physical proximity of other subjects, as the domestic spaces of city dwellers are crowded together in apartment buildings rather than in freestanding homes. Therefore, in the urban terrain, defining one's space against the larger social environment becomes crucial, while suburban living, at least during this historical period, guaranteed a certain amount of distance from neighbors. Evan Eisenberg suggests recorded music's main utility in densely populated locales may just be its protective dimensions: "The city is no place for listening to records. Half the time one has to use them as shields against other people's sounds. Music becomes a substitute for silence. (In the country music is the fulfillment of silence.) One does not freely choose when to listen, or even what to listen to, since the trespassing bass of a neighbor's rock, rap or disco records can be countered only by its like."[19] Even if Eisenberg overstates his point a bit here, construing technological listening solely in terms of its urban functionality, the question of sonic trespassing stresses the fluid sonic boundaries in the city. Where walls, curtains, and the like, can contain the visual, sound renders these borders permeable, making it hard to disregard the sonic provenances of one's surroundings. Therefore, in the city, sonic warfare would necessarily be aimed outward in an attempt to establish a discrete sonic domestic sphere as opposed to being a tool in the "war of the sexes" within the home. A new conception of hi-fi consumption in the period outlined by Keightley and beyond would have to look at varying geographical locations in order to more fully describe and theorize the use of sonic technologies in relation to domestic and public space. Moreover, this novel approach might further dwell on the use of sonic technologies by women. How does this recast the battle of the sexes invoked by Keightley? As we shall see, Darnell Martin's film *I Like It Like That* radically departs from the 1950s use of hi-fi equipment by portraying a woman who uses sonic technologies to recast her domestic and public space.

Sonic Publicity/Sonic Privacy   *I Like It Like That* (1994), the first Hollywood studio film directed by an African American woman, Darnell Martin, occupies a special place in contemporary black American cinematic production.[20] The film centers on Lisette, a black Puerto Rican woman who lives in the Bronx with her husband Chino and her three children, Little C., Mimi, and Peewee. By placing a black Puerto Rican woman at the center of its narrative and cinematic focus, *I Like It Like That* transcends the very male and racially narrow trends in mainstream black American cinema. In the early 1990s, cinematic representations of black subjects came mainly in the form of the "ghettocentric" genre exemplified by John Singleton's *Boyz in the Hood*, Mario Van Peebles's *New Jack City*, and the Hughes brothers' *Menace II Society*.[21] These films all portray poor black (male) youth in the urban centers of New York and Los Angeles coming to grips with a postindustrial landscape marked by the crack cocaine economy and the increased militarization of the inner city. While these films also feature black women, the focus is clearly on the plight of male youth; black women are, at best, foils for central male dilemmas and, at worst, mere cinematic enactments of male fantasies. Moreover, *I Like It* does not jibe well with the admittedly very minuscule niche of "black women's films" exemplified by *Waiting to Exhale* and *Set It Off*, for instance, which preceded it historically. While *I Like It Like That* is clearly constructed from a "woman's perspective," it does not privilege the same homosocial relationships that the other films do; instead the film portrays a female character's negotiation of her identity in relation to her family, friends, and workplace.

In addition, by focusing on a biracial Latina, the film also defies some of the rigid racial boundaries in Hollywood cinema.[22] Remarkably reminiscent of rules that constrained early black literary production, unwritten Hollywood rules required that black filmmakers only portray, in fairly traditional mimetic-cum-realist terms, their own supposedly immediate racial, gender, cultural, social, and geographical surroundings; more often than not this meant complying with fairly rigid notions of black American racial identity. By refusing to enact "mimetically" the director's ethnic background, *I Like It* threw a wrench in this Hollywood machinery. This uneasy relationship with the gender and racial codes of early nineties black cinema might explain why the film did not find a large audience in movie theaters, even if the film did enjoy some success on video and when shown on HBO.[23] This crossover between the cinema, video, and television—both network and cable—reflects a wider development within the current media landscape in the United States. Miriam Hansen proposes that the structural link between early cinema and contemporary practices for notions of cinematic spectatorship be rethought radically if they are to speak to current formations: "Those changes are the result of a combination of technological and economic developments that have displaced cinema as the only and primary site of film consumption. New electronic technologies propped onto television, in particular video playback, satellite, and cable systems, have shifted the venues for film viewing in the direction of domestic space and have profoundly changed the terms on which viewers can interact with films."[24] My aim is not to discern how these new media configurations are at play in *I Like It*'s narrative; nonetheless, these currents point to the contradiction in labeling the film unsuccessful in economic terms. The "success," or the lack thereof, of *I Like It* cannot be easily measured within the present fragmented media landscape, since we are unable to determine how many viewers actually saw the film on video — both legally and through bootlegs — and on cable television, because viewer statistics from these media do not have the same reliability as cinema ticket sales. Overall, these factors excavate *I Like It*'s complex relationship to the interlocking vectors of race, gender, urbanity, economics, and technology within the creative and commercial provenances of contemporary black cinema.[25]

The opening scene, emblematic of the film as a whole, features an extended shot, establishing all the major characters except Lisette and Chino. We see a street scene where people call down from their windows to play the numbers, spectators hang out on the street making comments on Alexis (Lisette's transgendered sister), and Chino's male friends (Angel, Chris, and Victor) flirt with two women on their way to the corner bodega. The viewer also encounters Magdalena, with whom Chino is having an extramarital affair, mocking the guys' courting rituals. This beginning crafts an image of the neighborhood that Chino and Lisette inhabit before actually showing the two protagonists. As the film progresses, this approach proves to be how Chino and Lisette are consistently represented to the viewers: always against the backdrop of their neighborhood and its inhabitants. In terms of sound, the film's beginning also sets the precedent for the remainder of the film: a musical soundtrack mixed with dialogues and environmental sounds (traffic, subway trains, and so on). While the opening scene situates the main characters and their community in the film, it also sets up the sonic narrative axis by combining music and nonmusical soundtracks. Hence the beginning scene not only invites the audience to become visual spectators but also, and perhaps more important, it calls attention to how this neighborhood sounds and addresses the audience as listeners.[26] Overall, the film magnifies the tension between its sonic and scopic axes, dislocating them at certain points and creating coherence at others.

After this initial scene the film cuts to Lisette and Chino's bedroom where they are engaged in sexual intercourse; far from being a "private" act, this activity is one in which the whole neighborhood and their children participate. While Chino checks the alarm clock hidden under the pillow to gauge the duration of their lovemaking—so far he has accomplished eighty-nine minutes—two of the children try to open the locked door and the downstairs neighbor knocks on her ceiling with a broom. Furthermore, Chino's friends, standing on the stoop in front of the open bedroom window, cheer him on by shouting "Go Chino! Go Chino!" and Magdalena, obviously jealous, angrily smashes a bottle against the wall of the apartment building. All of these factors contribute to the impression that the distinctions between private and public spaces are tenuous, at best, inasmuch as the entire neighborhood participates in this sexual act, routinely construed as the epitome of the private. The privateness of heterosexual sex represents, according to Lauren Berlant, one of the crucial spaces of contemporary American national culture: "Insofar as an American thinks that the sex he or she is having is an intimate, private thing constructed within the lines of personal consent, intention, and will, he or she is having straight sex, straight sex authorized by national culture; he or she is practicing national heterosexuality . . . protected by a zone of privacy."[27] Yet, it is not hetero sex per se that is "protected by a zone of privacy," but more specifically white, middle-class, hetero sex that occurs within wedlock; sex between people of color is often portrayed as deviant in relation to the state and national culture. If we survey the debates around "welfare queens," consistently depicted as a major threat to what remains of the U.S. welfare state, we encounter their sex acts—whether they are explicitly mentioned or implied through the emphasis on the number of children these women bear—as always already being "a drain" on the state's resources.[28] In addition, the numerous talk shows populating U.S. daytime television have made a habit of exploiting the sex lives of poor people regardless of their racial identities: nothing about their sex acts is private, they have to (or choose to) "stand trial" in front of the studio audience, psychological experts, and the national viewership. Thus, the "zone of privacy" invoked by Berlant appears somewhat more restricted and context-bound than suggested by her argument. The scene in *I Like It* seems to be playing with the vicissitudes of hetero sex as they relate to race and class in contemporary U.S. culture by underscoring the "nonprivateness" of Lisette and Chino's sex act, which, despite their state-sanctioned marital hetero status, is qualified by their income bracket, urban location, and racial identity.

While I do not want to imply that the semipublic sex act performed by Chino and Lisette at the start of the film should be construed as a meta-commentary on U.S. sexual politics, this scene can teach us something about this problematic by giving us a heterosexual sex act that is located at the intersection of private and public, and not positing this act as inherently deviant or, conversely, as clothed in nationally sanctioned privateness. The sonic boundaries are permeable: the open window, the kids behind the door, and the neighbor downstairs are all somehow involved in Lisette and Chino's lovemaking. While all parties can hear Chino and Lisette, none can be seen by or see the others; in other words, the publicity of this act is constituted primarily through sound — privacy is only available on the visual level, not the sonic one. Because there is not enough space for everyone to be atomized, most acts in this context become public in one way or another; ergo no one deems it unusual that Lisette and Chino are having sex in the afternoon with the windows open rather than under the mantle of privacy, that is, in the dark with the windows closed. Even their kids, while bored, do not seem to object to the act itself or even find it noteworthy. What this scene presents, then, is neither a private hetero sex act, as discussed by Berlant, nor a deviant public sex act, as usually reserved for people of color in U.S. public culture, but something that networks these two discourses. It is worth dwelling on the publicness that sound creates in this scene for a moment, as it points to different ways in which events can move from private to public and vice versa. In addition, events like Chino and Lisette's sex act can be an unwieldy admixture of both public and private, rather than merely one or the other. This current of sonic publicity sets up the narrative force of the film *in toto*, since one of Lisette's main goals is to create a private sonic space for herself, either through locking herself in her bathroom and blasting the radio, or using her Walkman, or pursuing a career in the music industry. As hard as she may try, however, she cannot get away from the sonic surroundings pushed on her by others, a situation that can be seen as an extended metaphor for Lisette's identity. In the beginning of the film, she does not have a space apart from her family and neighborhood; by the end of the movie, however, Lisette has forged an identity that extends beyond her immediate milieu, albeit not one that absolutely excludes her family and community.

When the film opens, Lisette appears as someone unable to influence the course of her life. Initially, this helplessness could be taken to signify Lisette's victim status, yet the film actually does an excellent job of not giving a stereotypical depiction of a poor woman of color; rather, Lisette, not satisfied with some aspects of her life and faced with an extreme situation (Chino's arrest), is forced to exert more control over her life than she has done thus far, especially in economic terms. When the couple exits the bedroom after Lisette tires of their sex marathon, the two children are fighting and in the process one of them accidentally knocks over the family stereo. In the following scene, Lisette can be seen carrying the broken stereo; it becomes a symbol for her life, denoting her lack of both private space and material possessions. When Lisette complains about her lack of material goods, Chino makes an empty promise about acquiring a new stereo for her, to which Lisette responds by emphatically stating how much she hates her life. Chino, after proclaiming his love for her, asks Lisette to cook for him, prompting her to take refuge in her sister Alexis's apartment downstairs in order to use Alexis's sound system, since her own stereo is broken. Once in Alexis's apartment, she and her sister start plotting ways to get a new stereo, considering that Chino—as Alexis remarks—is "the layaway king" and will thus most likely not procure the desired commodities. Alexis suggests that Lisette start modeling, but her plan is later greeted with jeers and sarcasm from Chino and the other neighbors. Taken together, these dynamics set in motion Lisette's pursuit of spheres not dominated by her family and neighbors, ensuring less financial dependence on Chino, whose bike messenger salary can barely support a family of five. In addition, the broken stereo introduces the film's strategy of using not only sound, but sound reproduction technologies—in this case the stereo system—as a central conduit for narrative conflicts.

The film imagines Lisette's yearning for a better life through her desire for a new stereo system that would allow her to create a sonic space of her own. Though the sonic reproduction apparatus may not bring absolute partition from her family and neighbors, it would provide her with a temporary sonic space in which to choose the music she plays and manage her immediate auditory locale. Lisette's limited influence on her aural technoecosystem amplifies her feelings about life in general; her stereo appears to be the only way she can distinguish herself from the folks and noises around her. After Chino tries to steal a stereo for Lisette from a neighborhood store during a power outage, he is incarcerated, an event that sets in motion Lisette's prolonged quest for financial and, as it turns out, sexual independence. Recorded music plays a crucial role in constructing and articulating this journey.

Eventually Lisette pursues the modeling career suggested by Alexis; however, when she arrives at the modeling agency she meets a female record company employee who is looking for a woman to accompany a record company executive to a dinner with the Mendez Brothers, a popular Latino singing group. When she appears at the dinner the executive (Price) is disappointed, since she is not the sort of "bimbo" he requested.[29] Nevertheless, Lisette persists and impresses the musical group, especially since they are one of her own favorites and she knows much more about their lives and music than does the record executive. Although Price initially refuses to hire Lisette, through her sheer determination and expansive knowledge of Latin music, she convinces him that she should occupy a permanent position as his assistant. On the car ride home Price plays a tape of a hot new group he plans to sign, but Lisette vetoes his decision because she has witnessed these performers being booed at a block party. Here Lisette effectively proves her insider knowledge of Latino music as a representative of the audience for Price's goods. He, conversely, is not a part of this audience and only understands the abstract laws of marketing, and thus Lisette becomes his link to the Latino/a community. After Lisette makes several suggestions on how to reshape the Mendez Brothers' image during their initial meeting, she continues to work with Latino artists. In two work-related scenes, one at a photo shoot and the other at a concert of Latino artists, Lisette changes the clothing and look of the performers. On her first workday Price asks Lisette whether she would have sex with the artist in the promotional photos they are producing. Initially Lisette is offended, yet she starts to dress and style the performer to resemble Chino, with whom she obviously would have sex. Price positions her as a Latina consumer: if the artist fulfills Lisette's sexual fantasies, he will be able to sell the artist's records. Thus Lisette is not only called upon as a member of the Latino record buying demographic, but also as a heterosexual woman, which intertwines her sexual and economic position in the narrative. Her job allows her to pursue monetary income and realize sexual fantasies, and until now, both of these aspects are still very much grounded in and around the incarcerated Chino. This is reflected in the images of this scene: Lisette's restyling of the performer is interspersed with corresponding images of Chino leaving jail. The cutting between Lisette's workplace and Chino's release from jail orchestrates not only Chino and the performer's visual resemblance but also their performance of the same movements, illustrating that, at this juncture, Lisette's career is integrally attached to bailing Chino out, rather than her own personal advancement. In sum, this scene visually and sonically—the soundtrack provides a point of cohesion for the manic editing—brings together a number of crucial components (Lisette's career, her sexual desire, her position as a Latina within the corporate workplace, her relationship to Chino) before the greatest moment of rupture in the narrative.

This moment occurs when Chino's friends, while visiting him in prison, tell him that they have witnessed Lisette engaging in sexual acts with Price in his Ferrari after driving her home from the meeting with the Mendez Brothers. To retaliate, Chino allows Magdalena's father to post his bail in return for his acceptance of the paternity of Magdalena's baby, although, as we learn later, his friend Angel actually fathered the child. When Lisette discovers this she writhes with anger and, screaming in front of a captive audience on her street, she vehemently denies the rumors about a tryst with Price. The scene ends with Lisette loudly proclaiming to all the people in the neighborhood that they have no life, unlike her, with her fulfilling new career in the music industry. Following this incident, Chino attempts to win Lisette back, but she ignores his attempts and moves in with her sister Alexis. In order to revenge Chino's infidelity, Lisette has sex with Price on his office floor, an act lasting less than a minute, after which he takes a telephone call—a gesture that once again underscores Lisette's lack of control with regard to her sonic environs. Even though sex with another man does not turn out to be the liberating experience she had hoped for, she still relishes conveying her adventure to Chino. The scene significantly realigns the power dynamics in the couple's relationship, as Lisette asserts her autonomy by engaging in an extramarital sexual act, just as Chino did with Magdalena. The sexual act, for Lisette, is not so much about her desire for Price, but about proving to herself and Chino that she, too, has sexual agency and desire. Furthermore, Lisette uses Price's institutional and monetary power (as a white record executive) to illustrate Chino's deficiency in both regards (as a Latino bike messenger). In this way, Lisette exploits a volatile situation to confront Chino with the newly redrawn parameters of her economic self-sufficiency and sexual agency.

The final scenes of the film further stress the correlation between Lisette's sexual desire, economic independence, and family relations. During Lisette's stay at her sister's apartment, they have an argument about Lisette's treatment of her children, in which Alexis accuses Lisette of neglecting the children in favor of her career, thereby replicating their own parents' behavior. Lisette, tired of being mistreated by her husband and children, nonetheless vows to concentrate primarily on professional matters. When Lisette grows weary of their conversation, she inserts a salsa tape into Alexis's boom box, whereupon Alexis responds by replacing the tape with one of her own, featuring Otis Redding's "Try a Little Tenderness," clearly intended as a parenting guide for her sister. Lisette protests, but Alexis reminds her that she is not in her own home and thus has no right to dictate the sounds flowing from the boom box. What begins as a demarcation of boundaries through the control over sound technology and as a primer in loving parenting—Alexis asserts her space by playing her own music instead of Lisette's—ultimately inspires Lisette's professional coup de grace: the next day Lisette suggests to Price that the Mendez Brothers record a remake of this sixties soul tune, one version in English and one version in Spanish, so that the song can "cross over" from a strictly Latin audience to the top of the pop charts.[30] For the look of the video, Price imagines Coney Island and beautiful girls, but Lisette is quick to counter: the women should not be "oiled-down video hos." In the discussion of the song and the video, Lisette brings both her identities as a Latina living in the States and as woman in a male-dominated recording industry into play, resisting a particular version of hegemonic femininity, "the oiled-down video ho," while signifying her Latina and African American identities in the bilingual versions of "Try a Little Tenderness."

Lisette eventually returns to her family after Alexis convinces her that she does not have to choose between "getting hers" and "trying a little tenderness." Alexis's first attempt to persuade Lisette to return to her children, using the way their own parents' treated them as nonentities when they were children, is unsuccessful. What ultimately convinces Lisette is the physical abuse Alexis suffers when she visits their parents, who violently reject her transgender status. When Lisette goes back to Chino and the children, she and Chino resolve to split the rent and their parenting duties equally to reflect their changing relationship. One night the couple decides to disclose to each other the details of their extramarital affairs. After their respective revelations Lisette is furious, since she only had sex with Price once, whereas Chino slept repeatedly with Magdalena. This is the "proper" ending of the narrative. The rest of the film shows the Linares family and Alexis dancing at a Coney Island video shoot for the Mendez Brothers' version of "Try a Little Tenderness" based on Lisette's idea. The final scene depicts everyone on the New York subway going home. Even if these last shots suggest that Lisette and Chino have reconciled, *I Like It* eschews any uncomplicated evocation of a traditional Hollywood cinema happy ending. More important, Lisette now mediates between her familial role and her newfound professional habitus. While this suggests a quasi-utopian moment, including an expanded version of family that makes room for transgendered Alexis and Lisette's monetary/sexual independence, the film does not represent it as such in order to resolve all the vexed issues raised in its narrative; instead, *I Like It* points to a utopian moment that requires continuous renegotiation. These two endings stage the complex intermingling of Lisette's sexual, monetary, and personal autonomy. And significantly, they achieve this feat through music and technology, as Lisette's knowledge of music enables her to assert these spheres of autonomy together. The bilingual re-recording of the Redding song and its music video companion, which, due to Lisette's influence, does not feature "oiled-down video hos," technicosonically transact the flow between the different spaces of Lisette's life. Initially, Lisette desired only a new stereo; by the end of the film, however, she has become a part of the production apparatus, ensuring not only increased control over her sonic environment but also influence on the way music is produced and marketed. In addition, *I Like It* makes the sonic sphere central to its narrative, using it to foreshadow later developments and as a general indicator of Lisette's transformation, which, in turn, emerges through the shifting spatialities of her immediate domestic and professional environments. Finally, the interface of sound and technology facilitates the film's double dénouement, which structurally performs the open-endedness of Lisette's fluctuating identifications.

Consuming Sonic Technologies

"An Auditory Free Territory in the Americas" Overall, Lisette inhabits three areas in which she can listen to and interact with music; all of these spaces reflect and/or sound her ability to inhabit an identity that detaches her, albeit not completely, from her family and neighbors.[31] The first of these areas is tied to the Walkman she sports for most of the film when not at home or work. The second is Lisette's bathroom, into which she locks herself several times during the narrative so she can listen to the radio undisturbed. Finally, she attains employment as an assistant to a record executive, and puts into practice her intimate knowledge of Afro-Caribbean music. As the film progresses, these spaces and their sonico-technological mediation become increasingly important as narrative vehicles in the articulation of Lisette's subjectivity. This current is apparent in Lisette's use of sonic reproduction technologies such as the Walkman and transistor radio to demarcate personal space.[32] Lisette's Walkman represents an individuated and mobile sonic space that allows her to escape and enhance her surroundings through her choice of music. Though the film does not depict Lisette actually listening to her Walkman very often, she is always seen wearing headphones when in transit; in other words, she can exert temporary control of her life through this device in a way that she is not able to in general, particularly at the beginning of the film.

Also, as Frances Aparicio shows in her book *Listening to Salsa*, in different contexts — such as a car — salsa can provide its listeners with a mobile cultural community: "The car . . . has become, in the context of U.S. Latinos, a mobile urban space of cultural production that allows us to recover (temporarily) our particular cultural specificity within the broader landscape of homogenized cities and public spaces."[33] The recovery of certain cultural artifacts within a hostile environment is certainly crucial, but cannot represent the only use value of listening to salsa in one's car. What if the listening subject — Lisette, for example — does not possess a car? For Lisette, her Walkman functions as her "mobile urban space of cultural production" (in lieu of a car stereo), which she uses anytime she is on the move, whether she is walking or riding the subway. In addition, the Walkman enables Lisette to assert her identity not only as a Latina within an urban context but also as a woman with an autonomous sonic space, something she cannot do in her home. While Aparicio focuses mainly on cultural identity, Lisette's case is marked just as much, if not more, by gender; the Walkman gives her the ability to withdraw from her family, which attempts to reduce her to the domestic categories of mother, wife, and homemaker. As Du Gay and his coauthors in *Doing Cultural Studies* suggest, the Walkman "can and is used in the home—for example, by members of high-density families living in relatively restricted domestic circumstances as a means of creating some personal space—but it is primarily designed and marketed for mobile private listening in public. It is this 'twist in the tale' that the Walkman adds to the conventional story of 'privatization'" (114).[34] Lisette deploys her Walkman mainly to achieve a "mobile private listening in public"; nevertheless, she makes use of other sonic technologies, such as transistor radios and boom boxes, to establish private sonic spaces within her home. While these two modes might not be perfectly congruent, they are part of the same continuum, which underlines the various ways in which sonic technologies differentiate individual and communal spaces in *I Like It*.

The Walkman, launched by Sony Enterprises in 1979, forms a principal ingredient in the long history of mobilization and privatization of sound reproduction technologies beginning with the advent of the phonograph in 1877. While the early phonograph was not quite as portable as later technologies, it did usher in an era of private music consumption, giving listeners the ability to enjoy recorded music at home.[35] While the privatization of musical consumption had already commenced with the increased commodification of the piano in nineteenth-century America, it came to full fruition with the phonograph and the various other audio technologies in its wake. Paul Théberge recounts how the piano and later the pianola, or player piano, were marketed to middle-class homes, arguing that this was in part due to the piano's durability, which lent itself to industrial manufacture and transport, and, in turn, allowed for musical listening pleasure to move from the concert hall and other public spaces to the confines of the home. A trajectory then continued by the phonograph, "the phonograph and its descendants have provided us with a cheap and plentiful distraction in the comfort of our own homes. It has made living in small, windowless, air-conditioned rooms a little easier, replacing shared Victorian pleasures of bandstand and music hall with the solitary delight of a private world of sound."[36] The issue of privatization in relation to sonic technologies, then, precedes discussions about the Walkman and remains one of the main complaints leveled at all modern audio technologies. Still, the Walkman seems to hold a particular place in this critique as it enables private consumption in public spaces. When earlier portable audio technologies such as transistor radios, portable cassette and record players, and boom boxes made possible the public consumption of recorded music, everyone in the vicinity of these technologies could not help but participate in these activities. The Walkman, by contrast, allows stationary or mobile listeners to hear music through their headphones, preventing other people who inhabit the same physical space from hearing the music playing on the machine. Even though this should have come as a relief, given general concern about the "noise pollution" created by earlier sounding technologies, the Walkman encountered massive hostility because it supposedly enabled its users to "cut themselves off" from their immediate environment — which, as we shall see, was not necessarily the case.[37] While earlier itinerant technologies, boom boxes for instance, were scrutinized because they subjected "innocent bystanders" to high decibels of "noise," the "silent" Walkman was ironically taken to task for its "antisociality."[38]

When the Walkman was first introduced in Japan, Sony did not intend it as a device for solitary listening, given that it came with outlets for two sets of headphones and was designed for two listeners. Research soon revealed that the Walkman was most often used by only one person, prompting Sony to slyly redraft their marketing campaign: couples riding tandem bicycles and sharing one Walkman were soon replaced by images of isolated figures ensnared in their private world of sound.[39] Thus the Walkman, the epitome of private music consumption on public display, came to be this sort of contraption not from its inception but through a process that involved both the efforts of Sony's marketing research department and their response to the ways in which the machine was put to use by the consumers, highlighting the shifting meanings of technologies and the ways they are absorbed into the cultural realm. Similarly, the phonograph was initially designed to primarily record sonic information, but was much more popular as a playback instrument. Since the late seventies this miniature listening device has become a permanent fixture — now often in the form of portable CD players, iPods, and other digital music players — in the public spaces of the Western world (especially in urban areas), although this technology is also widespread in non-Western countries, encompassing two major currents in contemporary social, political, and cultural life: mobility and privatization.[40] Or, as Iain Chambers writes, the Walkman "reveals itself as a significant symbolic gadget for the nomads of modernity, in which music on the move is continually being decontextualized in the inclusive acoustic and symbolic life of everyday life."[41] Instead of simply understanding the Walkman as a tool of capitalist individuation and compartmentalization, it might best be described as enabling subjects to perform sonic privacy in public, which is particularly pertinent within the context of increased urban population density. As listeners recalibrate one of their senses in order to establish some form of isolation, they still engage with their environments through their other senses. In certain ways the Walkman presents the "best of both worlds": it provides a sonic zone of privacy, a scarcity in the contemporary urban terrain (as can be inferred from the scene of Lisette and Chino's lovemaking, discussed above), and it also lets the users observe and interact with their surroundings.

Even so, Lisette's use of her Walkman to create a mobile private sonic space provides only one way in which sonic technologies negotiate private and public space. When in need of some seclusion, Lisette seeks refuge also in her miniscule bathroom in order to listen to music on a transistor radio. However, as the two scenes I will discuss show, the bathroom is not always a safe space: it takes on different characteristics depending on the (aural) context. In the first scene Lisette chooses to lock herself in the bathroom to get away from her kids, and in the second instance Chino bolts the door from the outside. By setting these scenes in the same physical location, the film suggests how spaces shift radically according to their usage. The earlier scene takes place after Lisette visits Chino in prison for the first time. When she leaves Alexis on the street, she is listening to her Walkman, which she removes once she enters the apartment, signaling her move from her "private" sonic space to the public sonic space of the living room that she shares with her three kids and mother-in-law. Her children, especially Little C, befuddled by the absence of their father, repeatedly scream: "Where is my father? Where is my father?" Overpowered by her own helplessness and the children's sonic onslaught, Lisette tries to recreate the effect of her Walkman by locking the bathroom door from the inside and blasting the radio. For Lisette the bathroom functions as an elaborate version of the Walkman effect, sonically shielding her from the outside world, only instead of putting on headphones she closes the door. However, Lisette marks her sonic territory even more explicitly than with a Walkman by not only attacking her mother-in-law and children with music flowing from the radio, but also constructing a forceful physical boundary—the locked bathroom door—

within the confines of her own home. Taken as a whole, this moment provides a much more aggressive construction of sonic space than Lisette's
Walkman use, which encodes her pending separation from her family in
order to recast the boundaries of her domestic and professional roles.

Lisette enters the bathroom; she covers her ears and turns on the radio
to strengthen the sonic boundaries between herself and her family on the
other side of the door. Her kids yell and kick energetically against the
door, so she turns the music up even louder in order to combat the noise
level from without, much in the same way Ellison deployed music as a
defensive buffer against his singing neighbor. Meanwhile, her downstairs
neighbor, angered by Lisette and her kids' noise level, starts knocking on
her ceiling with a broom, as she did in the film's opening scene. Lisette's
first reaction is to keep her hands over her ears and turn the music up
louder, but then she starts singing along with the song on the radio,
Marc Anthony's "Si Tu No Te Fueras" (If You Didn't Go), grabs a broom
and bangs it on the floor to the rhythm of the music. Initially a reaction
to her neighbor's thumping, Lisette stages an elaborate song-and-dance
number, the broom serving as her microphone and dance partner. This
dance oscillates between anger and jubilation: anger because it is directed
against her family and neighbor and jubilation due to Lisette's pleasure
in dancing to a favorite song that transports her into a different sonic
space, although she cannot fully escape the one she already inhabits. As
a result, this performance provides an audiovisual mélange of Lisette's
music and the noise generated by her family and the neighbor, creating
an auditory space that mixes all of them. The camera and the editing of
the film, which cut swiftly between all the participants, amplify this mix;
in addition, all the different sounds and noises grow louder on the film's
soundtrack, creating a sense of visual and sonic confusion. In this case,
the visual bolsters and magnifies the sonic, the camera cuts becoming
more rapid to complement the increased sonic density of the soundtrack.
Furthermore, as the kids outside and the neighbor downstairs become
more insistent, the camera synechdochally focuses on the attributes that
cause the racket. Instead of seeing the neighbor, we are shown her broom
knocking on the ceiling and the bathroom floor shaking, while hands
and feet insistently pound on the bathroom door, representing the children. The noises and their visual representations coexist with the song
on the radio, falling into and accentuating its rhythm, until Lisette turns
the volume so high that the external noise vanishes both sonically — now

we only hear Marc Anthony on the radio and Lisette singing along—and visually—no more children and neighbor, only Lisette blissfully dancing with her broom.

This moment dissolves any steadfast distinction between diegetic and nondiegetic sound: the sounds contained in the narrative and the ones outside the narrative of the film merge. The radio Lisette uses in the narrative generates music and the encroaching noise comes from the children and the neighbor. However, in this pivotal moment—when the outside noise is silenced by the song on the radio—the sounds emanating from the minuscule transistor radio become so loud as to suggest that they supersede the narrative but are still contained within it, since they are visually tied to the image of the radio. Lisette's autonomy as projected by the film, aurally and visually, is very brief. Altogether, Lisette's bathroom provides her with a space that works similar to the way in which salsa (as described by Herencia) functions in general. Herencia locates "the ear as the point of access to the commodity of salsa; the primary function: to break through the boundaries of the enclosure and declare an auditory 'free territory in the Americas' " (218). For Lisette this temporary free territory among the vast amount of dissonance around her is constituted as much by her position as a woman as it is a signification of her Afro-Latin heritage. Occurring during the first fifteen minutes of the film, this scene metaphorically foreshadows Lisette's striving not only to recast her bathroom, but her life as a whole, into "an auditory free territory."

Lisette's bathroom is adorned with posters of Celia Cruz and La India —two of the most prominent salsa performers, who have most consistently criticized traditional gender codes and patriarchy in their lyrics and performances—which transforms the room into a feminist Latina space. But in order to better understand the positions of Cruz and La India and how Lisette relates to them, we should briefly survey salsa and its history. Frances Aparicio delineates the genre's historical formation in the following manner:

As a specific historical-cultural expression, salsa was first produced during the 1960's in the Latina/o (mostly Puerto Rican) barrios of New York City. Puerto Rican working-class musicians had been avid listeners and students of the Latin popular music mostly performed by Cuban and Puerto Rican musicians during the 1950's. . . . While Latin music in New York had been heavily Cuban, after 1959, with the success of the Cuban revolution and with Fidel Castro's taking of Havana, Latin music in New York "would never be the same." The embargo on Cuba and the censorship of Cuban music in the United States led to some years of void and confusion among Latin musicians in New York, creating the need to mix musical forms. It is this syncretic tendency in Latin popular music that characterizes salsa's historical genesis. (*Listening to Salsa*, 79)

Salsa, far from being a "pure" musical genre, denotes a syncretic field that encompasses various Caribbean and Latin American musical forms refracted through the urban centers of the United States, particularly New York. Furthermore, the majority of previous musical practices that salsa draws upon already comprise an amalgamation of African rhythms, European harmonics, and Amerindian musical features; salsa also contains traces of African American soul, funk, and jazz genres.[42] It is no surprise, then, that this formation should come to full fruition in New York City and be articulated as its own musical formation where all these aspects collide both geographically and culturally.

Structurally, Salsa integrates one of the main components of most Afro-diasporic musics, call and response—which signifies the cultural and geographic convections of this genre, put in motion by various forms of migration within the African diaspora in the Western hemisphere, diasporas of a second order, if you will, and occasioned sonic dialogues for these different musical spheres to form the genre now known as salsa.[43] Instead of presenting us with a pristine and authentic preindustrial musical form, salsa blends various colonial and musical histories of Latin America and the Caribbean and their transformations within the urban centers of the United States. Mayra Febres stresses this point: "In this sense, it is more fitting that salsa be considered a 'translocal' phenomenon rather than a multinational one, as it cuts across national boundaries to create a community of urban locations linked by transportation, communication technologies, and the international market economy."[44] Salsa, then, supplies a "translocal" form of call and response enacted through musical forces, but the genre does not have the same meaning everywhere. In Puerto Rico, Aparicio tells us, it is considered a working-class form of music against which the middle class defines itself; conversely, in the States it functions "as a cohesive force among Latinos in general, syncretizing, in fact, an array of Latin American musical styles into its repertoire" (66). Thus Lisette's use of salsa, not only in her bathroom but also throughout the film, draws on the genre's characterization as "a cohesive force among Latinos" in the United States. By utilizing this genre of music, Lisette enacts and performs her identity as a Latina in the urban space of New York City, but as a working-class black Latina she also identifies with the raced and classed aspects of the genre. In her professional life as well as in her listening practices, Lisette actively intervenes in the gender politics of salsa, as, for example, when she speaks against using bikini-clad women in the Mendez Brothers video.

The posters of La India and Celia Cruz on her bathroom wall symbolically refer to Lisette's own position as a Latina attempting to reshape the gender politics of salsa.[45] The majority of lyrics by male salsa singers, according to Aparicio, depict women, black women in particular, in "the dualistic construct of the promiscuous, sexually superendowed black woman, or mulatta, on the one hand, and the pure, sexually unattainable virgin/mother figure, on the other" (155). While these lyrics are not necessarily representative of all salsa, they do form a major current therein, as many scholars of the genre are quick to emphasize; Jorge Duany, for instance, notes that salsa is "clearly a male's vision of the world . . . conceived and written by a man, and executed mostly by men."[46] Lisette struggles to locate herself within this scenario, attempting to negotiate between being a mother and a woman with sexual agency and bridging the putative gulf between the two. As the film demonstrates, Lisette grapples with understanding her sexuality and identity in her own terms and not only in those provided by her family and neighbors. In this way, Lisette's endeavors to carve for herself a position similar to the ones Celia Cruz and La India occupy within the male-dominated salsa industry: as women who engage with the genre even while they reformulate it to better fit their needs.

In the second bathroom scene, the room takes on a very different function from the one discussed above. Here, Chino picks up Lisette, throws her over his shoulder, and literally dumps her in the room, closes the door, and holds it shut from the outside. What ensues is a conversation about the "reasons" for Chino's infidelity. Unlike the first bathroom scene, which construed this space as a "free territory," here the room transacts literally and figuratively Lisette's enclosure and confinement. As this episode occurs in the same physical space—the bathroom—the two scenes point to how space per se is constantly recreated. Chino not only imprisons Lisette, but also tries to box her into the category of a "non-sexual person" by attempting to blame his affair on her supposed sexual shortcomings. Lisette, however, vehemently resists this confinement on both counts, first by fleeing her captivity with the help of a plunger, and second by pointing out Chino's own sexual limitations as well as her financial superiority, illustrating again the many ways in which sexual and monetary freedom are interconnected in *I Like It*'s narrative. Just like Celia Cruz and La India, Lisette attempts to redress the gap between the models of female sexual personhood, a career woman and a mother, instead inhabiting a space where she can be a sexual person and all these other things as well. The two scenes draw attention, in more ways than one, to Lisette's dialectical struggle for autonomy by staging the bathroom both as a sphere of freedom and enclosure.

If we return, for a moment, to the first scene, we can discern more clearly Lisette's attempt and success at negotiating and recreating the sexual, familial, and financial aspects of her life. The posters of the two performers stand in for the struggle over sexual and financial liberty of Latinas within a male-dominated recording industry; the Marc Anthony song, representing the male version of salsa, plays on the radio while Lisette lip-synchs and dances. Thus the visual and the sonic levels of action are contrapuntally superimposed upon each other. Yet this should not be construed as a simple dichotomy: male versus female salsa performers; instead, Lisette actively participates in salsa's ongoing gender dialogue as a form of "productive pleasure," as Aparicio notes (197–198). This is precisely what Lisette achieves in this scene and within the purview of the film as a whole. In the first bathroom scene, she visually and aurally augments Marc Anthony's male voice as it is articulated through this musical genre, providing a different constellation of the call-and-response structure of salsa. While she listens to his song "Si Tu No Te Fueras," Lisette also sings along with the lyrics thereby reshaping his male discourse into a bigendered one. In other words, Lisette does not so much replace Anthony's voice and lyrics on the soundtrack as she sings a duet with him, which converts the Linares' bathroom into a virtual space where the two voices—the recorded voice of Anthony and Lisette's extemporaneous "live" one—meet in a moment of productive pleasure.[47] The various levels of technological mediation should not go unnoticed here, since the song is being transmitted on the radio in its recorded form. Thus we have a recording, which is in and of itself the product of a complex technological process, coming through a radio and being accompanied by a "present" voice; still, this voice is only audible on the recorded soundtrack of the film, and it is only on the filmic level that Lisette's voice can be apprehended as live and present—that is, the film represents her voice as there, but it only reaches the viewers via recording and reproduction technologies, such as film sound and cinema speakers. Therefore the film offers a virtual space of the second order through the various technological mediations that make these transformations possible. These mediations enable Lisette's bathroom to metamorphose into a virtual sounding space wherein she can engage with, contest, and reshape the dominant meaning of salsa music, thus crafting her very own "auditory free territory in the Americas." Yet this "auditory free territory" remains contingent and context-bound, as we have seen in the shifting meanings of the two configurations of the bathroom and Lisette's relationship with her family, which does not move smoothly from complete immersion and dependence to absolute freedom but rather suggests a continual process.

Lisette's use of and engagement with the genre of salsa highlights a number of interlocking aspects of her subjectivity. Salsa—an amalgam of African, Native American, and European musical characteristics that only came together as a coherent genre in New York City—allows Lisette to imagine her ethnic identity, that of a Latina of mixed racial heritage, as marked by a number of different geographical and cultural locations. The music's capacity to incorporate these fluidities facilitates Lisette's multiple identifications: she embodies and is embodied by the genre of salsa as a Latina New Yorker. Nevertheless, the largely masculinist gender politics of the genre prevent any sort of easy identification: Lisette has to laboriously carve a space for herself in which she neither wholeheartedly dismisses salsa nor uncritically embraces the masculinist ethos of the music. Lisette's interaction with salsa echoes her quest to negotiate between her role in her family and her occupation in the music industry. Here, too, she achieves a balance, albeit an unwieldy and over-determined one, that resists subsuming either role in favor of the other. That the film manages to depict the conflicts of a working-class woman of color with this amount of complexity is remarkable, especially considering its place within mainstream Hollywood narrative cinema that routinely favors easy solutions and moral certainties. Furthermore, *I Like It* makes extensive use of sonic technologies to transact Lisette's exploration of personal and professional autonomy, foreshadowing Lisette's changing role vis-à-vis her family and workplace. Consequently, her pursuit of a private sonic space mutates into her new professional position, the workplace acting as an extension of the sonic space she creates in her home. In this way, *I Like It* renders analogous Lisette's struggle to become, first, an authority figure in the domestic sphere, second, a "sexual person" in her marriage, and third, a Latina to be taken seriously within the music industry. She moves from attempting to control her modes of sonic consumption — Walkman and transistor radio in the bathroom — to becoming a key player in the production process. The protagonist's consumption of Latin music grants her entry to the music industry, thereby establishing a place that ensures her voice will be heard in regard to what is transmitted through the sonic technologies she uses in her everyday life. In essence, Lisette fuses her old habits of consumption with her new position as a part of the production apparatus, creating a cluster that excavates the productivity of consumption, and vice versa.

Ellison, too, transforms consumption into production by creatively wielding his sonic apparatus to engage in a friendly "war of decibels" with his neighbor. Yet, these two cultural artifacts present us with rather different accounts of the sonic spatialities of the modern, even while both accent increased noise levels and show how sonic technologies magnify and counteract them within the urban terrain. In Ellison's context, sonic technologies are still somewhat of an anomaly and he relishes their "newness." *I Like It Like That*, in contrast, underlines the manifold ways in which these devices have become an integral part of the modern landscape. Ellison's "Living with Music" reveals that sonic technologies provide one of the central ways for subjects to negotiate shifting sonic public/private perimeters in cities, showing that proliferating noises can be kept at bay by establishing one's own sonic perimeters, all the while contributing to the very burgeoning of these sounds. These sound (re)production apparatuses provide the means to manage increasingly indistinct and overlapping sonic territories. *I Like It* goes one step further by portraying not only a woman's engagement with modern informational technologies (a rarity indeed) but also the explosive negotiation of privacy in public. Much more than *Invisible Man* and "Living with Music," *I Like It* focuses on the use of sound technologies against those closest to the listening subject, most likely the result of Lisette's gender, which does not grant her any privacy while it paradoxically confines her, both in material and discursive terms, to the domestic sphere. Lisette's ability to cohabit the apartment with her family and still have a semidistinct private sonic space translates, over the course of the film, to her ascent in the music industry and crucially depends on her utilization of the radio and Walkman. Using these technologies she can dwell in a number of different spaces simultaneously: her apartment, her neighborhood, her workplace, New York City, Latin America, and the Caribbean.

Sound technologies not only shape and reshape the temporality of modernity, they also significantly recast its spatiality. The city as the sine qua non of modern spatiality illustrates the varied ways in which these machines and their usage re/configure this sphere, adding an aural dimension to the generally visual considerations of modern geographical constellations. Both *I Like It like That* and "Living with Music" amplify the technological aurality of the modern urban terrain by dislodging the putative private/public bifurcation. Making music a clear marker that sets apart private spaces, whether this means singing neighbors or screaming kids, Ellison and Lisette utilize technologized music in this way. As both these works show, the manner in which subjects strategically employ recorded music to shape and reshape the private and public spaces they inhabit is germane to conjecturing how sound works in the field of the social. Accordingly, these texts draw our attention to the interface of sound, space, and subjectivity as they are mediated and created by modern sonic technologies, underlining how sound affects subjects in space and how subjects use sound to construct space in relation to the technological embodiment of these practices. Sonic technologies — with their attendant use and the sounds they transmit — allow for overlapping singular spatialities that are neither wholly random nor neatly discrete, instead coming together at certain points and falling apart at others; they enable us to apprehend these spatialities as intersecting without "losing sound" of their relationality. Or, to paraphrase Michel de Certeau, recorded music makes space, like a rented apartment, habitable. It transforms another listener's music into a space borrowed by a transient. Renters make comparable changes in an apartment that they furnish with sounds and memories, as do listeners of recorded music, into which they insert their own desires and their own listening practices.[48]

5

Sounding Diasporic Citizenship

The previous four chapters interrogated the crucial difference that sound recording and reproduction have made in
twentieth-century black culture and vice versa, focusing on
cultural utterances that explicitly address these questions in their content
and/or structure. This final chapter, in some ways, takes the importance
of sonic technologies for granted, instead centering on the fragmented
and at times contentious communities enabled by the global circulation
of African American popular music—which is to say, this chapter concerns itself not so much with the recording and/or reproduction apparatus per se as with the effects of these technologies' extensive infiltra-
tion of modern life worlds. Today, one would be hard pressed to find
any location around the globe where sonic technologies are not a forceful presence, and, given this widespread presence, these technologies do
not engender the same sorts of anxieties as they once did. Moreover, as
a result of the increased globalization of the recording industry, African
American music enjoys an unprecedented international popularity and
constitutes a movement that has spawned a plethora of related cultural
practices. Popular music, generally in the form of recordings, has and
still continues to function as one of the main channels of communication between the different geographical and cultural points in the African
diaspora, allowing artists to articulate and perform their diasporic citizenship to international audiences and establish conversations with other
diasporic communities.[1]

Surely, hip-hop represents an increasingly global cultural phenomenon, not only being consumed by various international audiences, but
also, and perhaps more important, functioning as a foil for a host of
identifications and cultural practices. As a direct outcome of its growing sonic and visual presence hip-hop has come to define what it means
to be black and "modern" within a global context and particularly in
youth cultures. Because of hip-hop's preeminence, Afro-diasporic youth
populations habitually identify with or define themselves against hip-
hop culture, creating identities suspended between the local and global.[2]
This chapter turns to that global context and scrutinizes the complexities set in motion by the presence of non-U.S. voices in hip-hop. While
international contributions may not have the same ramifications in the
States as they do abroad, black popular music, and hip-hop in particular,
serves as a global forum through which different black diasporic subjects
negotiate shifting meanings of blackness, as well as other forms of social
and political identification.[3] This negotiation, far from being uncomplicated or uncritical, entails facing the prominence of African American
cultural practices such as hip-hop within the continuum of the African
diaspora. The Haitian American rap group the Fugees, the black British
artist Tricky with his partner Martina Topley-Bird, and the Afro- and
Italian-German rap collective Advanced Chemistry all engage with hip-
hop, transmitting global messages in their music, lyrics, videos, record
covers, and promotional photographs that thematize the tricky singularities of Afro-diasporic identification. To this end, I will analyze the work
of these performers in order to conjecture a distinct manifestation of the
vicissitudes of Afro-diasporic subjectivity provoked by the becoming-
global of hip-hop.

Questions of citizenship have gained critical momentousness in recent
years as various forms of migration and immigration have brought with
them increasingly restrictive immigration laws, particularly in the Western world. These global developments necessitate concepts of citizenship
that allow for multiple spheres of belonging, rather than merely designating the parameters—both material and discursive—of a particular political community, although clearly we should not neglect the still very
much alive strictures of national attachment. Instead of simply insisting
on how the nation-state has been superseded by supranational entities,
or conversely, how the nation-state remains central to current constellations, we might do well to ascertain the ways in which transnational

movements work through the conduit of the nation-state and vice versa. While not concerned with citizenship directly, Giorgio Agamben's meditation on the volatile nature of modern sovereignty proves instructive in this context: *"The exception is what cannot be included in the whole of which it is a member and cannot be a member of the whole in which it is always already included.* What emerges in this limit figure is the radical crisis of every possibility of clearly distinguishing between membership and inclusion, between what is outside and what is inside, between exception and rule."[4] In Agamben's formulation, the exception and the rule always already contain one another, rather than serving as warring opponents in the fraught arena of modern political membership. This chapter concentrates on those citizens at the borders of the nation-state; those citizens, who, although abjected from the center, refuse to vanish, and in the process recast the very borders, imaginary and real, to which they are relegated. In this way, the forms of nonhegemonic citizenship discussed below are vital to current modalities of political association because they blur the edifice between inside and outside and show that, more often than not, the exception is, indeed, the rule.

The projects of the three groups in question insist on coarticulating the national and transnational instead of playing a zero-sum game with political identification; this fusion might be most accurately described as "diasporic citizenship," even if at first glance the two terms "diasporic" and "citizenship" seem almost antithetical.[5] Still, both "diaspora" and "citizenship" revolve around the problematic of belonging: where do subjects locate their political and cultural affiliations and how are these circumscribed by various political, economic, and cultural constraints?[6] The main difference lies in diaspora's emphasis on cultural belonging, where citizenship posits political and national affiliation as the sine qua non of membership. While citizenship, albeit in its most narrow definition, denotes a subject's affiliation with one bordered political community, diaspora always already implies belonging to at least two populations — the diasporic and the "home" communities — or what Paul Gilroy, in *The Black Atlantic*, refers to as "the inner dialectics of diaspora identification" (23).[7] This constellation is rendered even more overdetermined when we realize that Afro-diasporic identity, according to Ralph Ellison, is also a social formation of "passions."[8] Ellison argues that race, at least a strict biological version thereof, should not be construed as the primary logos or telos that connects the various cultures of the African diaspora because of the long histories of displacement encountered by peoples of African descent, for "it is not culture which binds the people who are of partially African origin now scattered throughout the world, but an identity of passions. We share a hatred for the alienation forced upon us by Europeans during the process of colonization and empire and we are bound by common suffering more than by our pigmentation" (263). In other words, often Afro-diasporic formations are communities in which subjects of African descent lean toward particular identifications in light of their shared histories of racism and colonialism. This also means that this distinctive version of diaspora is not predicated upon a return, even an imaginary one, to the "homeland."[9] Nonetheless, nowadays, over forty years after Ellison first wrote those lines, Afro-diasporic identity relies not only on political but on cultural channels of membership, because of the increased accessibility of African American cultural productions within the global marketplace. Hip-hop provides one of the most obvious examples of the tendential shift from the political to the cultural as it offers Afro-diasporic subjects an omnipresent cultural form through which to identify as black without having to fall back on strictly racialized ways of belonging, at least exclusively. In this sense, these Afro-diasporic "identities of passion" suggest prime examples of "coming communities" in Agamben's sense, rather than the identitarian machinations they are habitually perceived as: "Decisive here is the idea of an *inessential* commonality, a solidarity that in no way concerns an essence. Taking-place, the communication of singularities in the attribute of extension, does not unite them in essence, but scatters them in existence."[10] Hip-hop's centrality results from both the restructuring of the entertainment industry as global media conglomerates (such as Sony or BMG) and the genre's overall emphasis on a combative, and usually masculine, form of U.S. blackness. While race clearly forms an integral part of this diasporic identification, it eschews race as "pure" consanguinity, replacing it, at least partially, with race as cultural affiliation.

The question of diasporic citizenship, therefore, occupies the interstices of the nation-state and other forms of politicized community, for being a diasporic citizen entails culturally and politically aligning oneself with communities beyond the borders of the nation-state in which one dwells, in addition to negotiating legal and cultural positionalities in relation to this very nation-state. The metastasis in global formations of national affiliation has prompted sociologist Yasemin Soysal to suggest a "postnational" conception of citizenship that reimagines political membership as a mélange of the national and global. Soysal chides social scientists for their singular concentration on the national, arguing that "by omitting the global element and focusing on the nation-state as the unit of analysis, much of political sociology axiomatically privileges the nationally bounded model of citizenship and bypasses the reconfiguration of contemporary membership."[11] Still, contemporary considerations of transnationalism often pay scant attention to questions of citizenship, which misconstrues the situation, since "the transnational has not so much displaced the national, as resituated it and thus reworked its meanings."[12] Hence, any consideration of "postnational" membership should not exclude the national; rather, the national and the transnational should be understood as quasidialectical partners in the movement of globalization. Diasporic citizenship falls under the purview of Bruce Robbins and Pheng Cheah's term "cosmopolitical," which Robbins warns us not to think of "as universal reason in disguise." Instead he defines "cosmopolitical" "as a series of scales, as an area both within and beyond the nation (and yet falling short of 'humanity') that is inhabited by a variety of cosmopolitanisms."[13] While I subscribe to Robbins's differentiation of scales, which takes into consideration the nation but also looks beyond its immediate orbit, I would hesitate to locate a physical "area" in which these politics are practiced, especially since most "areas" in the world are occupied by nation-states. Additionally, cosmopolitical arrangements such as diasporic citizenship do not always have "real spaces" in which they can peacefully coexist with the ideological, administrative, and coercive practices of the nation-state.

Since these "real spaces" frequently do not occupy a specified place and must remain "coming in passion," the three groups (Advanced Chemistry, Tricky, and the Fugees) discussed in this chapter attempt to create a locale, even if only an imaginary one, in which the nation, as well as other political and cultural affiliations, can be articulated not as mutual exclusives, but as part of the same, even if at times aporetic, continuum. The musical projects of Advanced Chemistry, Tricky, and the Fugees utilize popular music to envision identifications and subjectivities that threaten the frequently very limited notions of political and cultural belonging within the realm of "real politics." The phrase "diasporic citizenship" excavates and magnifies this tension between the national and transnational, rather than subsuming one under the other. As opposed to a term like "hybridity," "diasporic citizenship" refuses to sublate the fraught and violent traffic between national and global assemblages; instead it raucously brings to the fore the tensions that require complex ways of mediating between contradictory forces as they are scripted and sounded through the bodies and psyches of Afro-diasporic subjects. For the purposes of my argument, the global circulation of hip-hop enacts this antinomy between diaspora and citizenship, not only because of its prominence, but also, and more significantly, due to its combative dimensions, which facilitate the confrontational articulation of these conflicts: "coming communities of passion."

"I Refugee from Guantanamo Bay Dance around the Border Like I'm Cassius Clay" When the Fugees appeared on the U.S. hip-hop scene in 1994 with their album *Blunted on Reality*, their success seemed highly unlikely.[14] The rap world, at the time dominated by the gangsta genre, did not seem ready for a crew of two male Haitians (Wyclef Jean and Prakazrel Michel) and an African American woman (Lauryn Hill), who dealt in consciousness rather than semiautomatic weapons and were generally the antithesis of the masculine outlaw that ran amok on various hip-hop records and in the accompanying music videos. The group's lyrics spoke of religion, slavery, immigration politics, the trappings of fame, and the joys of drug abstinence (hence the title of their debut album).[15] Also, the presence of a woman in the largely homosocial world of hip-hop (to this day the Fugees remain one of the few rap groups to feature a female performer) ensured "a female perspective," which although not at the center of the project, nonetheless dislodged the male centeredness not only of hip-hop but of most other popular music genres (with the exception of R&B and pop). Furthermore, the music contained on the album included hardcore hip-hop tracks; half-sung, half-rapped cuts; and the first hip-hop track that utilized an acoustic guitar as its main instrument. This musical experimentation further amplified the group's position on the margins of hip-hop culture.

After scoring a minor radio hit with a catchy remix of "Nappy Heads," the Fugees toured extensively. However, it was not until the release of their second album, *The Score* (1996), which remains one of the best-selling hip-hop albums of all time with worldwide sales in excess of eighteen million units, that the group skyrocketed to international stardom. Despite their success, the Fugees never lost their street credibility, so central to remaining "authentic" within the context of hip-hop culture. While criticisms of "selling out" were directed at the group, especially for their ubiquitous cover version of Roberta Flack's seventies hit "Killing Me Softly," their music was still aired on urban radio and written about in the hip-hop press.[16] This can be partially attributed to the group's shrewd use of remixes; for instance, when "Killing Me Softly" ruled all radio stations in the summer of 1996, they released a hardcore ragamuffin version of the track that circulated in clubs, which had little in common with the AOR (adult-oriented rock) compatibility of the original version.[17] In numerous interviews the group also proclaimed that the hip-hop community (read: young urban black and Latino audiences) were the listeners that were most important to them.[18] It is crucial for the argument that follows to keep in mind that the Fugees transmit their messages to a large transnational audience while maintaining their hip-hop integrity, which guarantees that their messages, musical and lyrical, are taken seriously, retaining a viable politicocultural currency even though thoroughly ensconced within the global music industry. While the success story of the Fugees, their subsequent demise, as well as their public bickering and innuendo provide a compelling narrative in and of itself, I want to focus on how the group has used their global renown to bring to the fore questions of citizenship, particularly the plight of refugees and diasporic identification in ways much more explicit than any other U.S.-based hip-hop act.[19]

Instead of erasing their "roots" in favor of a generic black or African American identity, a common practice for hip-hop artists, the Haitian background of two of its members, Wyclef Jean and Prakazrel Michel (Pras), was a focal point in the lyrics. Some of the best known rappers are of Caribbean heritage but do not present themselves as such: Notorious B.I.G., Busta Rhymes, and Doug E. Fresh are all of Jamaican descent, and Slick Rick, for instance, is British by way of Jamaica. The most extreme example of this tendency is AZ, a Dominican-born rapper, who makes derogatory references to the Spanish language in his lyrics. Other artists, such as Heavy D. (of Jamaican descent), separate their Caribbean and "black" hip-hop identity by recording reggae for the Jamaican market and rap for the American.[20] While the Fugees' insistence on the ethnic identity of the two Haitian members serves as the exception in hip-hop, it does not deviate from the practices of Haitians living in the northeast of the United States. According to Flore Zephir, who undertook extensive ethnographic research among this population, "Ethnic identity . . . was used by [Haitian immigrants] as a means to combat what they perceive to be a nefarious system of racial classification [in the U.S.], which places them at the bottom rungs of the social ladder. . . . [C]hoosing to remain ethnic and not to assimilate into a generic Black American population was a conscious decision on their part, and a situational response to the inferior status associated with Blackness in America."[21] In this spirit, the group deploys its name, lyrics, videos, and record sleeves to reconceptualize the role of refugees vis-à-vis modern nation-states in the global era. As opposed to portraying refugees as victims of or threats to national welfare, as is so often the case, the Fugees imagine refugees as heroic citizens who battle injustices from the borders of the nation-state, and in this way, the porous liminality of refugees emerges as a usable space from which to critique both internal and external repressive practices of modern political sovereignty.

Contemporary international refugee policy largely results from the atrocities committed by states against their own citizens during World War II, hence states could no longer be the lone agents trusted to ensure the physical safety of their citizens.[22] The present-day legal definition of "refugee" was devised during the 1951 United Nations Convention relating to the status of refugees; it defines "refugee" as a person who, "owing to a well-founded fear of being persecuted for reasons of race, religion, nationality, membership of a particular social group or political opinion, is outside of the country of his nationality and is unable or, owing to such fear, is unwilling to avail himself of the protection of that country; or, who, not having a nationality and being outside the country of his former habitual residence . . . is unable or, owing to such fear, is unwilling to return to it."[23] According to Jacqueline Bhabha, there are two major impediments to the implementation of the refugee declaration: first, states participate in the practice of the laws on a voluntary basis, which means that no country is legally required to implement them; and second, no international agency administers to what extent the law is executed by individual states, granting states the juridical and administrative power to determine when a person qualifies as a refugee within these particular precincts (6). Furthermore, the question of persecution is not adequately defined, resulting in ideologically inflected practices concerning the law's practical application. For example, Haitian refugees have habitually been refused refugee status by U.S. immigration agencies because they were deemed "economic migrants" as opposed to a politically persecuted group, while Cubans were accorded refugee status almost automatically as a result of their escape from "the clutches of communism." In essence, the lack of binding refugee laws renders this status the most fragile among the possibilities of political membership because of the at times capricious procedures against these subjects. Although not literally refugees themselves, the Fugees cast themselves in this role in order to signify the tenuousness of all forms of national membership, highlighting the way in which the refugee functions as the citizen's shadowy double, continually haunting the very foundations of the modern nation-state.

Not only do the representations of the Fugees recast the discursive configuration of refugees, but they also add the refugee to the archive of American national images. While immigrants, at least those deemed legal and productive, have attained a semisecure position in the U.S. national imaginary, refugees and illegal immigrants serve as constant scapegoats for a host of social ills.[24] Also, as Jacqueline Bhabha asserts, "the refugee par excellence was someone heroically seeking to assert his (typically male) individuality against an oppressive [communist] state" (8). This situation holds particularly true in the case of the United States, where the ideal refugee is one fleeing from a repressive "communist" state to the "land of the free." Other refugees, like Haitians, remain outside of this particular narrative, the effects of which are abundantly clear in the case of Haitian migrants. The Fugees dislodge this equation by depicting Haitian refugees, routinely lumped into the rubric of "economic migrants," as a heroic group that combats not only an oppressive state in Haiti and the U.S. support of this regime, but also U.S. immigration policy and everyday racism.

The cover of the first single from *The Score*, "Fu-gee-la," prominently features all three members' passports: Wyclef possesses the only Haitian passport; both Lauryn and Pras appear as American national subjects. Graphically superimposed upon the passport images is the group's logo: a circle that contains their name. Around the circle we see their second name, Refugee Camp (taken on specifically for this album), printed twice. Simulating a fence around a refugee camp, four lines with barbed wires extend outward to the edge of the cover. Initially it seems as if the passports divide the group: two are members of the richest nation in the Western hemisphere, and one belongs to the poorest, yet their representation as citizens first and foremost also equalizes them, since they are all subject to the legal and administrative machinations of the nation-state. Thus citizenship is not exhausted by the bestowal of rights on particular subjects, but represents a form of subjection to the laws of the politicoadministrative unit in question. What is more, the rights bequeathed upon the citizen can be taken away at any time; hence the need for an international refugee policy, even if fundamentally flawed. The visual interplay between the passports and the graphic representation of the barbed wire of refugee camps further elucidates this point by positioning citizenship and refugeedom as contiguous rather than mutually exclusive. This antinomy between the citizen and its phantom doppelgänger fuels the Fugees' project by articulating these two forces as part of the same discursive and material cosmos, and not, as occurs all too frequently, understanding them as strictly opposing categories. The Refugee Camp logo holds the image together by virtue of being superimposed and seems to carry a larger significance than the passports, or at least an equivalent one. Taken together, the name Refugee Camp, the logo, and the barbed wire indicate that regardless of national belonging, all three group members are refugees by association and solidarity, which, in turn, calls attention to the interdependence of the citizen and refugee within the ideological and repressive regimes of the nation-state. Consequently, refugee status suggests not only a legal and political condition but also a general modality of subjectivity inherent in the nation form itself.[25] Thus all citizens emerge as possible refugees, although clearly some are more likely to attain this status than others; the Fugees unearth this potential by staging themselves as refugees, which enables solidarity with, rather than abjection of, these political subjects, Haitian ones in particular. As Giorgio Agamben remarks: "If refugees represent such a disquieting element in the order of the modern nation-state, this is above all because by breaking the continuity between man and citizen, nativity and nationality, they put the originary fiction of modern sovereignty in crisis."[26] The Fugees, by dwelling in this abject category, always already buried in the crevices of "the fiction of modern sovereignty," desediment the overdetermined nexus between the people and the nation. Instead, the group zeroes in on the refugee as an integral component of modern political membership, asking the audience to examine the confines of their citizenship and how these are constituted by the abjection of those figures hovering at the borders, both literally and figuratively, of the nation-state.

While references to refugees are scattered all over the Fugees' oeuvre, the most sustained lyrical treatment of this subject can be found in the track "Refugees on the Mic" from their first album *Blunted on Reality*. The song begins with the following skit:

> Pras approaches Kim, starts talking to her and asks for her number.
> Kim's friend: "Hey yo Kim, ain't he Haitian?"
> Kim: "I don't know."
> Both of them: "Eeeeuuuw!!! Muthafucka Haitian!"
> Kim: "I don't think so. You stink, I cannot be talkin to no Haitian."
> Pras: "Hold up, man wait! Why y'all dissin me like that?"
> Kim: "I'm sorry, I just cannot be talkin to no fuckin Haitians."[27]

This scene economically illustrates American anti-Haitian prejudices, especially since it is articulated by an African American woman. The stench ascribed to Haitians in general through the conduit of one particular subject serves as a shorthand for centuries of U.S.-generated mythology about the second republic in the western hemisphere. In this sketch, Haitians appear as common-sensically inscribed abject objects, and whether Pras actually "stinks" is not the issue, for the olfactory component only crops up in the conversation after the two women's inquiry into Pras's national belonging. Therefore Pras's Haitian identity becomes the indicator, if not the reason, for his olfactory abjectness.

In Julia Kristeva's theorization of the abject, this category is not marked by specific characteristics, such as stinking or general filthiness, but by its antagonism to the "I," which bans the abject from its provenances in order to establish itself as an "I." Acknowledging the abjected would amount to nothing less than its own obliteration.[28] In Kristeva's words: "It is thus not lack of cleanliness or health that causes abjection but what disturbs identity, system, order. What does not respect borders, positions, rules. The in-between, the ambiguous, the composite" (4). In other words, the abject poses a threat insofar as it disfigures the presumed stability of the subject, which explains the vociferous reactions it engenders. Pras, cast in the role of the abject, becomes a representative of all Haitians, precisely because he threatens the safety of the two African American women as U.S. citizens. Despite their common racial identity, the two U.S. American women insist on relegating Pras to the realm of the abject by refusing to engage with him because of his Haitian background, which enables them to solidify their status as U.S. national subjects. As black females in the United States, Kim and her unnamed friend are not

exactly safely ensconced within the sphere of symbolic national belonging, since traditionally citizenship entails disembodiment as a precondition for access to the national sphere; the two are markedly made flesh by
virtue of their gender and race.[29] What this diasporic abjection enables,
then, is Kim and her friend's ascendancy to the disembodied realm of
rarified citizenship: by insisting on Pras's corporeality via his bodily odor,
the two women relinquish their own embodiment, constructing "a border" that places Haitians in the category of the abject.[30] This interchange
metonymically transacts both the general abjection of refugees from the
parameters of the modern nation-state and its particular consequences
for Haitian populations in the U.S., as much as it brings to the fore the
mechanics by which this group is continually positioned beyond the borders of the nation-state and the symbolic provenances of citizenship.

The Fugees both address the prejudices against Haitians in the States
and also reclaim the figure of the Haitian refugee not as an instantiation
of the abject but as a point of solidarity. "Refugees on the Mic" continues with the chorus of the track urging the refugees of the world to
unite:

> Yo check it out; I want all the refugees out there to put up your
> muthafuckin hands. You know you're a fucking immigrant, put up
> your hands. I'm-a start off this shit like this time around.
> "H" to the "a" to the "i" to the "t," I live or die nuthin but the darkside.
> Fugees on the mic, yeah, yeah. Yo refugees on the mic, oh yeah,
> oh yeah.

The chorus commences with a call to all refugees, then moves on to immigrants, not clarifying whether "immigrant" functions as a synonym
for "refugee" or as a different status altogether.[31] Afterward, the lyrics
mark the speaker's position as Haitian, ending with a merger of the
Fugees as a musical group and refugees as a political entity: refugees,
immigrants, Haitian refugees, and the Fugees share the same figurative
space. On the one hand, the Fugees cloak themselves in the guise of refu-
gees/immigrants, and on the other hand, they proclaim their solidarity
with this group. While both components are at play in these lyrics, the
latter has to be given greater import, since Wyclef is the only member
of the group who has actually emigrated to the United States; Pras, although Haitian, was born in the United States, and Lauryn is identified

as American. Therefore the chorus of "Refugees on the Mic" provides a rallying cry for solidarity with refugees rather than a mere description of the members' political status vis-à-vis the U.S. government, which, once again, highlights the complex traffic between the refugee and citizen within contemporary politics.

The politicosymbolic nature of the group's use of the refugee status also emerges in Lauryn Hill's verse on this track. As the only U.S. American in the group, Hill strategically wields Haiti's history to rebut the anti-Haitian sentiment in the opening skit. Hill commences by stating that she is a "Fugee on the Mic," then asserts her cultural and gender difference, in the end only to proclaim solidarity with the two Haitian group members: "I'm the girl Yankee rolling with the kids from Haiti." Finally, Hill unequivocally confronts the prejudices against Haitians brought to the fore in the skit: "My Haitian friends, they stink, says my Yankee one, but who was first . . . as soon as it came on—history you hypocrite!" This emphatic proclamation refers to Haiti's history as the first black republic in the Western hemisphere, an aspect usually downplayed by the U.S. narratives in favor of the perpetuation of abject images of Voodoo and AIDS. Hill alludes both to Haiti's history and the country's symbolic function for black struggle in the United States, which, as St. Clair Drake explains, "after 1791 Haiti became the kind of key symbol in the diaspora that Ethiopia was in Africa. . . . Toussaint L'Ouverture became a hero to black people in the United States, which achieved its independence only twenty five years before Haiti." [32] The fact that Hill serves as the historical consciousness underscores that empathy on the part of U.S. national subjects need not be impossible—both Hill and the two women featured in the opening skit are "Yankees"—since Hill is capable of empathizing with her Haitian friends due to her knowledge of Haiti's tumultuous history and its role as mobilizing force within the African diaspora, as opposed to the two "Yankee" women depicted in the skit, who simply redact the abjectness reserved for Haiti in official U.S. narratives. Thus Hill replaces diasporic abjection with diasporic identification.

For the most part, U.S. images of Haiti and Haitians have consisted of gross distortions, habitually featuring cannibalism, voodoo, zombies, or dictatorship. In recent years, Haiti as the source of the AIDS virus and as the producer of numerous "boat people" has been added to the U.S. national repository of images; while there exists no evidence to support the contention that Haiti is the origin of the AIDS virus, rumors still persist.[33] Both Paul Farmer and Robert Lawless have written extensive treatises about the long history of the dismal status Haiti and Haitians have occupied in the American imagination, which has not only spawned a multitude of stereotypes but also shaped American foreign policy toward Haiti since the nation's independence in 1804.[34] Although U.S. forces did not officially invade Haiti until 1915, the U.S. government played a key role in mediating, both politically and economically, Haiti's relation to the rest of the world throughout the nineteenth century; to cite one prominent example: immediately after independence, the U.S. government aided France in "orchestrating a diplomatic quarantine," since the country's status as the first black-governed republic posed a threat to the institution of slavery in the United States.[35] After some time, though, the United States became Haiti's chief economic trade partner, and while it initially had to compete with most western European nations for a share of the Haitian market, toward the end of the nineteenth century, the States had a quasi monopoly on the nation's foreign commerce; Haiti grew to be its most valuable economic ally in Latin and Central America. Generally, the American association with Haiti oscillated between diplomatic negligence, which repeatedly allowed repressive regimes to flourish, and heavy-handed economic interference, both of which ensured continued U.S. economic and political gains. By enabling foreign land ownership, the U.S. occupation of Haiti (1915–1934) significantly restructured the country's economy, securing its continued financial dependence. Although U.S. military occupation ceased in 1934, the U.S. government supported dictators François ("Papa Doc") Duvalier and Jean-Claude ("Baby Doc") Duvalier in a number of different ways.[36] In addition, Haitian labor has become increasingly vital for U.S. industries, since the country's poverty has guaranteed minimal labor costs.[37] While the States remained imbricated in Haitian economy and politics, peaking in the invasion of Haiti in 1994, the treatment of Haitian refugees has been marked by a volatile cocktail of benign neglect and/or aggressive rejection, even while, or perhaps because, Haitian immigration (primarily to Florida and New York) is more often than not a direct result of the covert and overt U.S. presence in Haiti.

There existed a brief period in the early sixties (during Kennedy's presidency) when Haitian refugees were encouraged to immigrate to the States, yet during the mid-sixties the emphasis shifted to "communist"

Cuba and the threat it posed to the United States as the premier "free" nation in the western hemisphere. François Duvalier, Haiti's dictator during this period, cooperated with the United States against Castro, and as a result the United States was able to "overlook" the atrocities committed by the Haitian government against its citizens and focus on using Haiti to strengthen its political position in the Caribbean.[38] This led to a long period in which Haitian migrants were denied political refugee status by the U.S. government and news media. According to Farmer, "The refusal to see Haitian asylum seekers as political refugees has its roots in U.S. foreign policy, which for decades decreed that only 'communist' nations could generate bona fide political refugees. Racism also played a role in the sorry welcome accorded to Haitians."[39] For example, in the years following the military overthrow of Jean Bertrande Aristide in 1991, the U.S. news media depicted the influx of Haitian refugees as mobs arriving on small boats to exploit the American economy—having therefore no valid reason to be "here"—while Cuban refugees appeared as political refugees fleeing from a communist regime. Before this juncture, Haitian refugees had the chance to plead their cases to the U.S. Immigration and Naturalization Services prior to being deported; in 1992, however, George H. W. Bush ordered that all Haitian refugees either be extradited or detained at Guantanamo Bay.[40] This ideological and political warfare against Haitian subjects forms the apex of official U.S. narratives concerning "the poorest nation in the western hemisphere."[41] Since Haiti's independence, U.S. government policy, with minor exceptions, has always intervened in the country's economy and politics, while simultaneously dismissing Haitian refugees in the United States on the basis of their alleged status as economic, and not political, migrants. In this case, according to Guy Goodwin-Gill, U.S. policy mirrors international practices; he states that " 'economic refugees'—the term generally disfavored—are not included [in international refugee law]. The solution to their problem, perhaps, lies more within the province of international aid and development."[42] Nonetheless, the construction of "fugitives from communism" as the sine qua non for all refugees comprises a uniquely American policy. As Jacqueline Bhabha explains, "This policy of privileging refugees from Communism is most clearly evinced in U.S. refugee policy and practice of [the cold war] but the effect of foreign policy on refugee admissions is evident in other jurisdictions too."[43] Furthermore, the a priori political persecution ascribed to Cuban refugees exposes the crassly ideological dimension of the treatment of Haitian refugees that is thinly veiled as juridical policy.

In "Refugees on the Mic" Pras's verse explores the U.S. government's positioning of the Haitian refugee as a persona non grata. Whereas, in the parts of the track discussed earlier, the Fugees present quotidian manifestations of these sentiments in the form of olfactory abjectness, this verse depicts a general anti-Haitian continuum in which everyday stereotypes go hand in hand with U.S. immigration policy: "Man, I went to court the other day to plead my innocence, they brought me in on charges of illegal residence: an alien in a foreign land, Uncle Sam wants me to go back to my land. . . . Gorillas [Guerrillas] in the mist where everything and the like becomes a risk. They put up they guard, they put up they fists, now I'm number one on they Muthafuckin hit-list." Here, Pras underscores the unstable nature of refugee existence (Haitians in particular) as a result of the perpetual peril of extradition, given that the U.S. state apparatus holds the right to classify refugees as legal or illegal residents and treat them accordingly. Consequently, the everyday hostility Haitians encounter in the United States is magnified by their shaky legal status and vice versa. If U.S. government tactics toward Haiti have largely been driven by stereotypes, then their rearticulation within the quotidian carries a different weight, enforcing governmental policy by barring Haitian subjects from the sphere of citizenship, which provides a different form of "public policy," one that locates Haitians outside the borders of the United States not by force but via commonsensical ideology. And while these lyrics are not as explicit as some of the other material in the track, viewed within a larger frame, the state and nonstate modes of discrimination presented here continually boost each other. Moreover, the use of "Go(uer)rillas in the Mist" conjures both types of "public policy" by referencing the film *Gorillas in the Mist*, starring Sigourney Weaver as Diane Fossey, a scientist on a mission to save mountain gorillas in Rwanda, and the 1992 rap album by the Lench Mob, *Guerrillas in the Mist*. According to Pras, both the U.S. government and the general public construe Haitian refugees as primates that threaten the status quo of the U.S. nation-state; consequently, deportation threatens. "Mist" alludes to the hegemonic images of Haiti as a wasteland, as well as to the ramifications of this ideological constellation for Haitians in the States. In this way, "mist" bears witness to life in the States for Haitians, who are forced to rework themselves from "gorillas" to "guerrillas" to combat the haze of government policies and stereotypes on a number of different fronts. Ergo the Fugees' music, videos, and record covers function as guerrilla practices in the mist of U.S. public culture; they call attention to the plight of refugees and the brittle character of modern citizenship, stressing, in the process, the plethora of political and economic links between the United States and Haiti in the western hemisphere.

Visible ReFugees Refugees also form the central motif in two of the music videos produced for songs from *The Score*. Both videos are mini-narrative films set to a Fugee soundtrack. *Fu-gee-la*, which I want to concentrate on here, opens with written credits—not usual in short form music videos—that convey the cinematic and/or televisual ambition of the video.[44] In large print we see "The Fugees Present The Score." Then the three group members are introduced through still shots taken from the narrative to follow and accompanied by written credits at the bottom of the screen. While this sequence resembles the generic conventions of a television show (the major characters are depicted frozen in action and not as part of a narrative), the video's plot as a whole aspires to be a miniaturized action film. The main generic divergence between an action film and this video are the interspersed performance sequences in which the group lip-synchs. The narrative, set on an unnamed Caribbean island, commences with a scene featuring a white and somewhat suspicious-looking man passing a metal briefcase under the table to a black man in military clothing at an outdoor café. Lauryn watches them from an adjacent table while she communicates with Pras and Wyclef via a microphone and earpiece wired to her body. Subsequently, Pras and Wyclef interrupt the covert exchange to steal the case and escape on their motorcycle. The two shadowy men then turn to Lauryn, seemingly accusing her of being an accomplice to the hijacking of the money. Lauryn immediately overturns her table, thrusting it in their direction, which allows her to flee the scene and join Wyclef on his motorcycle. With a group of soldiers on their trail, the Fugees, joined by others, resume their flight in a pickup truck, crashing through the barriers of a military checkpoint. After their driver has been shot by the military, the group completes their journey on foot. The final showdown comes when they reach the ocean just in time to see the small motorboat intended for their escape leaving the pier without them. In order to create a diversion, Lauryn opens the valuable metal case and throws the money it contains at the military pursuers; sufficiently distracted, the soldiers flock to the money, permitting the Fugees to reach the end of the pier. Switching from clear, standard 16 mm quality film to what seems like an old 8 mm projection, the final shots represent the group running toward their boat and jumping off the end of the pier. However, it is not quite clear whether they eventually catch up with the boat, since the last frame freezes the three group members floating in mid-air above the water.

We do get a glimpse, however, of the group's success through the performance sequence, which shows the trio singing and dancing in the same locales as the military pursuit shown in the narrative; this is a common feature in most music videos, one that periodically disrupts the plot.[45] Still, the group's refusal to include their victory within the scopic economy of the narrative flow suggests not only a general open-endedness, but more important, it amplifies the unstable position of refugees in relation to the modern nation-state: they are wanted neither in their home countries nor in the nations to which they flee. While displaying the group triumphantly joining the other "boat people" to sail away in search of a better life would have sufficed to draw attention to the political, cultural, and economic hardships faced by refugees, this deferral of visual and narrative closure by literally stopping the action, symbolically dramatizes the precarious state of refugees. Here, we are asked to consider whether the refugees will reach their ultimate destination and to witness the perils of fleeing their home country, which, within this particular configuration, cannot quite be a home. Consequently, *Fu-gee-la* registers the plight of refugees before their entry into the political and cultural economy of the United States (their most likely destination), which belies the figuration of refugees as rootless, featureless hordes that will become stinking "gorillas in the mist" and a supposed menace to the U.S. nation-state. The music video presents a two-front war against refugees, in both their countries of "origin" and those nations they seek refuge in, of which neither offers an even remotely safe haven from various forms of persecution.

As Wyclef explains, *Fu-gee-la* was intended to introduce *The Score* as a sonic feature film that recounts "the story of refugees in every country." The video presents the group members as mavericks who disrupt a corrupt exchange of monetary funds, actively participating in the sabotage of an operation that symbolically invokes—especially considering their ties to Haiti—the covert monetary funds channeled into so-called developing countries by the U.S. government in order to protect its political and economic interests.[46] Furthermore, the performance sequence of *Fu-gee-la* shows the group as "positive" role models—refugees who have overcome the odds placed against them—rather than mere victims of circumstance. Since in the performance they occupy the same spaces as those in which they were pursued by the military during the narrative of the video, we see them as heroic subjects who have reclaimed these formerly oppressive settings and now joyously celebrate their victory. Moreover, the lyrics of the song "Fu-gee-la" serve as a theme for the group's project and the video; the chorus sings: "Ooh lalala it's the way the way that we rock when we doin our thing. Ooh lalala it's the natural vibes that the refugees bring." The "ooh lalala's" in the lyrics initially register as still another instance of the general banality of pop lyrics; yet, within the overall architecture of the song and video, what emerges as the operative insight might just be the "banality" of the refugee, by which I mean the many ways in which refugees, in terms of sheer numbers as well as public discourse, have become integral components in the workings of the modern nation-state.

Ready or Not, the fourth video from the Fugees' second album, provides a companion piece to the *Fu-gee-la* video, functioning as the big-budget action film version of the earlier clip. Much like the first foray into the narrativization of the refugee experience, the video features the Fugees hounded by military forces, only this time the low-tech jeeps have been replaced by helicopters, jet-skis, and submarines. *Ready or Not* professes to stage the group's role as guardians of black cultural history and, according to the opening caption, fight intolerance and seek justice for the downtrodden.[47] While this quest carries clearly political undertones in the *Fu-gee-la* video, here it merely serves to highlight the group's shift from outsiders in the sphere of hip-hop to a world-dominating musical force, given that sociality beyond the immediate group vanishes from the representational radar and that the former video, at least symbolically, portrayed the Fugees' connection with other refugees. *Ready or Not*, in stark contrast, shows the Fugees without the cumbersome accoutrement of allies such as "boat people"; instead, this second clip shows them literally isolated, in a submarine—which in some sense serves as an apt allegory of the Fugees' success: they seize the hi-tech military apparatus in the same way they rise in the hierarchy of the global recording industry. The contradictions brought about by the different ways the Fugees present refugees in their oeuvre does not so much negate their general project, as it magnifies the contradictions, ruptures, breaks, and discontinuities involved in the construction of such an endeavor within the global capitalist culture industry. George Lipsitz points out that "for many musicians around the world, the 'popular' has become a dangerous crossroads, an intersection between the undeniable saturation of commercial culture in every area of human endeavor and the emergence of a new public sphere that uses the circuits of commodity production and circulation to envision and activate new social relations."[48] The Fugees are a prime example of this "dangerous crossroads": although thoroughly enmeshed within the music industry, they use their position to call attention to the status of refugees and dislocate the public image of this interstitial population. Nevertheless, as rudimentary as it may sound, we should not expect these "messages" to be either wholly libratory or utterly coopted by the global capitalist machinery; rather, we might do well to seek out their productive tensions, ones that bring to the fore the complexities of negotiating between representational politics and economic gain.

Whereas the U.S. news media customarily construct Haitian refugees as the mobile antithesis of the stationary and upstanding citizen, especially in terms of their supposed drain on the U.S. economy and their general abjectness, the Fugees direct our attention to the perspective of refugees. The *Fu-gee-la* video demonstrates that refugees need not necessarily be impoverished and smelly victims and/or "economic leeches"; instead, it imagines refugees as valiant warriors against corrupt political and military forces. Moreover, the Fugees' insistence on occupying the role of refugees claims this category as a constant mode of identity and identification, unmistakably rupturing hegemonic U.S. narratives of refugees as mere transients while putting under erasure commonsensical conceptualizations of citizenship that configure these subjects as aberrant exceptions to the smooth workings of nation-states. Within the public sphere of many Western nations, refugees appear as the political and economic limit cases that threaten their supposed coherency; the Fugees not only show how refugees are constitutive of this putative discreteness, what Agamben calls "the fiction of modern sovereignty," but also urge citizens to imagine themselves as refugees. "Dancing around the border," they project the refugee as citizen and vice versa, which, although not quite consequential in terms of policy, might just be a starting point in reconstructing the foundational tenets of contemporary political belonging both as a legal category and an ideological suturing point.

"Fremd im eigenen Land"   When Advanced Chemistry's first single "Fremd im eigenen Land" (Stranger in My Own Country) was released in the fall of 1992 against a backdrop of increased violence against people of color in the newly unified Germany, it caused quite an uproar. Until then, most other German hip-hop recordings either consisted of nonsensical party raps (Die fantastischen Vier, for instance), white German rappers attempting to prove how hardcore and ghetto they were (exemplified by the compilation *Krauts with Attitude*—a reference to the seminal L.A. gangsta rappers Niggas with Attitude), or Turkish rappers living in Germany (such as Islamic Force and Kingsize Terror). Advanced Chemistry consisted of two Afro-Germans, Torch and Linguist, and one Italian-German, Toni der Koch.[49] The group not only excelled in German-language freestyle rhyming but also positioned themselves as German citizens of color, something that had not previously occurred in such an explicit manner in German hip-hop. Before this historical juncture there had been articulations of Afro-German identity in German hip-hop, but only in the English language by the group Exponential Enjoyment. Furthermore, while there was a noticeable presence of Afro-Germans on German network television—Karin Boyd, Cherno Jobatey, and soccer players such as Jimi Hartwig—they did not address their audience as subjects of color. Often these public figures choose assimilation, refusing to make race an issue in their work: Jobatey, for example, states, "I do not make a *big deal* about the color of my skin."[50] For others, an option is the wholesale renunciation of German identity, the path followed by most Turkish youth. In contrast, Advanced Chemistry's strategy insists on a dual positioning, as Germans (legally and culturally) and as people of color.

In other words, the group claimed German citizenship without renouncing their racial embodiment, thereby obliterating traditional notions of citizenship, which require the transcendence of particularity as the prerequisite for national membership. Advanced Chemistry's tactics defy narrow notions of citizenship by presenting alternative versions that yield multiple modes of association in addition to pointing out different ways to negotiate between these. Thus Advanced Chemistry imagines a diasporic identity without renouncing full legal and cultural German citizenship. In doing so the group also reveals how whiteness functions as the implicit precondition for inclusion in the national citizenry within the German context.[51] This generally unarticulated normative whiteness, as Uli Linke notes, "permits Germans to exhibit race 'innocently,' without fear or guilt, and without having to publicly or (consciously) acknowledge their participation in a racial mythography, the Aryan aesthetic, which continues to colonize the German national imaginary even after Hitler."[52] By presupposing that being black *and* German need not appear as mutually exclusive, as they so frequently do in the hegemonic German mythography, Advanced Chemistry challenges the normative whiteness at the heart of German national culture. What is more, Advanced Chemistry pioneered an Afro-German cultural renaissance, which is only beginning to gain momentum now, over ten years after the group first made their musical and political interventions. While there has been a steady presence of people of color in German hip-hop since the beginning of the 1990s, most of these performers did not make their hyphenated subjectivities an integral part of their performative identities and texts.[53] Recent years, however, have seen the explosion of Afro-German hip-hop and R&B artists who address their German audiences as Afro-Germans, and Advanced Chemistry is often cited as a crucial influence. The most prominent examples of this trend are two benefit projects, Brother's Keepers and Sister's Keepers, both launched in 2001, commemorating the brutal, racially motivated murder of Alberto Adriano, a Mozambican man who lived in Dessau, as well as protesting neo-Nazi terror against people of color in Germany in general, which brought together a large group of Afro-German recording artists (including Torch).[54] While Advanced Chemistry was fairly isolated in its culturo-historical context, the group's work now has the wide-ranging effects not possible in the early 1990s.

In addition to serving as a mode of communication between different points in the African diaspora, hip-hop also highlights African American culture as the focal point of identification for black people in Germany and the rest of Europe. Since Afro-Germans do not have a coherent public history or culture, the dominance of African American cultural production, especially in the realm of popular music, represents a crucial frame for formulating black identity.[55] However, this identification is also accompanied by persistent white German assumptions that all black people are either African or African American. Tina Campt delineates this dialectic of identification: "This discourse is permeated with representations of African-American culture as the dominant point of reference for 'first world' black populations. . . . The predominance of these representations of African-American history and culture has come to define popular perceptions of blacks in the so-called 'first world.' In Germany, one effect of these representations of blacks is the popular perception that African Germans (as well as other blacks in Germany) as being either 'third-' or 'first-world' Others." [56] Frequently, this form of identification stems from the ignorance of white Germans, who assume all black subjects in Germany to be inherently non-German (meaning either African or African American). This enables them to situate Afro-Germans outside the German national community, thereby rendering this space de facto white. Advanced Chemistry dispels the myth of German whiteness and forges space for Germans of color by asserting their Germanness while also creating an Afro-diasporic identification with hip-hop.

Advanced Chemistry's third single "Kapitel 1" (Chapter 1) allegorically elucidates the history of German hip-hop, in addition to situating the group within hip-hop's history. Rapped by Torch, one of the Afro-German members of the group, the track blends his own biography into the history of German hip-hop and vice versa. The most striking aspect of this generic mix appears in the opening of this sonic history/autobiography:

> Ich weiß noch genau wie alles begann. The Message von "Melle Mel" war für mich wie ein Telegram und obwohl ich kein einziges Wort verstehen konnte, erkannte ich welches Feuer in seinen Worten brannte. . . . [D]ie Fackel in mir wurde sofort entfacht in einer Nacht über mein ganzes Leben nachgedacht ich erblickte den Pfad zur Geschichte, mein Kopf wippte nickte zur Geschwindigkeit des Taktes.

> I still know exactly how it all began. "The Message" by Melle Mel was like a telegram for me and although I could not understand a single word, I recognized the fire burning in his words. . . . [T]he torch within me was ignited immediately. My whole life passed before me in a single night, seeing the path of history, my head swayed, nodded to the speed of the measure. [57]

Here Torch recounts his first encounter with hip-hop via "The Message" by Melle Mel. [58] "The Message," generally considered to be the first "message rap," proffered socially conscious lyrics that considered the plight of poor black subjects in the South Bronx instead of calls to party and dance, like most rap records of the time.[59] In Germany, "The Message" was one of the first rap tracks to receive widespread radio airplay. It comes therefore as no surprise that "The Message" would be the cut that tunes Torch into hip-hop, because it was available within the global marketplace and mass media. Torch likens this track to a telegram: words sent from a distance, addressed directly to him, and harboring an urgency not signified by other media such as a telephone call, a letter, and the like. Still, in a twist that bears witness to Torch's situation as a native German speaker, and seemingly diverging from the case of a telegram, he is unable to discern the lyrics of this recording. The paradox lies in the glaring discrepancy between the intention of the producer and the moment of reception dramatized here, considering that "The Message" made history because of its "political" lyrics, yet Torch can discern only the manner in which the lyrics are delivered and not the content of the message; the medium is the message here. The lyrics also stage Torch's birth as a rapper ("Fackel" means *torch* in German); metaphorically a torch is ignited in this man, and he becomes a new persona, leaving behind his status as a hip-hop consumer to be reborn in flames as a producer. Although Torch, an Afro-German subject, cannot comprehend Melle Mel's English words (*the* message), he does receive *a* message through the music and the rapper's delivery, and, thus, sonorous signification and effect supersede linguistic meaning. The name Torch signifies this moment of the "monolingualism of the other," in which "nothing is untranslatable; but *in another sense*, everything is untranslatable, translation is another name for the impossible."[60] That this message reaches its recipient in a moment of productive catachresis, instead of via a simple and unmitigated one-way global cultural flow, only underscores the complexity of transnational cultural circuits. In fact, it is precisely this misunderstanding, this catachresis—which is "another name for the impossible"—that enables Torch to reinvent himself as an Afro-German rapper; in the process, Torch also becomes a diasporic citizen.

The encounter with hip-hop dramatized by Torch in "Kapitel 1" registers as an example of self-chosen identification with African American culture on the part of some Afro-Germans, rather than the global black identity imposed by white Germans. The two forms of identification are by no means interchangeable: Afro-German subjects might relate to black U.S. culture but not claim to be African American, whereas white Germans construct all black people as foreigners. However, Torch's inability to comprehend the lyrics of "The Message" and his German-language rapping clearly mark him as not African American. Thus Torch's identification with hip-hop offers an instance of "diasporic citizenship," in which being Afro-German and connecting with African American popular music become intertwined but not synonymous — which runs counter to the white German practice of grouping together all black subjects — because it shows a dialogue with African American culture that need not rest on the subsumption of difference. Instead of merely mimicking hip-hop, Torch and the other members of Advanced Chemistry appropriate the form in order to fill it with their own content.[61] This gesture underlines the difference between identity and identification as they appear in the psychoanalytic tradition.[62] The tension between identity, as an overarching factor, and identification, as a more context-bound version thereof, provide the subject with the parameters of its own subjectivity; for "identification is the detour through the other that defines the self."[63] For Advanced Chemistry, African American culture (in the guise of hip-hop) serves as the "detour" through which they establish an Afro-German identity: they *identify with* (identification) African American culture, but they do not *identify as* (identity) African American. The group does this, at least in part, because there are no precedents for articulating Afro-German identity, and African American culture serves as the dominant first-world conception of blackness. The members of Advanced Chemistry were all born in Germany, and, according to strict notions of national belonging, they are first and foremost German citizens; yet the group "chooses" to identify (culturally and politically) with African American culture, constructing an identification of "passions," in Ellison's sense, rather than one based on immediate cultural or "blood" ties. Conversely, mainstream German cultural and political discourses insist on rendering these two divergent avenues of Afro-diasporic belonging as interchangeable, so that the German national community remains white.

In order to locate the specificities of Advanced Chemistry's intervention into the internal borders of the German national community, I will briefly sketch some major points in the history of the African presence in modern Germany. Although a scattered presence of people of African descent in Germany can be traced from the Middle Ages onward, they did not form a sizable group until the end of the First World

War. The most famous Afro-German before the twentieth century was Ghanaian-born Anton Wilhelm Amo, who was given as a present to the duke Ludwig Rudolf von Wolfenbüttel in 1707. Amo studied at the University of Halle, then renowned for its support of progressive Enlightenment ideas, writing a dissertation entitled "The Rights of an African in Eighteenth-Century Europe." After teaching at Halle and Wittenburg and continuing his intellectual pursuits, Amo returned to Ghana where he became a goldsmith.[64] While Germany did not participate in African colonization efforts on the scale of Great Britain or France, the nation did have colonies in Cameroon, Namibia, Tanzania, and Togo from the time of the Congo Conference of 1884–1885 to the end of World War I. However, not many colonized subjects actually immigrated to Germany, since Great Britain had blocked the sea roads to the German colonies.[65] After World War I (1914–1918) a number of African soldiers remained stationed in the French-occupied Rheinland region. The soldiers' children, born to white German women and commonly referred to as "Rheinland bastards," generated an immense uproar. Although, numerically speaking, there were few Afro-Germans, the negative attention that their presence spawned, from newspaper articles to discussions in parliament, suggests that even in minuscule numbers, Afro-German children threatened Germany's self-image as an ethnically "pure" nation.[66] At the end of the nineteenth century and during the Weimar Republic (the time spanning the close of World War I and the beginning of the Third Reich in 1933), a small number of African subjects from the former colonies settled in Germany. When the National Socialist Party came to power it tolerated the presence of black subjects as most of them worked as actors in propaganda and feature films depicting a variety of African stereotypes.[67] Although Afro-Germans and Africans living in Germany were not persecuted by the Nazis to the same extent as Jewish subjects or communists, a large number were sterilized against their will and banned from educational facilities, enduring forced labor, or winding up in concentration camps.[68]

The next major stage in Afro-German history came in the aftermath of the Second World War due to the presence of African American soldiers in West Germany. The period immediately following World War II was different from the situation that existed during the Weimar Republic because racism could not be voiced as blatantly on account of Germany's recent genocidal past. After the war, most Germans, deprived of basic material goods, viewed U.S. soldiers, including African American military men, as saviors.[69] However, when there arose a need in the early fifties to integrate Afro-German children (so-called *Besatzungskinder*, or Occupation children) into German institutions, particularly schools and kindergartens, they were once again interpellated as large-scale social problems by the media and state apparatuses. Often Afro-German children were deemed less intelligent than white German children and/or simply incompatible with German culture; there was even a plan to have these children adopted by black people in the United States.[70] Throughout the sixties and seventies, the presence of Afro-German children in the popular media reflected their construction as dilemmas for German society and culture, rather than as subjects, or even members of the national community. More often than not, white German racism failed to be thematized, and black Germans were portrayed as strange limit cases that enabled Germany to imagine its citizenry as immaculately white.

This constellation shifted somewhat during the mid-eighties when the ISD (Initiative Schwarze Deutsche/Initiative of Black Germans) was founded in West Berlin. Before this there had been some organized groups of Africans living in Germany, various antiracist activities by progressive organizations, and associations by white German mothers of Afro-German children. The ISD, however, provided the first enunciation of an explicitly Afro-German subjectivity. The majority of members were young—in their teens and twenties—and their African fathers had either been students at German universities or had immigrated to West Germany during the sixties and seventies; there were also some members whose African American fathers were stationed in Germany during the cold war.[71] Later, the group, which became national, came to include African nationals who had spent the majority of their life in West Germany and older Afro-Germans who belonged to the immediate post–World War II generation.[72] The ISD was important insofar as it made it possible for Afro-Germans to identify as both black and German; in fact, the designation "Afro-deutsch" was coined by the ISD. This had not been conceivable before, as people of color were always already considered non-German by German mainstream cultural discourse.[73] The only routes previously available required either complete assimilation to or total denial of Germanness, and for many this meant overly romantic identifications with cultures (African American and/or various African cultures) they had hardly experienced. The public enunciation of the name/concept "Afro-German" enabled a new drafting of racial identity in Germany, a racial identity that "tainted" the whiteness of German national culture through its insistence on occupying the hyphen between *Afro* and *German* rather than configuring the two terms within a regime of mutual exclusivity.[74] As May Opitz argues, Afro-German identity presents a chance to make the "in-between world" usable.[75] In the United States, where hyphenated identities are not novel phenomena, this may not appear as revolutionary as in the German context, still bound by implicit and explicit assumptions of racial purity. In addition, according to Campt's discussion of the testimonies collected in the first anthology of Afro-German women's writing, *Farbe bekennen*, "the refusal of these women to accept a single racial identification is a form of resistance to hegemonic forms of [German] cultural and ideological domination, which seeks to impose an essentialized form of 'racial identity' on the basis of skin color."[76] Accordingly, Afro-German identity represents a rebuttal of German racial ideology just as much as it opens new spaces in the identity formation and articulation of black German subjects by its insistence on inhabiting Opitz's "in-between world" via punctuation, enabling Afro-Germans to "cling to the hyphen as a means of resisting dominant strategies of erasure and marginalization."[77]

"Fremd im eigenen Land" holds a pivotal place in the public articulation of a German national identity that is not exclusively white. The recording commences with news reports about violence against "foreigners" in the German town of Rostock, which segues into a mock news announcement of Advanced Chemistry's endeavor to fight against prejudice and racism. Then the song itself begins, suggesting an analogy between the official news reports in which people of color appear only as victims of racial violence and Advanced Chemistry's perspective as German citizens of color. Thus, at least in one way, "Fremd" takes on the position of a rapped news report, particularly since Germans of color have no access to the official, and still largely state-sponsored, televisual news apparatus. This current, fortified by the sample of the theme music from one of West Germany's longest running television news shows, *Report*, forms the core of the track's bassline, lending "Fremd" a cinema verité aura that bestows credibility upon the voices of the three rappers as German subjects of color.[78] Instead of being able to dismiss the problems addressed by the group as mere "paranoid ramblings," the use of this sample forces the audience to acknowledge the "objective" truth-value of the track.[79] The sample can also be heard as an ironic commentary on the way people of color are most habitually configured in the German news media: generally they appear in conjunction with large national problems such as unemployment, immigration, and crime. The sample, then, suggests that racism exists on the quotidian level as well as in more sensational arenas. Advanced Chemistry, using newscasts and the sample from *Report*, appropriates these signifiers of truthfulness and media power to redefine the manner in which Germans of color are interpellated by these ideological state apparatuses. Instead of mute ciphers besieged by an unwieldy mass of white violence, the members of Advanced Chemistry inscribe themselves as both potential victims of racist violence *and* German subjects of color who endure and combat more "mundane" forms of German racism. This is a key distinction, since it depicts racialized thinking not as a mere smudge on the tolerant veneer of German public discourse but as constitutive of both German national identity and the everyday lives of Afro-Germans.

In the early 1990s, the sensational examples of racism were violent racist attacks on people of color in mostly former East German cities such as Hoyerswerda and Rostock, but there were also numerous "incidents" in western Germany. The most prominent cases were the bombings/burnings of several shelters for asylum seekers; large spectator groups, including police officers, witnessed the events, but even these public servants chose not to intervene in extreme situations. In addition to these attacks, German newspapers reported (between 1991 and 1993) many incidents of racially motivated aggression directed at people of color: some were verbal, some caused minor physical harm to the victims, while some lead to death, as in the case of an Angolan man who was thrown off a moving train by a group of neo-Nazis. The majority of the reporting on these incidents, both in Germany and the United States, focused on the resurgence of Nazi sentiments among disenfranchised East German youth, constructing a primordial "German xenophobia."[80] The yoking of these two discourses (a new German lumpenproletariat and the supposed resurfacing of an innate German xenophobia) proved quite troubling, since it failed to consider two more historically and politically nuanced factors in this situation: the involvement of German parliamentary politics and the lack of discussion concerning German national identity within the public sphere by both the Right and the Left.[81] During the same period, parliamentary debates and party campaigns increasingly centered on questions of immigration and political asylum, with many politicians proclaiming that the then newly reunited Germany was not to be a nation of immigrants and that West Germany's hitherto liberal political asylum laws were no longer economically tenable due to the financial costs of reunification.[82] The Christian Democrats (CDU) in particular maximized these currents in their campaigns for both local and national elections, invoking slogans such as "Das Boot ist voll" (The boat is full) that referenced the supposedly overwhelming number of foreigners in Germany.[83] This, I contend, suggested to disenfranchised youth that their attacks served as valid reactions to and reflections of current political and economic circumstances. In other words, the political campaigns of the mainstream parties implicitly acknowledged the "truth" in the reasons for attackers' rage, even while they condemned the means by which this rage was publicly executed. Instead of punishing the attackers, however, the political parties chose to enforce stricter immigration laws.

In his verse on "Fremd," Linguist, the other Afro-German member, highlights the discrepancy between the political propaganda against asylum seekers and the nonintervention of the state in the violent attacks against people of color in the following manner:

Seit zwanzig Jahren leben wir hier und sind es leid zu schweigen. Progrome entstehen Polizei steht daneben, ein deutscher Staatsbürger fürchtet um sein Leben, in der Fernsehsendung die Wiedervereinigung, anfangs habe ich mich gefreut, doch schnell hab ich's bereut, denn noch nie seit ich denken kann, war's so schlimm wie heut! Politikerköpfe reden viel, doch bleiben kalt und kühl all dies paßt genau in ihr Kalkül man zeigt sich besorgt, begibt sich vor Ort nimmt ein Kind auf den Schoß, für Presse ist schon gesorgt mit jedem Kamerablitz ein neuer Sitz im Bundestag, dort erläßt man ein neues Gesetz. Klar, Asylbewerber müssen raus, und keiner macht den Faschos den Garaus!

Many will say that we are exaggerating, but after twenty years we are tired of being silent. Pogroms occur and the police just stand by, a German citizen is afraid for his life. The reunification is on TV. In the beginning I was happy about it, but regret came soon, because it's never been as bad as it is today. Politicians talk a lot, yet stay calm and collected. Going to the places where violent attacks against people of color have taken place, they pretend to be worried and put a child on their lap. Good publicity will guarantee a seat in parliament, where they have passed a new law. Asylum seekers have to leave, but no one fights the fascists.

Linguist here points out the hypocrisy with which German politicians approach the situation: on the one hand, they restrict asylum laws and deploy discourses concerning the alleged threat to German culture and economics posed by foreigners — read: people of color. On the other hand, they fail to take strong legislative and executive action against neo-Nazis; instead they opt to show only "emotional" support for victims of violent racist attacks. Rather than providing the means to stop the violence, German politicians sentimentalize the situation thereby absolving themselves of any responsibility. Moreover, since the Third Reich, German national identity has been a topic non grata in public debates, rendering Germanness interchangeable with Nazism. Because the German Left failed to formulate any alternative version of German national identity, when articulations of Germanness surface, they are usually accompanied by at least quasi-fascist undertones; for the Left, national identity can only be fascist, since it reactivates the only form of being explicitly German they recognize. David Rieff underlines this point in his exploration of West German liberals' and leftists' acute unease about their "Germanness," arguing that they choose to identify as European and cede Germanness to those who would render their self-fulfilling prophecy of an intrinsically fascist Germany true. He writes: "To well-intentioned Germans like my friends with their house in the south of France, talk of change [regarding German asylum laws] was, like the skinhead outrages, proof that Germany was still the same racist, xenophobic country they had always known it to be."[84] Also, by routinely using "Nazi" as a signifier for "evil," German leftists, in a similar fashion to politicians, place "Naziness" in a mythic space that only evil people (usually poor and uneducated, hence not leftist and/or educated) inhabit (as Linke notes in *German Bodies*, 175). Therefore, it comes as no great surprise that the articulation of German national identity takes the form of violence inspired by racism in this climate. Against this backdrop, Linguist urges the German mainstream political and media apparatuses to acknowledge their complicity as opposed to merely showing "emotional support" once the violence has already been perpetrated.

The passport becomes one of the main signifiers for citizenship in

"Fremd," allowing Advanced Chemistry a cultural claim to German citizenship. The opening lines of the rap read as follows: "Ich habe einen grünen Pass mit einem goldenen Adler drauf; dies bedingt, daß ich mir oft die Haare rauf" (I have a green passport with a golden eagle on it; often this causes me a lot of aggravation), and while they acknowledge the speaker's legal citizenship as a matter of fact, they also highlight the inherent problems of the speaking subject's German citizenship.[85] Still, the first couple of lines do not indicate the racial identity of the speaker; they merely establish that the subject carries a German passport and describe the difficulties eventuating from this marker of national identity. Once the speaker's position as a hyphenated German discloses itself, the function and importance of the passport become self-evident: "Warum ich der Einzige bin, der sich ausweisen muß, Identität beweisen muß. Ist es so ungewöhnlich wenn ein Afro-Deutscher seine Sprache spricht- und nicht so blaß ist im Gesicht?" (Why am I the only one who has to show his ID, to prove my identity? Is it so strange that an Afro-German speaks his own language, even if his face isn't pale?).[86] These lyrics stress the discordance between German citizenship as a legal status and a lived cultural identity, which forces the speaker to continually prove his legal citizenship due to the color of his skin. The German passport remains his only claim to national membership in the eyes of mainstream German culture. While this might not present a predicament as such, it becomes a problem when subjects of color are the only people who have to rely on their passports to authenticate their citizenship. This provides an instant in which "the passport is a technology that nationalizes bodies along racial lines," and in the process implicates " 'nation' and 'state' in discourses of race."[87] In the German context, the passport acutely racializes the German national community as white, since only nonwhite subjects have to invariably wield this technology within the national borders. This dilemma appears as even more multifaceted if we consider that "the historical burden of a technology such as the passport demands a 'nationalized' subject who might engage in legal mobility."[88] Routinely, this mobility refers to the movement across national borders; in this case, however, a German passport enables mobility within the confines of the German nation, because the passport as the technology of a nationalized subject is in constant tension with the scopic technology of racial classification, which positions people of color as always already beyond the pale of Germanness. In West Berlin, for instance, during the mid-eighties all "non-German-looking" subjects were required to show their passports at police checkpoints close to East Berlin for fear that they might be illegal immigrants. If subjects of color did not have "identification papers," they faced police custody until they provided proof of their legal status. In this context, the dialectic between interior and exterior mobility is reversed, creating a tension between "internal" and "external" transit particular to people of color in Germany.

This rift reveals the implicit whiteness of German cultural citizenship, placing all subjects of color always already beyond the confines of citizenship, or, as Torch phrases this dilemma: "Das Problem sind die Ideen im System: ein echter Deutscher muß auch richtig deutsch aussehen, blaue Augen, blondes Haar, keine Gefahr, gab's da nicht 'ne Zeit wo's schon mal so war?!" (The ideas in the system are the problem: a real German must look truly German, blue eyes, blond hair—no problem—wasn't there another time when the situation was similar?) Referencing the Third Reich, Torch attacks the hidden script of German citizenship, which, although never clearly articulated, thoroughly permeates German national culture. According to Etienne Balibar, "The 'external frontiers' of the state have to become 'internal frontiers' or—which amounts to the same thing—external frontiers have to be imagined constantly as a projection and protection of an internal collective personality, which each of us carries within ourselves and enables us to inhabit the space of the state as a place where we have always been—and always will be—'at home.'"[89] This interplay between internal and external borders proves crucial in this particular scenario, since the passport clearly shows that Afro-Germans are never "at home" in Germany; rather, they are dependent on the passport as proof of citizenship within the perimeters of the German nation-state because they do not a form a part of the (white) German "collective personality." Yet, the racial makeup of this collective personality is never unequivocally expressed for fear of harking back to Germany's fascist past, making this policing of the "internal frontiers" a problem only for people of color. Ergo Afro-Germans are constantly besieged by Germany's internal borders, while white Germans can delude themselves into thinking that there are only "external frontiers."

In part, these conceptions have their roots in German citizenship laws based on cultural and ethnic, rather than political, belonging. Rogers Brubaker distinguishes between the French legal concept of citizenship (*jus soli*) and the German version (*jus sanguinis*). Whereas the French citizenship model represents a territorial political community, German citizenship law is grounded in the idea that the national and monoethnic communities should be coterminous.[90] Put differently, only subjects of German descent can acquire citizenship status: subjects born and/or inhabiting "German soil" for a certain period of time are not eligible, unlike in France, the United States, and Canada. This rule creates ironies such as the granting of automatic citizenship to ethnic Germans who have never lived in Germany while refusing citizenship rights to second-generation immigrants.[91] Brubaker locates the divergence between these two forms of citizenship in nineteenth-century nationalism, arguing that Prussia's failure to assimilate Polish-descended immigrants lead to laws barring nonethnic Germans from citizenship. This guaranteed that "Germanness" would remain at the center of the newly formed German nation, which was hard enough to establish since Germany only became a unified nation at the close of the nineteenth century. In Brubaker's account, France had a better success rate at culturally "absorbing" immigrants; thus it constructed citizenship laws that reflected a belief in the assimilationist power of French political membership. In addition, Uli Linke shows how these laws were designed to bar subjects of color in the colonies from claiming German property and citizenship (*German Bodies*, 45). Although German citizenship laws have changed somewhat, the *jus sanguinis* principle still remains central. In addition, the ideological dimensions of German citizenship are deeply marked by notions of ethnic belonging, so that people of color, even if they possess German citizenship, are not seen as Germans but as foreigners; consequently, the legal and ideological aspects of German citizenship constantly fortify one another. "Fremd im eigenen Land" seeks to call attention to the lacunae between these two elements of German citizenship, to render it audible and visible in order for Germany to cease imagining itself, both culturally and legally, as an exclusively white nation.

As "Fremd" progresses, the recording reveals several typical white reactions to Torch's presence in Germany. These include amazement at Torch's ability to speak fluent German, questions about his origins in Africa or the United States, as well as comments about his hair. All these factors point to the small everyday occurrences of racism that usually fail to register on the radar of the news media. Stressing the way in which these seemingly insignificant encounters "matter" just as much as outright physical and/or verbal racist violence, Torch envisions a space for

Afro-Germans in the realm of German public culture. While the violence against people of color, especially in the early nineties, should not be downplayed, most racism in Germany is not overt. Often, everyday questions about one's "homeland" or addressing someone in "pidgin," although she or he is capable of speaking perfect standard German, constitute the bulk of racism, rather than more explosive occurrences of racially motivated brutality. Until recently there did not exist any Afro-German public forums, so the mainstream media focused on more overt racist attacks, rather than interrogating the more subtle forms of racialized thinking that so thoroughly permeate German culture and politics. Thus, Advanced Chemistry's choice to begin the lyrical component of their recording with "minor" and not "major" incidents of racism—especially when contrasted with the preceding news reports sampled on the track— suggests an important political choice that highlights the ways in which Afro-Germans perceive themselves within German culture. Moreover, this depiction provides a way in which the presence of Afro-Germans becomes quotidian; in other words, the claim to cultural citizenship results from the particularity Afro-Germans must have in order to endure these "little racisms," despite their status as German citizens. Paradoxically, Afro-German identity gets inscribed as German due to the racism faced by these citizens of color. Torch needs to constantly proclaim that he is indeed a German citizen precisely because a person of color who has spent all his life in Germany can still be viewed as a tourist or immigrant. Thus, rather than being an end unto itself, the passport represents a state-sanctioned symbol that enables Torch to declare cultural citizenship: Torch already possesses legal citizenship, but, as he contends, this means nothing if not accompanied by the acknowledgment of nonwhite Germans by mainstream German culture. Therefore the "internal" frontiers of the German nation-state have to be realigned in order to expose and abolish the monochrome tendencies of its "collective identity."

Advanced Chemistry fell prey to criticism because they were perceived to be distancing themselves from the many persons of color who did not hold German citizenship by insisting on their legal, and therefore privileged, status as Germans. The group responded to these censures by stating that they sought to present their own perspective instead of speaking for all people of color, thus proffering a totality that acknowledges internal differences. In addition, the group also suggested a different path to Germanness than that heretofore taken by ethnic minorities in post-

World War II German culture, who often refused to identify as German, thereby only reaffirming the implicit whiteness of German citizenship. This solidarity is evinced in "Operation Artikel 3," which criticizes German citizenship laws from the standpoint of noncitizens, represented by Italian German group member, Toni, who speaks as a "Gastarbeiter/guest worker." [92] In contrast to Toni, who is a German citizen as a result of one of his parents' German descent, most Gastarbeiter have not been naturalized since they lack German "blood." Toni's rhyme opens with a central contradiction inherent in the debates around immigration in Germany. On the one hand, politicians and the media loudly proclaim that the country cannot take any more immigrants as they pose a threat to German culture and take jobs away from Germans. Toni, in contradistinction, conjectures whether the postwar boom would have been possible at all without the contribution of immigrants:

> Somit denkt der Bürger, der Vorurteile pflegt, dass für ihn eine grosse Gefahr entsteht, er sie verliert, seine ihm so wichtige Lebensqualität leider kommt selten jemand, der frägt, wie es um die schlechtbezahlte, unbeliebte Arbeit steht. Kaum einer ist da, der überlegt, auf das Wissen Wert legt, warum es diesem Land so gut geht, dass der Gastarbeiter seit den 50ern unentwegt, mit Nutzem beitrug und noch beiträgt.

> Therefore the citizen who harbors prejudices thinks that s/he is in great danger of losing the famous German quality of life. Sadly no one asks about the state of low-paying and unpopular labor. Hardly anyone thinks about why the country is economically flourishing and how "guest workers" have contributed, and still contribute, to Germany's economic boom since the fifties.

"Gastarbeiter" first came to West Germany in the 1960s after the so-called *Wirtschaftswunder* (economic miracle), when the West German economy was booming and there was a surplus of employment but not enough laborers to fill the positions. Consequently, the West German government enticed unskilled and semiskilled laborers (mainly from Turkey, Italy, Greece, and former Yugoslavia) to come work in German factories.[93] The initial idea, shared by all parties involved, was for workers to return to their home countries after a certain period of time; yet, once the West German government stopped recruitment in 1973 as a result of the oil crisis, many workers resisted repatriation. They had brought their families, formed communities, and become accustomed to various aspects of life in the Federal Republic, especially in the urban centers of Berlin, Hamburg, Frankfurt, and Cologne. Notwithstanding their stability as comunities, these groups were not acknowledged as permanent members of German society (although the government recognized that a mass expulsion of guestworkers would not be feasible), and it was not until the mid-eighties that debates about Germany as a possibly multicultural society cropped up. Nevertheless, these debates assumed—and to a large extent still do—that the guest workers and their families were not an intrinsic part of the German social landscape. In the eighties, when mass unemployment became a fixture in West Germany, foreigners were blamed for occupying jobs that "belonged" to ethnic Germans. This, combined with an influx of asylum seekers from all over the world, resulted in virulent propaganda and violent attacks against all people of color during the early nineties.

These assaults and more subtle forms of German racism do not distinguish between foreigners and German nationals; all people of color are non-German by virtue of their pigmentation. Advanced Chemistry was criticized for differentiating between people of color who hold German citizenship and those who do not in the face of an extremely loaded political situation. This demarcation, however, proves to be one of their most salient political maneuvers. Since all nonwhite people are constructed as non-German by the mainstream media, Advanced Chemistry's insistence on being nonwhite *and* German provides a new space within the field of German national identity. Additionally, the group's bringing to the fore the diversity among people of color dislodges the homogenous lumping together of various groups' discordant experiences and histories. The combined articulation of Afro-German and guest worker identities carves out a niche previously nonexistent within German public discourses, enabling the creation of a "territory" that is not a mere antithetical foil to hegemonic German whiteness; rather, this category highlights the varied and complex formations of nonwhite German identities—whether citizens or "guests"—too often subsumed under the brutal equation nonwhite = non-German. This is not to argue that Advanced Chemistry "invented" Afro-German identity and/or shifted the political situation in early nineties Germany *tout court*; instead it suggests that within the social and political context in which that "Fremd" appeared, it gave voice to groups hitherto silent. Not only did "Fremd" posit a nonwhite German identity, but, by letting German subjects of color speak or rap themselves instead of being sensationalized by the news media, it magnified the complexity contained within this often unspoken ideological composite.

Advanced Chemistry and the Fugees deploy divergent strategies in imagining diasporic citizenship. Both groups want to make borders visible and audible, yet they choose different approaches in response to the varying sociopolitical contexts from which they articulate their projects. The Fugees, using the figure of the refugee, use their position in the United States to complicate and draw attention to the boundaries of the nation-state. If the Fugees' scheme consists of placing themselves on the border to "dance around [it] like Cassius Clay," then the members of Advanced Chemistry locate themselves squarely *inside* the border in order to fight German public discourse "like Cassius Clay." They adopt this modus operandi because, although they are German citizens de jure, German ideologies and practices often symbolically, and at times violently, place them beyond the precincts of the nation's border. Instead of using hip-hop as a distancing strategy from the German national scene, Advanced Chemistry appropriates the genre to assert its (Afro-)Germanness. Hip-hop facilitates the construction of an Afro-German identity that looks beyond the external German borders in order to redraw the (white) internal borders of German citizenship, in the process rendering Afro-German identity as "diasporic citizenship," which is situated at that dangerous line where the national bleeds into the transnational and vice versa. To this end, Advanced Chemistry performs an ideological voyage into the heart of the German imagined community, which, in the process, unmasks the implicit and explicit racial coherence contained in the ways Germany imagines itself and is imagined by the world at large.

"It's Maniacal, I Cuff the Mimetical"   The contemporary sociopolitical scene in the Western world is exemplified by, among other things, a growing chasm between classes that creates low-paying service jobs and high-salaried corporate labor, escalating unemployment rates, the militarization of inner cities, and the dismantling of the welfare state, as well as the increased privatization and surveillance of public space.[94] According to Simon Reynolds, these forces appear in current popular music in the form of the "real," which imagines no utopias, but "reality" in its most distorted and hardcore version: " 'Real' also signifies that the music reflects a 'reality' constituted by late capitalistic economic instability, institutionalized racism, and increased surveillance and harassment of youth by the police. 'Real' means the death of the social; it means corporations who respond to increased profits not by raising pay or improving benefits but by what Americans call downsizing" (*Slipping into Darkness*, 36). Contemporary black musical formations reflect, construct, and integrate this notion of the real in different fashions; most mainstream hip-hop and R&B acts suggest a hyperreality consisting of crass materialism as well as sexually explicit images and lyrics. These musical formations deflect these social forces by aligning themselves with the "gains" of late capitalism, emphasizing their readiness at playing and winning at this game of social and economic Darwinism, where only the business-savvy and physically fit survive to sell millions of records. Black British artist Tricky has taken a different track vis-à-vis these socioeconomic trends. The first words that Tricky utters on Massive Attack's debut album *Blue Lines*, "English upbringing, background Caribbean," summarize his own position as well as the musical geography of Massive Attack's album, which was produced by a multiracial collective from Bristol in the United Kingdom and musically incorporates reggae, soul, hip-hop, and house. Since then Tricky has appeared on Massive Attack's second longplayer *Protection*. In addition, he has produced three albums with his main collaborator Martina Topley-Bird: *Maxinquaye, Pre-Millennium Tension*, and *Angels with Dirty Faces*.[95] Tricky's music and lyrics, in contrast to mainstream hip-hop, provide soundscapes that constantly evoke a "real" suffused by paranoia and enclosure, while the lyrics speak of suffocation, death, nightmares, and drug psychosis. Accompanying these musical expeditions are an assortment of images depicting Tricky and Martina in numerous guises. The music, just like the images, plays with different conventions in order to suggest a new frame of representation for the gender and racial politics of contemporary black musical expression and diasporic citizenship.

Conversely, mainstream R&B and hip-hop imagine a version of the good life featuring sexually promiscuous, ice-donned, Versace- and Gucci-wearing, Cristal-sipping, Bentley-driving black subjects. This scenario falls into the purview of Paul Gilroy's conception of "a racialized bio-politics of fucking" that privileges the physical body as the site for freedom rather than the transcendence of the body through spirituality.

The transcendence of the body through spirituality, whether religious or secular, formed an integral part of earlier forms of black popular music such as soul and gospel.[96] The body Gilroy refers to gains its freedom *in* and not *through* sex, making sex an end unto itself rather than a means through which to acquire freedom. The "racialized bio-politics" is further compounded by the equation of sex and money in a number of R&B and hip-hop tracks, thus rendering sex, on the one hand, a mere physical exercise, and on the other, an object of monetary exchange. In addition, the consumption of designer clothes, jewelry, and expensive cars as well as the playa lifestyle have become the other staples in hip-hop and R&B culture's "bling bling" politics. Tricky and Martina, in contrast, imagine black subjects under erasure, subjects that cannot deal with the demands of conspicuous consumption and oversexualization. Their model of subjectivity is marked by failure, negativity, messiness, distortion, blurring of boundaries, drug psychosis, weariness, ugliness, and depression. These factors counterpose "a racialized bio-politics of fucking" with an aesthetics of "fucked-upness" that grows out of the representation of black diasporic subjects incapable of and/or unwilling to submit their psyches and bodies to the rigors of late capitalism, suggesting a different way of imagining and performing the black body politic, one that does not rest on the hubris of its discreteness or integrity. Rather, Tricky and Martina's conception of embodiment highlights its own deterritorialization and erodes any and all residual phantasms of completeness.

We should not, however, move too quickly to adopt Gilroy's terms without dwelling on some of the assumptions therein, particularly in regard to configurations of corporeality and subjective sovereignty. Gilroy seems to locate freedom only in those realms that transcend the body, where current black musical formations insist on the physical as *the* conduit for pleasure and the good life, raising some general questions about the nexus of freedom and embodiment. Put differently, why does Gilroy equate the body with "unfreedom"? While I do not want to defend some of the more excessive strands of "the good life" in these musical constellations, one might still try not to dismiss these longings as out of hand as does Gilroy, who seems to harbor a strictly pre-twentieth-century notion of Afro-diasporic liberation; nor might one almost celebrate them as some other critics do.[97] This notion of autonomy, one that Gilroy finds in spirituals, cruises the sphere of the ideal by going beyond the crude flesh in order to secure freedom in the afterlife. Since black subjects did not own their bodies either during slavery or in the slightly reformulated constellations of reconstruction and segregation, their liberty necessarily took on different forms than those of the masters.[98] Where the white and masculine Enlightenment subject secured his freedom via ownership of the self and property, black subjects were reduced to subhumanity due to their lack of possessions, even while they were equated with the body as the locus for their surplus value in these regimes of domination. These contradictions, at least substantially if not exclusively, led to the conception of personal sovereignty at the heart of Gilroy's critique: "I also want to mourn the disappearance of the pursuit of Freedom as an element in black vernacular culture, and to ask why it seems no longer appropriate or even plausible to speculate about the freedom of the subject of black politics in overdeveloped countries."[99]

But in what sense has freedom retreated from the Afro-modern culturopolitical landscape? And why should "freaky sex" not serve as an agent for liberation from the oppressive shackles of racialization? These questions never quite factor into Gilroy's analysis; instead, it hinges on a version of freedom as ideality and vice versa, which puts the argument in the neighborhood of a classical Enlightenment version of autonomy that completely erases the body. Moreover, the historical trajectory that Gilroy summons, where "love stories" of yesterday's classical soul have mutated into contemporary R&B's "sex stories," reads smoothly only if one neglects a large chunk of U.S. popular music history ("'After the Love Has Gone,'" 65).[100] This history includes a plethora of well-known double entendres, such as Bessie Smith's request to "put a little sugar in my bowl" or some lines recorded by Lucille Bogan in 1930, which leave little to the imagination, and make recent invocations of being "a freak like me" (Adina Howard and The Sugababes), "doing it anywhere," while making ample use of "peaches and cream" (112), or "feeling a little bulk on you" (NEXT) seem tame in comparison: "I got nipples on my titties as big as the end of my thumb . . . I fucked all night and feel like fucking all morning."[101] These lyrics metonymically redact the presence of "sex stories" alongside "love stories" in the blues and later R&B, Barry White, Blowfly, or Millie Jackson, for instance. And these sex stories should not be understood as any less "free" than the love stories Gilroy exalts to such ideal, if not idealist, heights; they just insist on the body as the nexus of freedom instead of a transcendence thereof. In a context where black subjects were denied ownership of their bodies for so long, sex stories might just be as liberating as love stories. Gilroy apparently dismisses these ludic invocations because of their current hegemony, yet his argument unwittingly descends into the realm of nostalgia and unnecessary prudishness by dismissing all sexually explicit scenarios in contemporary black music as cryptofascist. Despite some of Gilroy's salient critiques of the rampant (hetero)sexism, such as the insistence on calcified notions of what constitutes a proper family and physical body within these Afro-biopolitics, too many factors get lumped in together so as to undermine his general points about gender and sexuality in these constellations. For instance, the early nineties R&B preoccupation with cunnilingus (invoked by Gilroy), given the paucity of spaces for the discussion of female sexuality, surely should not be construed as synonymous with the virulent masculinist dimensions of hip-hop. Generally, Gilroy seems unwilling to listen to contemporary R&B as the genre of popular music most forcefully concerned with female sexuality, which weakens the force of his points by disallowing the uses of "freaky sex" beyond the merely biopolitical. Recently, Tricia Rose has argued that in the face of relentless stereotyping and/or silencing of black female narrated and sexually explicit material might provide spaces of freedom, since "refusing to make desires, pleasures and terms of intimacy known will not reduce sexually objectifying, male-empowering representations and treatment of women."[102] While Rose does not go as far as suggesting that sexually explicit materials are the sole answer to the way black female libidinality is coded within various representational regimes, not addressing these currents will not effect any changes either, since the masculinist images in hip-hop and beyond will remain intact. Overall, Gilroy's arguments remain relevant because they call attention to the shifting notions of physicality and embodiment in black popular music; however, their limitations are evident in the quasimoralizing of these transformations, which fail to carefully calibrate the uses of "freaky sex," especially for black female performers.

Tricky's music has been characterized as "trip-hop," a term he himself is loath to use. While Tricky's aural oeuvre displays some characteristics of this genre, defined mainly by slow-motion hip-hop beats and spherical sounds, the parameters of this genre do not do Tricky's distorted aural sculptures justice. As Greg Tate explains, "Gall and nakedness plus ganja make Tricky the mutant offspring of Chuck Berry, Lee Scratch Perry, and Richard Hell—a dub wise, black punk rocker on a future-primitive soundtrip."[103] The sonic language moves between mutations of hip-hop beats, guitar ruminations associated more with the genre of alternative rock, twisted torch songs, backward tape effects, and modes of delay and echo, as well as the use of environmental noise, not as a moodsetter but as the basis of rhythm tracks. For example, on the ambient remix of "Pumpkin" the only sound heard except the voice is that of a motorcycle engine, which runs counter to the soothing environmental sounds—tingling synthesizers, rain forest sounds, animals such as whales or dolphins, soft chanting by non-Western peoples, for example—associated with this genre. In fact, this mix inverts the main goal of ambient music, designed as a comforting soundblanket to protect subjects from the noise created by the fragments of late capitalism, converting the noises that ambient music tries to shield its listeners from into music by rendering the noises of late capitalism pleasurable. On "My Evil Is Strong," we hear Tricky and Martina hoarsely whispering lyrics about evil accompanied by backward loops of guitars and a stretched-out drum loop, which paints a very distorted sonic image of an enclosed musical space that manages to turn its own musical askewness into aestheticized anxiety. Tricky consciously misuses the sampler to distort the sounds of the past and blow them to pieces to fit his own needs, as opposed to using them to signify their recognizability, as much of hip-hop does.[104] Utilizing noises and sounds against their traditional connotations adds a sonic layer of "fucked-upness" to the ones in the images and words, creating a cluster of dissonance that represents a black diasporic subject under erasure. Furthermore, Tricky's records have gotten progressively bleaker and less user-friendly. *Maxinquaye*, even though austere in music and lyrics, sported pop and funk sensibilities and worked within a somewhat song-oriented musical format. However, with each following album Tricky's sounds have become more and more distorted, almost completely dispensing with melody and coherent lyrical formulations. *Angels with Dirty Faces*, the last Tricky album on which Martina appears, offers hardly any snatches of melody or funky elements; rather, the tracks consist of minimal noises combined with Tricky and Martina's whispers.[105] These musical landscapes represent a diasporic subject under erasure in the sense that these sounds consciously undermine the wholeness and presence of the musical text.

One of the most salient features of the music media's coverage of Tricky thus far has been the constant reference to his marijuana consumption.[106] But the weed he consumes is a far cry from the kind that generated the spaced-out hippiesque experience for which this drug is best known in pop culture; as Simon Reynolds explains: "These days smoking isn't a mellow, Marleyesque affair. With their much higher THC content, superbreeds like skunk are near-hallucinogenic, offering a sensory intensification without euphoria, tinged with jittery, nerve-jangling paranoia."[107] These superbreeds of marijuana, unlike alcohol, for instance, fail to entail an escape into sociality, since this sphere has been thoroughly corrupted by various late-capitalist tendencies; instead they construct a retreat into a paranoid dismantled self. Rather than offering a diversion or redemption from the "reality" of late-capitalist structures, the drugs, and their representations in Tricky's music, intensify and distort "reality" itself, transforming it into a bad dream. As opposed to the "ghetto fabulous" pretensions of other black popular music, this mode of engagement — the voluntary and involuntary failure to seek an escape that envisions life as more bearable — posits that there is no "good life" in late capitalism and the only way to cope with this lack is to magnify and distort the negative aspects of global capitalism. And this magnification, via the channel of chemical mind alteration, serves to blur the boundaries of coherent black subjectivity by eroding the self only in relation to itself; it does not interpellate a social group (the posse being the most prominent) as in most hip-hop, where the combination of weed and various forms of alcohol are mainly configured as party favors and/or another code of hypermasculine armor. The only form of nonindividuated sociality suggested by Tricky's sonic and visual practices is the couple, although it hardly provides a safety net from the real, functioning instead in much the same way as the self, as a clearing ground for "dysfunction."

Martina Topley-Bird has appeared on most of Tricky's early releases; in fact, on the debut album her voice commanded the most sonic space, and Tricky himself was only heard occasionally. The vocal interplay between Tricky and Martina worries the distinction between lead/background and female/male singer in several significant ways. In the history of popular music women are often heard as background singers for male artists, while there are hardly any examples of men singing background for female singers.[108] With Tricky and Martina, the distinction between lead and background vocals is disrupted by Martina, singing lead, and Tricky, not singing so much as whispering in the background. Thus Tricky's voice realigns the gendered hierarchies frequently found within popular music. Finally, on some tracks the duo takes turns singing/rapping lead in different parts, often switching lyrics, as opposed to singing distinct single parts. Greg Tate interprets Martina's role in the Tricky universe as follows: "Martina's position in the music might seem marionettish, but it's really that of a confessor priest–type sister. Her role is to interpret, alter, and redeem this black man's inner child" ("Trick Baby," 77). However, Tricky has a similar function for Martina: their interaction is far from unidirectional, as their voices complement each other and overlap, rather than having distinct positionalities/ personalities within the sonic architectonics of the individual tracks, making it difficult to distinguish where one voice begins and the other ends. Together, Tricky and Martina's voices sound a black diasporic subject whose boundaries are blurred and frayed, rather than concrete and finite. Their voices, in conjunction with the dissonant sounds, provide a space in which both their egos merge to create a new one that is not centered and whole but distorted and fractured — a centerless ego — one that is witnessing its own falling apart, a movement further underlined by Tricky's January 1997 live performance in New York, where he chose to perform in almost complete darkness for the duration of the concert, reminiscent of the way jazz musicians such as Miles Davis performed with their backs to the audience.[109] Although the visual component of the concert was scant, to say the least, practically the entire audience insisted on looking at the stage, which seems to exemplify Tricky's strategy of dramatizing his own disintegration and thereby commanding the attention of his audience both visually and musically.

Tricky's musical and imagistic politics should be contextualized within a wider framework of different black musics produced in the last thirty years, since they resemble those of other black male "geniuses" such as Miles Davis, Charlie Parker, or Jimi Hendrix. Like Tricky, these musicians constantly reinvented themselves musically and ran up against the boundaries of "black music" within their particular historical framework. Tricky's most direct influence, albeit not with respect to his dark and destructive aspects, seems to be Prince. Prince's frequent reincarnations pushed his music and images beyond the limits of what was previously acceptable for any mainstream black artist: he changed his image and music slightly with the release of every new album, in addition to presenting himself as consciously androgynous.[110] Like Prince, Tricky utilizes numerous musical genres to shape his own sonic aesthetics and defy the generic conventions most black artists have to comply with under the pressure of major record label demands and expectations. Tricky's work

echoes Prince not only in his musical experimentation but also in the
different ways he imagines himself publicly: appearing as an astronaut
landing in London, as Jesus or the devil, or covered in gold paint, or as
a baby laying in a crib. In videos and press photos, Tricky and Martina
are often seen in distorted forms of drag, partaking in what Isaac Julien
and Kobena Mercer describe as the long history of theatricalizing traditional gender roles in black popular music: "George Clinton's Parliament
and Funkadelic, Cameo, and Prince, for instance, destabali[ze] the signs
of race, gender and sexuality; such artists draw critical attention to the
cultural constructedness, the artifice, of the sexual roles and identities
we inhabit. In this way they remind us that our pleasures are political
and that our politics can be pleasurable."[111] The twist that Tricky and
Martina give to Julien and Mercer's analysis is that they radically mark
their performances as messy and incomplete, not only for the sake of performance itself but to distort the porous boundaries of traditional gender
roles even further. Throughout these images and the music, Tricky and
Martina convey that they do not have the strength—psychic, physical,
sexual, musical—to make the performance complete; instead they aes-
theticize and eroticize their own failure to comply with narrow and rigid
heterosexual gender identities.

On the cover for the "Overcome" single, for example, Martina and
Tricky stage a twisted inverse of the heterosexual bride and groom scenario. Martina wears a suit and a top hat, while holding a cigarette; Tricky,
on the other hand, sports a wedding dress askew, allowing the viewers to
see his jeans and shoes underneath. Bright red lipstick is smeared across
his face and he holds a revolver in each hand.[112] This "terrorist drag"
is striking because it makes no effort to conceal its "dragness"; rather,
it accents its own performativity by calling attention to the "failure" of
cross-dressing.[113] The wedding scenario is a key component here as well,
for it connotes the moment in which heterosexual romance traditionally
becomes state- and church-sanctioned. As a result, the picture mocks
the conventions of heterosexual union by showing a couple that refuses
to perform heterosexuality in its most hegemonic incarnation, thus excavating the violence inherent in the manifold ways in which state and
nonstate discourses—think, for instance, of relentless apotheosis of marriage in Hollywood cinema or U.S. television—continually police and
enforce the boundaries of proper couplehood. Moreover, in the lyrics on
all three albums, heterosexual romance does not appear as a refuge from

the strains of late capitalism but is just as "fucked-up" as everything else. In "Suffocated Love" Tricky sings, "I keep her warm, but we never kiss / she cuts my slender wrists / I keep her warm, but we never kiss / she says I'm weak and immature." Similarly, in "Christiansands," Tricky questions some of the main clichés of monogamous heterosexual romance: "You and me, what does that mean? / Always, what does that mean? / Forever, what does that mean?" Here, heterosexual romance could not be further from functioning as a safe haven from the damages created by late capitalist society; instead, it is as embattled and distorted as other social formations, if not even more so.

"Abboan Fat Tracks," to take another example, features Martina chanting the following lines: "I fuck you in the ass, just for a laugh / I ride the premenstrual cycle / Forget about the Michael." Here, instead of Tricky singing, Martina sings lines that are coded as specifically masculine in order to garner shock value from the unusualness — even in the era of *Bend over Boyfriend* videos — of a woman stating that she wants to fuck a man up the ass and not vice versa.[114] The mention of her "premenstrual cycle" calls attention lyrically to Martina's voice as feminine and creates a glaring rift between the enunciating voice and the content of enunciation, which refuses to be subsumed either musically or lyrically. This linguisticosonic juxtaposition enacts a different form of what Judith Halberstam describes as "female masculinity," since these lyrics position Martina as "masculine" despite her "feminine" voice.[115] Here, Martina's "female masculinity" enables her to take on the role of the sexual aggressor instead of simply functioning as a foil for masculinist fantasies — the role women are habitually relegated to in hip-hop. The anal domain serves as one of the most forceful dislocations of the heterosexual matrix, even if articulated from within putatively hetero contexts such as the Tricky/Martina scenario, since, according to Leo Bersani, "if the rectum is the grave in which the masculine ideal (an ideal shared — differently — by men *and* women) of proud subjectivity is buried, then it should be celebrated for its very potential of death."[116] Thus the anus supplies another way to dislodge the precincts of traditional heterosexual representational economies by means of Martina cast in the role of penetrator, a position usually reserved for men whether gay or straight. Instead, Tricky and Martina declare: "How things are together we'll destroy / and then we can destroy what we are," both "burying" their "proud subjectivities" in the annals of the posterior. This obliteration, rather than dispensing with the heterosexual couple per se, stages its implosion, in the process illustrating that sexual explicitness need not always serve the "lower" purposes ascribed to it by Gilroy. Put differently, Tricky and Martina's sex story does not so much interpellate a hetero self that takes the fit body as its logos, but utilizes sex as a way to detonate both the body politic of hip-hop and traditional configurations of heterosexual coupling in which "the bio-politics of fucking" give way to *fucking* with these very categories.

Lee Edelman notes that "sodomy . . . gets figured as the literalization of the 'preposterous' precisely insofar as the practice of giving precedence to the posterior and thus as confounding the stability or determinacy of linguistic or erotic positioning," linking the invocation of the anal as the locus for the dismantling of a self-same (sexualized) subjectivity, as discussed above, with other lyrical and imagistic instances of "fucked-upness," or in Edelman's terms, "preposterousness" in Tricky and Martina's cosmology.[117] The video for "Christiansands" further exemplifies their distrust of rigid gender identities and heterosexual bonds. It begins with a shot of Tricky, his fingernails adorned with gold nail polish, sitting across from Martina in a bus station. The music features a doubling of their voices, as most of the lines are sung by both of them on the soundtrack, but they are lip-synched in the video by Tricky alone; Martina, wearing a red dress, only mimes the lines she sings by herself. In the second half, the video cuts between Martina, now wearing a three-piece suit and fedora hat, while she mimes Tricky's words and Tricky performs his own voice. This adds a visual layer to the aural doubling of their voices: Martina now functions as Tricky's double and stand-in. Where Tricky was lip-synching his own and Martina's voices in unison, Martina now mimes his words. At some point Martina stops performing Tricky's words and is seen in the same red dress she wore in the beginning of the video. As the video progresses Tricky gets up and fidgets around and a group of three background singers wearing a single interconnected sequined garment appears, but their voices are inaudible to the listeners. The group resembles 1960s black female vocal groups such as the Supremes or Martha Reeves and the Vandellas and can be taken to ironically signify upon the uses of black women background singers in a variety of popular music genres, especially when contrasted to the dominant role Martina's voice occupies in the duo's musical figurations.[118] In his book *Are We Not Men?* Phillip Brian Harper contends that black background singers, particularly black women, as parts of white musicians' performances register primarily on the visual level. Harper argues that white artists often use black backup singers not as individual subjects but as composites for an authenticity constituted mainly by their racial identity.[119] The somewhat random appearance of the three singers in Tricky's video would seem to visually enact Harper's point since they do not sing or even lip-synch, but only provide a visual point of reference in the video.

While this is under way, we see Tricky climbing up the walls, until the video comes to a close with another shot of Tricky's painted fingernails, as he sits on the other side of the room from Martina, just as in the opening shot. Overall, music serves as the only mode of communication between the two subjects; they do not look at each other or acknowledge each other's presence for the duration of the video. The soundtrack functions as the channel for the blurring of their gender and musical identities, for it provides both Tricky and Martina with the means to embody and feed off each other without having to do so visually. Although Tricky and Martina take on stereotypical characteristics of the other gender—Tricky wearing nail polish and Martina a suit—they never make the shift complete so as to suggest a process of becoming rather than being. However, they do embody each other's voices by visually enacting the vocal parts of the other person: Tricky by performing by himself the parts that he and Martina sing together in the video and Martina by miming some, but not all, of the lines that Tricky sings. The lyrics of "Christiansands" reflect this aural (dis)embodiment: "I'll master your language; in the meantime I create my own." In the video, Martina attempts to master Tricky's language and, vice versa, to create a new language that fails to give us a clear map of where one voice ends and the other begins. By "fucking with" the at times unyielding performances of race and gender in black popular music, the duo unearths the fissures hidden in the maintenance of these categories and highlights the massive amount of ideological and physical labor needed to make it seem as if these ruptures were not always already gnawing at its margins.

The gender distortion of Martina's and Tricky's singing personas and Martina's vocalized "female masculinity" also make themselves evident in their cover versions, as most of the songs were performed by male voices in the original recordings and delivered by Martina in the new versions. Their cover versions include African American hip-hop tracks such as Eric B. and Rakim's "Lyrics of Fury," Slick Rick's "Children's Story," and Public Enemy's "Black Steel in the Hour of Chaos."[120] These three choices for covers represent the archetypes of "new school" hip-hop MCS: Slick Rick is widely admired for his storytelling capabilities, Chuck D. stands for the agitated political MC, and Rakim is revered as a wordsmith.[121] Thus the cover versions represent a hip-hop history lesson, while also redefining the articulations of iconic figures of recent black popular music. Their cover version of Public Enemy's "Black Steel in the Hour of Chaos" achieves its most dramatic effect through the gender shift in the main voice and its general musical resignification of the track. The track chronicles a black male subject getting a letter from the government asking him to join the army, an invitation he refuses because of the racist policies of his country. Not only does the black man rebuff the call; he also threatens to fight the government itself with "black steel." In Tricky's version, Martina is the lead voice and enunciates the lines "a brother like me" and "they cannot understand that I am a black man" repeatedly, although they only appear once in the original. Through the repetition of these lines in which Martina refers to herself as a man, she sonically inscribes her gender difference, which is ironic, since Public Enemy's vision, while not excluding women in an explicit fashion, contains no references to women, in part because women are excluded from the military draft in most Western countries. (Public Enemy's early oeuvre is replete with explicitly antifeminist statements, which does not detract from the group's sonic and political impact but should nonetheless be noted.) Thus Public Enemy's masculine and black nationalist call for armed black resistance mutates into a cross-gender testimony of solidarity by virtue of Martina singing these lyrics. Instead of changing Public Enemy's words to fit her own situation, Martina shifts their meaning through the "femininity" of her own voice. However, in this particular case, the femininity of Martina's voice registers chiefly in relation to the masculinity of Chuck D.'s voice in the earlier rendition. Not simply dismissing Public Enemy, Martina's voice creates a space in which she, as a black woman, can practice resistance alongside black men. Having a female voice refer to herself as a brother and black man makes the marginalization of women in the original audible/hearable—it sounds the absence in the original, in addition to amplifying her presence in the cover version, especially considering the habitual equation of the military and militarism in general, both materially and discursively, with masculinity. But the sounding of "feminine lack" should not be heeded as mere ideology critique but also as an opening bid for a conversation between feminism and black nationalism. The alterity inscribed by Martina's voice sounds not only in terms of gender but also in terms of nationality, for she raps/sings/intones with an obviously crisp British accent. On the one hand, her performance unearths the Americanness of the original, and on the other hand, Martina's voice transposes Public Enemy's call for armed resistance against white supremacy into one that includes black British (female) subjects, not just African Americans. As with the gender blurring discussed above, the Britishness of Martina's delivery opens a space for black British voices and subjectivity on the map of the popular musical practices of the black Atlantic. Tricky and Martina create a transatlantic dialogue around black resistance, making the track relevant not only to African American men but also to other subjects in the African diaspora. It is as if Tricky and Martina comply with one of the members of Public Enemy, Flavor Flav, who commands London "to make some noise," in the beginning of the original "Black Steel." Accordingly, the repetition of "I got a letter" in Tricky and Martina's version can be taken to refer to Public Enemy's track itself. In the original, Public Enemy received "a letter" from the American government; Tricky and Martina, on the other hand, receive an American letter in the form of "Black Steel," which they respond to by radically diversifying its signification.

The musical construction of this cover version also highlights the divergences from the original. Where the Public Enemy version of "Black Steel" is a stripped-down hardcore hip-hop track that consists mainly of a drum and a piano loop laid under the raps of Chuck D., Tricky and Martina's version sounds more like a runaway from the land of indie rock, with its wall of guitars, than the fugitive from the American government Public Enemy had in mind. Tricky himself sees a link between his musical and racial identities, which he describes in the following fashion: "Both of them are still in me: the white guy making black music and the black guy making white music—it was all integrated from way back."[122] Thus the explicit use of a musical idiom mainly considered "white"— alternative rock—in a cover version of the most explicitly militant and black nationalist of all hip-hop crews—Public Enemy—can be heard as a deliberate move to assert his biracial identity through sound by placing them side by side. Rather than treating the two musical and racial spheres as separate, Tricky and Martina provide us with a "fucked-up" version of them wherein worlds sonically collide as opposed to coexisting peacefully. Overall, they fail to perform and conform to the versions of masculinity, blackness, and Americanness generated by Public Enemy. However, in achieving this feat Martina and Tricky create their own, albeit very different version, of black resistance that reconstructs the signification of Public Enemy's "Black Steel" even while it could not exist without this initial formulation, in terms of gender, race, and musical genre.

With the global distribution of sound recordings and MTV, black popular music has become an immensely influential international arena. Martina and Tricky's version of Public Enemy's "Black Steel in the Hour of Chaos" serves as one example that illustrates the dialogues taking place in this domain and complicates notions of community membership in significant ways. In our case, Tricky and Martina identify as black British through the "Britishness" of their voices and also as black diasporic subjects since they articulate their political and musical solidarity with Public Enemy by remaking their song. Furthermore, Tricky identifies himself as biracial in his use of the musical genres rock and hip-hop, which are usually considered racially and culturally distinct, if not mutually exclusive, especially for black mainstream artists. Finally, Martina and Tricky reconstruct rigid gender roles through their cover versions and in various other musical and visual aspects of their work. All of these factors taken together musically and visually imagine new forms of diasporic citizenship that do not separate these different ways of belonging and becoming but represent them as part of a fractured whole.

Tricky and Martina depart from the practices of diasporic citizenship of both Advanced Chemistry and the Fugees; the primary difference lies in the abstraction of their musical, lyrical, and imagistic performances. Where the Fugees use their lyrics, record covers, and videos to reclaim the vilified position of refugees and Advanced Chemistry writes lyrics concerning the cultural citizenship of Afro-Germans, Tricky and Martina construct apocalyptic panoramas in which issues of citizenship rise or rather fall from the emotional, cultural, racial, sexual, and musical debris provided by the sociopolitical situation in the contemporary Western world. In some sense, then, their version of diasporic citizenship can be called postdiasporic, since they are clearly in dialogue with diasporic practices such as hip-hop but do not specify their relation to this culture in the same explicit manner as do both of the other groups. In interviews, Tricky tells stories about his engagement with hip-hop as a black British teenager, like those of Torch in "Kapitel 1" by Advanced Chemistry; the

Fugees also engage with hip-hop, constructing themselves as the "positive saviors" of this art form. However, Tricky's role vis-à-vis hip-hop represents a dismantling rather than a guardianship: Tricky and Martina blow the genre apart in order to show the seams — musical and ideological — that hold the form together. The Fugees and Advanced Chemistry, to be sure, appropriate this sonic form and make it their own by adding new musical styles and content, but they still insist on the discreteness of hip-hop. Thus Tricky and Martina create a popular fantasy in which they "cuff strictly mimetical" representations of gender, race, sexuality and musical genres in order to suggest a "maniacal" black subjectivity. In other words, they emphasize the pain and negativity of negotiating between different poles of identification instead of concealing them. As we have seen, the Fugees place themselves on the border and Advanced Chemistry inside it. Tricky and Martina's diasporic citizenship, however, turns inward, showing, in its focus on the psyche and the couple, how the border "cuts" particular minoritized subjects within the framework of the modern nation-state and its global networks in a different way than the more explicitly "political" narratives of the other two groups.[123] Tricky and Martina not only "fuck with" diasporic identification as it relates to questions of blackness and the nation-state in the West but also explode both the individuated person and couple as subject from within these structures, thus underscoring the messiness of these categories, which cannot be subsumed by either celebratory incantations of hybridity or determinist notions of oppression.

Between things does not designate a localizable relation going from one thing to the other and back again, but a perpendicular direction, a transversal movement that sweeps one *and* the other away, a stream without beginning or end that undermines its banks and picks up speed in the middle.

—Gilles Deleuze and Felix Guattari

Outro

Thinking Sound/Sound Thinking

(Slipping into the Breaks *Remix*)

It seems that much recent work in literary and cultural studies desires nothing so much as to affirm and perform its professionalism while at the same time mimicking the disciplinary maneuvers of history and sociology respectively. As a consequence, the various critical interventions of the last thirty years have been absorbed and made safe at an accelerating velocity, while daring and adventurous models that query the status quo remain few and far between. Following a period of balkanization, customarily referred to as the culture wars, we have now entered another stage, where different subdisciplines exist in quasi isolation, producing virtually identical insights, in effect ushering us from the hazardous struggles of the crack wars to the assumed safety of a Prozac nation. Splintered fractions have retreated to their different gated communities of semihomogeneity not all that different from the countless suburbs defined by the same yet oh-so slightly different strip malls that populate the U.S. landscape, producing nothing less than the suburbanization of literary and cultural studies. Assorted historicisms, incantations of domination and resistance, litanies of race, gender, class, and sexuality, to name but a few, insist too often on the radical specificity of their claims even though these very particularities appear strikingly alike across a wide array of spatiotemporal configurations and have frequently calcified into dogmas of uninflected positivism in which arguments can only pertain to such a microparticularized sliver of the universe that any and all dialogue with other times, localities, cultures, and so on is dismissed a priori. Still, it is also hard to swallow the wholesale renunciation of these accounts either in the name of a universal old-school notion of the aesthetic, a knee-jerk redaction of poststructuralism, or a return to the classical tenets of Marxism and psychoanalysis, since these arguments serve as reactive rejoinders rather than reformulations of the disciplines in question, let alone alternatives to the problematics they seek to circumvent. Too often, these polemics against identity politics and historicism provide little in the way of novel methodologies or critical models, appearing instead as not much more than sparsely disguised tactics to keep the barbarians at the gate.

This impasse results in part from the tenor of crisis in the U.S. humanities, especially as it pertains to their raison d'être in a posthumanist university and world at large, wherein these putative certainties offer a leg to stand on in a hostile environment. And, despite the general lip service paid to interdisciplinary maneuvers in our contemporary institutional and intellectual ecologies, they are habitually taken as handicaps, since the supposedly clearly delineated methods and objects of yesteryear have given way to a threatening multiplicity of approaches and cultural forms. Rather than openings that facilitate fresh institutional configurations and imaginings of unorthodox intellectual endeavors, the lack of obvious focus and the absence of a conceptual and institutional center have lead to retrenchment. Nevertheless, this lack could prove to be the humanities' strongest asset in the current climate, as it presents a chance to leave behind old beliefs in order to invent nondisciplinary disciplines that are always in the throes of becoming, where limits are not preset but are negotiated within the contexts of the intellectual project in question. Making this instability usable might instigate potential forms of literary and cultural studies instead of reproducing current practices while simultaneously and repeatedly bemoaning their shortcomings. In what follows, I will not offer any wholesale homeopathic remedies, not even partial ones, nor embrace interdisciplinarity as a relativistic free-for-all. I do, however, want to think about, through, and with this current deadlock vis-à-vis the intellectual and methodological strategies of *Phono-*

graphies: Grooves in Sonic Afro-Modernity. I do this not in the spirit of tendering my approach as the shining beacon of a newly invigorated literary and cultural studies but as an example of reflecting, if only messily and cursorily, this conundrum within the confines of a particular intellectual trek within the current humanities.

In its earliest incarnation *Phonographies* was a fairly straightforward affair, each chapter contained a reading of one twentieth-century African American literary text concerned with the cultural dimensions of sound technologies. At the time, producing analyses of canonical written works, rather than examining the popular musical practices I thought were ripe for my special brand of exegesis, provided the easiest path to achieve my goals within the disciplinary confines of an English department; after all, my training had been primarily in the analysis of literary texts. The two dimensions of my project, however, appeared contradictory, if not mutually exclusive. Suffice it to say, this structure did not last very long; it was soon replaced by an amalgamation of literature (with its lofty heights) and popular culture (with its ephemeral speed). Once this new *Phonographies* began to take its present shape one of my central challenges was how to think these two spheres together without losing the texture of either. In what ways could popular practices and artifacts resituate and reformulate canonical literary texts? And how could techniques of literary studies cast fresh light on contemporary popular music and film? Although it sounds deceptively simple, it has been a much rougher terrain to negotiate than I had initially assumed. While it may seem obvious to expand a project in literary studies just by using other cultural forms as contemporaneous evidence, doing so without reflecting the process itself barely reconstructs how things are done — it just adds a slightly hip flavor to the same old tools of the trade. Including nonliterary artifacts, I believe, should not serve only as an end in itself but as an aid in reformatting these, at times rusty, utensils. Otherwise what's the use? Or, as Samuel Delany has said, "We must be willing to understand how cleaving to a certain dead rhetoric forces us to go on repeating empty critical rituals associated with past authority and perpetuating the anxiety that what we take pleasure in will not be sufficiently welcomed, the two interacting in a way that does not overcome the problem but only produces a self-fulfilling prophecy."[1] In my case, avoiding self-fulfilling prophecies necessitated experimenting with different forms of analysis and modes of writing, in addition to a variety of juxtapositions across media and historical periods, so that extratextual forms contaminate literary texts and vice versa.

For instance, the first chapter I wrote, "In the Mix," discusses W. E. B. Du Bois's *The Souls of Black Folk* in relation to the practices of disc jockeying without allowing one to dominate the other. There would have been nothing simpler than to create a causal link between these two factors, either positioning Du Bois's notion of double consciousness as a form of DJing *avant la lettre* or, conversely, reading the mixing of two records as a present reformulation of the earlier concept. This brand of inquiry would have just affirmed the already accepted rubrics that discipline both Du Bois and DJing, where one remains in the institutionally sanctioned annals of literary canonicity and the other safely occupies the messy popular terrain, and never the twain shall meet. Instead, I wanted to ask what would happen if these components were thought together without the safety net of an a priori historical connection. This approach eschews simply applying Du Bois's superstructural concepts to the raw base of DJing, the traditional modus operandi in literary and cultural studies, but ascertains how DJing unearths new potentialities in the Du Boisian text and vice versa. Critical concepts from the archive of "theory" are regularly applied to a host of cultural artifacts: here we have a Marxist consideration of mainstream Hollywood cinema, and in that corner, a psychoanalytic reading of a canonical novel, and even though there exists no need to dismiss these endeavors, they do beg the question: is that enough? Clearly not, for once again neither camp is transformed in this encounter, the theoretical frame/cultural case still remain lodged in their predetermined positions. While I would not go quite as far as Kodwo Eshun, who contends that "you don't really need any Heidegger, because George Clinton is already theoretical," his perspective is refreshing since it does not presume that popular practices direly need the help of theory to be conceptual. And if you don't believe me, please call R. Kelly, the German electronic music label Mille Plateaux, or Nina Simone.[2] Still, there is no reason to choose: why not conjecture what Heidegger can learn from George Clinton without simply reversing the logic that deems one more abstract than the other in the first place? In other words, what if Du Bois and DJing cohabit this chapter not because there exists some nebulous and predetermined correlation between them, either historical or scholarly but, to put it briefly, because the act of thinking them together establishes both the logic and reasoning for doing so? Hence, the fusion attains an originary status within the confines of this particular argument, shifting the emphasis to the manner in which Du Bois's text and DJing infiltrate each other, using Du Bois as a way into the practice of DJing and rethinking *Souls* as a form of textual mixing. Nonetheless, despite this permeation, the two components are surely not congruent or even symmetrical. Consequently, not assuming that these linkages preexisted the confines of the argument forced me to conceive of my method not as cinema verité but more along the lines of a speculative narrative.

In a different place Eshun offers the following observation: "In Cult-Stud, TechnoTheory, and CyberCulture, those painfully archaic regimes, theory always comes to Music's *rescue*. The organization of sound is interpreted historically, politically, socially. Like a headmaster, theory teaches today's music a thing or 2 about life. It subdues music's ambition, reins it in, restores it to its proper place, reconciles it to its proper belated fate."[3] For the project as a whole, this insight enabled me to think with sound, rather than thinking *about* sound with the help of critical theory; my newfound approach is closer to one that, according to Jacques Attali, "makes mutations audible. It obliges us to invent categories and new dynamics to regenerate social theory, which today has become crystallized, entrapped, and moribund."[4] The practice of DJing itself served as my guide in this murky topography, since DJs mix records not according to primary content, but for the various dimensions of rhythm, timbre, texture, and the overall "feel" of the tracks in question. Rather than putting my faith only in the protocols of literary studies that do not even register these features' existence, much less deploy them, I chose to intermingle the two in order to fashion different methodologies. Infusing techniques of close textual reading and historical contextualization, for instance, with the much more vague, but nonetheless useful, parameters of DJing that are a potential of experience but often resist the explanatory strictures of critical discourse, opened up and reinvented the function of the literary in *Phonographies*. This wrested Ralph Ellison's *Invisible Man* from its primary place as a literary text to be mined, read, and contextualized within the traditional strata of literary and social history, revealing, instead, a theory of the intersectionality of sound, technology, and black subjectivity. Appropriating DJing for or translating DJing into the languages of literary studies implies not so much its wholesale importation — pretty much an impossibility — as an embrace of certain forms of chaos or entropy in which lacunae, fractures, and inconsistencies are allowed to spawn their own skewed logics and velocities, generating their becomings only in the milieu of the *between* invoked in the epigraph by Deleuze and Guattari. The acclimatization of DJing was further aided by concepts such as Hortense Spillers's notion of "the crosscurrents and discontinuities" of literary genealogy; Walter Benjamin's "monadic shrapnel" that blasts open the putative continuum of linear historical time; and Edouard Glissant's "opacities," because they do not simulate cohesion, clarity, or meaning but accentuate the contained rhythmic chaos of the world much in the same way as DJs. In the context of *Phonographies*, thinking sound unearths the singular potentialities of both the literary and the sonic, which, as opposed to affirming and perpetuating their institutionally sanctioned being, exalts their becoming. Process, not structure, is the rule of this game.

DJing acutely draws attention to questions of technology, the second crucial aspect of *Phonographies*, since record players serve as the DJ's instruments. DJing also brings into crisis the modes of critical discourse about information technologies, where machines appear as either material limit cases frozen in time and space or discursive constructs always already waiting to be appropriated. Surely, DJing represents a prime instance of a technology used against its intended function of reproducing prerecorded sound material mimetically. DJing is habitually construed as a resistant art form that underscores how already existing technologies modify their function according to usage, which, although constituting a significant shift in practice, leaves the apparatus itself unsullied; a record player is still a record player, only now it also acts as an instrument and not a simple playback device. What remains uninterrogated is the variable materiality of the apparatus itself, since the machine, by definition, becomes a different creature via its reconfigured usage. If one consults the histories of sound technologies, these ruptures appear not as aberrations but as *the* defining features. The phonograph itself was initially anticipated to serve as an office instrument for recording letters, not reproducing music, and the Walkman was conceptualized by Sony as a device for two listeners rather than the individuating mechanism it has become, since these aspects only emerged in the practices of consumers.

These are just some brief examples of many that worry, and perhaps negate, both the productivist lens of the history of technology that approaches these machines primarily from the vantage point of the captains of industry and the appropriation model favored by cultural studies that only takes in what is done with these gadgets by users. What authorizes the notion of an originary function and conversely appropriative reconfigurations if these alleged aberrations represent not so much the fringes of these technologies but, instead, have come to define their major utilities? Thus the interplay between the materiality of the apparatus and its discursive dimensions ceases to transact the binary drama it has hitherto enacted and splinters into a series of relational singularities that refuse to signify any ontological consistency before and beyond. The phonograph always already harbors the potentiality of either reproducing music or serving as a musical instrument, since, to put it in the crudest terms, the machine does not necessitate structural changes to take on these configurations. Nevertheless, these practices also significantly revise the materiality of the apparatus while contemporaneously altering the idea of materiality per se, which in this constellation is only instantiated and invented in the course of singularization. Instead of a dialectical sparring between the transcendental material and cultural mediation, the history of sound technologies offers singular materialities, throwing us into the orbit of "monadic shrapnel," "crosscurrents and discontinuities," and "opacities." How else to fathom the phonograph's becoming an instrument in the hands of hip-hop DJs in New York City? That transformation was enabled by, but cannot be reduced to, the mixing routines developed almost contemporaneously in gay clubs also in New York and the sound system culture of Jamaica — itself based on the importation and reinvention of African American recorded music, which was then brought back to New York by Jamaican immigrants who became hip-hop DJs. Linearity and historical causality don't quite do justice to this fragile and discordant cluster. Here, I am advocating not the abandonment of the historical as much as its reimagining vis-à-vis singularity.

I have thus far not explicitly addressed questions of racial difference, even though my project concerns itself primarily with cultural practices that often bear the mark, and perhaps burden, of the "Afro" prefix. After all, the title of this volume, *Phonographies: Grooves in Afro-Modernity*, does not so much invite as make an argument about the particular Afro-diasporic provenances of various sound technologies in its very utterance. And one of the questions I have been asked most frequently is, What makes this project specifically black? As with most other questions, the answer is deceptively simple yet boundless: everything and nothing.

Surely, *Phonographies* concerns itself with black culture given that all the "primary" artifacts discussed were authored by subjects rumored to be of African origin; after that the situation gets a little more tricky — and I'm only being mildly facetious here. This situation raises some general procedural questions about the status of minority discourse in the contemporary academy. If black studies is to remain institutionally and intellectually relevant, then black specificity and its sibling identitarian logic are in dire need of recalibration, without resorting to some of the facile critiques launched from outside the discipline that clamor for the dismantling of the field in its entirety. Instead of pressing black cultural production into the straitjacket of particularity, might we begin fathoming its singularity, which, rather than erasing differences — as in our old friend, colorblind universalism — takes these not as all there is but only as part of this unruly equation. If black culture continues to be reduced to its particularity, then any analysis of it will only affirm the already known. To argue that what I term "sonic Afro-modernity" pertains only to black culture seems "wrong" — I am using this term both advisedly and explicitly here — on so many different fronts (empirically and conceptually, for instance) that I cannot even begin to list them, let alone provide provisional discussions of their erroneousness. In the most crass empirical terms, confronted with the "crosscurrents and discontinuities" of black popular music, one would be hard pressed to formulate an argument only in the tongue of particularity and specificity; how else to explain the immense global popularity of hip-hop, a genre that, at least lyrically, consists of little more than a performance of African American particularity? Still, permutations of this form can be found in the most nonmelanated spaces of the globe, which, while not abolishing U.S. black specificity, nonetheless obliges us to ask just how useful identitarian thinking remains in this and any other context when it serves as the only or even the main mode of conceptualizing black culture. To argue that black popular musics and their multifarious technological instantiations are only relevant to black people and not to American culture at large, or numerous other global cultural architechtonics, simply misses the point, all the points.

In the sound of "sonic Afro-modernity," one cannot relinquish the concept of modernity to the Habermas-lite variant of this conglomerate that conceives of this field solely in terms of enlightenment, rationality, democracy, and so on. Modernity has also given us terror, colonialism, slavery, genocide, and the like, as Aimé Césaire, Hannah Arendt, Theodor Adorno, W. E. B. Du Bois, Simone de Beauvoir, and Frantz Fanon, among others, have shown. If modernity does indeed include these "other" experiences, why do such astute critics as Homi Bhabha and Paul Gilroy still insist on using phrases such as "countermodernity" or "otherwise than modernity"? Perhaps we need to excise the "otherwise" and "counter" from this volatile compound, even if only for experimental purposes that enable alternative avenues for thought in the absence of these conceptual safety nets. In the place of an unrelenting particularity appears a careful attention to the singularity of every cultural utterance, which does not signify so much the obliteration of particularity as such as it reshuffles the heuristic deck of cards this generation's minority intellectuals have been dealt. In other words, if singularity is thought of not as merely immanent to itself but as also always already relational — a symbiosis of Deleuze and Guattari's singularity and Edouard Glissant's poetics of relation — then this model succeeds both in ascertaining the specificity of the cultural performance in question and potentially networking it with everything else in the cosmos. In practical terms, the notion of a relational singularity suspends, and perhaps even nullifies, the in spite of/because of white supremacy (or patriarchy, the heterosexual matrix, etc.) bifurcation that haunts minority discourse in the Anglo-American humanities and social sciences. Consequently, *Phonographies* does not present black culture's complicated rapport with sound technologies as a series of exploitative practices within the recording industry, or, conversely as a heroic narrative of resistance, but as textured singularities that move in and out of these particularities yet loudly refuse to be reduced to them. Generally, I have attempted to surmise the conditions of im/possibility put in motion by the interfacing of sound technologies and Afro-diasporic culture without resorting to celebratory boosterism or a laundry list of oppressions. This methodology should not and cannot lead to a complete denial of their existence but conjures a different model of conceptualizing minority discourses, releasing them from their preordained cell of marginality to conjecture how these technocultural practices are indicative of and shape modernity as such.

It is crucial, I insist, that this dismantling of particularism and identitarian logic come from within the intellectual and institutional confines of minority discourse, since the critique from without — if we must draw such reactive boundaries — too frequently leaves the general/particular partition intact by replacing a series of specificities with a return to universalism: just another name for the particular projected onto a larger screen. As Sylvia Wynter suggests, "The present definition, *minority/majority*, if accepted as a brute fact, empowers mainstream literary scholarship to continue to see itself . . . as so ordered by the given nature of things rather than secured by the institutionalized directive signs of an order of discourse."[5] Wynter compels us not to make minority discourse the paradoxical end unto itself that it has become by merely rehearsing its own particularity and in the process leaving the general discursive architecture untouched. Instead of merely occupying an enclosed chamber in this shaky edifice, Wynter asks that we redraw the foundational blueprints. In the chapter that engages this problematic most directly I use the catchphrase "I am I be" — taken from hip-hop group De La Soul — as a shorthand that garners its argumentative and evocative force via juxtaposition and facilitates the amplification of the putative abyss between subjectivity and identity within current academic debates. To this end, the refrain "I am I be" attempts to reframe this impasse by insisting on the minoritarian as a crucial vicinity from and through which to theorize some dynamics of the modern — period — no prefixes or suffixes. Earlier Afro-diasporic intellectuals such as Zora Neale Hurston, James Baldwin, Ralph Ellison, and Audre Lorde fully realized this dilemma; we could do far worse than follow their intellectual lead, without duplicating some of their blind spots and shortcomings. Abandoning certain constraining features of particularity and identity thinking unbolts the cell and opens up to new spheres of both intellectual and institutional procedures that do not endeavor to reproduce how things supposedly are but imagine how things could be. Or, to put it in the words of two other key players in *Phonographies*, the black British musicians Tricky and Martina: "How things are together we'll destroy / and then we can destroy what we are."

Here, Brian Massumi's sagacious words should serve as directives not only in the register of minority discourse, but for literary and cultural studies in general: "Critical thinking disavows its own inventiveness as much as possible. Because it sees itself as uncovering something it claims was hidden or as debunking something it desires to subtract from the world, it clings to a basically descriptive and justificatory modus operandi. . . . The balance has to shift to *affirmative* methods: techniques which embrace their own inventiveness and are not afraid to own up to the fact that they add (if so meagerly) to reality."[6]

Outro

Somewhere far away, I already discern concerns about the viableness of these ideas, especially with regard to institutional constraints ("But what about tenure committees, deans, and all those other 'evil forces' that keep us from doing work we really want to do?"), which merely detract from the fact that our disciplinary superegos — or maybe they are ids in drag? — and their attendant subtle policing mechanisms at times lag behind the flexibility, and yes, inventiveness of the current university environment. And possibly, just possibly, the fact that I hear these voices among many others in my head just testifies to my own disciplinary superego. But that discussion needs to take place *sotto voce* in another time and place. I have tried to follow this dictum of affirmative methods when and where possible in writing and thinking *Phonographies*, even when I did not have the vocabulary to announce that this is what I was indeed doing, or when the specific venture was doomed to failure. This exemplar of intellectual inquiry departs from current hegemonic formations without ceding the field altogether to closet positivists, identitarian gatekeepers, conservative poststructuralists, and other such strange creatures. The crucial point, however, remains that this work could have only been carried out within the strictures and freedoms of current formations in the humanities, to which I remain dedicated in spite of and because of myself. Does *Phonographies* succeed in carrying out the claims outlined here? Right now, I am not sure whether this is even a relevant question. I — and all that this entails — have moved, busy slipping into the breaks, where thinking is never quite safe but always sound, looking around but also listening, touching, feeling, smelling, tasting. Maybe I'll hear you there, and if not, that's okay, too.

Notes

Intro

1 Delany, quoted in Dery, "Black to the Future," 192. The editors of a recent collection, and one of the first anthologies concerned with the intersectionality of race and technology, phrase this conundrum as follows: "*Technicolor* presents a full spectrum of stories about how people of color produce, transform, appropriate, and consume technologies in their everyday lives. In order to locate these stories, we found it necessary to use a broader understanding of technology, and to include not only those thought to create revolutions (e.g., information technologies), but also those with which people come in contact in their daily lives. For when we limit discussions about technology simply to computer hardware and software, we see only a 'digital divide' that leaves people of color behind" (Nelson, Tu, and Hines, "Introduction: Hidden Circuits," 5).

2 For a different version of this question, one that engages questions of (post)humanity more explicitly than I do here, see my essay "Feenin," which forms the basis of a forthcoming project about technologies of humanity.

3 For a general history of African American music, see Southern, *The Music of Black Americans* and *Readings*. The best writings on the history of the American music industry are Russell Sanjek's *From Print to Plastic* and *American Popular Music*. For a consideration of the commodification of black popular music by largely white-owned corporations, see Cashmore, *The Black Culture Industry*.

4 For the sake of economy, I will hereafter refer to sound recording and re-

production as sonic technologies unless I want to stress specific aspects of one or the other.

5 For further arguments regarding the constitutiveness of blackness to U.S. culture, see Morrison, *Playing in the Dark*, and Ellison, "What Would America Be Like without Blacks?"

6 For a comprehensive overview regarding different conceptions of modernity in relation to politics, culture, and history, see Hall et al., *Modernity*.

7 On the imbrication of the modern and the anthropological primitive, see Fabian, *Time and the Other*, and Cruz, *Culture at the Margins*.

8 See Spillers's forthcoming *The Idea of Black Culture*.

9 Judy, *(Dis)Forming the American Canon*. I will return to these debates in chapter 1. In addition to Judy's work, the reader might also consult the oeuvres of James Baldwin, Aimee Cesaire, W. E. B. Du Bois, Frantz Fanon, Ralph Ellison, Zora Neale Hurston, and Audre Lorde as antecedents as well as those of the following contemporary critics: Houston Baker, Lindon Barrett, Kevin Bell, Homi Bhabha, Jennifer Brody, Abena Busia, Hazel Carby, Nahum Chandler, Angela Davis, Samuel R. Delany, Kodwo Eshun, Henry Louis Gates Jr., Ruth Wilson-Gilmore, Paul Gilroy, Edouard Glissant, Stuart Hall, Michael Hanchard, Wilson Harris, Saidiya Hartman, Mae Henderson, Sharon Holland, Robin Kelley, Wahneema Lubiano, Deborah McDowell, Nathaniel Mackey, Fred Moten, Alondra Nelson, Hortense Spillers, James Snead, Gayatri Spivak, Greg Tate, Cheryl Wall, and Sylvia Wynter.

10 Ellison, *Invisible Man*, 9.

11 Generally, the terms "ephemerality" and "materiality" do not designate ontological or empirical truths, not even half-truths, as much as markers in the cultures and histories of sonic technologies. Moreover, as my argument "develops" it will become apparent that these initially contrasting forces commingle in a number of significant ways, and this book represents a nonlinear genealogy of the variety and intensity of these blurrings.

12 See, for instance, Mowitt, "Music in the Era"; Chion, *Audio-Vision*; Attali, *Noise*; Paulson, *The Noise of Culture*; Eshun, *More Brilliant Than the Sun*; Gitelman, *Scripts, Grooves, and Writing*; Bull, *Sounding Out the City*; Gilbert and Pearson, *Discographies*; Corbett, *Extended Play*; Lastra, *Sound Technology*; Altman, *Sound Theory/Sound Practice*; Rose, *Black Noise*; Sterne, *The Audible Past*; Gracyk, *Rhythm and Noise*; Kittler, *Gramophone, Film, Typewriter*; and Kahn, *Noise, Water, Meat*. For texts that consider the impact of sound technologies in non-Western contexts, see Ahmed, *Daybreak Is Near*; Jones, *Yellow Music*; Mientjes, *Sound of Africa!*; Manuel, *Cassette Culture*.

Notes

13 See Spillers, "Cross-Currents, Discontinuities."

14 Baraka, *Black Music*, 199.

15 I am drawing here on the concise redaction of these debates in Gilbert and Pearson's *Discographies*, 38–53.

16 This versioning of the term "Enlightenment" is Sterne's, *The Audible Past*, 2.

17 For examples from the archive of "new musicology" that attempt to de-absolutize music, see Durant, *The Conditions of Music*; Leppert, *The Sight of Sound*; McClary, *Feminine Endings*; and the essays collected in *Music and Society* edited by Leppert and McClary. Take for instance David Morton's recent comprehensive history of sonic technologies, which closes with the following prophetic statement about the virtual transmission of music via the Internet: "Sound recording activities will continue, but today's sound recorders and tangible sound recording media may well disappear, and the history of sound recording as physical artifact will end" (*Off the Record*, 187). Even though this will seem obvious, isn't there still a need for material objects such as computer hard-drives, software, user interfaces, servers, CDs etc., in the digital transmission of music? It seems that the quest for the holy grail of immaterial sounds has not yet receded from our critical horizons.

18 Attali, *Noise*, 3.

19 In a different place Attali concretizes these prognostic tendencies by asserting that the political organization of the nineteenth century is clearly audible in the music of the eighteenth century (*Noise*, 4).

20 This paragraph is inspired by (and is my humble attempt at a tribute to) the stylistic force and explosive beauty of Avital Ronell's oeuvre, which enacts what many musicians and the critics Gayatri Spivak, Gilles Deleuze, and Hortense Spillers have known for long: style might not be everything, but surely it goes a long way. See in particular Ronell's *Crack Wars, The Telephone Book*, and *Stupidity*.

21 Agamben, *The Coming Community*, 10.

22 Deleuze and Guattari, *A Thousand Plateaus*, 348. The terminology around this concept is somewhat confusing in the Deleuze and Guattari cosmos, since, in addition to *refrain* (as in Massumi's translation) and *ritournelle* (as in the original French version of Deleuze and Guattari's book, *Mille Plateaux*, and the term used by several other translators of Deleuze's work), Guattari utilizes *ritornello* in his solo work. See his "Ritornellos and Existential Affects." Ronald Bogue tenders the following succinct definition of this concept-metaphor: "The refrain territorializes chaos in forming a milieu; it deterritorializes them in a territory proper; and deterritorializing forces constantly play through the territory, thereby opening it to the cosmos as a whole. . . . Music takes

the refrain as its content and transforms it by entering into a process of 'becoming' that deterritorializes the refrain" (*Deleuze on Music and the Arts*, 33).

23 This is a reference to Nick Hornby's 1996 novel *High Fidelity* and its 1999 filmic incarnation, which codify the music geek, or trainspotter as he — and it is almost always a he — would be called in the United Kingdom, as an emotionally stunted, record-collecting, and best-of-list-obsessed white man in his early thirties.

24 Mis-Teeq, "It's Beginning to Feel Like Love."

25 On "making language stutter," see Mackey, *Discrepant Engagement*, 251 and passim; Deleuze, *Proust and Signs* and "He Stuttered." For musical examples that emphasize the stuttering of speech through studio tricknology, listen to the genre of dub reggae, Chaka Khan's "My Love Is Alive," or Ellen Allien's "Sehnsucht."

26 Glissant, *Poetics of Relation*.

1 Hearing Sonic Afro-Modernity

1 I am not singling out Baker and Gilroy because they condemn sound technologies more vociferously than other critics do, but because their arguments explicitly link questions of modernity to black music.

2 Gilroy, *The Black Atlantic*, especially the first and third chapters.

3 In *The Jazz Revolution*, Kathy Ogren shows how the new technology of electrical recording and the national distribution of "race records" altered both the jazz and blues genres in the 1920s. For a fascinating account concerning the role of phonograph records in the dissemination of jazz in 1930s China, see Jones, *Yellow Music*.

4 Baker, *Modernism and the Harlem Renaissance*, xiv.

5 Bhabha, *The Location of Culture*, 243.

6 Bhabha uses "otherwise than modernity" in describing the cultures and subjectivities usually relegated to the margins of modernity (*Location of Culture*, 6). I have changed his term in order to reflect the integrality of "minority cultures" to modernity and the modernity of the cultural practices themselves. Bhabha's original phrase suggests a greater difference between modernity and the cultural practices he is concerned with than his analysis actually reveals.

7 Walter Benjamin, in his influential artwork essay, holds that the advent of mechanical reproduction of art has had two significant structural effects on art's authenticity: first, mechanical reproductions are more autonomous of the original than manual reproductions; second, mechanical reproductions can be viewed in contexts that the original is unable to reach. See "The Work of Art," esp. 222–223.

8 In *Orality and Literacy*, Walter Ong shows writing to, indeed, be a tech-

nology since it requires nonhuman tools (81–83). However, this assumes that speech is not technological and that the human body is natural.

9 Kittler, *Gramophone, Film, Typewriter*, 7. Here and throughout I deploy the term "phonograph" even when referring to machines not habitually associated with this designation to underscore the linkage and leakage of sound and writing in sonic technologies. The "actual" machines in question were termed gramophones once discs replaced cylinders in the early twentieth century and "phonograph" was later neglected in favor of more generic terms such as "record player" and currently "turntable." In other words, "phonograph" refers to a technocultural assemblage rather than circumscribing one empirical "thing."

10 See Gellat, *The Fabulous Phonograph*, 17–32. While the technohistory of *The Fabulous Phonograph* is useful, the book is also glaringly Eurocentric in its focus and tone. On the first page, jazz is dismissed in favor of a "more ambitious and durable repertoire," i.e., Western classical music (11). The entire book grants jazz one paragraph, and the contributions of black people to the phonograph industry are all but elided. For more recent histories of sound recording and reproduction that do take into account black music, see Morton, *Off the Record*; Kenney, *Recorded Music in American Life*; Millard, *America on Record*; and Chanan, *Repeated Takes*. For a cultural historiography of the early years of the phonograph as it relates to other writing technologies, see Gitelman, *Scripts, Grooves, and Writing Machines*. In addition to these texts, I have also consulted Read and Welch, *From Tin Foil*, and Lubar, *Info Culture*, for the following discussion of the early history of the phonograph.

11 Among the other uses Edison foresaw for the phonograph were to tell time, play music like a music box, teach elocution, store aural family memories, record telephone messages and conversations, and aid in language acquisition. The reproduction of music represented only one of ten possible uses envisioned by Edison. See Edison, "The Phonograph and Its Future," 69.

12 Millard, *America on Record*, 24.

13 In "A Voice without a Face," David Laing writes: "For a variety of technical and economic reasons [the phonograph] was not a success. When the revival of sound recording occurred it was primarily through the disc, a format incapable of facilitating homemade recordings, but a more effective instrument for relaying music and light entertainment" (5).

14 See Read and Welch, *From Tin Foil*, 105–118, and Millard, *America on Record*, 42–45.

15 Gitelman, *Scripts, Grooves, and Writing Machines*, 97–147. See also Levin, "For the Record"; Laing, "A Voice without a Face"; Adorno, "The Curves of the Needle" and "The Form of the Phonograph."

16 Taussig, *Mimesis and Alterity*, 199. See also Pietz, "The Phonograph in Africa."

17 Philip Auslander has shown that the very idea of liveness is not only contingent on recording and reproduction but a direct product of these formations, since the formulation "live" in this sense does not enter the annals of dictionaries until the 1930s and is generally defined as that which can be recorded. Auslander, *Liveness*, 51–53. This also echoes, although not in the same terms, Walter Benjamin's notion of the aura introduced to the art work in the age of mechanical reproduction.

18 Laing, "A Voice without a Face."

19 Some of the other routes taken in coming to grips with the disjuncture between the "ephemerality" and "materiality" brought about by the phonograph include depicting the sounds on the surface of records as a form of angelic inscription or hieroglyphic script. See Levin, "For the Record," 38 and 40–41; Adorno, "The Form of the Phonograph," 60; and Gitelman, *Scripts, Grooves, and Writing Machines*, 281.

20 Derrida, "Signature Event Context," 315.

21 In *Of Grammatology*, Derrida makes a similar claim about an expanded field of writing: "And thus we say 'writing' for all that gives rise to an inscription in general, whether it is literal or not and even if what it distributes in space is alien to the order of the voice: cinematography, choreography, of course, but also pictorial, musical, sculptural 'writing'" (9).

22 Here I am drawing on Derrida, *Speech and Phenomena*, 70–87.

23 Thompson goes on to distinguish this mediated interaction from "face-to-face interaction, in which the space-time coordinates of the participants are the same or very similar. ['Tele-aural'] quasi-interaction involves different sets of space-time coordinates which must be spliced together by recipients" (*The Media and Modernity*, 95). I have changed Thompson's original "tele-visual" to "teleaural" in order to highlight my concern with sound and not visuality. Michael Chanan asserts that sound recording is a central aspect of modernity because "it separates the space and time of audition from the place and time of performance, paradoxically giving the experience of modernity a sound in the very act of preserving the voice that fades as it sings" (*Repeated Takes*, 21).

24 Douglas Kahn terms this phenomenon the "deboning" of the human voice; he writes: "Thus, the presence produced by the voice will always entail a degree of delusion because of a difference in the texture of the sound: the speaker hears one voice, others hear it deboned" (*Noise, Water, Meat*, 7).

25 On the extensive intersection of modern informational technologies and the supernatural, see Sconce, *Haunted Media*. For discussions focused

specifically on the phonograph, see Connor, "The Modern Auditory I"; Sterne, *The Audible Past*; Taussig, *Mimesis and Alterity*.

26 Lastra, *Sound Technology and the American Cinema*, 123–153. Most of the essays collected in Altman, *Sound Theory/Sound Practice*, argue along the "nonidentity" line.

27 See also Peggy Phelan's argument about the ontological priority and nonreproductive nature of "live" performance (*Unmarked*, 146–166).

28 In a similar vein, Theodore Gracyk argues that recordings "create a 'virtual' space and time in which a performance is represented as taking place" (*Rhythm and Noise*, 53).

29 See Deleuze, *Difference and Repetition*, where he makes the following claim: "Repetition thus appears as difference without a concept, repetition which escapes indefinitely continued conceptual difference. It expresses a power peculiar to the existent, a stubbornness of the existent in intuition, which resists every specification by concepts no matter how far it is taken" (13–14).

30 Moten describes the ensemble as the "improvisation *of* singularity and totality *through* their opposition" (*In the Break*, 89).

31 See Snead, "Repetition as a Figure of Black Culture."

32 Kittler further shows Derrida's dependency on phonography for his conception of writing: "All concepts of the trace, up to and including Derrida's grammatological *ur*-writing are based on Edison's simple idea. The trace preceding all writing, the trace of pure difference still open between reading and writing, is simply the gramophone needle" (33).

33 Levinas, "The Transcendence of Words," 147.

34 For a crisp delineation of how the sonorous has been abjected in the history of Western thought, see Gilbert and Pearson, *Discographies*, 38–53. For a critique of Derrida on this point, see Dolar, "The Object Voice."

35 There are many places in the Deleuze and Guattari galaxy where these thoughts appear and disappear. The reader might sound out "1837: Of the Refrain" in *A Thousand Plateaus*, Guattari's essay "Ritornellos and Existential Affects," or Deleuze's discussion of Peirce in *Cinema 2*. For secondary sources besides Massumi, consult Bogue, *Deleuze on Music and the Arts*, and Smith, "Deleuze's Theory of Sensation."

36 Massumi, *Parables for the Virtual*, 258–259n11.

37 It should be noted that these forces are not apprehended by a preformed subject as in phenomenology but bring a subjective opacity into becoming through their very machinations. Thus it also provides a different take on the sublime from the one outlined by Kant in his third critique. At the center of the concept of the dynamically sublime lies the imagination (*Vorstellungskraft*), which in the case of the sublime fails to mediate between sensual perceptions (*sinnliche Wahrnehmung*) and

understanding (*Verstand*). Generally, the imagination molds sensual perceptions (external stimuli) into regular forms via understanding, thus creating a smooth synthesis between understanding and sensual perceptions. However, when the subject experiences the *unvergleichliche Grösse* (the absolutely great) in nature (for Kant the sublime can only appear in nature and not in the work of art as in Adorno and Lyotard), the perceptions are too strong to be shaped into conventional forms by the imagination. This triggers a feeling of unpleasure (*Unlust*) that can be overcome if the subject is granted bodily safety and free thought vis-à-vis the "unvergleichliche Grösse." Ultimately, this moment of unpleasure causes the subject to recognize the a priori law of reason (*Vernunft*) that precedes all and exceeds everything. The subject, by virtue of transcending this moment of negativity, realizes that the sublime is in fact intrinsic to its being and not to nature—its vastness only activates the sublime within the subject—thus actualizing the subject's full human potential.

Therefore, what we might call an aesthetic perception of power results in the triumph of reason and the unlimited autonomy of the subject. Initially the dynamically sublime indicates an articulation of radical alterity, but in the final instance all otherness is delimited and subsumed by the all-encompassing dominance of transcendental reason. See Kant, *Kritik der Urteilskraft*, 64–207. Deleuze's theorization of sensation appears precisely in this breach, which, here, rather than being sublated by sensible perceptions and/or reason remains open, enabling sensation and perception to coexist. On Deleuze and the Kantian sublime, see Smith, "Deleuze's Theory of Sensation."

38 Barrett, *Blackness and Value*. I focus on Barrett here because his reformulation of the writing and/as freedom constellation is the most pertinent for my argument about the field of sonic Afro-modernity.

39 Alden Nielsen offers a crucial rejoinder to Barrett, coming to the conclusion that "chant, and indeed all orature, bodies itself forth in the garb of the mark, inscription, calligraphy" (*Black Chant*, 30).

40 For works emphasizing the centrality of orality to black culture, see Gilroy, *The Black Atlantic*; Baker, *Blues, Ideology*; Levine, *Black Culture, Black Consciousness*; Gates, *The Signifying Monkey*; Glissant, *Caribbean Discourse*.

41 Glissant, *Caribbean Discourse*, 248.

42 "Speakerly text" is the phrase employed by Henry Louis Gates, Jr. to describe how "to represent the speaking black voice in writing" (*The Signifying Monkey*, xxv–xxvi and passim).

43 As Daphne Duval Harrison points out, "Blacks were heard on records as early as 1895, when George W. Johnson recorded 'Laughing Song' on

an Edison phonocylinder. There were also Victor recordings by the brilliant young comedian Bert Williams; a 1902 recording by the Dinwiddle
Colored Quartet; recordings by Carol Clark, a vocalist who sang so-
called plantation melodies; the Fisk Jubilee Singers singing their 'sorrow
songs'; and coon songs by a few black minstrel men" (*Black Pearls*, 44).
On the twenties and the recording of black music (jazz and blues, in particular) see Ogren, *The Jazz Revolution*; Jones, *Blues People*; and Kenney,
Recorded Music in American Life. For discussions of other genres and
nonmusical recordings in the period, see Higginbotham, "Rethinking
Vernacular Culture," and Oliver, *Songsters and Saints*. Moreover, in the
twenties, records were being produced in American colonies such as the
Philippines and in the Caribbean. See Dixon and Godrich, *Recording
the Blues*, 13. According to Michael Chanan, shellac, the most popular
material for the production of phonograph discs from the end of the
nineteenth century to the middle of the twentieth, was imported from
Asia: "Shellac itself comes from the secretion of a tropical beetle, the
lac, common in India and Malaysia; a substance known from early times
and used by the ancient Egyptians and Chinese as both a glue and a
polish. Shellac discs survived almost unchanged until the 1940's, when
the Allied countries were cut off from sources of supply in the Far East
and found a replacement in vinyl" (*Repeated Takes*, 28). For accounts
of the use of the phonograph in colonial contexts, particularly as an instrument of ethnography in Latin America and Africa, see Pietz, "The
Phonograph in Africa," and Taussig, *Mimesis and Alterity*.

44 Millard, *America on Record*, 85–87.

45 Here I am not arguing that black performers created any monolithic
category of blackness or that all white depictions of blackness were the
same; I am merely establishing the underlying assumptions and uncer-
tainties involved in bringing together the voice and racial identity of any
performer of "coon songs."

46 Jay's *Downcast Eyes* remains the most expansive survey of the role of
the ocular in the West since antiquity, especially in terms of philosophy.
Jonathan Crary (in *Techniques of the Observer*) traces how vision was
disassociated from the other senses in order to become par excellence
the disembodied sense of reason.

47 Du Bois, *The Souls of Black Folk*, 5 (emphases mine).

48 In *Race Men*, Hazel Carby scrutinizes the implicit masculinist ideology
of Du Bois's conception of racial uplift at the turn of the century and
the shadow it has cast on twentieth-century African American political and intellectual culture. About the notion of double consciousness,
Carby writes: "While double-consciousness is, indeed, a product of the
articulation between race and nation, I would argue that we need to

revise our understanding of how this double-consciousness works in order to understand how gender is an ever-present, though unacknowledged, factor in this theory. For Du Bois, the gaining of the 'true self-consciousness' of a racialized and national subject position is dependent upon first gaining a gendered self-consciousness" (37).

49 Fanon also highlights the inadequacy of ontology when it encounters blackness: "Ontology—once it finally admitted as leaving existence by the wayside—does not permit us to understand the being of the black man" (*Black Skin, White Masks*, 110).

50 Hortense Spillers notes the centrality of visuality in Du Bois's theorization of racial subjectivity: "One is . . . struck by the importance of the *specular* and the *spectacular* here, which is precisely where Du Bois placed the significance of the look regarding the 'seventh son' (" 'All the Things You Could Be,' " 346).

51 Wiegman, *American Anatomies*, 31. Frantz Fanon refers to this phenomenon as the "racial epidermal schema." See *Black Skin, White Masks*, 112. Here I draw mainly on Wiegman because she explicitly links the privileging of vision in Western modernity to questions of race. For more general delineations of the "hegemony of vision," see Mowitt, "Music in the Era of Electronic Reproducibility"; Crary, *Techniques of the Observer*; Lowe, *The History of Bourgeois Perception*; Levin, *Modernity and the Hegemony of Vision*.

52 Du Bois's and Fanon's projection of racial formation suggest instances of what Fred Moten calls "a kind of black anticipatory doubling of some fundamental conceptual apparatuses of psychoanalysis: of the primal scene and of the mirror stage that might . . . be seen to operate at the level of a *racial* as well as a sexual determination that is marked in the black tradition though largely unmarked or occluded in psychoanalysis" (*In the Break*, 176).

53 The image of the shadow was also employed by a number of other turn-of-the-twentieth-century black writers such as Charles Chesnutt in *The Marrow of Tradition* and Pauline Hopkins in *Contending Forces*. Francis Watkins Harper goes so far as to equate shadows with black subjects by entitling her novel *Iola Leroy; or, Shadows Uplifted*. Clearly, these uses of the shadow are reflected in and refracted through Ellison's *Shadow and Act*. Du Bois also envisions racial difference as the veil that separates black from white subjects.

54 Butler, *The Psychic Life of Power*, 112. Here, we might also note that Fanon clearly forestalls this Althusserian gesture from within the psychoanalytic paradigm through his important addition of "sociogeny" to the Freudian archive of ontogeny and phylogeny. See *Black Skin*, 11.

55 Du Bois also lists the gift of spirit and physical labor in this context.

56 Gibson, "Introduction," xv.

57 On the vision of the blind, see, for instance, Paulson, *Enlightenment, Romanticism and the Blind in France.*

58 Ansell-Pearson, *Viroid Life*, 15. Ansell-Pearson develops these "poisoned" ideas through a reading of Nietzsche's *On the Genealogy of Morals.*

59 Only after completing this chapter did I come across a similar discussion of *gift* in Du Bois in Ronald Radano's masterful book, *Lying Up a Nation.*

60 In "Plato's Pharmacy" Derrida asks whether "the *pharmakon* isn't . . . a poisoned present?," playing on the English and German significations of "gift" (77). Derrida also discusses "gift" as analogous to the pharmakon in a lengthy footnote (130–131).

2 "I Am I Be"

1 The quoted phrase in the title of this chapter is from De La Soul, "I Am I Be."

2 For a concise overview of the status of the subject in the U.S. humanities in the aftermath of the linguistic turn, see Smith, *Discerning the Subject.*

3 Here I have in mind the proliferation of "minority discourses," as both intellectual endeavors and institutional formations, such as African American studies, Asian American studies, gay and lesbian studies, and women's studies in the U.S. academy since the 1960s. Nevertheless, I would also caution against reading this proliferation in any uncomplicated manner, given that the institutional structures of these discourses, although often construed as taking over, are shaky at best.

4 Any debate about the recent history of the U.S. academic humanities might benefit from consulting Spillers's magisterial "The Crisis of the Negro Intellectual." For Wynter's arguments, see "Columbus, the Ocean Blue" and "On Disenchanting Discourse." See also Judy, *(Dis)Forming the American Canon*, especially chapter 1.

5 See Barbara Christian's "The Race for Theory." Although this essay now seems somewhat dated, especially its polemical edge, we should not move too quickly to dismiss the arguments therein, questions of institutional reproduction in particular. Cheryl A. Wall, while paying close attention to the politics of theory as it is positioned against black feminist criticism, suggests a less exclusionary path by insisting on the usefulness of theory as one of the many forms of interpretive inquiry for dislodging Afro-diasporic women's writing from the mimetic and sociological. See her "Taking Positions."

6 Benjamin, "The Work of Art."

7 I habitually invoke the locution black studies as opposed to more speci-

fied forms of Afro-diasporic thought to keep concerns of institution-
ality in mind, since neither of these forces can be disarticulated from
the other. Furthermore, while I focus primarily on black studies for the
purposes of this argument, many of these points pertain to other forms
of racialized "minority discourse" in the U.S. academy as well.

8　The phrase used as the title to this section, "listen around corners," references the following statement from the prologue of *Invisible Man*: "To
see around corners is enough (that is not that unusual when you are invisible). But to hear around them is too much; it inhibits action" (13).
While hearing around corners might mitigate activity, although I would
doubt that, certainly it does not prohibit critical thinking.

9　Sundquist, *Cultural Contexts*, 115.

10　Robert Stepto reads the prologue in the tradition of authenticating pref-
aces of slave narratives. See *From behind the Veil*, 175. Moreover, we
should also note in passing Ellison's versioning of the last line—by way
of Genesis—from Du Bois's "Forethought" to *Souls*, "need I add that I
who speak here am bone of the bone and the flesh of the flesh of them
that live within the Veil?" (2).

11　Wynter, "On Disenchanting Discourse," 452.

12　This intimates yet another Du Boisian residue in *Invisible Man*, particularly with regard to the scopic; Du Bois writes, "They approach me in
a half-hesitant sort of way, eye me curiously or compassionately, . . .
instead of saying directly, How does it feel to be a problem?" (3).

13　Hall, "The After-Life of Frantz Fanon," 23.

14　Connor links urbanization to the increased noise level produced in cities
and argues that this creates a new way of being in the world that engages
a high level of sonic stimuli ("The Modern Auditory I," 209–212).

15　Martin Jay offers the following formulation of the *lux/lumen* bifurcation: "Perfect linear form was seen as the essence of illumination, and it
existed whether perceived by the human eye or not. Light in this sense
became known as *lumen*. An alternative version of light, known as *lux*,
emphasized instead the actual experience of human sight." These two
conceptions of light and sight have cast their shadows over philosophy,
aesthetics, and optics in the history of the West since Greco-Roman antiquity. See *Downcast Eyes*, 29.

16　Derrida, "White Mythology," 243.

17　Vasseleu, *Textures of Light*, 12.

18　See Deleuze and Guattari, *A Thousand Plateaus*, 167–191. See also the
pertinent distinction between "reflexive faces" and "intensive faces" in
Deleuze, *Cinema 1*, 87–101. Since Deleuze writes about the cinematic
close up, we might think of Ellison's scene as providing a phonographic
close up; in fact, Deleuze's description of the intensive face gels almost

too well with Armstrong's phonographic figuration: "we find ourselves before an intensive face each time the traits break free from the outline, begin to work on their own account, and form an autonomous series which tends towards a limit or crosses a threshold" (89).

19 De La Soul, "I Am I Be."

20 Spillers, "Mama's Baby," 80.

21 Schwarz, *Listening Subjects*, 7.

22 See Schwarz, *Listening Subjects*, and Silverman, *The Acoustic Mirror*. For Lacan's formulation of the mirror stage, which at this point has become such a lingua franca of contemporary criticism that it is almost not necessary to give a citation, see "The Mirror Stage."

23 Gallop, *Reading Lacan*, 59.

24 Silverman, *The Acoustic Mirror*, 80–86, and Schwarz, *Listening Subjects*, 16–17.

25 See Derrida, "Violence and Metaphysics," 84–92. He writes: "Everything given to me within light appears as given to myself by myself. Henceforward, the heliographical metaphor only turns away our glance, providing an alibi for the historical violence of light: a displacement of technico-political oppression in the direction of philosophical discourse" (92).

26 In *Discographies* Jeremy Gilbert and Gilbert Pearson discuss drugs as cultural technologies (138–140).

27 Frith, *Performing Rites*, 157.

28 In *The Cinematic Body*, Steven Shaviro dismantles the repressive and phobic tendencies of the psychoanalytic machine within Anglo-American film theory, where this archetype has exerted a marked influence; he draws the following conclusion: "Psychoanalytic film theory has taken on all the attributes of a religious cult, complete with rites and sacred texts. Twenty years of obsessive invocations of 'lack,' 'castration,' and 'the phallus' have left us with a stultifying orthodoxy that makes any fresh discussion impossible. . . . The psychoanalytic model for film theory is at this point utterly bankrupt; it needs not to be refined and reformed, but to be discarded altogether" (ix). Amen, to that. One might also consult Deleuze and Guattari's *Anti-Oedipus* and the relevant chapters on Freud in *A Thousand Plateaus*.

29 Snead, "Repetition as a Figure of Black Culture," 69.

30 Deleuze, *Difference and Repetition*, 23.

31 Quotations will hereafter be cited parenthetically in the text.

32 This phrase is also employed in Nahum Dimitri Chandler's essay "Originary Displacement," discussed below.

33 Chandler, "Originary Displacement," 249–250.

34 Wynter, "Beyond the Word of Man," 641. Wynter also lists the native,

woman, worker, mad, and unfit as further ontological others; however, she insists that the designation "nigger" holds a particularly volatile position in this disposition.

35 On the idealization of the other in the name of particularity, see the first three chapters of Rey Chow's *Ethics after Idealism*.

36 Still, it is crucial to remember that this happens largely within fields of inquiry that are explicitly racialized, and not with gender studies, for instance—at least not to the same degree—which can aspire to some form of universality. One of the main reasons for this development emanates from the grip that what Paul Gilroy terms "raciology" still holds on so many facets of intellectual and everyday life in the Western world. See his *Against Race*, 11–53. Although the prison house remains largely metaphorical here, even while it often produces insidious forms of institutional confinement in U.S. academe, we should not forget how this form of theoretical incarceration mirrors the current large-scale imprisonment of people of color in the United States. Still, this should not be taken to imply that these two forces are synonymous, or even closely comparable, just relational. For an astute analysis of the current California prison system and "the prison-industrial complex" in general, see Gilmore, *Golden Gulag*, and Davis, "Race and Criminalization."

37 Surely, this is not to argue that the subject is not always already catachrestic, but that this endeavor excavates its general figuration as catachresis. The notion of catachresis has been most forcefully formulated in Gayatri Spivak's work, see *Outside in the Teaching Machine*. Spivak gives the following definitions: "The unendorsable naming of the discovery of the repetition of origin as 'graphematic,' by way of 'writing' as a catachresis, is the double bind that founds all deconstruction" (131); "the name of 'woman,' however *political*, is, like any other name, a catachresis. . . . 'woman' as the name of writing must be erased insofar as it is a necessarily historical catachresis" (137); and "One of the offshoots of the deconstructive view of language is the acknowledgement that the political use of words, like the use of words, is irreducibly catachrestic" (161). The concept was introduced to current critical idioms through Derrida, "White Mythology."

38 Spillers, "The Crisis of the Negro Intellectual," 92.

39 Smith, *Discerning the Subject*, xxix.

40 Tom Cohen formulates this retreat as follows: "Turning away from the sterile formalism of linguistic analysis, one could not disassociate a return to the political from a return to re-asserted agency of the subject (this time, socially constructed). To a degree such reclaimed 'subjectivities' and their associated motifs . . . involved a return to familiar names and mimetic epistemological models." Cohen, *Ideology and In-*

scription, 5. While *Ideology and Inscription* is a fine book, it at times lends itself too well, even if not quite expressly figured in the text, to a certain antiminoritarian retrenchment that crops up increasingly under the mantle of minority discourse lacking analytical "rigor" and/or theoretical sophistication. Cohen's antiminoritarian tendencies are fully articulated in an article about Toni Morrison's *Sula* in which he sees fit to dismiss all previous readings of this text as "regressive" due to their putative insistence on identity politics (6). Cohen writes: "Certain 'Nietzschean' implications of *Sula* (the character or work) seem to have escaped the critical guardians of this canon, who often assume a strict relation between *mimetic* writing styles and the empowerment of 'minority' communities in general and African-American writing in particular" (6). Cohen shelves all prior engagements with Morrison's novel in one sentence without actually engaging them (these might include: Houston Baker, Barbara Smith, Deborah McDowell, and Hortense Spillers, to name only the most prominent), but he also completely denigrates (I'm using this term advisedly here) African American intellectual labor as a mere protective mimesis, i.e., not as intellectual labor at all. While the disavowal and neglect of minoritarian scholarship seems vitriolic enough, although not a rarity in the current climate, Cohen's discussion of *Sula* works over much of the same ground as Deborah McDowell's 1988 article "Boundaries."

41 Spivak, *Death of a Discipline*, 70.

42 Butler, *The Psychic Life of Power*, 11.

43 Glissant, *Poetics of Relation*, 191.

44 In a similar fashion, Gayatri Spivak suggests the following conception of the subject: "A subject-effect can be briefly plotted as follows: that which seems to operate as a subject may be part of an immense discontinuous network of strands that may be termed politics, ideology, economics, history, sexuality, language, and so on. (Each of these strands, if they are isolated, can also be seen as woven from many strands.) Different knottings and configurations of these strands, determined by heterogeneous determinations which are themselves dependent on myriad circumstances, produce the effect of an operating subject." *In Other Worlds*, 204.

45 Deleuze and Guattari, *A Thousand Plateaus*, 348.

46 Deleuze and Guattari are primarily concerned with "pure and intense sonorous material that is always connected to its own abolition — a deterritorialized musical sound" (*Kafka*, 6). In this way, given the emphasis on unformed, unstructured, and asignifying sound matter, this conception of sonic rupture represents the antithesis of Emanuel Levinas's insistence on the wordness of the aural, as I discussed in chapter 1.

47 Deleuze and Guattari contend that sound draws primarily from the fountain of expression and not content (similar to Glissant's distinction between texture and nature), even though this opposition is surely not absolute: "Thus, we find ourselves not in front of a structural correspondence between two sorts of forms, forms of content and forms of expression, but rather in front of an expression machine capable of disorganizing its own forms, and of its forms of contents" (*Kafka*, 28).

48 Hopefully it is sufficiently clear that I am in no way suggesting an uncomplicated contrast between language and the sonic, rather than highlighting their different properties.

49 The quotation is from Glissant, *Poetics of Relation*, 190. In relation to the sonic, Glissant's image of "weaving fabrics" finds its acoustic counterpart in the work of disc jockeys (see my chapter 3), who weave sonic fabrics in order to create a textured sounding mix that is not concerned exclusively with the nature of its components.

50 Deleuze, *Pure Immanence*, 30.

51 While Glissant's differentiation between nature and texture is crucial, it should only occasion a first step in the exhuming of nature within texture and vice versa.

52 Levinas, "The Transcendence of Words," 147.

53 In one of his earliest engagements with Levinas's thought, Jacques Derrida delineates why for Levinas speech and sound function as harbingers of radical alterity, where vision always already violates the other. Later in the same essay, Derrida censures Levinas's idealization of speech as presence (for different reasons than I do) and his neglect of the secondariness of writing. "Violence and Metaphysics," 98–103.

54 On the social-scientification of black life, see Kelley, *Yo' Mama's Disfunktional*, 15–42; on the problem of sociological thinking in the institutional histories of black studies, see Judy, "Untimely Intellectuals."

55 This represents a minor terminological divergence from Homi Bhabha's notion concerning minority cultures as "otherwise than modernity" and Paul Gilroy's positioning of the African diaspora as "a counterculture of modernity." While I wholeheartedly endorse their general analyses, which stress the integrality of minority configurations to Western modernity, using these phrases seems to leave Western modernity unsullied by the very real economic, cultural, philosophical, and political contributions of minority cultures. See Bhabha, *The Location of Culture*, 6, and Gilroy, *The Black Atlantic*, 1–41.

3 In the Mix

1 For a different consideration of Afro-modern time, see Hanchard, "Afro-Modernity."

Notes

2 Jameson, *The Political Unconscious*, 9.

3 "The Brotherhood," as it appears in the text, bears striking resemblance to the Communist Party in its "scientific" theory of history and its attempt to uplift the dispossessed masses. While the text invites analogy to the Communist Party, it does not suggest one-to-one mimesis.

4 Valerie Smith believes this to mark a crucial turning point in the protagonist's life trajectory: "The sequence of events that culminates in Tod Clifton's murder precipitates the invisible man's thorough and lasting reexamination of himself and his relation to authority and ideology" (*Self-Discovery*, 104).

5 For discussions of the culture of zoot suits, see Cossgrove, "The Zoot Suit and Style Warfare," and Kelley, "The Riddle of the Zoot."

6 *Nomen est omen*, since *Tod* means death in German, which inscribes Tod's demise in his proper name; its repetition in the passage quoted above would sonorically signify his multiple deaths.

7 Ellison refers to CPT in an earlier part of the novel: "If you made an appointment, you couldn't bring them any slow c.p. (colored people's) time" (163).

8 Robert O'Meally argues of this scene, "Blues singers *are* historians in the sense that they, like all artists, project the lasting themes, forms, and images of their culture." However, Ellison does not mention blues singers in this particular passage; rather, he refers to a variety of instruments (trumpets, trombones, saxophones, and drums) and the lyrics the protagonist hears, and overall the historicity is not so much constituted through the agency of a human subject — the blues singer — as it is through the process of recording itself. See O'Meally, *The Craft of Ralph Ellison*, 90.

   Houston Baker, commenting on the same section, stresses the issues of sound recording rather than focusing on individual blues singers: "Indeed, the very fact that the protagonist hears a *recorded* blues (one designed for commercial duplication and sale) speaks to the historical and literary historical possibilities of the single, imagistic figure, or trope. For if the blues heard by the invisible man *are* history, they are not constituted as such in any simple sense. The economics that these recorded blues signal [are] a modern, technological era of multinational corporations, mass markets, and advertised commodities." See Baker, *Blues, Ideology*, 62. Although the recorded blues are surely dependent on capitalist structures for recording, distribution, and advertising, they should not be reduced to these factors, especially in light of this particular chapter of *Invisible Man*. Instead, one might suggest that recorded blues gains its power as a major location for black history precisely because it is widely disseminated. Even if this does not admonish the exploitative tendencies in the early history of the music industry, it does provide a certain surplus, which cannot be subsumed or erased by unequal access to the means of musical production.

9   Benjamin, "On the Concept of History," 257. I have altered the translation of Benjamin's text where necessary, most markedly the title, since the German ("Über den Begriff der Geschichte"), contains no references to either "theses" or "the philosophy of history." Benjamin's original typed manuscript bears no title at all, but this is the designation used by the compilers of Benjamin's work in German and his more recent English language translators.

There are a plethora of congruences between Ellison and Benjamin besides the ones elaborated here; a future project will have to interrogate the hashish/reefer pharmacopoetics in their respective oeuvres. Also, one would be hard-pressed not to notice the Ellisonian echo in the following lines from the first thesis, the one that describes Wolfgang von Kempelen's — who was also one of the first inventors to construct a speaking machine — supposedly automated chess player: "A system of mirrors created the illusion that this table was transparent from all sides" (253). On Von Kempelen, see Lastra, *Sound Technology*, 31–35. I discuss Ellison's mirrors and their relevance for the protagonist's invisibility in chapter 2.

10   See also my discussion of Giorgio Agamben's thoughts on this coevalness of the exception and the rule in chapter 5.

11   Benjamin uses the term "Stillstellung," which, especially when contrasted to "Stillstand"–the term closer to the English "cessation" — connotes an active force in the shaping and production of this interruption.

12   Gilles Deleuze offers the following definitions of "folds": "Straight lines are all alike, but folds vary, and all folding proceeds by differentiation.... Folds are in this sense everywhere, without the fold being a universal. It's a 'differentiator,' a 'differential.' " Deleuze, *Negotiations*, 156.

13   For an astute discussion of Hegel's views regarding Africa and history, see Snead "Repetition as a Figure," esp. 59–67.

14   Here is how the *Oxford English Dictionary* defines this particular dimension of the term: "b. Phr. *in the* (or *a*) *groove* (cf. 2c above). GROOVY *a.* 3. Hence *groove* is used to mean: a style of playing jazz or similar music, esp. one that is 'swinging' or good; a time when jazz is played well; more widely, one's predilection or favourite style, BAG *n.* 1d; something excellent or very satisfying. *slang* (orig. *U.S.*)."

15   They describe the colloquial dimension of groove in the following fashion: "In the vernacular a 'groove' refers to an intuitive sense of style as process, a perception of a cycle in motion, a form or organizing pattern being revealed, a recurrent clustering of elements through time. Groove and style are distilled essences, crystallizations of collaborative expec-

tancies in time." Feld and Keil, *Music Grooves*, 109. Diedrich Diedrichsen discusses the notion of the groove along similar lines: "The groove is not harmonic, it does not entail synchronicity; it is polyrhythmic and able to incorporate dissonances without resolving them" (*Freiheit macht arm*, 109; translation mine).

16 The models of "Being" and "Relation" in Glissant are complex and opaque. Put simply, the first designates a closed single totality, while the latter projects an open and singular genus thereof. Glissant offers the following formula: "(of) Being [vs.] (of) beings" (*Poetics of Relation*, 186).

17 The title of this section comes from Indeep, "Last Night a DJ Saved My Life."

18 Perhaps, in addition to the oeuvres of Spinoza, Hume, Bergson and Nietzsche, we can think of the musical bars in *Souls* as a precedent for Deleuze and Guattari's reproduction of Sylvano Bussoti's radically disrupted musical score on the first page of *A Thousand Plateaus*.

19 With this assertion, I follow the lead of German media and literary theorist Friedrich Kittler, who locates nineteenth- and twentieth-century German (not exclusively, but for the most part) literature in a wider network of different informational media. Kittler sums up his methodology as follows: "Traditional literary criticism, probably because it originated in a particular practice of writing, has investigated everything about books except their data processing" (370). "All libraries are discourse networks, but all discourse networks are not books. In the second industrial revolution, with its automation of the streams of information, the analysis of discourses has yet to exhaust the forms of knowledge and power. Archaeologies of the present must also take into account data storage, transmission, and calculation in technological media" (*Discourse Networks*, 369). See also Kittler, *Gramophone, Film, Typewriter* and my discussion of Kittler in chapter 1.

20 Eshun, *More Brilliant*, 188.

21 Claiming moral and ethical superiority under the auspices of "true Christianity" has a long tradition in African American letters, particularly in slave narratives and literature produced in the immediate aftermath of slavery. For the best known examples see Harriet Jacobs's and Frederick Douglass's slave narratives, Jerena Lee's spiritual narrative, and Harriet Wilson's novel, *Our Nig*.

22 The canonical secondary literature on the Harlem Renaissance does not always acknowledge *Souls* as a major influence on the formal dimensions of the writers producing during this period; rather, the authors cite Du Bois as an instrumental political activist and editor of *The Crisis* magazine. The two most widely read studies of the Harlem Renaissance are Nathan Huggins's *The Harlem Renaissance* and Levering Lewis's *When*

Harlem Was in Vogue. In the more recent scholarship on this period, Houston Baker's *Modernism and the Harlem Renaissance* is unique in its attempt to take into account the literary-aesthetic significance of Du Bois's text.

23 Bell, "Genealogical Shifts," 96. Arnold Rampersad deems *Souls* the most influential text in twentieth-century African American literary production. See Rampersad, *The Art and Imagination of W. E. B. Du Bois*, 89. In addition, Jean Toomer's *Cane* (1923), widely considered to be one of, if not *the*, most formally inventive text of the Harlem Renaissance, bears a number of structural and thematic resemblances to *Souls*. *Cane* consists of different literary genres — short story, novella, and drama — which are held together by epigraphic poems much in the same way that the musical and poetic epigraphs provide a guiding thread through Du Bois's text. For other current writings placing Du Bois in dialogue with various political, cultural, social, philosophical, literary, and historical discourses, see Chandler, "Originary Displacement"; Zamir, *Dark Voices*; Bell, Grosholz, and Stewart, *W. E. B. Du Bois on Race and Culture*.

24 Eric Sundquist pushes Du Bois's argument further by professing that "the labor of slavery that built much of white America, in this view, is one with the labor of cultural striving and nation building that created African America and preserved it." See Sundquist, *To Wake the Nations*, 537. Seeing these two forms of labor as one undercuts Du Bois's rhetorico-political strategy, since he clearly seeks to emphasize the cultural and spiritual labor of slavery above, beyond, and over the economic one. The reason for this hierarchy is that black subjects could exert more control over their cultural labor than their economic labor, especially during slavery, but also in its pseudo-reconstructed shadowy aftermath. By privileging the cultural and spiritual over the economic realm, cultural and political functions are served that are otherwise rendered obsolete when these forms of labor are equated. Sundquist's linking of these forms of labor also denies Du Bois the space to assert the cultural and spiritual superiority of black folk in the United States. Moreover, these musical and religious endowments are closer to "aneconomic" versions of the gift than "sweat and brawn." As Derrida says in his consideration of this subject, the gift "must not circulate, it must not be exchanged, it must not in any case be exhausted, as a gift, by the process of exchange, . . . the gift must remain *aneconomic*." Derrida, *Given Time*, 7.

25 In the second of his two cinema books concerned with the post–World War II "time image," Deleuze imagines the temporal prism thus: "What we [hear] through the pane or crystal is time, in its double movement of making presents pass, replacing one by the next while going toward the

future, but also of preserving all the past, dropping it into an obscure depth. . . . From the indiscernibility of the actual and the virtual, a new distinction must emerge, like a new reality which was not preexistent" (*Cinema 2: The Time-Image*, 87). The reader should remember that for Deleuze *the virtual* encapsulates not an empirical category set off against *the real*, as it often is in quotidian parlance, but an event horizon that is in perpetual to-and-fro tension with the actual. In fact, Deleuze prefers the movement of *actualization*, marking a persistent flux and adjacency to *becoming*, over any clear distinction between these two fields so central to his vitalist ontology. Deleuze also deems this crystal to be directly related to acoustic properties and a prima facie example of the refrain (92–93).

26 Brewster and Broughton, *Last Night a DJ Saved My Life*, 111. See also Stolzoff, *Wake the Town*, especially 41–64.

27 I use "M[aster of] C[eremony]" here so as not to confuse the reader, since the person who talks over records and eggs on the crowd is referred to as the DJ in the Jamaican context and the person who spins the records is called the selector.

28 Brewster and Broughton, *Last Night a DJ Saved My Life*, 124–164.

29 Roker, "Diatribe," 6. "Box" in this quote refers to the portable boxes DJs carry their records in; these boxes function as sonic libraries or discotheques. In DJ-speak one of the highest terms of praise for a record is to assert that it has not left one's box for a long time; meaning that the DJ cannot or does not want to stop playing this record.

30 Simon Reynolds deems DJs to be closer to critics than musicians, emphasizing their "trainspotter" and record collector homosocial behavior as much as the more stereotypical ludic ones associated with this group, an observation that is important because, like Roker's observations on the same subject, it calls attention to the pedagogic and archival dimensions of DJing. Reynolds, *Generation Ecstasy*, 271–276.

31 Miller, "Cumulus," 3.

32 Robert Stepto has already analyzed the significations of Du Bois's changes with regard to form as well as content. He attributes the majority of the shifts and resignifications in *Souls* to Du Bois's reaction to Booker T. Washington. See *From behind the Veil*, 53–59. For the purposes of my argument, it suffices to note that this connection adds yet another layer to the mix as it manifests itself in Du Bois's text.

33 Not all DJs mix records according to their beats (or "beatmatch," as it is called in DJ circles). However, within the traditions of mixing records in a club environment, beatmatching is the most common practice to achieve a mix.

34 The most common records employed in DJing are extended-play twelve-

inch singles, which usually contain different extended DJ mixes of tracks and were "invented" specifically for the practice of DJing. "Ten Percent" by the group Double Exposure, which appeared on the New York Disco label Salsoul in 1976, is considered to be the first record available commercially in this format. See Porschardt, DJ Culture, esp. 122–125. See also Collin, Altered State, 13.

35 Mudede, "The Turntable," 4.

36 CD mixers never established themselves as central to the club environment, so the new Final Scratch™ software, which allows DJs to connect their turntables to a PC with digital data and manipulate MP3 files as they would vinyl records, has become increasingly popular.

37 Schafer uses "schizophonia" to mark the splitting of sounds from their sources; see The Soundscape, 90.

38 In recent years, mix CDs — CDs that feature DJs mixing records — have become a submarket in many dance music genres. As most people will not always have access to the DJs they are interested in experiencing in a club environment, these records enable them to hear and — if they are "bedroom DJs" — copy, some of the techniques in their own homes. Some of the most interesting records of this kind have appeared in the DJ Kicks series, featuring a host of artists from different genres and DJing styles.

39 This does not mean that the DJ has to take all of these factors into account at all times. In most forms of club music — hip-hop, house, techno, and jungle, for example — in which the art of DJing is taken most seriously, the DJs focus on the beat, since the main ingredient of these musics is the rhythm.

40 According to Gilbert and Pearson, "as sound, the vibrations of all musics are capable of being communicated to the whole body," especially on the lower frequencies that not only speak for you but to you (Discographies, 45).

41 In "Spirituals and Neo-Spirituals" Zora Neale Hurston vehemently objects to Du Bois's classification of all spirituals as "sorrow songs": "The idea that the whole body of spirituals are 'sorrow songs' is ridiculous. They cover a wide range of subjects from a peeve at gossipers to Death and Judgment" (344). This is a valid criticism of Du Bois's terminology but not of his political project. While "sorrow songs" might not be an accurate term vis-à-vis the thematic scope of these artifacts, it achieves Du Bois's goal of elegiacally inscribing the memory of slavery and futurity of sonic blackness in these songs. Moreover, the structural features of Souls enact many of the adorning and improvisatory principles Hurston ascribes to "negro expression." This is just to say that Du Bois and Hurston might not be as opposed to each other aesthetically, at least in this case, as they and perhaps we would like to think.

Notes

42 Durant, *Conditions of Music*, 98. In this study, Durant traces the changing functions of musical notation in relation to symphonic music since
the seventeenth century. This is crucial since it highlights the ways in
which the Western system of musical notation is tied to particular and
shifting musical formations rather than being a universal sonic language.

43 Radano, "Denoting Difference," 508. In the "Afterthought" to *Souls* Du
Bois singles out the collections of spirituals compiled by abolitionists
Thomas Wentworth Higginson and Lucy McKim respectively (205).

44 "Writing down" acquires a particular resonance in relation to the title
of Friedrich Kittler's *Aufschreibsysteme 1800/1900*. David Wellbery, in
his introduction to the English translation (*Discourse Networks*) of this
work, shows that the German title "can be most literally translated as
'systems of writing down' or 'notation systems.' It refers to a level of material deployment that is prior to questions of meaning. . . . In Kittler's
view, such technologies are not mere instruments with which 'man' produces his meanings, . . . Rather they set the framework within which
something like 'meaning,' indeed, something like 'man,' becomes possible at all" (xii).

45 Kojin Karatani describes the discourse of the "noble savage," of which
the interest in spirituals partakes, as follows: "Then, in Romanticism
of the late eighteenth century, the attitude changed; an aesthetic stance
towards the other—the ambivalent worship towards those who are
deemed intellectually and ethically inferior—came into existence. Europeans began to discover 'sacred savages' externally, and 'sacred medieval
people' internally." Karatani, "Uses of Aesthetics," 149.

46 Cruz, *Culture at the Margins*, 5.

47 Cruz interrogates the importance of spirituals to the formation of
African American institutions of higher learning, Fisk, Tuskegee, and
Hampton, to name the most prominent. Clearly the Fisk Jubilee Singers
represent a crucial part of this assemblage (*Culture at the Margins*, 164–
188).

48 Radano writes: "Yet as these sounds submitted to the effects of writing,
so did they bring about changes in the notations themselves. Seeking
to capture the peculiarities of African American vernacular singing, the
transcribers altered staff notations to obey a new logic that exceeded the
confines of common time and well-tempered scales. . . . Seeking to master, notation succumbed, only to amplify black difference" ("Denoting
Difference," 525).

49 For the most influential argument concerning the syncretism of slave
culture in general and spirituals in particular, see Levine, *Black Culture,
Black Consciousness*.

50 Gibson, "Introduction," xvi.

51   Hebdige, *Cut 'n' Mix*, 142.

52   Hebdige, *Cut 'n' Mix*, 142.

53   See Marsh, *The Story of the Jubilee Singers; With Their Songs*, 5.

54   Here, "symbiosis" draws on Keith Ansell-Pearson's use of this concept to designate how hitherto separate life-forms and/or technologies contaminate each other to form new, albeit unstable, entities that are integral to both biological and technological "development," rather than auxiliary to its becoming. See Ansell-Pearson, *Viroid Life*, 132–134.

55   David Levering Lewis, in his sweeping biography of Du Bois's early life, encapsulates this interplay between music and poetry in the epigraphs, when he writes: "He twinned them [music and poetry] in this manner in order to advance the then-unprecedented notion of the creative parity and complementarity of white folk and black folk alike. Du Bois meant the cultural symbolism of these double epigraphs to be profoundly subversive of the cultural hierarchy of his time." Lewis, *W. E. B. Du Bois*, 278.

56   Fabian, *Time and the Other*, 143.

57   Du Bois's disruption of the text and the ordering of the page and Ellison's "lower frequencies" anticipate the claims Avital Ronell makes for the innovative typographic structure of her *Telephone Book*: "Your mission . . . is to learn how to read with your ears. . . . [Y]ou are being asked to tune your ears to noise frequencies . . . to crack open the closural sovereignty of the book, we have feigned silence and disconnection" (xv).

58   Oddly enough, Du Bois's remixing of the two spirituals is strikingly similar to a current musical genre known as "mash up" in which bedroom producers take the a capella vocals of one song and play it over the musical track of another and distribute their creations via the Internet.

59   Paul Anderson remarks that "music offered itself to Du Bois's imagination as not only a haunted site of memory but as an energizing site of utopian anticipation" (*Deep River*, 5).

60   Brewster and Broughton, *Last Night a DJ Saved My Life*, 119. In their *Reggae: The Rough Guide*, Steve Barrow and Peter Dalton proffer the following concise redaction of dub reggae's three main historical stages and movement from margin to center: "First there was the so-called 'instrumentals,' not originally conceived as such, but becoming so by removal of the vocal track. Initially these instrumentals were strictly for soundsystem play, but before too long they were being issued commercially. Versions on which the contribution of the studio engineer was more obvious then emerged around the end of 1968, and by 1970 these remixes — called 'versions' — were appearing on B-sides of most Jamaican singles. . . . During 1973–74 record buyers in Jamaica became accustomed to checking labels not just for the producer or artist, but also for the engineer" (199).

61 Kodwo Eshun holds that the temporality of echo in dub significantly changes the perception and sensation of listening: "Your ear has to chase the sound. Instead of the beat being this one event in time, it becomes a series of retreating echoes, like a tail of sound. The beat becomes a tail which is always disappearing around the corner and your ear has to start chasing it" (*More Brilliant*, 064). Even though the Ellisonian "listening around corners" is in full effect, I would place the emphasis on the multiplicity of the one here, since dub mixes, as Eshun points out, disperse and refigure the one into echnoness, another name for singularity. For a brilliant reading of the gendered place of Echo (the feminine counterpart to Narcissus) in Ovid's *Metamorphoses* and psychoanalytic discourse, among other things, see Spivak, "Echo."

62 Gordon, *Haunted Matters*, 8. For a suggestive discussion of blackness and death in the machinery of the U.S. nation, see Holland, *Raising the Dead*, especially chapter 1. In addition, Freud lists the following Du Boisian factors in his discussion of the uncanny double (indebted to Otto Rank): "mirror-images, shadows, guardian spirits, the doctrine of the soul, and the fear of death" ("The Uncanny," 142).

63 Benjamin, "Über den Begriff der Geschichte," 251. Translation mine. These sentences are included in the recent translation by Edmund Jephcott and others in vol. 4 of Benjamin's *Selected Writings*, 390.

64 Benjamin, "The Task of the Translator," 255; "Die Aufgabe des Übersetzers," 52.

65 Benjamin, "The Task of the Translator," 258; "Die Aufgabe des Übersetzers," 57. Translation modified.

66 The field of thought opened by Du Bois and Benjamin concerning echo, haunting, temporality, and translation also makes several appearances in Deleuze's theater of *Difference and Repetition*. At several moments in the argument, Deleuze makes echo a key player in this drama, for instance, when he states: "Reflections, echoes, doubles, and souls do not belong to the domain of resemblance and equivalence" (1). See also the invocation of echoing later in the same text when Deleuze defines "repetition as difference without a concept" (13) and in his discussion of Plato's cave (65). While I have generally been influenced by Deleuze's idea of repetition (and Snead's, discussed in the previous chapter), here I want to draw the reader's attention to "souls" and "echoes" as instantiations of the singular in Du Bois and Deleuze.

67 See also the discussion of rhythm in Deleuze's *Difference and Repetition*, 20–21, and *Francis Bacon*, especially 39–70.

68 Du Bois, "Sociology Hesitant," 44. In his introduction to the special issue of the journal *boundary 2* that comprises Du Bois's piece and other essays, Ronald Judy reads this tension between primary and secondary

rhythm as a style of singularity. See Judy, "Introduction," 33. According to Ronald Bogue, Deleuze also projects rhythm as a singular relation between two forces: "Rhythm, in short, is difference, or relation—the in between whereby milieus communicate with one another, within themselves (as collections of submilieus), and with chaos. Rhythm is not a secondary byproduct of a milieu's measure, but a primary constituent of that milieu" (18). I should note that I am not advocating a simple and/or originary privileging of rhythm as marker of African American (musical) difference as occurs so often; rather, I am attempting to make its formal properties usable for a theorization of the temporalities of sonic Afro-modernity. For a critical genealogy of how rhythm came to be heard as an enactment of radical black alterity, see Radano, *Lying Up a Nation*, chapter 5.

4 Consuming Sonic Technologies

1   The end of the nineteenth century and beginning of the twentieth continued the revolution in informational technologies commenced in the 1830s with the invention of the telegraph and photographic camera. Samuel Morse constructed the rudiments of the electric telegraph in 1837; Alexander Graham Bell is usually credited with the production of the first functional telephone in 1876; Thomas Edison and Charles Cros are both acknowledged for providing blueprints of the phonograph in 1877. The first functional wireless radio appeared in 1910. For a concise history of these technological developments that takes into account their effects on American culture, see Lubar, *InfoCulture*. For a different consideration of the shifting sonic contours of modernity, see Thompson, *The Soundscape of Modernity*.

2   See, for example, Soja, *Postmodern Geographies*; Massey, *Space, Place and Gender*; Harvey, *The Condition of Postmodernity*; Jameson, *Postmodernism; or, The Logic of Late Capitalism*; and Keith and Pile, *Place and the Politics of Identity*. All these writings address questions of spatiality as they intersect with various political, cultural, economic, and social formations. None, however, discusses the role of sound as a factor in the construction of space.

3   Smith, "Soundscape," 238.

4   Leyshon, Matless, and Revill, *The Place of Music*, 4.

5   Soja, "The Spatiality of Social Life," 92–93.

6   J. McGregor Wise gives the following definition of social space: "Social space is the space created through the interaction of multiple humans over time. There is never a single social space, but always multiple social spaces. Social spaces are always open and permeable, yet they do have limits." This conceptualization of social space, while not as determin-

ist as Soja's model, also does not possess the same analytical nuances. *Exploring Technology and Social Space*, xiii.

7   Schafer, *Book of Noise*, 25.

8   Berland, "Toward a Creative Anachronism," 33–34. See also Berland, "Locating Listening." It should be noted here that I take Berland's points to be concerned with certain historically formulated structures of vision and hearing and not biological or ontological absolutes. Generally, however, it seems harder to distinguish the ontological from the historical, or at least the point where one bleeds into the other, than current critical idioms would like to think.

9   Connor, "The Modern Auditory I," 209.

10 The title of this section comes from Ellison, "Living with Music," 195. I have not been able to locate any critical studies of his essay. Both Robert O' Meally's influential book-length study of Ellison's oeuvre and biography (*The Craft of Ralph Ellison*) and Robert Cataliotti's monograph concerning the role of music in the history of African American literature (*The Music of African American Literature*) fail to mention "Living with Music."

11 See the collection of Ellison's correspondence with Albert Murray, in Callahan and Murray, *Trading Twelves*.

12 See Morrison's *Jazz*; Wilson's *Ma Rainey's Black Bottom*; and Marshall's *Praisesong for the Widow*. For McKay, see *Home to Harlem* and for Baldwin, see *Another Country*.

13 Hughes, *I Wonder as I Wander*, 69. I thank Erik Dussere for bringing this text to my attention.

14 Theodore Gracyk distinguishes three different kinds of "noise." First, noise is any sound that disrupts communication. Second, all sounds that disturb or distract are perceived as noise. Finally, any sound that causes physical harm is taken to be noise. Gracyk, *Rhythm and Noise*, 103–104.

15 Corbett, *Extended Play*, 42.

16 Keightley, " 'Turn it down!' she shrieked," 152. David Morton shows how pervasive the ideology of high fidelity was during the first fifty years of the U.S. recording industry, particularly in relation to classical music, while also highlighting the many ways in which the recording was enhanced by such factors as microphone placement and later tape editing, which were not concerned with reproducing sound faithfully as much as using recording technology to maximum effect. Morton, *Off the Record*, 13–47.

17 Ellison, *Shadow and Act*, 3–23. Ellison also evokes radio building when commenting on the role of music in his life, linking both his status as a musician and radio hobbyist with his proclivity for creating things (9).

18 Susan Douglas writes at length about radio hams in the 1920s, argu-

ing that this activity allowed mostly white middle-class young men to feel they could exert a certain amount of control over the apparatus. Douglas, *Listening In*, 55–82. Not everybody grants the hobby as much libratory potential as Ellison or Douglas: take, for instance, Theodor Adorno's (typically) damning indictment of the radio hobbyist as the sine qua non of "regressive listening." He writes: "Of all fetishistic listeners, the radio ham is the most complete. It is irrelevant to him what he hears or even how he hears; he is only interested in the fact that he hears and succeeds in inserting himself, with his private equipment, into the public mechanism, without exerting even the slightest influence on it." Adorno, "On the Fetish Character of Listening," 54.

19 Eisenberg, *The Recording Angel*, 44.

20 Leslie Harris's *Just Another Girl on the IRT* was released the previous year, and although no major Hollywood studio backed the film, it received a fairly wide release compared to other "independent" films directed by black women such as Julie Dash or Cheryl Dunye. Other Hollywood films centered on black women include *Waiting to Exhale*, *Set It Off*, *Beloved*, *Soul Food*, and *How Stella Got Her Groove Back*, all directed by men; the exceptions include Cassie Lemmons's *Eve's Bayou* and *The Caveman's Valentine*; Maya Angelou's *Down in the Delta*; and Gina Prince-Blythewood's *Love and Basketball*.

21 *Sugar Hill, Juice, Jason's Lyric*, and *Straight Outta Brooklyn* are some other examples of this black cinematic trend. For a consideration of the "ghettocentric" genre, see Todd Boyd's *Am I Black Enough for You*, chapter 4, "Young, Black, and Don't Give a Fuck"; and Watkins, *Representing*, especially 169–231.

22 In this way, the film can be seen as a precursor to films directed by African Americans that do not primarily feature black characters, at least in any facile notion of representation. Recently three films directed by African Americans appeared that featured either no major black characters (Carl Franklin's *One True Thing*, the Hughes brothers' *From Hell*, F. Gary Gray's *The Italian Job*, and Forest Whitaker's *Hope Floats*) or only one major black character (F. Gary Gray's *The Negotiator*). Interestingly, two of these directors previously worked on films centered on black women; Gray directed *Set It Off* and Whitaker *Waiting to Exhale*.

23 Martin has since directed some episodes of the NBC police drama *Homicide*, on which John Seda, who played Chino in the film, had a recurring role. Martin also directed another feature, *Prison Song* (which never received a theatrical release), as well as some episodes of the HBO series *Oz* (1997–2003), on which Lauren Velez, Rita Moreno, and John Seda, all *I Like It* alums, were featured as actors.

24 Hansen, "Early Cinema, Late Cinema," 135.

Notes

25 Spike Lee's *Do the Right Thing* (on which Martin worked as an assistant cinematographer) seems to be *I Like It*'s most clear precursor in recent (black) cinema; Lee's use of sonic technologies, in particular, invites a comparison between the two films. However, the gender politics of the two films could not be more different, since in Lee's film only male figures (Radio Raheem and Mr. Senor Love Daddy, for instance) occupy public sonic spaces, while the female characters are relegated to the home. In some ways, then, *I Like It* provides an extended sonic and visual critique of Lee's project by working over a similar terrain, but staging a female seizing of public space through sound technologies.

26 For a general discussion concerning the role of soundtracks in classical Hollywood cinema, see Gorbman, *Unheard Melodies*.

27 Berlant, *The Queen of America Goes to Washington*, 79–80.

28 For a particularly insightful consideration of the vilification of "welfare queens," see Wahneema Lubiano, "Black Ladies, Welfare Queens, and State Minstrels." In this essay about the "narrative ideological battle" (330) in the Hill-Thomas case, Lubiano brilliantly counterposes discourses around "welfare queens" as "moral aberrations" and "economic drains" (338) with narratives about "black ladies" who in the media are represented as power-hungry "overachievers" (333).

29 Griffin Dune plays Price, which would not necessarily be worth mentioning had he not depicted the main character in *After Hours*, a mid-eighties Scorsese film. His role in that film—as a "white-bred" business man who gets lost in the "dark" NYC night life—is almost resumed in *I Like It*, where he plays a stereotypically white-bred record executive. In one of the most intertextually resonant scenes, Price drives Lisette to her home in the Bronx in his Ferrari.

30 In popular music "crossover" is the designation for the move of "particular musics" to a "general audience." More often than not this refers to certain performers' recordings moving from generically specific charts, such as jazz or dance, to the pop charts, which are not bound by generic concerns but measured solely in terms of sales and airplay. For a discussion of crossover as it relates to African American popular music, see Harper, *Are We Not Men?* especially chapter 4, "Class Acts: The 'Street,' Popular Music, and Black-Cultural Crossover" (74–102).

31 The title of this section is from Juan Carlos Herencia, "Notes towards a Reading of Salsa," 218.

32 When I use the term "Walkman," I am not referring only to Sony's Walkman but to portable stereos in general. I do this because in everyday speech in the United States, "Walkman" has become a generic term for all these devices regardless of their name brand. "Personal stereo" seems to be the designation of choice in Great Britain.

33 Aparicio, *Listening to Salsa*, 227–228.

34 Michael Bull, in his monograph about the Walkman, contends that this device perfectly encapsulates, among other things, the thorough technologization of the urban experience as it enables the management of contingencies of everyday life in the city. Bull, *Sounding Out the City*.

35 In its early stages as both a mobile recording and reproduction apparatus, the phonograph was also used for ethnographic field recordings. See Brady, *A Spiral Way*.

36 Millard, *America on Record*, 1.

37 As Andre Millard remarks, personal stereos actually shield the listener from "noise pollution," as opposed to causing it. However, one could also argue that due to louder volumes and closer proximity to the ear, the Walkman and its connected headphones cause more acute sonic health threats. Millard writes: "One very important function of the portable personal stereo is that it acts to drown out the oppression of noise in our society. Putting on the soft plastic earphones and playing a tape instantly cuts out the background noise of modern life" (*America on Record*, 326).

38 Currently, cell phones seem to have replaced the Walkman as the annoying auditory technology du jour. Whenever I have discussed the early hostile reception of the Walkman in my classes, the students were puzzled by these reactions, since this gadget has become such a "natural" part of their ecology. Cellular phones, however, elicit similar responses from students now as the Walkman did in the late 1970s.

39 Du Gay et al, *Doing Cultural Studies*, 58–59.

40 For a discussion of the Walkman in non-Western contexts, see Chow, "Listening Otherwise."

41 Chambers, "A Miniature History of the Walkman," 2.

42 See the account of Afro-Latin music in Boggs, *Salsiology*, particularly "The Roots" (7–22).

43 As Juan Carlos Herencia postulates: "Salsa as a genre is constituted as an instance of combination, as the site of a transnational amalgamation reworked by a national group. . . . The combination of Puerto Rican, Cuban and U.S. American rhythms, among others, in New York, like any other work consisting of all manner of choral gestures, of the convocations of the sonero, of the exclamations of the sonera, delineates the map of salsa. Such is the genre of salsa: a space for the debate, negotiation, representation and rehearsal of national forms and identities in the process of movement and consumption" ("Notes towards a Reading of Salsa," 196–197).

44 Febres, "Salsa as Translocation," 180. Furthermore, in order to become and continue being a "translocal phenomenon" salsa crucially depends

on technological transmission as it is mediated by the recording industry.

45   Before her death, Celia Cruz was the *grande doyenne* of salsa; she collabo-
rated with Wyclef Jean of the Haitian American rap group, the Fugees
(discussed in detail in chapter 5), on a new version of the Cuban classic
"Guantanamera." India, on the other hand, represents a new generation
of female salsa performers, having become one of the most popular artists in recent years. For an analysis of La India, see Puelo, "Una verdadera
cronica del Norte: Una noche con la India."

46   Duany, "Popular Music in Puerto Rico," quoted in Puelo, "Una verdadera cronica," 225.

47   In fact, most contemporary recorded duets (or any other musical collaborations for that matter) do not require that the performers inhabit
the same physical space; rather, their performances are spliced together
in the studio, creating the same virtual effect as Lisette's interaction with
Marc Anthony. The most notable examples of this trend can be found in
the duets of deceased performers and their children: Natalie Cole with
Nat King Cole and Hank Williams Jr. with Hank Williams. Theodore
Gracyk makes the point that all recordings approach this virtuality: "The
recording creates a virtual space and time in which a performance is
taking place." Gracyk says this about Natalie Cole's recording with her
father: "The emotional impact does not rest in its constructed 'subject'
alone (how the duet sounds); its affective power turns on our knowledge that it *is* a product of studio wizardry, that Natalie is singing to
the memory of her father, not with him in the studio." See *Rhythm and
Noise*, 53 and 85.

48   De Certeau, *The Practice of Everyday Life*, xxi.

5   Sounding Diasporic Citizenship

1   Peter Linebaugh remarks, "The ship remained perhaps the most important conduit of Pan-African communication before the appearance of
the long-playing record" (as quoted in Gilroy, *The Black Atlantic*, 13).
In the contemporary moment we might add CDs, twelve-inch singles,
MP3s, and videos to the repertoire of black Atlantic sounding channels.
Mark Anthony Neal notes, "The hip-hop tradition has emerged as a
digitized aural facsimile of the traditional black urban landscape"; Neal
also believes "hip-hop artists [to] have reclaimed the critical possibilities of popular culture, by using popular culture and the marketplace
as the forum to stimulate a broad discussion and critique about critical
issues that most affect their constituencies." Neal, *What the Music Said*,
161. This chapter investigates the international dimensions of this for-

mulation. While studies that address the internationalization of hip-hop are still rare, the recent anthology *Global Noise*, ed. Mitchell, is a first step in this direction.

2   Malcolm Waters defines globalization "as a social process in which the constraints of geography on social and cultural arrangements recede and in which people become increasingly aware that they are receding" (*Globalization*, 3). Ashcroft, Griffiths, and Tiffin, the authors of *Key Concepts in Post-Colonial Studies*, emphasize slightly different factors in their notion of globalization, defining it as "a process whereby individual lives and local communities are affected by economic and cultural forces that operate world-wide. In effect it is the process of the world becoming a single place" (110). They go on to distinguish different schools of thought that either celebrate globalization for bringing prosperity to the world population, reject it on the grounds of an unequal balance of power and economic resources between the first and the third worlds, or simply analyze this social formation without renouncing or embracing any particular paradigm (110–111). See also the essays collected in Featherstone, *Global Culture*; Appadurai, *Modernity at Large*; and Wilson and Dissanyake, *Global/Local*.

3   While public culture in the United States by and large still remains insular in the "era of globalization," U.S. cultural products can be found and are consumed almost everywhere in the world, particularly Hollywood cinema, television series, and popular music. Many exceptions to the United States' insular public culture stem from Central and Latin America and are usually geared toward "immigrant" communities rather than mainstream markets. Norman Stolzoff makes a similar case for the Jamaican engagement with African American R&B in the 1940s, when he writes: "The dialogue between American and Jamaican musical cultures was based on the hegemony of black American cultural forms more than on equality" (*Wake the Town*, 39).

4   Agamben, *Homo Sacer*, 25.

5   The concept of diaspora is thoroughly discussed in Gilroy, *The Black Atlantic*; Hall, "Cultural Identity and Diaspora"; Clifford, "Diasporas"; and Tölölyan, "Rethinking Diasporas."

6   For general overviews of contemporary and historical debates concerning citizenship, see Mouffe, *Dimensions of Radical Democracy*; Beiner, *The Citizenship Debates*; and Shafir, *Theorizing Citizenship*. In their essay "Citizens and Citizenship," Stuart Hall and David Held hold that questions of belonging form the central tenet of citizenship: "Who belongs and what does *belonging* mean in practice? Membership, here, is not conditional: it is a matter of right and entitlement" (175).

7   This should not be taken to mean that members of diasporic commu-

nities necessarily feel that they "belong" to the country they live in, but rather that their presence requires some form of engagement even if these subjects identify solely with their "homeland(s)" and vice versa.

8 Diasporas, conversely, do not rest only on right or entitlement but are, at least partially, communities of choice. On diaspora and passion, see Gilroy, "There Ain't No Black in the Union Jack," 159, and Ellison, "Some Questions and Some Answers," 264.

9 Abena Busia formulates this problematic in the following way: "The homeland, which in the mind of the child becomes an imagined homeland, is a place not to which one will not return but to which one *cannot* return" ("Re:locations," 271).

10 Agamben, *The Coming Community*, 18–19.

11 Soysal, *Limits of Citizenship*, 6.

12 Rouse, "Thinking through Transnationalism," 380.

13 Robbins, "Actually Existing Cosmopolitanism," 13.

14 The title to this section is from the Fugees, "Ready or Not," *The Score*. Paul Farmer writes of the Guantanamo naval base where a number of Haitian refugees were detained: "Guantanamo, an otherwise full-fledged military base, is located roughly a third of the way between Haiti and Florida on the island of Cuba. In 1903, Guantanamo was leased 'indefinitely' to the United States for $2,000 per year, and, by the terms of the lease, is not subject to Cuban laws" (*The Uses of Haiti*, 264). This space has reentered the U.S. national imaginary in the aftermath of September 11, 2001, as an international prison camp for alleged Muslim terrorists. "Cassius Clay" was the name of the world heavyweight champion Mohammed Ali before he joined the Nation of Islam.

15 It is important to note that hip-hop is far from historically uniform and that in the late eighties, the pinnacle of "consciousness rap," the Fugees would have fit quite comfortably into a landscape populated by rappers with strong "political" lyrics, such as Public Enemy, or with Afrocentric worldviews, such as X-Clan and Lakim Shabazz or "The Native Tongues" (De La Soul, A Tribe Called Quest, and Queen Latifah, for example), who specialized in playful lyrics and soundscapes without the gangsta posturing of the mid-nineties. Nevertheless, this should not be taken as a qualitative distinction, but rather as a marker of historical and cultural contingencies within hip-hop. The best scholarly discussion of the historical and aesthetic parameters of "gangsta rap" remains Robin Kelley's "Kickin' Reality, Kickin' Ballistics."

16 The Fugees released five singles from *The Score*; in addition to "Killing Me Softly," they cover Bob Marley's "No Woman, No Cry," while two cuts ("Fu-gee-la" and "Ready or Not") were based on the hooks of Teena Marie's "Ooh LaLa" and the Jackson Five's "Ready or Not." Due to these

borrowings the group was accused of merely recycling old hits instead of constructing new ones; however, their creative reimaginings of these songs would disprove these allegations. Their version of "Killing" was not only based on Flack's recording, but also reinterpreted the song as a hip-hop battle cry rather than a simple love song. Furthermore, the rhythm track of the Fugees' version paid homage to the hip-hop group A Tribe Called Quest, as the beat was culled from their 1990 single "Bonita Applebum."

17 Raggamuffin is a musical mélange of hip-hop and dancehall reggae.

18 In an interview with the British magazine *The Face*, the group asserted that they would rather kill their grandmothers than feature a white person in one of their videos. After a barrage of criticism, the Fugees attributed this statement to their "pro-black politics." Yet this can also be interpreted as an attempt, even if unconscious, to hold on to their credibility with an urban black audience in light of their immense success, which is usually accompanied by accusations of "selling out."

19 In his solo work Wyclef shifts his emphasis from refugees to the carnival as the locus for diasporic citizenship. Wyclef's first solo album provides a sonic rendering of the popular annual West Indian carnival in New York. The title of that album still contains the refugee element: *Wyclef Jean Presents the Carnival: Featuring the Refugee All-Stars*, but the lyrics and videos do not explicitly address the politicized identity of particular migrants. Instead, Wyclef attempts to construct a new world diasporic continuum interfacing various points in the Caribbean with African America. For Wyclef the carnival represents a site where all these musical and cultural aspects converge, where "anything can happen." While the use of "refugee" seems more overtly "political" than "carnival," both terms provide clusters of meaning through which constantly changing sounds and images of the African diaspora emerge. The carnival, rather than relying on a more legal definition of citizenship, opens the field for questions of cultural citizenship. Viewed in tandem, "the carnival of refugees" underscores the overdetermined nexus between questions of cultural belonging and political membership.

20 For a discussion of the tension between U.S. American and Caribbean black identities during the 1960s, see Cruse, *The Crisis of the Negro Intellectual*, 420–448.

21 Zephir, *Haitian Immigrants*, 146–147.

22 Bhabha, "Embodied Rights," 5.

23 *United Nations Convention Relating to the Status of Refugees* Art. 1 (2). As quoted in Bhabha, "Embodied Rights," 9–10.

24 While propaganda against immigrants crops up again and again, I would argue that the basic view of the United States as a nation of immigrants

remains firmly ingrained in the national imaginary. This runs counter to the German situation that I discuss later, where the nation imagines itself as ethnically and culturally homogeneous. Bonnie Honig argues that immigrants in the United States are caught in a tug-of-war between the "xenophobic" and "xenophilic." On the one hand, immigrants serve as productive subjects who restore values that the U.S. populace has lost. On the other hand, they function as those who economically deplete the U.S. welfare state. See Honig, "Immigrant America?"

25 To use an Agambian formulation of this constellation: refugeedom is a potentiality of citizenship per se and not merely its exception, especially since, "at the limit, pure potentiality and pure actuality are indistinguishable, and the sovereign is precisely this zone of indistinction" (*Homo Sacer*, 47). See also the essays collected in Agamben, *Potentialities* (for instance, those on 161–162 and 177–184) and *The Coming Community* (35–44).

26 Agamben, *Homo Sacer*, 131.

27 The transcription of the skit and the lyrics of "Refugees on the Mic" are mine.

28 Kristeva, *The Powers of Horror*, 1–15.

29 According to Lisa Lowe, among others, traditional Western conceptions of citizenship and publicness require individuals to sublate their embodiment through their participation in the polity: "The abstraction of the *citizen* is always in distinction to the particularity of *man's* material condition" (*Immigrant Acts*, 25). Lauren Berlant formulates this problematic, especially as it pertains to people of color and women in the United States, as "the logic of [the] dialectic between abstraction in the national public sphere and the surplus corporeality of racialized and gendered subjects" ("National Brands," 178).

30 Kristeva argues that the abject functions both as a limit and a border. And while, at least in this context, she does not refer to national borders, I am choosing to literalize her argument to underscore the contiguity between corporeal boundaries and the borders of the body politic (*The Powers of Horror*, 9).

31 Here, the Fugees rely on a general and commonsense definition of "refugee," as opposed to a strict legal one. Guy Goodwill-Gill defines the ordinary usage of refugee as "signifying someone in flight, who seeks to escape conditions or personal circumstances found to be intolerable" (*The Refugee in International Law*, 3). The legal definition stipulated by most states specifically requires political persecution.

32 Drake, "Diaspora Studies and Pan-Africanism," 452.

33 A glaring instance can be found in the film, based on the novel by Terry McMillan, *How Stella Got Her Groove Back*, released in August 1998.

Therein, the main character, a forty-year-old woman, returns from a vacation in Jamaica, where she engaged in an affair with a man half her age. One of her sisters, pointing out the foolishness and desperation of this tryst, states that "those people" all have AIDS anyway, to which her other sister responds: "That's Haitians, not Jamaicans." Wyclef Jean condemned this scene during his performance at the MTV Music Video Awards, held in Los Angeles on September 10, 1998. As a result, the studio cut this scene from the international and video/DVD versions of the film.

34 For an excellent study about Haiti and AIDS that bridges the gap between ethnography and political economy, see Paul Farmer, *AIDS and Accusation*. See also Robert Lawless, *Haiti's Bad Press*.

35 Farmer, *AIDS and Accusation*, 166. See also Lawless, *Haiti's Bad Press*, 107–134.

36 In his introduction to Paul Farmer's *The Uses of Haiti*, Naom Chomsky details the military and foreign aid given to Haiti by the Reagan administration during "Baby Doc's" reign.

37 As Farmer notes, "by 1978, 'exports' from offshore assembly operations had surpassed coffee as [Haiti's] number one export" (*AIDS and Accusation*, 188). Largely, these plants produce goods such as baseballs and dolls for which the individual components or materials are imported from the United States.

38 See Alex Stepick, *Pride and Prejudice*, 99–112.

39 Farmer, *The Uses of Haiti*, 350. Farmer also shows that between 1981 and 1991 the United States refused asylum to 24,559 Haitian refugees, granting only eight cases of political asylum during this period (267).

40 Stepick, *Pride and Prejudice*, 108.

41 In 1983 Haiti's per capita income was estimated at $315 (Farmer, *AIDS and Accusation*, 183).

42 Goodwin-Gill, *The Refugee in International Law*, 3.

43 Bhabha, "Embodied Rights," 8.

44 Fugees, *Fu-gee-la*, dir. Guillet.

45 "Performance sequence" designates the parts of music videos that portray the performers lip-synching the songs on which the video is based. As a general rule, these sequences do not form a part of the narrative, but function as distancing devices, reminding viewers that they are watching a music video rather than a feature film. Intermingling narratives with performance sequences is currently one of the most popular formats for music videos. While videos in the past either depicted a performance or a plot containing the performance of the song, a number of newer ones combine the two. Videos that consist only of action sequences, in which the music functions as a soundtrack, remain a rarity. For a gen-

eral overview of the generic, aesthetic, economic, and political dimensions of music videos consult the essays collected in Frith, Goodwin, and Grossberg, *Sound and Vision.*

46 Haiti is just the most obvious example in the context of the Fugees: the U.S. funding of oppressive regimes in Nicaragua, Iraq, the Philippines, Afghanistan, and El Salvador are just as pertinent.

47 The initial caption of the video reads: "Chapter Two. . . . In the year of the rat, The Fugees' quest for justice and battle against intolerance continues."

48 Lipsitz, *Dangerous Crossroads,* 12.

49 On Advanced Chemistry, see von Felbert, "Die Unbestechlichen."

50 Cherno Jobatey, quoted in Koch, *"Medien mögen's weiß,"* 76. Translation mine. "Big deal" was rendered in English within Jobatey's quote. It was not until 1994, when the television station Pro 7 touted Arabella Kiesbauer as the first black talk show host in Germany, that race became a clearly articulated factor in the presentation of a public figure. Francine Jobatey traces the post–World War II representations of Afro-Germans within the West German public sphere. She argues that most Afro-German public figures either took the roles of clowns, making humorous references to their racial identity (Roberto Blanco, an extremely popular singer and variety show host) or were presented by the media as completely German, that is, no mention was made of their racial identity (the teenage singer Ramona, for instance). See Jobatey, "From *Toxi* to TV."

51 The literature on whiteness, particularly in U.S. contexts, is expansive and steadily growing. See Dyer, *White*; Frankenberg, *White Women*; Harris, "Whiteness as Property"; Hill, *Whiteness*; Lipsitz, *The Possessive Investment*; and Ware, *Beyond the Pale.* For a discussion of whiteness in the German context, see Linke, *German Bodies.* Linke's important book, while thoroughly chronicling the manifold discursive and material configurations of race, blood, and kinship that permeate so many aspects of post–World War II German culture and society, also runs the risk of reducing people of color to mere victim objects, since she neglects to take into account the ways in which people of color respond to these forces.

52 Linke, *German Bodies,* 113.

53 Hear also albums by Meli, AsD, Glashaus, Sekou the Ambassador, Chima, Joy Denelane, Bintia, Xavier Naidoo, Sammy Deluxe, J-Luv, and Afrob. Torch himself reemerged in 2001 with a solo CD featuring the other two members of Advanced Chemistry on selected cuts. In their definitive history of German hip-hop, *20 Jahre Hip-Hop in Deutschland,* Sascha Verlan and Hannes Loh cite Torch and Advanced Chemistry as both pioneers of the art of German language rapping and as forerun-

ners to the explosion of hip-hop as the public voice of multicultural Germany.

54 During the summer of 2001 Brother's Keepers' "Adriano" was a top five hit in Germany, and the video was in heavy rotation on the two major music video outlets, MTV Germany and Viva.

55 This is not limited to black Germans, but also includes Turkish and white Germans who appropriate hip-hop styles. There exist numerous musical productions and videos, which feature non–African Americans in typical hip-hop wear attempting to be as American as possible.

56 Campt, "African German/African American," 77–78.

57 Advanced Chemistry, "Kapitel 1." The translations of Advanced Chemistry's lyrics are all my own. Instead of trying to convey the rhymes and wordplays, I opted for literal translations, choosing to indicate the aspects that get "lost" in translation but are germane to my argument when neccessary.

58 "The Message," which appeared on Sugarhill Records in 1982, was actually credited to the DJ Grandmaster Flash and not the rapper Melle Mel.

59 For a discussion of "The Message" and many of the "message raps" that followed in its aftermath, see Toop, *Rap Attack Two*, 120–125.

60 Derrida, *Monolingualism*, 56–57. However, we should not assume that the flow of information goes both ways, as it is highly unlikely that English-speaking audiences will hear Advanced Chemistry's raps. While the non-English-speaking world is used to hearing lyrics they can only partially understand, Anglophone countries remain hesitant about embracing other languages in popular music.

61 Chaos, an African American techno artist from Detroit, renders an ironic reversal of the Afro-German identification with black U.S. culture. In this track, Chaos identifies with German culture, imagining himself as "Afrogermanic" through the constant repetition of the lines "I am Afrogermanic" and "Ich schwarz Deutsch." Chaos, "Afrogermanic." This goes back to the influence of German group Kraftwerk on the predominantly black American techno genre. Kodwo Eshun argues that Kraftwerk functioned as a way for African American musicians to construct themselves as aliens in the United Sates: "In Techno Kraftwerk is the delta blues. . . . So Europe and whiteness generally take the place of origin. And Black Americans are synthetic; the key to Techno is to synthesize yourself into a new American alien." See *More Brilliant*, 178.

62 Diana Fuss differentiates these two concepts thus: "Identification is the psychical mechanism that produces self-recognition. Identification inhabits, organizes, instantiates identity" (*Identification Papers*, 2). Although squarely located within psychoanalytic cultural criticism, Fuss furnishes a framework for thinking identification beyond the merely

psychic. Still, it is surprising that the text makes no reference to literal "identification papers" such as passports and identity cards. This obvious connection would have provided a more overdetermined version of the argument linking the psychic apparatus and more explicitly political formations.

63 Fuss, *Identification Papers*, 2.

64 On Amo, see Sophocle, "Anton Wilhelm Amo"; Martin, *Schwarze Teufel*, 308–327); and Oguntoye et al., *Farbe bekennen*, 17–19. For a brief discussion of Amo's philosophical writings, see Judy, *(Dis)forming*, 43–48.

65 Although not many Africans from German colonies migrated to Germany, as Carol Aisha Blackshire-Belay shows, there were sizable populations of Afro-Germans in the colonies themselves. See "Historical Revelations," 106–111.

66 The estimated number of biracial children born in the aftermath of World War I is eight hundred to one thousand. Given the massive media and government attention, the actual and symbolic effects are in no way commensurate. For an in-depth discussion of the intertwining of sexual and racial stereotypes concerning the French African soldiers, white German women, and Afro-German children, see Lester, "Blacks in Germany," 113–119. See also Oguntoye, *Eine Afro-deutsche Geschichte*, and El-Tayeb, *Schwarze Deutsche*. For a delineation of the presence of black soldiers in Germany spanning the last eighty years, see Little, "The Black Military Experience."

67 See, for example, the personal testimonies of Frieda P. and Anna G., whose father came from Cameroon to Germany in 1891. The sisters spent their entire life in Germany and write about their experiences during the Weimar Republic and the Third Reich (Oguntoye et al., *Farbe bekennen*, 65–84).

68 For a sustained discussion of Afro-Germans during the Third Reich, see Campt, *Other Germans*. Susann Samples holds that Afro-Germans and African nationals were not as heavily and publicly persecuted as a group because their numbers were relatively small and represented the "ultimate shame" of the "Aryan nation" in the eyes of the National Socialists. Enforced sterilizations were undertaken, not as mass organized events, but covertly. See "African Germans in the Third Reich" and Reiner Pommerin's monograph, *Sterilisierung der Rheinlandbastarde*. See also the fascinating autobiography—chronicling his trials as an Afro-German during the Third Reich—of former *Ebony* magazine managing editor Hans Massaquoi, *Destined to Witness*.

69 Lester argues that African American soldiers in an army segregated until 1951 were treated "better" in Germany than in their home country. Furthermore, she argues that being stationed in Germany often

provided black soldiers with the first chance to experience unrestricted interactions with white people. See Lester, "Blacks in Germany," 120.

70 A majority of the Afro-German children during this period were born out of wedlock, their fathers returning home to the United States, which created a number of problems for the mothers, since they were forced to deal with the situation by themselves and were often ostracized by their family and friends. For a detailed historical study of Afro-German children in post–World War II West Germany and the United States, see Muniz, *Zwischen Fürsorge und Ausgrenzung*.

71 See Little, "The Black Military Experience," 189–191.

72 In East Germany, the first major influxes of black people were African students on scholarships from socialist "sister countries." This was a common practice during the sixties and seventies in most socialist countries. Students from newly independent African states that declared themselves socialist were granted scholarships in European socialist nations, so that they would return to their home countries and help transform them into strong socialist states. There were also numerous laborers from Cuba and African socialist countries that came to work in factories and were often put in housing separate from Germans. See Farah, *Schwarz-Weisse Zeiten*.

73 In her autobiography, Ika Hügel-Marshall recounts how the ISD changed her identification from a generic black identity, abjected by German national discourse, to Afro-German, highlighting the tricky dialectic between imposed and chosen subjectivities. See Hügel-Marshall, *Daheim unterwegs*, 93–94.

74 Here, I do not mean to imply that the effects of the term/concept "Afro-German" hold true in every case; rather, I am drawing on the pertinent literature (Oguntoye, Opitz, and Schultz; Blackshire-Belay; Campt), as well as my own observations and experiences, to make an argument that remains generalizable but not necessarily universal. Thus the articulation created a space for Germans of African descent in which they were able to publicly envision their identity in ways hitherto impossible.

75 Oguntoye, Opitz, and Schultz, "Title," 141.

76 Campt, "Afro-German Cultural Identity," 113. This analogy does not presume that Afro-German and African American identities are interchangeable or even closely comparable. As Campt rightly remarks, Afro-German identity construction rests much more on mediating between black and white identification rather than choosing one or the other, as is the case with racial identification and classification in the States. The main reason for this distinctive form of identity construction among Afro-Germans comes from the lack of an established ethnic history and community, which form the principal pillars in African American

ethnic identification. "Afro-German Cultural Identity," 124. Also, most Afro-Germans are biracial and grow up in a largely white environment, making it hard to construct an exclusionary form of racial identification.

77 Brody, "Hyphen-Nations," 159.

78 *Report*, similar to *60 Minutes* in the United States, is a long-running hour-long newsmagazine aired every two weeks on German public television. These production techniques reference the "wall of noise" created by the Bomb Squad for Public Enemy's oeuvre that combines everyday noises and sound snippets from the news media with beats culled from James Brown records. Public Enemy serves as Advanced Chemistry's U.S. counterpart, especially since Torch's voice and delivery so clearly evoke those of Chuck D. I thank Fred Moten for pointing out this similarity in his response to an earlier version of this chapter.

79 One of the main problems confronting Afro-Germans in everyday life comes from the denial of racism by white Germans. As the personal testimonies in Oguntoye, Opitz, and Schultz, *Farbe bekennen*, note in many different places, often when Afro-Germans bring up the question of racism with their white friends or family members, they are dismissed and accused of "paranoia" or "sensitivity" (145–221). This ignorance and/or willful denial also extends into the realm of politics, since Afro-Germans are not recognized as an official minority by the German government.

80 Besides the Holocaust, these incidents bring lynching to my mind, especially in the violent coupling of burned nonwhite bodies and white spectatorship.

81 Uli Linke recounts the intense reactions of left-leaning intellectuals to her argument about the violence that haunts both right and left political formations in Germany. These opponents prefer to codify racist violence as a problem of the uncontrollable sub-proletariat (*German Bodies*, 212–214).

82 Rogers Brubaker holds that the image of West Germany as a nonimmigrant nation dominated debates regarding immigration. This, he goes on to assert, should not be taken as having any bearing on the reality of the presence of nonwhite subjects; rather it serves as "a political-cultural norm, an element of German self-understanding." Thus, although factual evidence points toward the exact opposite, immigrants of color in Germany are largely placed beyond the ideological borders of the ideal German nation. Brubaker, *Citizenship*, 174.

83 The Swiss government first used the phrase "Das Boot ist voll" during the Third Reich to highlight the rising number of Jews within its borders.

84 Rieff, "The Tuscany Fraction," 12.

85 Until recently West German passports were green and featured a golden

eagle, the national emblem of the former Federal Republic of Germany and now of the reunited Germany.

86 *Ausweisen* comes from *Ausweis*, which is an official identity card. Although the verb *ausweisen* could be translated as "to identify," it literally means to show one's ID, in other words, to officially (in the state-sanctioned way) identify oneself. *Ausweisen* also connotes deportation, which gains added dimensions in the debate on the repatriation of political asylum seekers in Germany at that time.

87 Mongia, "Race, Nationality, Mobility," 554.

88 Mongia, "Race, Nationality, Mobility," 554.

89 Balibar, "The Nation Form," 95. Balibar draws on the early nineteenth-century works of Johann Gottlieb Fichte to construct this argument. See also the more topical discussion of Fichte in Balibar, "Fichte and the Internal Border."

90 In the following discussion of German citizenship, I draw mainly on Brubaker, "Immigration" and *Citizenship and Nationhood in France and Germany*. See also Barbieri, *Ethics of Citizenship*, particularly chapter 3.

91 Most German "ethnics" outside of Germany's borders live in the former eastern bloc nations, Russia or Romania, for example, and are naturalized immediately upon their arrival provided they prove their German heritage. When these subjects come to Germany, they are not classified as immigrants, but are called *Aussiedler* (out settlers), which signifies a mere change of location and not a shift in political membership.

92 Advanced Chemistry, "Operation Artikel 3."

93 William Barbieri summarizes the initial situation as follows: "German recruiters saw the arrangement as an opportunity to build up the German economy through labor obtained with a minimum of financial investment and social costs. Policymakers in the countries providing the workers viewed recruitment as a chance to siphon off unemployed workers, bring in foreign currency, and gain trained workers who on their return would help develop their home country. And the workers themselves were confronted with the allure of good jobs that would allow them to provide for their families and improve their economic status upon their return" (*Ethics of Citizenship*, 28).

94 The title of this section is from Tricky, "Brand New You're Retro," *Maxinquaye*.

95 If this were not enough output for a time span of three years, Tricky also released one full-length record, *Nearly God*, and one EP of collaborations, *Tricky Presents the Grassroots*. In the following analysis I limit my discussion to the work Tricky produced with Martina, although his oeuvre is far larger than these recordings. According to Simon Reynolds, *Maxinquaye* is not only a reference to Tricky's mother; rather,

Tricky has presented two versions of the genesis of that evocative title: " 'Quaye, that's a race of people in Africa, and "Maxin," that's my mum's name.' . . . Elsewhere, he's said that Quaye was his mother's surname. I prefer the first version because it makes it into a sort of place name: the lost Motherland" (*Generation Ecstasy*, 333). This is crucial since in a number of ways Tricky insists on claiming the maternal and the feminine as forceful locations from and through which to imagine a non-hegemonic subjectivity.

96   Gilroy, " 'After the Love Has Gone,' " 55. I refer to this essay in the collection *Black Public Sphere* rather than the later version in Gilroy's monograph *Against Race*, since the word "fucking," which is important to my argument, has been edited out of the later version.

97   Mark Anthony Neal notes that "the high visibility of *haute couture* fashions and other emblems of conspicuous wealth within hip-hop served to stimulate desire and consumption that transcended the structural realities of many black urban youth; processes that were often construed as forms of resistance against the invisibility and misery associated with black urban life" (*What the Music Said*, 150). Perhaps this version too easily accepts current formations as resistant, where Gilroy sees only commodification.

98   For a brilliant reading of the continuities between slavery and "freedom" in relation to the domination of black subjects in the nineteenth-century United States, see Hartman, *Scenes of Subjection*.

99   Gilroy, "After the Love Has Gone," 55.

100   Gilroy does gesture toward this history but claims that currently there exist no discourses to counter this recent all-encompassing sex machine as in earlier periods. See *Against Race*, 197.

101   This recording, along with a host of other "explicit" blues songs from this period, can be found on the compilation *Raunchy Business: Hot Nuts and Lollipops*.

102   Rose, "Two Inches or a Yard," 320–321.

103   Tate, "Trick Baby," 77.

104   Greg Tate gives this description of Tricky's revolutionary use of sampling: "His use of the sampler is mad stylish, distinctively his own, identifiable enough to qualify as an original voice on the instrument. Attribute this to his pushing the sampler's capacity for distortion, dissonance, and discontinuity" ("Trick Baby," 77). A sampler transforms analog sonic information into digital information, thereby allowing for infinite mutations and recombinations of the musical material. Andrew Goodwin describes this device as follows: "Digital sampling computers are relatively new machines that digitally encode any sounds, store them, and enable the manipulation and reproduction of those sounds within

almost infinite parameters and no discernible loss of sound quality"
("Sample and Hold," 216). Tricia Rose analyzes the pivotal role of sam-
pling within hip-hop in *Black Noise*, particularly chapter 3, "Soul Sonic
Forces" (62–98).

105 The only track approaching song status on the album is the first single
"Broken Homes."

106 For some examples of music journalistic reports on Tricky, see Storms,
"Tricky: Die magischen Kanäle"; Roberts, "Watching Channel Zero";
Reden, "Tricky: Fremd in jedem Land"; Melville, "The Trickster"; Gonzales, "Weeded, Wicked & Wise"; Cohen and Krugman, "The Madness
of King Tricky"; Ali, "Tricky."

107 Reynolds, "Slip into Darkness," 36.

108 John Corbett describes the interaction between lead and background
vocals as follows: "By providing a harmonic 'bed,' it literally supports the
singular voice, which is constructed as the central point around which
the background vocals are laid as the foundation. And these vocals are
commonly held to be an 'expressive' supplement to the single voice"
(*Extended Play*, 64).

109 In this way, Tricky and Martina's "negative" performances are more akin
to rock and jazz, or even beatnik traditions, than they are to R&B or hip-
hop, where darkness and psychosis are generally eschewed rather than
celebrated as integral parts of the destructive genius narrative.

110 For a brief discussion of androgyny in the history of popular music, see
Savage, *Time Travel*, 156–162. In *The Sex Revolts*, Simon Reynolds and
Joy Press argue that most post–rock 'n' roll forms of popular music ideologically rest on rebellions against the feminine. It is all the more striking
then that Tricky utilizes "the feminine" to construct his rebellion against
the strict categories of black identity and music. In the documentary
contained on the 2002 DVD compilation of Tricky's music videos, *The
Rough Guide*, Tricky explains that masculine men are far less interesting
than feminine ones.

111 Mercer, *Welcome to the Jungle*, 141.

112 Phil Johnson gives this description of the images: "The selling of the
album cannily maximized *Maxinquaye*'s cross-genre potential by cloak-
ing the artist and his muse, Martina, in gender-bending mufti for publicity shots. . . . Tricky's distinctive, sallow, drugged-up face was painted
and preened, with a Clockwork Orange false eyelash here, a smear of lipstick there, and his skinny body dressed in drag, while Martina was made
to be the groom to his bride in the celebrated wedding shots" (*Straight
outa Bristol*, 133).

113 Muñoz, *Disidentifications*, 93–115.

114 *Bend over Boyfriend* is a successful semieducational video series fre-

quently advertised in the *Village Voice* that instructs women on how to anally penetrate their male partners with dildos and strap-ons.

115 Halberstam, *Female Masculinity*. This is how Halberstam describes the limitations of her project: "While much of this book has concentrated on the masculinity in women with sexual variance, I also think the general concept of female masculinity has its uses for heterosexual women" (268). Still, might we also ask how both straight and queer femmes (who do not visually embody the masculine in the same way as the tomboys or butch lesbians that are Halberstam's subjects) deploy masculinity?

116 Bersani, "Is the Rectum a Grave?" 222.

117 Edelman, *Homographesis*, 183–184.

118 The ironic invocation of background singers as mere eye candy has a fairly long history in popular music, beginning with Robert Palmer's "Addicted to Love," which features a group of very similar-looking models boredly pretending to be Palmer's backup band. This already ironic use of the models has been spoofed by rapper Tone Loc in "Wild Thing," who only used white models, and Shania Twain's all-boy "band" in "Man! I Feel Like a Woman!" I thank Michael Hanchard for pointing this out.

119 Harper, *Are We Not Men?* 177–182.

120 Martina and Tricky also covered Siouxsie and the Banshees' "Tattoo" and "Judas" by Depeche Mode on the *Nearly God* album.

121 "New school hip-hop" generally designates the period in the mid- to late 1980s in which samplers widely displaced DJs as the main source of musical production.

122 Tricky, quoted in Johnson, *Straight outta Bristol*, 136.

123 Spillers, "Who Cuts the Border?"

Outro

1 Delany, *Shorter Views*, 270.

2 Eshun, *More Brilliant*, 190.

3 Eshun, *More Brilliant*, 4.

4 Attali, *Noise*, 4.

5 Wynter, "On Disenchanting Discourse," 461.

6 Massumi, *Parables for the Virtual*, 12–13.

Works Cited

Aaliyah. "One in a Million." *One in a Million*. Blackground/Atlantic Records. 1996.

Adorno, Theodor W. "The Curves of the Needle." Translated by Thomas Y. Levin. *October* 55 (1990): 49–55.

———. "The Form of the Phonograph Record." Translated by Thomas Y. Levin. *October* 55 (1990): 56–61.

———. "On the Fetish Character in Music and the Regression in Listening." *The Culture Industry*. 1938. New York: Routledge, 1991.

Advanced Chemistry. "Fremd im eigenen Land." 1992. *Advanced Chemistry*. 360°/IRS Records, 1995.

———. "Kapitel 1." *Advanced Chemistry*. 360°/IRS Records, 1995.

Agamben, Giorgio. *The Coming Community*. Translated by Michael Hardt. 1990. Minneapolis: University of Minnesota Press, 1993.

———. *Homo Sacer: Sovereign Power and Bare Life*. Translated by Daniel Heller-Roazen. 1995. Stanford, Calif.: Stanford University Press, 1998.

———. *Potentialities: Collected Essays in Philosophy*. Edited and translated by Daniel Heller-Roazen. Stanford, Calif.: Stanford University Press, 1999.

Ahmed, Ali Jimale. *Daybreak Is Near . . . Literature, Clans, and the Nation-State in Somalia*. Lawrenceville, N.J.: Red Sea Press, 1996.

Ali, Lorraine. "Tricky." *Option: Music and Culture* 70 (September–October 1996): 77–81.

Allien, Ellen. "Sehnsucht." *Berlinette*. B-Pitch Control Records, 2003.

Althusser, Louis. "Ideology and Ideological State Apparatuses (Notes towards an Investigation)." In *Lenin and Philosophy and Other Essays*, translated by Ben Brewster, 127–186. 1970. New York: Monthly Review Press, 1971.

Altman, Rick. "Material Heterogeneity of Recorded Sound." In *Sound Theory/Sound Practice*, edited by Rick Altman, 15–31. New York: Routledge, 1992.

—————, ed. *Sound Theory/Sound Practice*. New York: Routledge, 1992.

Anderson, Paul Allen. *Deep River: Music and Memory in Harlem Renaissance Thought*. Durham, N.C.: Duke University Press, 2001.

Ansell-Pearson, Keith. *Viroid Life: Perspectives on Nietzsche and the Transhuman Condition*. New York: Routledge, 1997.

Appadurai, Arjun. *Modernity at Large: The Cultural Dimensions of Globalization*. Minneapolis: University of Minnesota Press, 1996.

Aparicio, Frances R. *Listening to Salsa: Gender, Latin Popular Music, and Puerto Rican Cultures*. Hanover, N.H.: Wesleyan University Press, 1997.

Ashcroft, Bill, Gareth Griffiths, and Helen Tiffin. *Key Concepts in Post-Colonial Studies*. New York: Routledge, 1998.

Attali, Jacques. *Noise: The Political Economy of Music*. Translated by Brian Massumi. 1977. Minneapolis: University of Minnesota Press, 1985.

Auslander, Philip. *Liveness: Performance in a Mediatized Culture*. New York: Routledge, 1999.

Baker, Houston. *Blues, Ideology, and Afro-American Literature: A Vernacular Theory*. Chicago: University of Chicago Press, 1984.

—————. *Modernism and the Harlem Renaissance*. Chicago: University of Chicago Press, 1987.

Baldwin, James. *Another Country*. New York: Vintage, 1960.

Balibar, Etienne. "Fichte and the Internal Border: On Addresses to the German Nation." In *Masses, Classes, Ideas: Studies on Politics and Philosophy before and after Marx*, 61–84. New York: Routledge, 1994.

—————. "The Nation Form: History and Ideology." In *Race, Nation, Class: Ambiguous Identities*, edited by Etienne Balibar and Immanuel Wallerstein, 86–106. London: Verso, 1991.

Baraka, Amiri (LeRoi Jones). *Black Music*. New York: William Morrow, 1968.

—————. *Blues People: Negro Music in White America*. New York: William Morrow, 1963.

Barbieri, William A. *Ethics of Citizenship: Immigration and Group Rights in Germany*. Durham, N.C.: Duke University Press, 1998.

Bardin, Brantley. "Sugar Hill." *Details Magazine* (November 1998): 150–153, 199.

Barrett, Lindon. *Blackness and Value: Seeing Double*. New York: Cambridge University Press, 1999.

Works Cited

Barrow, Steve, and Peter Dalton. *Reggae: The Rough Guide*. New York: Penguin, 1997.

Beiner, Ronald, ed. *Theorizing Citizenship*. Albany: State University of New York Press, 1995.

Bell, Bernard W. "Genealogical Shifts in Du Bois's Discourse on Double Consciousness as the Sign of African American Difference." In *W. E. B. Du Bois on Race and Culture: Philosophy, Politics, Poetics*, edited by Bernard Bell, Emily Grosholz, and James B. Stewart, 87–108. New York: Routledge, 1996.

Bell, Bernard W., Emily Grosholz, and James B. Stewart. *W. E. B. Du Bois on Race and Culture: Philosophy, Politics, Poetics*. New York: Routledge, 1996.

Benjamin, Walter. "Die Aufgabe des Übersetzers." In *Illuminationen: Ausgewählte Schriften*, edited by Siegfried Unseld, 50–62. 1923. Frankfurt am Main: Suhrkamp, 1980.

——. "On the Concept of History." Translated by Edmund Jephcott and others. In *Selected Writings*, vol. 4, *1938–1940*, edited by Howard Eiland and Michael Jennings, 389–400. 1940. Cambridge, Mass.: Harvard University Press, 2003.

——. "The Task of the Translator." Translated by Harry Zohn. In *Selected Writings*, vol. 1, *1913–1926*, edited by Marcus Bullock and Michael Jennings, 253–263. 1923. Cambridge, Mass.: Harvard University Press, 1996.

——. "Theses on the Philosophy of History." In *Illuminations*, edited by Hannah Arendt, translated by Harry Zohn, 253–264. 1940. London: Fontana, 1973.

——. "Über den Begriff der Geschichte." In *Illuminationen: Ausgewählte Schriften*, edited by Siegfried Unseld, 251–261. 1940. Frankfurt am Main: Suhrkamp, 1980

——. "The Work of Art in the Age of Mechanical Reproduction." In *Illuminations*, edited by Hannah Arendt, translated by Harry Zohn, 319–253. 1936. London: Fontana, 1973.

Berland, Jody. "Locating Listening: Technological Space, Popular Music, and Canadian Mediations." In *The Place of Music*, edited by Andrew Leyshon, David Matless, and George Revill, 237–258. New York: Guilford Press, 1998.

——. "Toward a Creative Anachronism: Radio, the State and Sound Government." In *Radio Rethink: Art, Sound and Transmission*, edited by Dan Lander and Diana Augatis, 33–44. Banff, Alberta: Walter Phillips Gallery, 1994.

Berlant, Lauren. "National Brands/National Body: *Imitation of Life*." In *The*

Phantom Public Sphere, edited by Bruce Robbins, 173–208. Minneapolis: University of Minnesota Press, 1993.

———. *The Queen of America Goes to Washington: Essays on Sex and Citizenship*. Durham, N.C.: Duke University Press, 1997.

Bersani, Leo. "Is the Rectum a Grave?" In *AIDS: Cultural Analyis/Cultural Activism*, edited by Douglas Crimp, 197–222. Cambridge, Mass.: MIT Press, 1988.

Bhabha, Homi. *The Location of Culture*. New York: Routledge, 1994.

Bhabha, Jacqueline. "Embodied Rights: Gender Persecution, State Sovereignty, and Refugees." *Public Culture* 9 (1996): 3–32.

Blackshire-Belay, Carol Aisha, ed. *The African-German Experience: Critical Essays*. Westport, Conn.: Praeger, 1996.

———. "Historical Revelations: The International Scope of African Germans Today and Beyond." In *The African-German Experience: Critical Essays*, edited by Carol Aisha Blackshire-Belay, 89–123. Westport, Conn.: Praeger, 1996.

Blondie. "Rapture." *Autoamerican*. Chrysalis Records, 1980.

Boggs, Vernon W. *Salsiology: Afro-Cuban Music and the Evolution of Salsa in New York City*. New York: Excelsior, 1992.

Bogue, Ronald. *Deleuze on Music and the Arts*. New York: Routledge, 2003.

Boyd, Todd. *Am I Black Enough for You? Popular Culture from the "Hood" and Beyond*. Bloomington: Indiana University Press, 1997.

Brady, Erika. *A Spiral Way: How the Phonograph Changed Ethnography*. Oxford: University of Mississippi Press, 1999.

Brewster, Bill, and Frank Broughton. *Last Night a DJ Saved My Life: The History of the Disc Jockey*. New York: Grove, 1999.

Brody, Jennifer DeVere. "Hyphen-Nations." In *Cruising the Performative: Interventions into the Representation of Ethnicity, Nationality, and Sexuality*, edited by Sue-Ellen Case, Philip Brett, and Susan Leigh Foster, 149–162. Bloomington: Indiana University Press, 1995.

Brother's Keepers. *Adriano (Letzte Warnung)*. Cologne: Nitty Gritty Music/WEA, 2001.

Brubaker, Rogers. *Citizenship and Nationhood in France and Germany*. Cambridge, Mass.: Harvard University Press, 1992.

———. "Immigration, Citizenship, and the Nation-State in France and Germany." In *The Citizenship Debates*, edited by Gershon Shafir, 131–164. 1990. Minneapolis: University of Minnesota Press, 1998.

Bull, Michael. *Sounding Out the City: Personal Stereos and the Management of Everyday Life*. New York: Berg, 2000.

Busia, Abena P.A. "Re:locations—Rethinking Britain from Accra, New York, and the Map Room of the British Museum." In *Multicultural*

States: Rethinking Difference and Identity, edited by David Bennet, 267–281. New York: Routledge, 1998.

Butler, Judith. *The Psychic Life of Power: Theories in Subjection*. Stanford, Calif.: Stanford University Press, 1997.

Callahan, John F. "Chaos, Complexity, and Possibility: The Historical Frequencies of Ralph Waldo Ellison." In *New Essays on Invisible Man*, edited by Robert O'Meally, 55–94. Cambridge: Cambridge University Press, 1988.

Callahan, John F., and Albert Murray, eds. *Trading Twelves: The Selected Letters of Ralph Ellison and Albert Murray*. New York: Random House, 2000.

Campt, Tina M. "African German/African American — Dialogue or Dialectic." In *The African-German Experience: Critical Essays*, edited by Carol Aisha Blackshire-Belay, 71–88. Westport, Conn.: Praeger, 1996.

———. "Afro-German Cultural Identity and the Politics of Positionality: Contests and Contexts in the Formation of a German Ethnic Identity." *New German Critique* 58 (1993): 109–126.

———. *Other Germans: Black Germans and the Politics of Race, Gender, and Memory in the Third Reich*. Ann Arbor: University of Michigan Press, 2003.

Carby, Hazel. *Race Men*. Cambridge, Mass.: Harvard University Press, 1998.

Cashmore, Ellis. *The Black Culture Industry*. London: Routledge, 1997.

Cataliotti, Robert H. *The Music in African American Fiction*. New York: Garland, 1995.

Chambers, Iain. "A Miniature History of the Walkman." *New Formations* 11 (1990): 1–4.

Chanan, Michael. *Repeated Takes: A Short History of Recording and Its Effects on Music*. London: Verso, 1995.

Chandler, Nahum Dimitri. "Originary Displacement." *boundary 2* 27.3 (2000): 249–286.

Chaos. "Afrogermanic." *Interstellar Fugitives*. UR Records, 1998.

Chesnutt, Charles. *The Marrow of Tradition*. 1901. Ann Arbor: Michigan University Press, 1969.

Chion, Michel. *Audio-Vision: Sound on Screen*. Translated by Claudia Gorbman. 1990. New York: Columbia University Press, 1994.

Chow, Rey. *Ethics after Idealism: Theory — Culture — Ethnicity — Reading*. Bloomington: Indiana University Press, 1998.

———. "Listening Otherwise, Music Miniaturized: A Different Type of Question about Revolution." *Discourse* 13.1 (1990–91): 15–29.

Christian, Barbara. "The Race for Theory." In *The Nature and Context of Minority Discourse*, edited by Abdul JanMohamed and David Lloyd, 37–49. New York: Oxford University Press, 1990.

Clifford, James. "Diasporas." *Cultural Anthropology* 9.3 (1994): 302–338.

Cohen, Jason, and Michael Krugman. "The Madness of King Tricky." *Raygun* 40 (October 1996): 33–40.

Cohen, Tom. *Ideology and Inscription: "Cultural Studies" after Benjamin, De Man, and Bakhtin.* New York: Cambridge University Press, 1998.

———. "Politics of the Pre-figural: *Sula*, Blackness, and the Precession of Trope." *Parallax* 8.1 (2002): 5–16.

Collin, Matthew, with contributions by John Godfrey. *Altered State: The Story of Ecstasy Culture and Acid House.* London: Serpent's Tail, 1997.

Connor, Steven. *Dumbstruck: A Cultural History of Ventriloquism.* New York: Oxford University Press, 2000.

———. "The Modern Auditory I." In *Rewriting the Self: Histories from the Renaissance to the Present*, edited by Roy Porter, 203–223. New York: Routledge, 1997.

Corbett, John. *Extended Play: Sounding Off from John Cage to Dr. Funkenstein.* Durham, N.C.: Duke University Press, 1994.

Cossgrove, Stuart. "The Zoot Suit and Style Warfare." *History Workshop Journal* 18 (fall 1984): 77–91.

Crary, Jonathan. *Techniques of the Observer: On Vision and Modernity in the Nineteenth Century.* Cambridge, Mass.: MIT Press, 1990.

Cruse, Harold. *The Crisis of the Negro Intellectual: A Historical Analysis of the Failure of Black Leadership.* 1967. New York: Marrow Quill, 1984.

Cruz, Jon. *Culture on the Margins: The Black Spiritual and the Rise of American Cultural Interpretation.* Princeton: Princeton University Press, 1999.

Davis, Angela Y. "Race and Criminalization: Black Americans and the Punishment Industry." In *The House That Race Built*, edited by Wahneema Lubiano, 264–279. New York: Vintage, 1997.

De Certeau, Michel. *The Practice of Everyday Life.* Translated by Steven Rendall. Berkeley: University of California Press, 1984.

Delany, Samuel R. *Shorter Views: Queer Thoughts and the Politics of the Paraliterary.* Hanover, N.H.: Wesleyan University Press, 1999.

De La Soul. "I Am I Be." *Buhloone Mindstate.* Tommy Boy Records, 1993.

Deleuze, Gilles. *Cinema 1: The Movement-Image.* Translated by Hugh Tomlinson and Barbara Habberjam. 1983. Minneapolis: University of Minnesota Press, 1986.

———. *Cinema 2: The Time-Image.* Translated by Hugh Tomlinson and Robert Galeta. 1985. Minneapolis: University of Minnesota Press, 1989.

———. *Difference and Repetition.* Translated by Paul Patton. 1968. New York: Columbia University Press, 1994.

———. *Francis Bacon: The Logic of Sensation.* Translated by Daniel W. Smith. 1981. Minneapolis: University of Minnesota Press, 2003.

————. "He Stuttered." In *Essays Critical and Clinical*, translated by Daniel W. Smith and Michael A. Greco, 107–114. 1993. Minneapolis: University of Minnesota Press, 1997.

————. *Negotiations: 1972–1990*. Translated by Martin Joughin. 1990. New York: Columbia University Press, 1995.

————. *Proust and Signs: The Complete Text*. Translated by Richard Howard. 1964. Minneapolis: University of Minnesota Press, 2000.

————. *Pure Immanence: Essays on A Life*. Translated by Anne Boyman. 1995. New York: Zone Books, 2001.

Deleuze, Gilles, and Felix Guattari. *Anti-Oedipus: Capitalism and Schizophrenia*. Translated by Robert Hurley, Mark Seem, and Helen R. Lane. 1972. Minneapolis: University of Minnesota Press, 1983.

————. *Kafka: Towards a Minor Literature*. Translated by Dana Polan. 1975. Minneapolis: University of Minnesota Press, 1986.

————. *A Thousand Plateaus: Capitalism and Schizophrenia*. Translated by Brian Massumi. 1980. Minneapolis: University of Minnesota Press, 1987.

Delgado, Celeste Fraser, and Jose Esteban Muñoz, eds. *Everynight Life: Culture and Dance in Latin/o America*. Durham, N.C.: Duke University Press, 1997.

Derrida, Jacques. *Given Time*, vol. 1, *Counterfeit Money*. Translated by Peggy Kamuf. 1991. Chicago: University of Chicago Press, 1992.

————. *Monolingualism of the Other; or, The Prosthesis of Origin*. Translated by Patrick Mensah. 1996. Stanford, Calif.: Stanford University Press, 1998.

————. *Of Grammatology*. Translated by Gayatri Chakravorty Spivak. 1967. Baltimore, Md.: Johns Hopkins University Press, 1974.

————. "Plato's Pharmacy." In *Dissemination*, translated by Barbara Johnson, 65–171. 1968. Chicago: University of Chicago Press, 1981.

————. "Signature Event Context." In *Margins of Philosophy*, translated by Alan Bass, 307–330. 1971. Chicago: University of Chicago Press, 1982.

————. *Speech and Phenomena and Other Essays on Husserl's Theory of Signs*. Translated by David Allison. 1967. Evanston, Ill.: Northwestern University Press, 1973.

————. "Violence and Metaphysics: An Essay on the Thought of Emanuel Levinas." In *Writing and Difference*, translated by Alan Bass, 79–153. 1964. Chicago: University of Chicago Press, 1978.

————. "White Mythology: Metaphor in the Text of Philosophy." In *Margins of Philosophy*, translated by Alan Bass, 207–271. 1971. Chicago: University of Chicago Press, 1982.

Dery, Mark. "Black to the Future: Interviews with Samuel Delany, Greg Tate, and Tricia Rose." In *Flame Wars: The Discourse of Cyberculture*, edited by Mark Dery, 179–222. Durham, N.C.: Duke University Press, 1994.

Diedrichsen, Diedrich. *Freiheit macht arm: Das Leben nach dem Rock 'n' Roll.* Cologne: Kiepenheuer und Witsch, 1993.

Dixon, Robert, and John Godrich. *Recording the Blues.* New York: Stein and Day, 1970.

Dolar, Mladen. "The Object Voice." In *The Gaze and Voice as Love Objects,* edited by Renata Salecl and Slavoj Žižek, 7–31. Durham, N.C.: Duke University Press, 1996.

Douglas, Susan. *Listening In: Radio and the American Imagination.* New York: Random House, 1999.

Drake, St. Clair. "Diaspora Studies and Pan-Africanism." In *Global Dimensions of the African Diaspora,* edited by Joseph E. Harris, 451–514. Washington, D.C.: Howard University Press, 1983.

Du Bois, W. E. B. "Sociology Hesitant" (1905). *boundary 2* 27.3 (fall 2000): 37–44.

———. *The Souls of Black Folk.* 1903. New York: Penguin, 1989.

Du Gay, Paul, Stuart Hall, Linda James, Hugh Mackay, and Keith Negus. *Doing Cultural Studies: The Story of the Sony Walkman.* London: Sage and Open University Press, 1997.

Durant, Alan. *Conditions of Music.* Albany: State University of New York Press, 1984.

Dyer, Richard. *White.* New York: Routledge, 1997.

Edelman, Lee. *Homographesis: Essays in Gay Literary and Cultural Theory.* New York: Routledge, 1994.

Edison, Thomas A. "The Phonograph and Its Future." In *Thomas Edison and Modern America: A Brief History with Documents,* edited by Theresa M. Collins and Lisa Gitelman, 69–75. 1878. New York: Bedford, 2002.

Eisenberg, Evan. *The Recording Angel: Explorations in Phonography.* New York: McGraw-Hill, 1987.

Ellison, Ralph. *Invisible Man.* New York: Random House, 1952.

———. "Living with Music." In *Shadow and Act,* 187–198. 1955. New York: Vintage, 1995.

———. "Some Questions and Some Answers." In *Shadow and Act,* 261–272. 1958. New York: Vintage, 1995.

———. *Shadow and Act.* New York: Vintage, 1995.

———. "What Would America Be Like without Blacks?" In *Going to the Territory,* 104–112. 1970. New York: Vintage, 1995.

Eshun, Kodwo. *More Brilliant Than the Sun: Adventures in Sonic Fiction.* London: Quartet Books, 1998.

Works Cited

El-Tayeb, Fatima. *Schwarze Deutsche: Der Diskurs um "Rasse" und nationale Identität, 1890–1933.* Frankfurt am Main: Campus Verlag, 2001.

Fabian, Johannes. *Time and the Other: How Anthropology Makes Its Object.* New York: Columbia University Press, 1983.

Fanon, Frantz. *Black Skin, White Masks.* Translated by Charles Lam Markman. 1952. New York: Grove Press, 1967.

Farah, Ahmed. *Schwarz-weisse Zeiten: Ausländerinnen in Ostdeutschland vor und nach der Wende.* Bremen: IZA, 1993.

Farmer, Paul. *AIDS and Accusation: Haiti and the Geography of Blame.* Berkeley: University of California Press, 1992.

———. *The Uses of Haiti.* Monroe, Me.: Common Courage Press, 1994.

Featherstone, Mike, ed. *Global Culture: Nationalism, Globalization and Modernity.* London: Sage, 1930.

Febres, Mayra Santos. "Salsa as Translocation." In *Everynight Life: Culture and Dance in Latin/o America*, edited by Celeste Fraser Delgado and Jose Esteban Muñoz, 175–188. Durham, N.C.: Duke University Press, 1997.

Felbert, Oliver von. "Die Unbestechlichen." *Spex* (March 1993): 50–53.

Feld, Steven, and Charles Keil. *Music Grooves.* Chicago: University of Chicago Press, 1994.

Frankenberg, Ruth. *White Women, Race Matters: The Social Construction of Whiteness.* Minneapolis: University of Minnesota Press, 1993.

Freud, Sigmund. "The Uncanny." In *The Uncanny*, translated by David McClintock, 121–161. 1919. New York: Peguin, 2003.

Frith, Simon. *Performing Rites: On the Value of Popular Music.* Cambridge, Mass.: Harvard University Press, 1996.

Frith, Simon, Andrew Godwin, and Lawrence Grossberg, eds. *Sound and Vision: The Music Video Reader.* New York: Routledge, 1993.

The Fugees (Refugee Camp). *Fu-gee-la.* Directed by Guy Guillet. In the series for *The Score . . . Bootleg Versions.* Columbia Music Video/Sony Enterprises, 1996. Music video.

———. "Fu-gee-la." Ruffhouse/Columbia Records, 1995.

———. *Ready or Not.* Directed by Marcus Nispel. In the series for *The Score . . . Bootleg Versions.* Columbia Music Video/Sony Enterprises, 1996. Music video.

———. *The Score.* Ruffhouse/Columbia Records, 1996.

———. *The Score . . . Bootleg Versions.* Columbia Music Video/Sony Enterprises, 1996. Music video series.

The Fugees (Tranzlator Crew). *Blunted on Reality.* Ruffhouse/Columbia Records, 1994.

Fuss, Diana. *Identification Papers.* New York: Routledge, 1995.

Gallop, Jane. *Reading Lacan*. Ithaca: Cornell University Press, 1985.

Gates, Henry Louis, Jr. *The Signifying Monkey*. New York: Oxford University Press, 1986.

———. "Writing, 'Race,' and the Difference It Makes." In *"Race," Writing and Difference*, edited by Henry Louis Gates Jr., 1–120. Chicago: University of Chicago Press, 1985.

Gellat, Roland. *The Fabulous Phonograph, 1877–1977*. 3rd rev. ed. 1955. New York: Macmillan, 1977.

Gibson, Donald. "Introduction" in Du Bois *The Souls of Black Folk*. New York: Penguin, 1989. vii–xxxv.

Gilbert, Jeremy, and Ewan Pearson. *Discographies: Dance Music, Culture and the Politics of Sound*. New York: Routledge, 1999.

Gilmore, Ruth Wilson. *Golden Gulag*. Berkeley: University of California Press, forthcoming.

Gilroy, Paul. " 'After the Love Has Gone': Bio-politics and Etho-poetics in the Black Public Sphere." In *Black Public Culture*, edited by Public Culture, 49–76. Chicago: University of Chicago Press, 1994.

———. *Against Race: Imagining Political Culture beyond the Color Line*. Cambridge, Mass.: Harvard University Press, 2000.

———. "Analogues of Mourning, Mourning the Analogue." In *Stars Don't Stand Still in the Sky: Music and Myth*, edited by Karen Kelly and Evelyn McDonnell, 260–271. New York: New York University Press, 1999.

———. *The Black Atlantic: Modernity and Double Consciousness*. Cambridge, Mass.: Harvard University Press, 1993.

———. *Small Acts: Thoughts on the Politics of Black Cultures*. London: Serpent's Tail, 1993.

———. *"There Ain't No Black in the Union Jack": The Cultural Politics of Race and Nation*. 1987. Chicago: University of Chicago Press, 1991.

Gitelman, Lisa. *Scripts, Grooves, and Writing Machines: Representing Technology in the Edison Era*. Stanford: Stanford University Press, 1999.

Glissant, Edouard. *Caribbean Discourse*. Translated by J. Michael Dash. 1981. Knoxville: University of Virginia Press, 1989.

———. *Poetics of Relation*. Translated by Betsy Wing. 1990. Ann Arbor: University of Michigan Press, 1997.

Gonzales, Michael. "Weeded, Wicked & Wise." *VIBE* (April 1997): 82–85.

Goodwin, Andrew. "Sample and Hold: Pop Music in the Digital Age of Reproduction." In *On Record: Rock, Pop, and the Written Word*, edited by Simon Frith and Andrew Goodwin, 258–273. New York: Pantheon, 1990.

Goodwin-Gill, Guy. *The Refugee in International Law*. 2nd ed. New York: Oxford University Press, 1996.

Gorbman, Claudia. *Unheard Melodies: Narrative Film Music*. Bloomington: Indiana University Press, 1987.

Works Cited

Gordon, Avery. *Haunted Matters: Haunting and the Sociological Imagina-tion*. Minneapolis: University of Minnesota Press, 1997.

Gracyk, Theodore. *Rhythm and Noise: The Aesthetics of Rock*. Durham, N.C.: Duke University Press, 1996.

Green, Richard C., and Monique Guillory. "Question of a 'Soulful Style': Interview with Paul Gilroy." In *Soul: Black Power, Politics, and Pleasure*, edited by Richard C. Green and Monique Guillory, 250–265. New York: New York University Press, 1998.

Guattari, Felix. "Ritornellos and Existential Affects." In *The Guattari Reader*, edited by Gary Genesko, 158–171. 1990. London: Blackwell, 1996.

Halberstam, Judith. *Female Masculinity*. Durham, N.C.: Duke University Press, 1998.

Hall, Stuart. "The After-life of Frantz Fanon: Why Fanon? Why Now? Why Black Skin, White Masks?" In *The Fact of Blackness: Frantz Fanon and Visual Representation*, edited by Alan Read, 13–37. Seattle: Bay Press, 1996.

———. "Introduction: Who Needs 'Identity'?" In *Questions of Cultural Identity*, edited by Stuart Hall and Paul du Gay, 1–17. London: Sage, 1996.

———. "What Is This 'Black' in Black Popular Culture?" In *Stuart Hall: Critical Dialogues in Cultural Studies*, edited by David Morley and Kuan-Hsing Chen, 465–475. 1992. New York: Routledge, 1996.

Hall, Stuart, and David Held. "Citizens and Citizenship." In *New Times: The Changing Face of Politics in the 1990's*, edited by Stuart Hall and Martin Jacques, 173–190. London: Verso, 1990.

Hall, Stuart, David Held, Don Hubert, and Kenneth Thompson, eds. *Modernity: An Introduction to Modern Societies*. London: Blackwell, 1996.

Hanchard, Michael. "Afro-Modernity: Temporality, Politics, and the Afri-can Diaspora." *Public Culture* 11.1 (1999): 245–268.

Hansen, Miriam. "Early Cinema, Late Cinema: Transformations of the Pub-lic Sphere." In *Viewing Positions: Ways of Seeing Film*, edited by Linda Williams, 134–152. New Brunswick: Rutgers University Press, 1995.

Harper, Francis. *Iola Leroy; or, Shadows Uplifted*. 1892. New York: Oxford University Press, 1988.

Harper, Philip Brian. *Are We Not Men? Masculine Anxiety and the Problem of African American Identity*. New York: Oxford University Press, 1996.

Harris, Cheryl. "Whiteness as Property." *Harvard Law Review* 106.8 (June 1993): 1710–1745.

Harrison, Daphne Duval. *Black Pearls: Blues Queens of the 1920's*. New Brunswick: Rutgers University Press, 1988.

Hartman, Saidiya V. *Scenes of Subjection: Terror, Slavery, and Self-Making in Nineteenth-Century America*. New York: Oxford University Press, 1997.

Harvey, David. *The Condition of Postmodernity*. Cambridge: Blackwell, 1989.

Hebdige, Dick. *Cut 'n' Mix: Culture, Identity and Caribbean Music*. New York: Methuen, 1987.

Herencia, Juan Carlos Quintero. "Notes towards a Reading of Salsa." In *Everynight Life: Culture and Dance in Latin/o America*, edited by Celeste Fraser Delgado and Jose Esteban Muñoz, 189–222. Durham, N.C.: Duke University Press, 1997.

Higginbotham, Evelyn Brooks. "Rethinking Vernacular Culture: Black Religion and Race Records in the 1920s and 1930s." In *The House that Race Built*, edited by Wahneema Lubiano, 157–177. New York: Vintage, 1997.

Hill, Mike, ed. *Whiteness: A Critical Reader*. New York: New York University Press, 1995.

Holland, Sharon P. *Raising the Dead: Readings of Death and Black Subjectivity*. Durham, N.C.: Duke University Press, 2000.

Honig, Bonnie. "Immigrant America? How Foreignness 'Solves' Democracy's Problems." *Social Text* 16.3 (fall 1998): 1–27.

Hopkins, Pauline E. *Contending Forces: A Romance Illustrative of Negro Life North and South*. 1900. New York: Oxford University Press, 1988.

Hornby, Nick. *High Fidelity*. New York: Riverhead Books, 1996.

Hügel-Marshall, Ika. *Daheim unterwegs: Ein deutsches Leben*. Frankfurt am Main: Fischer Verlag, 1998.

Huggins, Nathan Irvin. *Harlem Renaissance*. New York: Oxford University Press, 1971.

——, ed. *Voices from the Harlem Renaissance*. New York: Oxford University Press, 1976.

Hughes, Langston. *I Wonder as I Wander*. 1956. New York: Hill and Wang, 1993.

Hurston, Zora Neal. "Spirituals and Neo-Spirituals." In *Voices from the Harlem Renaissance*, edited by Nathan Irvin Huggins, 344–347. New York: Oxford University Press, 1976.

I Like It Like That. Directed by Darnell Martin. Columbia Pictures, 1994.

Indeep. "Last Night a DJ Saved My Life." *Last Night a DJ Saved My Life*. Sound of New York Records, 1983.

Jacobs, Harriet. *Incidents in the Life of a Slave Girl*. In *The Classic Slave Narratives*, edited by Henry Louis Gates Jr., 335–515. New York: Penguin, 1987.

Jay, Martin. *Downcast Eyes: The Denigration of Vision in Twentieth-Century French Thought*. Berkeley: University of California Press, 1993.

Works Cited

Jameson, Fredric. *The Political Unconscious: Narrative as a Socially Symbolic Act*. Ithaca, N.Y.: Cornell University Press, 1981.

———. *Postmodernism; or, The Logic of Late Capitalism*. Durham, N.C.: Duke University Press, 1989.

Jobatey, Francine. "From *Toxi* to TV: Multiculturalism and the Changing Images of Black Germans." In *The African-German Experience: Critical Essays*, edited by Carol Aisha Blackshire-Belay, 13–36. Westport, Conn.: Praeger, 1996.

Johnson, Phil. *Straight outa Bristol: Massive Attack, Portishead, Tricky and the Roots of Trip-Hop*. London: Hodder and Stoughton, 1996.

Jones, Andrew F. *Yellow Music: Media Culture and Colonial Modernity in the Chinese Jazz Age*. Durham, N.C.: Duke University Press, 2001.

Judy, Ronald A. T. *(Dis)Forming the American Canon: African-Arabic Slave Narratives and the Vernacular*. Minneapolis: University of Minnesota Press, 1993.

———. "Introduction: On W. E. B. Du Bois and Hyperbolic Thinking." *boundary 2* 27.3 (fall 2000): 1–35.

———. "Untimely Intellectuals and the University." *boundary 2* 27.1 (spring 2000): 121–133.

Kahn, Douglas. *Noise, Water, Meat: A History of Sound in the Arts*. Boston, Mass.: MIT Press, 1999.

Kant, Immanuel. *Kritik der Urteilskraft*. 1790. Frankfurt am Main: Suhrkamp, 1974.

Karatani, Kojin. "Uses of Aesthetics: After Orientalism." Translated by Sabu Kohso. *boundary 2* 25.2 (summer 1998): 145–160.

Keightley, Kier. " 'Turn it down!' she shrieked": Gender, Domestic Space, and High Fidelity, 1948–59." *Popular Music* 15.2 (1996): 149–177.

Keith, Michael, and Steve Pile, eds. *Place and the Politics of Identity*. New York: Routledge, 1993.

Kelley, Robin D. G. "Kickin' Reality, Kickin' Ballistics: 'Gangsta Rap' and Postindustrial Los Angeles." In *Race Rebels: Culture, Politics, and the Black Working Class*, 183–227. New York: Free Press, 1994.

———. "The Riddle of the Zoot: Malcolm Little and Black Cultural Politics During World War II." In *Race Rebels: Culture, Politics, and the Black Working Class*, 161–182. New York: Free Press, 1994.

———. *Yo' Mama's Disfunktional: Fighting the Culture Wars in Urban America*. Boston: Beacon Press, 1997.

Kenney, William Howland. *Recorded Music in American Life: The Phonograph and Popular Memory, 1890–1945*. New York: Oxford University Press, 1999.

Khan, Chaka. "My Love Is Alive." *I Feel For You*. Warner Brothers Records, 1984.

Kittler, Friedrich. *Discourse Networks, 1800/1900*. Translated by Michael Metteer, with Chris Cullen. 1985. Stanford: Stanford University Press, 1990.

———. *Gramophone, Film, Typewriter*. Translated by Geoffrey Winthrop-Young and Michael Wutz. 1986. Stanford: Stanford University Press, 1999.

Koch, Ralf. "*Medien mögen's weiß*": *Rassismus im Nachrichtengeschäft*. Munich: Deutscher Taschenbuch Verlag, 1996.

Kristeva, Julia. *The Powers of Horror: An Essay on Abjection*. Translated by Leon Roudiez. 1980. New York: Columbia University Press, 1982.

Lacan, Jacques. "The Mirror Stage as Formative of the Function of the I." In *Ecrits: A Selection*, translated by Alan Sheridan, 1–7. 1966. New York: Norton, 1977.

Laing, David. "A Voice without a Face: Popular Music and the Phonograph in the 1890's." *Popular Music* 10.1 (1991): 1–9.

Lastra, James. *Sound Technology and the American Cinema: Perception, Representation, Modernity*. New York: Columbia University Press, 1999.

Lawless, Robert. *Haiti's Bad Press*. Rochester, Vt.: Shenkman Books, 1992.

Lee, Jerena. "The Life and Religious Experience of Jerena Lee." In *Sisters of the Spirit*, edited by William Andrews, 25–48. 1836. Bloomington: Indiana University Press, 1986.

Lemke Muniz de Faria, Yara-Colette. *Zwischen Fürsorge und Ausgrenzung: Afro-deutsche "Besatzungskinder" im Nachkriegsdeutschland*. Berlin: Metropol, 2002.

Leppert, Richard. *The Sight of Sound: Music, Representation, and the History of the Body*. Berkeley: University of California Press, 1993.

Leppert, Richard, and Susan McClary, eds. *Music and Society: The Politics of Composition, Performance and Reception*. Cambridge: Cambridge University Press, 1987.

Lester, Rosemarie K. "Blacks in Germany and German Blacks: A Little-Known Aspect of Black History." In *Blacks and German Culture*, edited by Reinhold Grimm and Jost Hermand, 113–134. Madison: University of Wisconsin Press, 1986.

Levin, David Michael, ed. *Modernity and the Hegemony of Vision*. Berkeley: University of California Press, 1993.

Levin, Thomas Y. "For the Record: Adorno on Music in the Age of Its Technological Reproducibility." *October* 55 (1990): 23–47.

Levinas, Emanuel. "The Transcendence of Words." In *The Emanuel Levinas Reader*, edited by Sean Hand, 144–149. London: Blackwell, 1989.

Levine, Lawrence. *Black Culture, Black Consciousness*. New York: Oxford University Press, 1977.

Lewis, David Levering, ed. *The Portable Harlem Renaissance Reader*. New York: Penguin, 1994.

———. *W. E. B. Du Bois: Biography of a Race, 1863–1919*. New York: Henry Holt, 1993.

———. *When Harlem Was in Vogue*. New York: Vintage, 1979.

Leyshon, Andrew, David Matless, and George Revill, eds. *The Place of Music*. New York: Guilford Press, 1998.

Linke, Uli. *German Bodies*. New York: Routledge, 1999.

Lipsitz, George. *Dangerous Crossroads: Popular Music, Postmodernism and the Poetics of Place*. London: Verso, 1994.

———. *The Possessive Investment in Whiteness: How White People Profit from Identity Politics*. Philadelphia: Temple University Press, 1998.

Little, Monroe H. "The Black Military Experience in Germany: From the First World War to the Present." In *Crosscurrents: African Americans, Africa, and Germany in the Modern World*, edited by David McBride, Leroy Hopkins, and C. Aisha Blackshire-Belay, 177–196. Columbia, S.C.: Camden House, 1998.

Loh, Hannes, and Sascha Verlan. *20 Jahre Hip Hop in Deutschland*. Höfen: Hannibal, 2000.

Lowe, David. *The History of Bourgeois Perception*. Chicago: University of Chicago Press, 1982.

Lowe, Lisa. *Immigrant Acts: On Asian American Cultural Politics*. Durham, N.C.: Duke University Press, 1996.

Lubar, Steven. *Info Culture: The Smithsonian Book of Information Age Inventions*. Boston: Houghton Mifflin, 1993.

Lubiano, Wahneema. "Black Ladies, Welfare Queens, and State Minstrels." In *Race-ing Justice, En-gendering Power*, edited by Toni Morrison, 323–363. New York: Pantheon Books, 1993.

Mackey, Nathaniel. *Discrepant Engagement: Dissonance, Cross-Culturality and Experimental Writing*. 1993. Tuscaloosa: University of Alabama Press, 2000.

Manuel, Peter. *Cassette Culture: Popular Music and Technology in North India*. Chicago: University of Chicago Press, 1993.

Marsh, J. B. T. *The Story of the Jubilee Singers, with Their Songs*. 1881. New York: Negro University Press, 1969.

Marshall, Paule. *Praisesong for the Widow*. New York: Plume, 1983.

Martin, Peter. *Schwarze Teufel, edle Mohren: Afrikaner in Geschichte und Bewusstsein der Deutschen*. Hamburg: Junius Verlag, 1993.

Massaqoui, Hans. *Destined to Witness: Growing up Black in Nazi Germany*. New York: HarperCollins, 1999.

Massive Attack. *Blue Lines*. Virgin Records, 1991.

———. *Protection*. Virgin Records, 1994.

Massumi, Brian. *Parables for the Virtual: Movement, Affect, Sensation.* Durham, N.C.: Duke University Press, 2002.

Massey, Doreen. *Space, Place, and Gender.* Minneapolis: University of Minnesota Press, 1994.

McClary, Susan. *Feminine Endings: Music, Gender, and Sexuality.* Minneapolis: University of Minnesota Press, 1991.

McDowell, Deborah E. "Boundaries; or, Distant Relations and Close Kin— *Sula.*" In *The Changing Same: Black Women's Literature, Criticism, and Theory*, 100–117. 1988. Bloomington: Indiana University Press, 1995.

McKay, Claude. *Home to Harlem.* 1928. Northeastern University Press, 1987.

Melville, Caspar. "The Trickster." *Touch: The Street Culture and Music Monthly* 65 (December 1996–January 1997): 52–58.

Melvin, Harold, and the Blue Notes. "Wake Up Everybody." *Wake Up Everybody.* Philly International Records, 1975.

Mercer, Kobena. *Welcome to the Jungle: New Positions in Black Cultural Studies.* New York: Routledge, 1994.

Mientjes, Louise. *Sound of Africa!: Making Music Zulu in a South African Studio.* Durham, N.C.: Duke University Press, 2003.

Millard, Andre. *America on Record: A History of Recorded Sound.* Cambridge: Cambridge University Press, 1995.

Miller, Paul D. "Cumulus from America. Cartridge Music: Of Palimpsest and Parataxis; or, How to Make a Mix." *http://homestudio.thing.net/revue/content/spooky.htm*, 2004.

Mills, Jeff. *Mix-Up, Vol. 2.* Sony Records, 1996.

Mis-Teeq. "It's Beginning to Feel Like Love." *Eye Candy.* London: Telstar Records, 2003.

Mitchell, Tony, ed. *Global Noise: Rap and Hip-Hop outside the U.S.A.* Middletown, Conn.: Wesleyan University Press, 2002.

Mongia, Radhika Viyas. "Race, Nationality, Mobility: A History of the Modern Passport." *Public Culture* 11.3 (1999): 527–556.

Morrison, Toni. *Beloved.* New York: Plume, 1987.

———. *Jazz.* New York: Plume, 1992.

———. *Playing in the Dark: Whiteness and the Literary Imagination.* New York: Vintage, 1992.

Morton, David. *Off the Record: The Technology and Culture of Sound Recording in America.* New Brunswick, N.J.: Rutgers University Press, 2000.

Moten, Fred. *In the Break: The Aesthetics of the Black Radical Tradition.* Minneapolis: University of Minnesota Press, 2003.

Mouffe, Chantal, ed. *Dimensions of Radical Democracy: Pluralism, Citizenship, Community.* London: Verso, 1992.

Mowitt, John. "Music in the Era of Electronic Reproducibility." In *Music and Society: The Politics of Composition, Performance and Reception*, edited by Richard Leppert and Susan McClary, 173–197. Cambridge: Cambridge University Press, 1987.

Mtume. "Juicy Fruit." *Juicy Fruit*. Epic Records, 1983.

Mudede, Charles. "The Turntable." http://www.ctheory.net/text_file .asp?pick=382. 2003.

Muñoz, Jose Esteban. *Disidentifications: Queers of Color and the Performance of Politics*. Minneapolis: University of Minnesota Press, 1999.

Murray, Albert. *Stomping the Blues*. New York: McGraw-Hill, 1976.

Neal, Mark Anthony. *What the Music Said: Black Popular Music and Black Public Culture*. New York: Routledge, 1999.

Nearly God. *Nearly God*. Durban Poison, Island Records, 1996.

Nelson, Alondra, Thuy Linh N. Tu, and Alicia Headlam Hines. "Introduction: Hidden Circuits." In *Technicolor: Race, Technology, and Everyday Life*, edited by Alondra Nelson and Thuy Linh N. Tu with Alicia Headlam Hines, 1–12. New York: New York University Press, 2001.

Nielsen, Alden Lynn. *Black Chant: Languages of African American Postmodernism*. New York: Cambridge University Press, 1997.

Ogren, Kathy. *The Jazz Revolution*. New York: Oxford University Press, 1989.

Oguntoye, Katharina. *Eine Afro-deutsche Geschichte. Zur Lebensituation von Afrikanern und Afro-Deutschen in Deutschland von 1884 bis 1950*. Berlin: Hoho Verlag Christine Hoffman. 1997.

Oguntoye, Katharina, May Opitz, and Dagmar Schultz, eds. *Farbe bekennen: Afro-deutsche Frauen auf den Spuren ihrer Geschichte*. 1986. Frankfurt am Main: Fischer Taschenbuch Verlag, 1992.

Oliver, Paul. *Songsters and Saints: Vocal Traditions on Race Records*. New York: Cambridge University Press, 1984.

O'Meally, Robert. *The Craft of Ralph Ellison*. Cambridge, Mass.: Harvard University Press, 1980.

Ong, Walter. *Orality and Literacy: The Technologizing of the Word*. New York: Routledge, 1982.

Paulson, William. *Enlightenment, Romanticism and the Blind in France*. Princeton: Princeton University Press, 1987.

———. *The Noise of Culture: Literary Texts in a World of Information*. Ithaca: Cornell University Press, 1988.

Phantom/Ghost. "Perfect Lovers" (Unperfect Love Mix by Tobias Thomas and Superpitcher). *Perfect Lovers*. Ladomat, 2001.

Phelan, Peggy. *Unmarked: The Politics of Performance*. New York: Routledge, 1993.

Pietz, William. "The Phonograph in Africa. International Phonocentrism from Stanley to Sarnoff." In *Poststructuralism and the Question of His-*

tory, edited by Derek Attridge, Geoffrey Bennington, and Robert Young, 263–285. Cambridge: Cambridge University Press, 1987.

Porschardt, Ulf. *DJ Culture*. Hamburg: Rogner und Bernhard bei Zweitausendundeins, 1995.

Public Culture, ed. *Black Public Sphere*. Chicago: University of Chicago Press, 1994.

Puelo, Augosto C. "Una verdadera cronica del Norte: Una noche con la India." Translated by Celeste Fraser Delgado. In *Everynight Life: Culture and Dance in Latin/o America*, edited by Celeste Fraser Delgado and Jose Esteban Muñoz, 223–228. Durham, N.C.: Duke University Press, 1997.

Radano, Ronald. "Denoting Difference: The Writing of Slave Spirituals." *Critical Inquiry* 22.1 (1996): 506–544.

———. *Lying Up a Nation: Race and Black Music*. Chicago: Chicago University Press, 2003.

Rampersad, Arnold. *The Art and Imagination of W. E. B. Du Bois*. Cambridge, Mass.: Harvard University Press, 1976.

Read, Oliver, and Walter Welch. *From Tin Foil to Stereo: The Acoustic Years of the Recording Industry 1877–1929*. 1959. Gainesville: University of Florida Press, 1994.

Reden, Sven von. "Tricky: Fremd in jedem Land." *Spex* (May 1998): 32–36.

Reynolds, Simon. "Slipping Into Darkness." *The Wire: Adventures in Modern Music* 148 (June 1996): 32–35, 62.

———. *Generation Ecstasy: Into the World of Techno and Rave Culture*. New York: Little, Brown, and Company, 1998.

Reynolds, Simon, and Joy Press. *The Sex Revolts: Gender, Rebellion and Rock 'n' Roll*. Cambridge, Mass.: Harvard University Press, 1995.

Rieff, David. "The Tuscany Fraction." *Transition: An International Review* 61 (1994): 4–16.

Robbins, Bruce. "Actually Existing Cosmopolitanism." In *Cosmopolitics: Thinking and Feeling beyond the Nation*, edited by Bruce Robbins and Pheng Cheah, 1–19. Minneapolis: University of Minnesota Press, 1998.

Roberts, Tod C. "Watching Channel Zero." *URB Magazine* 50 (June–July 1995): 50.

———. Review of *Nearly God* and *Tricky Presents the Grassroots*. *URB Magazine* 50 (August–September 1996): 69.

Roker, Raymond Leon. "Diatribe." *URB Magazine* 55 (September–October 1997): 6.

Ronell, Avital. *Crack Wars: Literature, Addiction, Mania*. Lincoln: University of Nebraska Press, 1992.

———. *Stupidity*. Urbana: University of Illinois Press, 2002.

———. *The Telephone Book: Technology, Schizophrenia, Electric Speech.* Lincoln: University of Nebraska Press, 1989.

Rose, Tricia. *Black Noise: Rap Music and Black Culture in Contemporary America.* Hanover, N.H.: New England University Press, 1994.

———. " 'Two Inches or a Yard': Silencing Black Women's Sexual Expression." In *Talking Visions: Multicultural Feminism in a Transnational Age,* edited by Ella Shohat, 315–324. Boston, Mass.: MIT Press, 1998.

Samples, Susan. "African Germans in the Third Reich." In *The African-German Experience: Critical Essays,* edited by Carol Aisha Blackshire-Belay, 53–69. Westport, Conn.: Praeger, 1996.

Sanjek, Russell. *American Popular Music and Its Business: The First Four Hundred Years.* Vol. 3. New York: Oxford University Press, 1988.

Sanjek, Russell, and David Sanjek. *American Popular Music Business in the 20th Century.* New York: Oxford University Press, 1991.

———. *From Print to Plastic: Publishing and Promoting America's Popular Music (1900–1980).* New York: Institute for the Studies in American Music, 1983.

Savage, John. *Time Travel: Pop, Media and Sexuality, 1976–1996.* London: Chatto and Windus; 1996.

Schafer, R. Murray. *Book of Noise.* Wellington: Price Milburn, 1970.

———. *The Soundscape: Our Sonic Environment and the Tuning of the World.* Rochester, Vt.: Destiny Books, 1977.

Schwarz, David. *Listening Subjects: Music, Psychoanalysis, Culture.* Durham, N.C.: Duke University Press, 1997.

Sconce, Jeffrey. *Haunted Media: Electronic Presence from Telegraphy to Television.* Durham, N.C.: Duke University Press, 2000.

Shafir, Gershon, ed. *The Citizenship Debates.* Minneapolis: University of Minnesota Press, 1998.

Shaviro, Steven. *The Cinematic Body.* Minneapolis: University of Minnesota Press, 1993.

Silverman, Kaja. *The Acoustic Mirror: The Female Voice in Psychoanalysis and Cinema.* Bloomington: Indiana University Press, 1988.

Sister's Keepers. "Liebe und Verstand." Nitty Gritty Music/WEA, 2001.

Smith, Daniel W. "Deleuze's Theory of Sensation: Overcoming the Kantian Duality." In *Deleuze: A Critical Reader,* edited by Paul Patton, 29–56. London: Blackwell, 1996.

Smith, Paul. *Discerning the Subject.* Minneapolis: University of Minnesota Press, 1988.

Smith, Susan J. "Soundscape," *Area* 26 (1994): 232–240.

Smith, Valerie. *Self-Discovery and Authority in Afro-American Narrative.* Cambridge, Mass.: Harvard University Press, 1987.

Snead, James A. "Repetition as a Figure of Black Culture." In *Black Litera-*

ture and Literary Theory, edited by Henry Louis Gates Jr., 59–79. New York: Methuen, 1984.

Soja, Edward. *Postmodern Geographies: The Reassertion of Space in Critical Social Theory*. London: Verso, 1989.

———. "The Spatiality of Social Life: Towards a Transformative Retheorization." In *Social Relations and Spatial Structures*, edited by Derek Gregory and John Urry, 90–127. New York: St. Martin's, 1985.

Sophocle, Marilyn. "Anton Wilhelm Amo." In "The Image of Africa in German Society," special issue, *Journal of Black Studies* 23.2 (1992): 182–187.

Southern, Eileen. *The Music of Black Americans*. New York: Norton, 1971.

———, ed. *Readings in Black American Music*. New York: Norton, 1971.

Soysal, Yasemin. *Limits of Citizenship: Migrants and Postnational Membership in Europe*. Chicago: University of Chicago Press, 1994.

Spillers, Hortense J. " 'All the Things You Could Be by Now If Sigmund Freud's Wife Was Your Mother': Psychoanalysis and Race." *Critical Inquiry* 22.4 (1996): 223–259.

———. "The Crisis of the Negro Intellectual: A Postdate." *boundary 2* 21.3 (fall 1994): 65–116.

———. "Cross-Currents, Discontinuities: Black Women's Fiction." In *Conjuring: Black Women and Literary Tradition*, edited by Marjorie Pryse and Hortense J. Spillers, 249–261. Bloomington: Indiana University Press, 1985.

———. *The Idea of Black Culture*. London: Blackwell, forthcoming.

———. "Mama's Baby, Papa's Maybe: An American Grammar Book." *Diacritics* 17.2 (1987): 65–81.

———. "Who Cuts the Border? Some Readings on 'America.' " In *Comparative American Identities: Race, Sex, and Nationality in the Modern Text*, edited by Hortense J. Spillers, 1–25. New York, Routledge, 1991.

Spivak, Gayatri Chakravorty. *Death of a Discipline*. New York: Columbia University Press, 2003.

———. "Echo." In *The Spivak Reader*, edited by Donna Landry and Gerald Maclean, 175–202. New York: Routledge, 1996.

———. *In Other Worlds: Essays in Cultural Politics*. New York: Routledge, 1988.

———. *Outside in the Teaching Machine*. New York: Routledge, 1993.

Stepick, Alex. *Pride and Prejudice: Haitians in the United States*. Boston: Allyn and Bacon, 1998.

Stepto, Robert B. *From Behind the Veil: A Study of Afro-American Narrative*. Urbana: University of Illinois Press, 1979.

Sterne, Jonathan. *The Audible Past: Cultural Origins of Sound Reproduction*. Durham, N.C.: Duke University Press, 2003.

Works Cited

Stolzoff, Norman. *Wake the Town and Tell the People: Dancehall Culture in Jamaica*. Durham, N.C.: Duke University Press, 2000.

Storms, Christian. "Tricky: Die magischen Kanaele." *Spex* (April 1995): 34–37.

Sundquist, Eric, ed. *Cultural Contexts for Ralph Ellison's Invisible Man: A Bedford Documentary Companion*. Boston: Bedford Books, 1995.

———. *To Wake the Nations: Race in the Making of American Literature*. Cambridge, Mass.: Belknap/Harvard University Press, 1993.

Tate, Greg. "Trick Baby." *Village Voice*, December 3, 1996, 77.

Taussig, Michael. *Mimesis and Alterity: A Particular History of the Senses*. New York: Routledge, 1993.

Théberge, Paul. *Any Sound You Can Imagine: Making Music/Consuming Technology*. Hanover, N.H.: Wesleyan University Press, 1997.

Thompson, Emily. *The Soundscape of Modernity: Architectural Acoustics and the Culture of Listening in America, 1900–1933*. Cambridge, Mass.: MIT Press, 2002.

Thompson, John B. *The Media and Modernity: A Social Theory of the Media*. Stanford University Press, 1996.

Tölölyan, Kachig. "Rethinking Diaspora(s): Stateless Power in the Transnational Moment." *Diaspora* 5.1 (1996): 3–32.

Toomer, Jean. *Cane*. Edited by Darwin Turner. 1923. New York: Norton, 1988.

Toop, David. *The Rap Attack 2: African Rap to Global Hip Hop*. 1984. New York: Serpent's Tail, 1991.

Tricky. *Angels with Dirty Faces*. Island Records, 1998.

———. *Christiansands*. Island Records, 1996. Directed by Shawn Mortensen. Music video.

———. Live performance, New York, Irving Plaza, January 13, 1997.

———. *Maxinquaye*. Island Records, 1995.

———. *Overcome*. Island Records, 1995.

———. *Pre-Millennium Tension*. Island Records, 1996.

———. *The Rough Guide*. Island/Universal, 2002. DVD.

———. *Tricky Presents the Grassroots*. Payday, London Records, 1996.

Various artists. *DJ Kicks* (Mix CD Series). Studio K7 Records, 1996–2005.

———. *Raunchy Business: Hot Nuts and Lollipops*. Columbia Records, 1991.

Vasseleu, Cathryn. *Textures of Light: Vision and Touch in Irigaray, Levinas, and Merleau-Ponty*. New York: Routledge, 1998.

Wall, Cheryl A. "Taking Positions and Changing Words." In *Changing Our Own Words: Essays on Criticism, Theory, and Writing by Black Women*, edited by Cheryl Wall, 1–15. New Brunswick: Rutgers University Press, 1990.

Ware, Vron. *Beyond the Pale: White Women, Racism and History*. London: Verso, 1991.

Watkins, S. Craig. *Representing: Hip-Hop Culture and the Production of Black Cinema*. Chicago: University of Chicago Press, 1998.

Waters, Malcolm. *Globalization*. New York: Routledge, 1995.

Weheliye, Alexander G. "Feenin: Posthuman Voices in Black Popular Music." *Social Text* 71 (summer 2002): 21–47.

Wiegman, Robyn. *American Anatomies: Theorizing Race and Gender*. Durham, N.C.: Duke University Press, 1995.

Wilson, August. *Ma Rainey's Black Bottom*. 1984. New York: Plume, 1988.

Wilson, Rob, and Wimal Dissanyake, eds. *Global/Local: Cultural Production and the Transnational Imaginary*. Durham, N.C.: Duke University Press, 1996.

Wilson, Harriet E. *Our Nig; or, Sketches from the Life of a Free Black*. 1859. New York: Vintage, 1983.

Wise, J. McGregor. *Exploring Technology and Social Space*. Thousand Oaks, Calif.: Sage, 1997.

Wynter, Sylvia. "Beyond the Word of Man: Glissant and the New Discourse of the Antilles." *World Literature Today* 63.4 (1989): 637–647.

———. "Columbus, the Ocean Blue, and Fables That Stir the Mind: To Reinvent the Study of Letters." In *Poetics of the Americas: Race, Founding, and Textuality*, edited by Bianard Cowan and Jefferson Humphries, 141–202. Baton Rouge: Louisiana University Press, 1997.

———. "On Disenchanting Discourse: 'Minority' Literary Criticism and Beyond." In *The Nature and Context of Minority Discourse*, edited by Abdul JanMohamed and David Lloyd, 432–469. New York: Oxford University Press, 1990.

Zamir, Shamoon. *Dark Voices: W. E. B. Du Bois and American Thought, 1888–1903*. Chicago: University of Chicago Press, 1995.

Zephir, Flore. *Haitian Immigrants in Black America: A Sociological and Sociolinguistic Portrait*. Westport, Conn.: Bergin and Garvey, 1996.

Index

Index

Double consciousness, 12, 40–43, 47, 65–66, 84, 89–92, 103
Doug E. Fresh, 151
Douglass, Frederick, 84
Drake, St. Clair, 147
Du Bois, W. E. B., 6, 9, 38–39, 81, 207, 234 n.55; on black music, 86–87; on "dark" and "blue," 43; on double consciousness, 12, 40–42, 65–66, 84; on the gaze, 41–43; and gender, 219 n.48; influence on *Invisible Man,* 222 n.12; and labor, 230 n.24; and Lacan, 41; on lynchings and looking, 42; and mash-ups, 234 n.58; and mixing, 83, 88–89; and Sartre, 41; on "second sight," 40, 44, 70; on "sorrow songs"/spirituals, 84–85, 92–105, 232 n.41; *The Souls of Black Folk,* 12, 41, 73, 82–105, 202–3, 230 n.23; on sound and hearing, 43–44; and visuality, 220 n.50
Du Gay, Paul, 134
Durant, Alan, 93; on musical notation, 233 n.42
Duvalier, François ("Papa Doc"), 158
Duvalier, Jean-Claude ("Baby Doc"), 158

Edelman, Lee, 192
Edison, Thomas Alva, 52: and the phonograph, 26–28, 215 n.11
Eisenberg, Evan, 123
Ellison, Ralph, 6, 9, 34, 38–39, 43, 89–90, 101, 104–5, 203, 208; and Benjamin, 228 n.9; on diaspora, 147–48; *Invisible Man,* 12–14, 17, 47–64, 70–71, 73–82, 84, 113, 143; "Living with Music," 14, 106–123, 143; on "passions," 147, 169; on sound technologies, 47–49, 52–56, 107–8, 237 n.17
Eshun, Kodwo, 202–3, 248 n.61; on the mix, 83

Fabian, Johannes, 99–100
Fanon, Frantz, 207; on ontology, 220 n.49; on vision and racism, 41–42
Farmer, Paul, 158–59
Febres, Marya, 139
Ferrier, Kathleen, 116
Film: black filmmakers, 124, 238 nn.20, 22; and gender, 123–24; "ghettocentric," 124; and race, 123–24
Flack, Roberta, 151
Fossey, Diane, 160
Foucault, Michel, 66
Freud, Sigmund, 66, 103; on the uncanny and the double, 235 n.61; and "sorrow songs," 96
Frith, Simon, 61–62
"Fucked-up(ness)," 187, 190–93, 195–96; and "fucking (with)" 183–85, 192–93, 197
Fugees, the, 146, 150, 182, 196–97, 243 n.14; and boat people, 162–64; and Haiti, 151–65; "Killing Me Softly," 151; and refugees, 152–55
Fuss, Diana, 248 n.62

Gamble, Kenny, 17
Gates, Henry Louis, Jr., 218 n.42
Gellat, Roland, 215 n.10
Gender: and Du Bois, 219–20 n.48; and film, 123–24; and hip-hop, 150, 188–95, 254 n.112; and music, 254 n.110; and sound, 123–24
Germany: African American soldiers in, 249 n.69; African presence in, 169–82; and citizenship, 165–82; guestworkers in, 252 n.93; and immigration, 244–45 n.24, 251 n.82; and Nazis, 170, 175; and neo-Nazis, 173; race and music in, 165–69; and whiteness, 166, 172. *See also* Afro-German(s)
Gibson, Donald, 44
Gift, in Du Bois, 44
Gilroy, Paul, 192, 207; *The Black Atlantic,* 147; on black music and

Index

Judy, Ronald: on blackness and writing, 5–6; on (il)legibility, 38
Julien, Isaac, 190

Kahn, Douglas, 215 n.23
Kant, Immanuel, 34; on the sublime, 217 n.37. *See also* Sublime
Karatani, Kojin, 233 n.45
Keightley, Keir, 118–23
Kelly, R., 202
Kennedy, John F., 158
King Tubby, 103
Kittler, Friedrich: on Derrida, 217 n.32; on literature and media, 229 n.19; on the phonograph, 33–34; on writing, 25, 233 n.44
Koestler, Arthur, 114
Kraftwerk, 248 n.61
Kristeva, Julia, 155, 245 n.30

Labor: cultural and economic, 86–87, 230 n.24; German importation of, 252 n.93
Lacan, Jacques: and Du Bois, 41; and the mirror stage, 57–58; and psychoanalytic concepts, 62
La India, 138, 140–41
Laing, David, 29; on the phonograph, 215 n.13
Lastra, James, 31–32
Lawless, Robert, 158
Lefebvre, Henri, 109
Lench Mob, 160
Levinas, Emmanuel, 34, 69–71
Linguist (Advanced Chemistry), 174–75
Linke, Uli, 166, 175, 178, 251 n.81
Lipsitz, George, 164
Lorde, Audre, 208
L'Ouverture, Toussaint, 157
Lowe, Lisa, 245 n.29

Mackey, Nathaniel, 17, 39
Marijuana, 187–88
Marshall, Paule, 6, 113
Martin, Darnell, 14, 106–112, 123–44
Martina (Topley-Bird), 146, 183–

84, 187–97, 208, 252–53 n.95, 254 nn.109, 110, 112. *See also* Tricky
Marxism, 200
Massive Attack, 183
Massumi, Brian, 208: on perception vs. sensation, 35–36
Materiality, 104; vs. ephemerality, 7–8, 20, 88, 212 n.11, 216 n.19
Mayfield, Curtis, 43
McKay, Claude, 113
Melle Mel, 167–69
Melvin, Harold, 1, 17
Mercer, Kobena, 190
Millard, Andre: on "coon songs," 39; on Edison, 26
Mille Plateaux (record label), 202
Mis-Teeq, 17
Mix, and mixing, 13, 73, 83–84, 96; and double consciousness, 89–92; dub, 102–3; in Du Bois, 88–89; as education, 88–89; in hip-hop, 87
Modernity, Western, 9, 11–13, 23, 206–7; and blackness, 3–6, 22, 11–12, 44–45; and *Invisible Man*, 47; and minority cultures, 214 n.6, "modern spatialities," 106–112; and music, 22, 64; "otherwise than," 226 n.55; sonic, 50; and sound recording, 216 n.23; and temporality, 104, 144; theories of, 4; and the universal, 66; as urbanization, 106; and vision, 40–45, 50, 64; and Western texts, 99
Monad, 79
Morrison, Toni, 6, 39, 83, 113
Morton, David, 213 n.17
Moten, Fred, 32–35, 95, 220 n.52; on race and psychoanalysis
Mtume, 1
Mudede, Charles, 90
Music: and African American literature, 39; and androgyny, 189–90, 254 n.110; crossovers, 239 n.30; and legibility, 7; vs. noise, 114–20; and orality, 36–40; popular, 2–4; and space, 110–12; videos, 246 n.45

Index

Shaviro, Steven, 223 n.28
Siano, Nicky, 87
Silverman, Kaja, 62: on the acoustic mirror stage, 57–59; on the maternal voice, 58
Simone, Nina, 202
Singleton, John, 124
Singularity, 16
Slick Rick, 151, 193–94
Smith, Bessie, 185
Smith, Paul, 67
Smith, Susan, 108–9
Smith, Valerie, 227 n.4
Snead, James, 33; on "the cut," 63
Soja, Edward, 109–10
Sonic, the: and the archival, 88; and blackness, 5; and the linguistic, 10; and the subject, 49–50; and the temporal, 99–100
Sonic Afro-modernity, 6, 7–8, 10, 12, 16, 23, 45, 47, 70, 101, 105, 108, 113, 206; and Du Bois, 86; and the subject, 51
"Sorrow Songs," 84–85, 88, 92, 96, 232 n.41. See also Spirituals
Souls of Black Folk, The (Du Bois), 12, 41, 82–105, 202–3, 230 n.23
Sound: in Deleuze and Guattari, 225 nn.46–47; diagetic vs. nondiagetic, 138; ephemerality vs. materiality of, 7–8, 20, 88, 212 n.11, 216 n.19; in film, 31–32; and gender, 122–24; and hearing, 43–44; in Invisible Man, 47–48, 50–51; and literature, 22; and purity, 118–20; and race, 123–24; recording/reproduction of, 3, 15–16, 30–36, 106, 145, 216 n.23, 218 n.43, 241 n.47; and source, 7–8, 118–21; and space, 106–44; system(s), 117–21, 128–29; technologies of, 2–4, 8, 17, 19–21, 47–48, 50–51, 106–12, 114, 143, 145; in urban terrain, 106; and writing in black culture, 36–40
Soysal, Yasemin, 148–49
Space: domestic sphere, 143–44;

"modern spatialities," 106–112; perception and construction of, 106; private and public, 106–44; "real," 149; social, 236–37 n.6; and sound, 106–44
Spillers, Hortense J., 46, 56, 67, 79, 204; on Du Bois, 220 n.50
Spirituals, 92–105, 233 n.47. See also "Sorrow songs"
Spivak, Gayatri Chakravorty, 67; on the subject, 225 n.44
Stepto, Robert, 82, 222 n.10, 231 n.32
Stern, Richard, J., 121–22
Subject, the, 223 n.37; and black studies, 67–72; dissolution of, 47; and double consciousness, 47; and identity, 47; and minority discourse, 47; and the sonic, 49–50; and sonic Afro-modernity, 51; in Spivak, 225 n.44; in structuralism and poststructuralism, 46
Subjectivity: and embodiment, 37; vs. identity, 12–13; in Invisible Man, 47–69; and race, 185
Sublime, the, 217–18 n.37. See also Kant, Immanuel
Suburbanization, of literary and cultural studies, 199–201
Sundquist, Eric, 93, 230 n.24
Supremes, The, 192
Symons, Arthur, 97–98

Tate, Greg, 186, 189, 253 n.104
Taussig, Michael, 28
"Technological re/production," 2, 7
Technology: and black cultures, 3; and "the human," 2; information, 22; in the nineteenth century, 236 n.1; and race, 211 n.1; of reproduction, 86; sound, 2–4, 8, 17, 19–21, 47–48, 50–51, 106–12, 143
Temporal and temporality, 77–81; and DJing, 89; of dub, 235 n.61; and modernity, 104, 144; and the sonic, 99–100
Théberge, Paul, 134

Alexander G. Weheliye

is an assistant professor of English
and African American studies at
Northwestern University.

*Library of Congress Cataloging-in-
Publication Data*

Weheliye, Alexander G.
Phonographies : grooves in sonic Afro-
modernity / Alexander G. Weheliye.
p. cm.
Includes bibliographical references and
index.
ISBN 0-8223-3577-8 (cloth : alk. paper)
ISBN 0-8223-3590-5 (pbk. : alk. paper)
1. Popular music—Social aspects—
History—20th century. 2. Sound—
Recording and reproducing—Social
aspects. 3. Blacks—Music—20th
century—History and criticism.
4. African Americans—Music—20th
century—History and criticism.
5. Music and literature—
United States. I. Title.
ML3916.W46 2005
781.64′089′96073—dc22
2004028461